More Praise for *H*

"Here is an introduction to the Bible perfectly suited for students in our current cultural moment! Written with an inviting style and plenty of helpful pop culture references, Fentress-Williams does not simply introduce the Bible; she shows readers how to use their imagination, creativity, and literary sensibilities. Insights from the study of poetry lead the way to encountering scripture as a collection of imaginative and imagination-provoking writings that explore the identity of God's people in God's world. The best parts of standard and emerging critical scholarship are here (including African American, Latinx, and womanist interpretations), but an emphasis on the diversity of the Bible's voices invites readers to enter into their own ongoing dialogue with the biblical texts."

—Brad E. Kelle, professor of Old Testament and Hebrew, Point Loma Nazarene University, San Diego, CA; author, *Telling the Old Testament Story: God's Mission and God's People* (Abingdon Press, 2017)

"Judy Fentress-Williams, a seasoned teacher and skillful preacher, here uses her considerable gifts to offer an insightful 'literary and theological introduction to the whole Bible.' Readers will benefit from her light (but deft) coverage of scholarly debates, her selective (but pervasive) incorporation of contemporary culture, and her evocative (but foundational) attention to genre, story, and poetry. The result? An introduction that not only describes but serves to inculcate a holy imagination."

—Brent A. Strawn, professor of Old Testament, professor of Law, Duke Divinity School, Duke University, Durham, NC

"Fentress-Williams issues a welcome invitation to read with imagination and gives us the tools to read with understanding. As she walks through each biblical text, she points out analogies between ancient myths, Negro spirituals, and the Superman franchise. She explains various literary types such as charter myths and chronotypes, and describes the way literary techniques such as metaphor and parallelism create tension and beauty. And throughout, she beckons us to engage (not erase) the text's theological and literary complexity. The reader emerges with a fuller sense of what the biblical texts mean and why they matter."

—Melody Knowles, vice president of academic affairs, associate professor of Old Testament, Virginia Theological Seminary, Alexandria, VA

"You hold one of the best introductions to the Bible ever written! Clear, compelling, accessible, and memorable—these words come from a master teacher. Come, sit at her feet, and allow your mind—and life—to be enriched!"

—Matthew Schlimm, professor of Old Testament, University of Dubuque Theological Seminary, Dubuque, IA

"In *Holy Imagination: A Literary and Theological Introduction to the Whole Bible*, Judy Fentress-Williams presents a thoroughly engaging contemporary overview of the Old and New Testaments that creatively illumines their major sections and constituent books. The author's approach is certain to enhance appreciation of the Bible's artistry and theological sophistication, and to promote greater awareness of the various methodologies, established and emerging, employed in its interpretation. It is a creative, novel, and timely addition to the growing body of introductions to Scripture."

—Hugh Rowland Page Jr., professor of theology and Africana studies, University of Notre Dame, Notre Dame, IN

"Fentress-Williams helps us do exactly what we need to: fall in love with the Scriptures. Her love for the Bible, exemplified in her approach to it, inspires us to a greater, deeper love."

—Jacqueline E. Lapsley, professor of Old Testament, Princeton Theological Seminary, Princeton, NJ

JUDY FENTRESS-WILLIAMS

HOLY IMAGINATION

A Literary and Theological Introduction to the Whole Bible

Abingdon Press
Nashville

HOLY IMAGINATION:
A LITERARY AND THEOLOGICAL INTRODUCTION TO THE WHOLE BIBLE

Library of Congress Control Number: 2020948568

ISBN: 978-1-4267-7531-4

21 22 23 24 25 26 27 28 29 30—10 9 8 7 6 5 4 3 2 1
MANUFACTURED IN THE UNITED STATES OF AMERICA

ACKNOWLEDGMENTS

There is a sense in which a book never feels like it is complete, but there is a moment when it is time to let it go. I cannot do so without thanking the institutions and people who supported me in this work.

I am grateful for the generosity of Virginia Theological Seminary's Dean and President Ian Markham and Dean of the Faculty Melody Knowles. They made my time of study possible at the Gladstone Library in Wales, where I worked on a preliminary draft of the book. That support continued with the Meade Seminar, which met regularly to read chapter drafts. Thank you to Tia Johnson, Melody Knowles, Paula Lewis, Johnny President, Kathy Staudt, Riley Temple, and Cynthia Wood-Turner for your thoughtful recommendations and great questions.

I owe a debt of gratitude to the Alfred Street Baptist Church and its pastor, the Rev. Dr. Howard-John Wesley, for his support of this project and the opportunity to teach Bible in a context that is culturally, theologically, and intellectually relevant. I am indebted to those who attend Tuesday night Bible study and my beloved Seasoned Saints who participate in the Wednesday mid-day Bible study. You all are a constant source of encouragement and inspiration.

Special thanks goes to my editors. Paul Franklyn, my editor at Abingdon Press, was a wonderful support, encouraging and coaching in the writing of this book. He saw what was ahead of me when I could not. Mel Krothe and Linda Lanam are astute readers who reviewed drafts of the manuscript and made insightful suggestions.

This book is dedicated to my family: my husband of almost thirty years, Kevin Williams, MD, who brings laughter to my life; my daughter,

Samantha, whose voice, with her insistent and challenging questions about the Bible, spoke to me as I wrote; and my thoughtful son, Jacob, who shares my love for story.

I write these words in a moment of national turmoil. The violent deaths of George Floyd and Breonna Taylor and Ahmad Aubery have resulted in an outcry stoked by a longstanding history of oppression, injustice, and institutional racism. I can think of no better time to invoke our Holy Imaginations so that we might envision an identity that honors the full humanity of every child of God.

CONTENTS

Part Three—The Letters

Part Four—Revelation

INTRODUCTION
FALLING IN LOVE WITH SCRIPTURE

Read these poems to yourself in the middle of the night. Turn on a single lamp and read them while you're alone in an otherwise dark room or while someone else sleeps next to you. Read them when you're wide awake in the early morning, fully alert. Say them over to yourself in a place where silence reigns and the din of the culture—the constant buzzing noise that surrounds us—has momentarily stopped. These [words] have come from a great distance to find you.[1]

When I teach the year-long Old Testament Interpretation course, I end the first lecture and the last lecture with this quotation from Edward Hirsch's book, *How to Read a Poem: And Fall in Love with Poetry.* I read it because I want them to fall in love with scripture. I read it because I want them to read the text both "day and night" like the person described in Psalm 1 who delights in the study of Torah. I read it to them because these words come to us from a great distance, and I do believe they seek to "find us."

Language is complicated. Words can mean more than one thing, and this passage from a book about poetry informs my students that the words of scripture not only come a long way to find us but, like a poem, must be read with attention. Poetry does not yield meaning easily, and it doesn't promise to make sense. "In my not so humble opinion,"[2] readers of the Bible would be better off if they approached scripture like poetry.

1. Edward Hirsch, *How to Read a Poem: And Fall in Love with Poetry* (New York: Harcourt, 1999), 1.

2. In the movie *Harry Potter and the Deathly Hallows, Part 2,* Albus Dumbledore says, "Words are, in my not so humble opinion, our most inexhaustible source of magic" (Steve Kloves and J. K. Rowling [Warner Brothers, 2011]).

When we read poetry, we know that we will have to look past the words on the page and find the images, tropes, sounds, and metaphors that are meaning-full. Readers of poetry understand that poets often use words or phrases that have double meaning, which, even when contradictory, are a part of the poem. The surplus of meaning in poetry is the reason a poem is never mastered or finished.

This type of writing invites, rather demands, the imagination. We must accept that we will only get so close but that this is close enough. Our imagination spans the gaps left by sparse language and incomplete narratives. Imagination affirms that what we experience in the reading of a poem transcends the transmission of information through words. The point of the poem is the encounter itself. Before we know all there is to know about the author and context and the events that led to the poem's composition, the reading of a poem is an event to itself. We will return again and again, with more information and perhaps more experiences. The words are the same, but we are not; and for that reason, there are always new discoveries.

With this understanding, we conclude that there is no such thing as an "unimaginative" reading of scripture. There are only readings that acknowledge the imaginative universe that shape them and those that do not. This literary principle looks for a surplus of meaning in symbolic language and invites the reader to use their imagination in the act of reading, just as the creators and curators of scripture used their imaginations to tell the stories of a God who called, formed, and redeemed them again and again.

Because it is a theological text, the Bible is inviting us to imagine God and God's work in the world. In many African American preaching traditions, preachers will refer to their sanctified imagination. It's a signal to the audience that they are following the text's invitation to engage the text imaginatively, to see themselves in the story and to apply the tenets of the text to their current situation. In this way, preachers of this hallowed tradition have encouraged their communities to imagine aspects of God into their current circumstances, equipped with an existential knowledge of a God who acts in real time, facilitated by a text that is imaginatively written.

THE
OLD TESTAMENT

Part One

THE ORIGIN OF IDENTITY

CHAPTER 1
GENESIS

From the beginning, the Bible presents itself to us as a diverse and multi-voiced text. It all begins with two versions of the creation story in Genesis 1:1–2:4a and 2:4b–3:24. The creation accounts are a part of the first section of Genesis, known as the primeval history, in chapters 1–11. These first eleven chapters are mythic in genre and proportion. They describe the origin of the created world, the first humans and their families, and the events that started things on their trajectory to the world we know in the time of the compilers and editors. The primeval history offers the story of creation, the expulsion from Eden, Cain's murder of Abel, the flood, and the tower of Babel.

The narrative units are held together by a string of genealogies, which carry the narrative from Adam and Eve to Terah in the land of Haran. These stories tell us how things were, how they came to be, and they also explain how things are. From the stories in this time before time, we learn about the origin of the various nations, languages, and peoples. The stories share themes of limitation and separation.

God calls and makes a covenant (a promise) to Terah's son Abram in Genesis 12, and this begins the second section of Genesis known as "the Ancestors." In Genesis 12–50, the focus of the book shifts from the universal to a particular family and certain members of this particular family. The patriarchs and matriarchs—Abraham, Sarah, Hagar, Isaac, Rebekah, Jacob, Leah, Rachel, Zilpah, and Bilhah—all have encounters with the promise that God makes to Abraham in Genesis 12, and in their stories we encounter not only the story of a people called by God, but we are exposed to the various ways in which this family and other families over time respond to God's promise.

OUTLINE	THEMES
1–11 The primeval history	Universal origins Boundaries established and crossed Increasing separation from God
12–50 The Ancestors	God's Covenant Threat to the promise "Chosenness"

Genesis 1–11: The Primeval History

In popular culture, every superhero has an origin story. Whether it is Black Panther or Wonder Woman, the origin story of the superhero describes how the hero obtained their powers, discloses their secret identity/alter ego, and explains their motivation. The origin story is the point of reference that helps us to make sense of how the characters operate, and why they do what they do.

The first eleven chapters of Genesis are known as the primeval history, and they are our origin stories. They take place in "that time," which is distinct from "this time," and like present-day origin stories, they are our point of orientation, answering the questions of who we are, where we come from, and what it means to be human with all our strengths, limitations, and motivations. The origin stories in the Bible are overtly theological. God plays a dominant role as the creator, and humans (the creation) play a significant role in the tale. Told and retold, origin stories speak to how things began, and how these events inform our identities, secret and known.

Genesis 1:1–2:4a: Creation the Musical

When God began to create the heavens and the earth—the earth was without shape or form, it was dark over the deep sea, and God's wind swept over the waters. (CEB)

The first story of creation is a "heavenly liturgy"[1] characterized by repetition and arranged by days. In this account, God, *elohim*, is cosmic and creates simply by speaking, "Let there be. . . ." There is an order in this

1. Claus Westermann, *The Genesis Accounts of Creation* (Minneapolis: Fortress, 1964), 6.

creation, and order seems to be one of the goals of creation. God subdues the primordial chaos by imposing limits and boundaries to water, land, and sky. The repeated phrase "there was evening and there was morning" moves the narrative along, forming a chronological structure. On each day of creation, God speaks something new into existence. God's creation is pronounced as good (days 1, 3, 4, 5, and 6). Days 1 through 3 correspond to days 4 through 6.

Day 1 light	Day 4 Sun, moon, and stars
Day 2 Sky	Day 5 Water creatures and birds
Day 3 Dry land, seas	Day 6 Land creatures

On the last day of God's activity, humanity appears. The humans, both male and female, made in God's image and after God's likeness (Gen 1:27), are instructed to be fruitful and to rule over the created order. After the creation is complete, God rests and in so doing creates the Sabbath. This seventh day of rest is the culmination of God's work of creation.

Genesis 2:4b-25: In the Garden (Part 1)

The stability of the first account eludes us in the second one. Opening with a run-on sentence that leaves the reader breathless, the second account begins in a garden in the center of the world, the point from which four rivers extend in the four directions. Like the first story, it takes us to a "before" time—before the world became what it is now. And in that place, the Lord God, *YHWH elohim*, formed a man from the dust of the ground, and "breathed into his nostrils the breath of life" (KJV). With that, *adam* comes to life. Everything in this second account seems to happen based on the needs of this *adam*. If the first creation story can fit into a chart, the second story is best expressed by concentric circles.

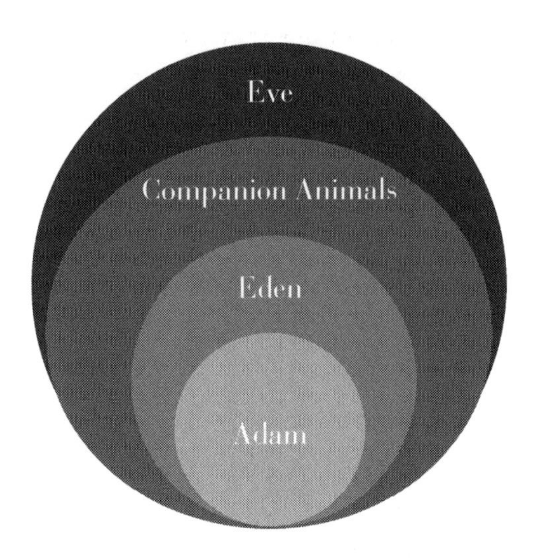

In contrast to the first story where the humans have dominion over the earth, the *adam* in this account is instructed to tend to and care for the created world. *Adam* is placed in a garden for shelter, and given trees for food. In addition to the trees for food, two trees are named, the tree of life and the tree of the knowledge of good and evil (2:9). Only the second one is forbidden, which leaves the reader to wonder: (1) why the first one is mentioned at all, and (2) why is there a forbidden tree in the story? The purpose of the trees will come later in the story, but their mention at this point can be seen as a literary feature as the storytellers prepare the audience for what is to come.

The creator determines that the first human, *adam*, is lonely and in need of companionship. A "counterpart-companion" (*kenegdo*, like one who is an opposite) is needed to avert a solitary existence. God creates the animals, presumably to meet this need, and the man names them. However, when the exercise of naming all the creatures is complete the "counterpart-companion" was "nowhere to be found" (2:20). Now God puts the man to sleep, removes a rib and "builds" a woman from it. Upon seeing her, the man declares, "this one finally is bone from my bones and flesh from my flesh" (2:23a). The depiction of the deity adjusting and adapting as things progress stands in contrast to the way God is depicted in the first account as cosmic, organized, and knowing. The woman comes into the narrative via a circuitous route, but she is celebrated as the culmination of creation, and the story concludes with the man and woman together, and in their natural state, "naked" and not "embarrassed."

There is ample evidence that the two stories are distinct and originate from separate sources: they have different sets of vocabulary and names for God, different terms for the act of creation, names for male and female, and so on. The humans come at different times and in different ways, and they have different relationships to the created order. Moreover, the stories of creation are structured differently; the first is based on time and is ordered by periods of time, that is by days. The second story is spatially oriented, beginning with a man in a garden in the center of the universe. The stories can be classified differently by genre, and they have different theological orientations: In the first, a cosmic God is omnipotent, ordered, and creates by speaking. In the second story, God is intimate and appears to adjust based on the needs of the man. Scholarly consensus asserts that first story comes from the Priestly source, known as "P," and the second from the Jahwist, known as "J."

Genesis 1:1–2:4a—Priestly Writer	**Genesis 2:4b–3:24—Jahwist Writer**
God: *elohim*	Lord God: *YHWH elohim*
Create: *bara'*	Form: *yatsar*
Six days of creation	garden of Eden
Humans created together, male and female in God's image and likeness	Adam first, then animals, and then the woman, who is later named *haya*, Eve
Humans are the last act of creation.	The man is the first in creation and the woman is last.
Seventh day, Sabbath	Eden
God is cosmic and creates by speaking. Separation of water from sky, land from sea, day from night, and so on	God is relational, forms the adam and breathes into his nostrils. Boundaries: the tree of the knowledge of good and evil is forbidden.
Humans have dominion over creation.	Humans tend and care for the garden.
The watery deep: *tahom*	Four rivers: Tigris, Euphrates (known), and the Pishon and Gihon (unknown).
Time: days	Space: Eden in the center of the world

Once the sources have been identified, the next question for Western readers is, What next? If they are not to be read as consecutive stories, what is the reader to do with these different accounts? Does one have more weight than the other? How do two accounts complicate our understanding of these stories as historical? Where is the meaning when there are two messages? Does the fact that the first story was composed after the second one matter?

"Encountering an ancient text not only as a historical source but also as a literary artifact entails an important paradigm shift."[2] When we move from our understanding of scripture as a simple attempt at a historical document, we open the door to greater possibilities and new understandings. If scripture is exclusively a historical source, we find ourselves either looking to scripture to be historically accurate or we focus on the components of scripture, such as original sources and archaeological evidence in the hope that these elements can assist us in a historical reconstruction. This pursuit has its own rewards, but often ignores the riches the Bible has to offer as story. When we engage the Bible as story,

1. We acknowledge that the compilers of the Bible were storytellers —composers who exercised some intentionality in the way they told and organized stories.
2. We acknowledge the fluidity between oral and written cultures, which causes us to see the written text differently.
3. We acknowledge that we are also storytellers and that our stories, like those of our predecessors, are intentional and serve a purpose.

The Bible's account of what takes place in the two accounts teaches us that the Bible may be many things, but it is not singular. True to their form as origin stories, the early chapters of Genesis will make use of literary tools in an attempt to convey they truth.

> A dialogic reading is rooted in the observation that the Bible is made of more than one voice and that these voices are in conversation with

2. Hanna Liss and Manfred Oeming, eds. *Literary Construction of Identity in the Ancient World: Options and Limits of Modern Literary Approaches* (Winona Lake, IN: Eisenbrauns, 2010), vii.

> each other. The text has a "proclivity to make connections" between stories. Reading the Bible dialogically can be compared to reading music written in parts. The reader of this music may focus on one part, aware that there are other parts to the song. Each musical line works with the other parts to make music. In scripture, the variety of voices, vocabulary, motifs and symbols work toward meaning in dialogue with other parts, which always makes room for new meaning to be found in the text.[3]

As our origin stories, the two creation accounts are tasked with telling us about the beginning of all beginnings, namely how the world came to be, the characteristics of God, the nature of humanity, and the order of the world. This is more than one narrative can convey, so more than one perspective is required. It is more than can be contained in a single structure, so additional models are needed. The two stories in dialogue tell us that God the creator has a plan and that same God is flexible. God is cosmic and intimate. Humans were created as equals in the image of God and they are intended to be in relationship with one another. Humanity's rule over the earth is tempered by the command to serve and tend to it. The first creation story, with its seven-day structure, is defined temporally, while the second is spatially oriented. Thus the created world and our existence is limited and defined by time and space. Our universe is ordered, but the threat of chaos is present.

James Weldon Johnson's poem "The Creation" combines elements from both creation stories to emphasize God's tenderness in forming the man out of clay:

> And there the great God Almighty
> who lit the sun and fixed it in the sky,
> who flung the stars to the most far corner of the night,
> who rounded the earth in the middle of his hand;
> This great God,
> like a mammy bending over her baby,
> kneeled down in the dust
> toiling over a lump of clay,
> till he shaped it in is his own image;
> Then into it he blew the breath of life,
> and man became a living soul.
> Amen.
> Amen.[4]

3. Judy Fentress-Williams, *Ruth*, Abingdon Old Testament Commentaries (Nashville: Abingdon Press, 2012), 14–15.

4. James Weldon Johnson, *God's Trombones: Seven Negro Sermons in Verse* (New York: Penguin, 1976), 20.

In addition to the stories of creation, the primeval history contains stories about the expulsion from Eden, the flood, Cain and Abel, and the spread of humanity throughout the known world. There are some recurring themes in these stories, such as limits, boundaries and the crossing of them, and increasing separation from God. We will explore these themes as we sample a few stories in the primeval history.

Source Criticism and the Pentateuch

Source criticism, also known as literary criticism, is a historical-critical approach to the Bible that acknowledges the presence of multiple literary sources in the Pentateuch and aims to identify and date these sources. Once sources are identified and isolated, the reader/interpreter can begin to detect patterns that may reflect the worldview and theology of the community behind the "writer." As sources are dated, the reader or interpreter has information that can inform our understanding of how the various traditions were combined into the text as we have it now.

J = Jahwist	E = Elohist	P = Priestly	D = Deuteronomist
The Jahwist is named for its use of YHWH (JHWH in German), as the divine name.	The Elohist uses *elohim* for God.	The Priestly source uses *elohim* for God, along with other titles.	
The Jahwist is known for anthropomorphic depictions of God, and tends to have a fairly low opinion of humanity.	E is a fragmentary source—there is not a lot of it. It is often combined with "J" material. Some scholars refer to J/E as a combined source.	P is associated with the religious leaders, as it is concerned with ritual, observance of law, dietary laws, ancestry, and so on.	D is the source responsible for the book of Deuteronomy alone (and also influenced the books of Joshua, through Kings).
Date: tenth century BCE Origin: South/Judah	Date: ninth or eighth century BCE Origin: North/Israel	Date: sixth century BCE Origin: Exilic	Date: eighth or seventh century BCE Origin: North/Israel

Genesis 3:1-24: In the Garden (Part 2)

The third chapter of Genesis continues the second creation story (J). At the end of chapter 2, the first human (*adam*) and his companion (*haya*) are in the garden, the two of them "naked" (*'arumim*) and not "embarrassed" (Gen 2:25). Genesis 3 begins with a description of the serpent, the most clever (*'arum*) of the creatures God made. Hebrew readers would notice the wordplay between *naked* and *clever*. Their juxtaposition places the cleverness of the serpent over and against the nakedness, that is, vulnerability, of the woman and man. From a literary perspective, they are no match for the serpent, who invites the humans, specifically the woman, into a theological dialogue: did God really say that you shouldn't eat from any tree in the garden (Gen 3:1)? The question is intriguing on many levels. If read at face value, it is problematic because in Genesis 2, God gives the instructions about the tree to the man before the woman is created. We have no account of how the woman received instructions regarding the tree. Her response is not an accurate reflection of what is recorded in Genesis 2 (Eve's version adds a prohibition of touching the tree). The serpent's words not only dismiss God's warning, "You won't die"; but promises, "God knows that on the day you eat from it, you will see clearly and you will be like God, knowing good and evil" (Gen 3:5). The word for knowing, *yada'*, does not refer exclusively to head knowledge, rather it encompasses all kinds of knowing and experiences. The serpent's promise is not limited to some kind of additional cognitive ability or level of discernment. Rather the serpent promises experiences: good and evil, from A to Z.

The story of the encounter between the serpent and the woman is a sensual one in that four of the five senses are mentioned or implied. She hears the voice of the serpent and "saw the tree was beautiful with delicious food and that the tree would provide wisdom, so she took some of its fruit and ate it" (touch and taste). The encounter between the serpent and the woman is further complicated because when she succumbs to the invitation to take the fruit, the text tells us "and she also gave some to her husband, who was with her, and he ate it."

If Adam was with her, was he there during the conversation between Eve and the serpent? If he was, why did the serpent address Eve? Why did Adam say nothing? If he arrived on the scene when the conversation was in progress, why didn't he speak up? The order of events in this narrative challenges our understanding of what makes sense. However, when we remember the genre of this material fits origin stories, we are able to think about the function of the characters in the overall movement of the story and we are helped by reading another ancient creation story.

In the *Epic of Gilgamesh*, the role of the woman sheds light on what may be going on in Genesis 3. In this ancient Babylonian story, the woman Shamhat comes to the man named Enkidu, takes him from the animals, and they engage in sexual activity for a week. When he returns, the animals run away from him and tell him he is a human now. Enkidu's sexual encounter with Shamhat changes his status in the created order. In the *Epic of Gilgamesh*, the woman is associated with sexual knowledge and civilization.

The dialogue between the two accounts helps us to understand the ordering in Genesis 2, in which God creates the first man and then the animals and then the first woman. This ordering preserves the story of the man and the animals together before the woman, and it associates the woman with knowledge and civilization. In Genesis 3, the woman is drawn to the forbidden fruit, because of its aesthetic desirability, because it looked good for food, and because she wanted to be wise. The reference to wisdom suggests that the woman in Genesis 3 is fulfilling more than one function in the story. She is both the companion of the man who takes the fruit and she is Woman, writ large, representing woman wisdom. The serpent speaks to the woman because women are affiliated with wisdom and civilization—that which separates humans from animals. Wisdom is personified as a woman (see also Prov 1–9). Read this way, it makes sense that the serpent addresses the woman. In her role as purveyor of wisdom and knowledge, she would naturally want to know.

Another literary reading invites us to think about the location of the man and woman in the garden symbolically. Gardens in the ancient Near East were walled, protected environs. In this garden, the humans are naked because they have no need of clothing and they are nourished by the fruit trees within the garden. All their needs are supplied. This Edenic space evokes the womb. It is only upon leaving the womb that the humans need clothes and a means of securing sustenance. Outside of Eden they must fend for themselves. The concept of Eden as a womb also explains why Eve, the one who will give birth, is the conduit for their expulsion. It is at the end of the story that the man names his companion *Haya,* "life," "because she is the mother of everyone who lives" (Gen 3:20).

Neither of these readings, which pay attention to the function of the first woman, Eve, in the story, lends strong support to the theological doctrine of original sin and the fall.

> The fall is a concept that developed from a reading of Genesis 3, asserting that Eve and Adam's disobedience forever changed human nature, passing down corruption to their descendants, as some kind of epigenetic transmutation. The idea was developed approximately two centuries before the Christian era by Jewish interpreters (see Sirach 25:24, "Sin began with a woman"), and later dropped, only to be retrieved by Paul in his rhetorical explanation of Christ's work of redemption.

To the extent that the stories in the primeval history tell us how things were and how things are, the account in Genesis 3 tells us that, given the opportunity, we—and all humans—will eventually transgress the boundaries God has laid out for us. No one can remain in Eden or the womb forever. Thus, from a dialogic perspective, the taking of the forbidden fruit in the garden is less a moment in chronology and more an example of chronotope. It is the moment upon which the narrative hangs, and this is not just a moment for Adam and Eve. It is the existential and inevitable moment for all of us, their descendants.

> In Dialogic Criticism, chronotope describes the way time, space, and character are constructed in relation to one another in story. It operates out of the assumption that the world does not make sense from a single perspective or vantage-point. It asserts that events are multi-layered.[5] Science fiction describes this interaction between time and space as the time-space continuum. Sometimes time dominates space,

5. Sue Vice, *Introducing Bakhtin* (Manchester: Manchester University Press, 1998), 202.

> and sometimes space takes precedence over time, so much so that an event can forever change the way one thinks about one or the other. In recent history, 9/11 is a time stamp that speaks to an event. The date signifies an event that happened once, even though the calendar event of September 11 occurs every year. When Americans reference 9/11, they mean *that* 9/11, and the event carries meaning into the past and future.

The expulsion and exile of the woman and man from the garden means they have left the point of orientation to which they may not return. The remainder of the primordial history can be characterized by the theme of disorientation and increasing separation. It is also shaped by recurring genealogies, known as *toledot* formulas, which we find posited between narrative units. They move the larger narrative along, both connecting each generation with the next while continuing the theme of increasing separation. This has the effect of reinforcing the idea that each generation chooses to transgress or violate God's boundaries. As a result of their disobedience, Adam and Eve must leave the garden and forfeit access to the tree of life. They will not live forever, and their existence will only be continued through procreation.

Genesis 4:1-26: Cain and Abel

The births of Cain and Abel confirm that the humans, like the plants God made, are capable of being "fruitful." Eve has two sons, Cain, which means "gain," and Abel, meaning "breath" or "puff." Abel's name is a "spoiler alert" to the reader—he will not last. The brothers have occupations. Cain is a farmer, a tiller of the ground, living out the role placed on his father. The younger brother is a shepherd. The action in the story revolves around acts of sacrifice and God's response to them. At this point in the narrative, there is no mandate for offerings/sacrifice. There are no guidelines provided on what type of sacrifice God expects, and the reader has no basis upon which to determine the appropriateness of either sacrifice. The narrative focuses on God's responses. Abel's offering, "his flock's oldest offspring with their fat," is received "favorably" by the LORD, and there is a lack of favor for Cain's grain offering. In this story, God is not a vegetarian! God's lack of favor for Cain's offering causes Cain's face to fall. God responds to Cain by engaging him in dialogue:

> Why are you angry, and why do you look so resentful? If you do the right thing, won't you be accepted? But if you don't do the right thing, sin will be waiting at the door ready to strike! It will entice you, but you must rule over it. (Gen 4:6-7)

The LORD's words do not address the sacrifice, but Cain's response pertains to the unexplained circumstances he finds himself in. He has a choice. He can "do the right thing" or not, and he is warned about "sin . . . lurking at the door" (NRSV) with its "desire . . . for you." The depiction of sin as a crouching animal is a powerful image. The word *desire* in this story is the same word used to describe Eve's desire for her husband in Genesis 3:16 and connotes a longing or perhaps an instinct.[6] It may require some effort to "do the right thing" when sin is lying in wait. In this story, Cain succumbs to sin and kills his younger brother Abel. Again, God responds to Cain by engaging him in dialogue, this time with an inquiry about Abel: "Where is your brother Abel?" to which Cain responds, "I don't know; am I my brother's guardian?" (Gen 4:9b). The second part of Cain's response has come to represent the human tendency of indifference toward others. Of interest in this story is the fact that God asks Cain a question to which he already has an answer, as he presumably did in Genesis 3:9 when he asked Adam where he was. God knows Abel is dead because his "blood is crying to me from the ground" (Gen 4:10). The Hebrew word for blood is in the plural—Abel's "bloods" cry out, suggesting that Abel's death is also the death of his progeny and all their potential. We should also note that the first murder in the Bible is fratricide, and if we are all descendants of Adam, then any murder is within the family. If we are Eve and Adam's children, there are no outsiders—only relatives.

6. Part of Eve's punishment for eating the forbidden fruit is increased pain in childbearing: "you will desire your husband, but he will rule over you." The juxtaposition of pain in childbearing with desire for her husband established an uncomfortable dynamic between the two. Sexual desire is unavoidable, and for Eve, this desire comes with the burden of pregnancy and painful childbirth.

Perhaps the most important learning from this story is the role God plays in it, namely in the unexplained element of Cain's offering being rejected. This preference for one over the other is an ongoing motif in scripture. The dialogue in this story is not focused on why some are "favored" or chosen while others are not. Rather the narrative is interested in how we respond when we are not chosen, or when there is no favor for our work.[7] God's rationale for choosing one offering and not another may not be clear, but God is persistent in showing up for Cain, inviting him into conversation and relationship. Even in his punishment, which is exile, God provides for him just as God provided for Adam and Eve when they left the garden.

Genesis 6:5–9:27: The Flood

Consistent with the theme of increased separation from God, the flood story presents the reader with a creation gone bad, prompting God to push the "reset" button. The account in Genesis is a composite of two complete, separate accounts. Both the Jahwist and Priestly accounts, have striking similarities to other ancient Near Eastern flood traditions,[8] resulting in one story with details that do not fit together easily. For the Jahwist, the reason for the flood is humanity's proclivity to sin; "The LORD saw that humanity had become thoroughly evil on the earth and that every idea their minds thought up was always completely evil" (Gen 6:5). This writer, who is prone to describe God anthropomorphically goes so far as to say, "The LORD regretted making human beings on the earth, and he was heartbroken . . ." (Gen 6:6). The Priestly writer has a different reason; "In God's sight, the earth had become corrupt and was filled with violence" (Gen 6:11). Both writers supply a reason for the flood, yet neither of these reasons is enough to offset the scope of divine violence that is the destruction of all of God's creation, save a man, his immediate family, and

7. Stephen Lewis Fuchs, *What's in It for Me? Finding Ourselves in Biblical Narratives* (Sandy, UT: Aardvark Global, 2014), 10–11.

8. *The Epic of Gilgamesh* and the *Enuma Elish*.

a group of animals. The flood is the reversal of creation, and the undoing of the order. This story is literarily and theologically complex.

The Story

God's destruction of the world by flood moves from the motivation for the flood to preparation for the event and resolution. Almost as soon as it is established that God will destroy the world, a plan is put in place to prevent total annihilation. The earth will recover and a remnant of living creatures will survive so that the world can begin again. Noah is chosen and commissioned to build the ark and curate the animals.[9] "Noah did everything the LORD commanded him" (Gen 7:5). The specifications for the ark, building materials, and dimensions are given, and the text is careful to note in the Jahwist/J tradition that "the LORD closed the door behind them" (Gen 7:16), emphasizing God's agency in the salvation of humanity. In one tradition (J) the flood consists of rains that last 40 days and nights. In the Priestly version, the waters of primordial chaos return as the "springs of the deep sea erupted and the windows of the skies opened" (Gen 7:11), and waters were on the earth for 150 days. The ark finally rests on Mount Ararat, from which Noah and his family eventually emerge. Noah offers a sacrifice and God affirms a covenant never to destroy the world by flood again.

Ark and Covenant

Humanity and life on earth are preserved in the ark that Noah builds at God's command. It is designed by God and secured by God, and the attention given to the details around its specifications may intend to offset the horror of the flood. The scope of destruction is not to be avoided. Rather, the preservation of humanity is tied to God's covenant, which is made before the flood (Gen 6:18) and affirmed after the flood (Gen 9:9-17). Structurally, God's destruction is surrounded by covenant. The community in Babylonian exile received and shaped this story from their own experience

9. In the Priestly tradition Noah gathers a pair of each kind of animal (male and female). According to the Jahwist (J), he takes a pair of unclean animals and seven pairs of clean animals.

of chaos. God's covenant before and after the flood is a reassuring word that they will not be utterly destroyed. Covenant is a legal agreement that outlines the terms of engagement between two parties, and it is one of God's signature acts. In the Old Testament, God engages in one covenant after another, trying to maintain a relationship with God's people. The covenant in this story is unique because it doesn't ask anything of the people. In Gen 6:18, God's covenant promises a relationship and in Gen 9:12-17, God's covenant is cosmic. It is with Noah and his descendants and the whole world. Marked by the sign of the rainbow, God promises, "there will never again be a flood to destroy the earth" (Gen 9:11). The followers of the Canaanite deity Baal saw the rainbow as an archer's bow in the sky demonstrating Baal's military prowess. Israel is aware of this symbolism and in the Israelite remix, the rainbow has a double meaning. YHWH has the power to release chaos; nevertheless, this God chooses self-restraint.

The story is a reminder that primordial chaos[10] never went away completely and that God's ordered world can come undone. In its final form, the reasons for the flood do not make God's destruction palatable. Rather, the story and the flood itself has an ark in its midst that preserves the covenant people. From a literary perspective, the ark functions like another Eden, another womb from which living things will emerge. Moreover, it foreshadows other arks that we will encounter in the Torah, namely the ark that will preserve the infant Moses from Pharaoh's death order and the chest that will preserve the law of the LORD in Exodus. For the community in exile, God's covenant, God's promise to keep them, is the ark that will preserve them.[11]

10. Genesis 1:2 states that when God began creating, the earth was "without shape or form, . . ." which many interpreters understand to be some state of chaos. In that same verse there is reference to the "deep sea," which bears resemblance to Tiamat, the goddess who is subdued by Marduk who divides her body and uses one half to form the sky and the other half to form the seas, fed from subterranean waters. In the flood account, the mythical waters of chaos return.

11. The word for the basket Moses is placed in, *tebah*, is the same word for the ark in the Noah story. The chest into which the law is placed, although translated as ark or chest, comes from the Hebrew word *'aron.*

Genesis 11:1-9: Tower of Babel

"All people on the earth had one language and the same words." Babel is the charter myth about different languages and the dispersion of humanity "over all the earth," and the origin of different languages. Consistent with one theme in the primeval history, it is a story about the crossing of boundaries. In this one, the humans begin construction on a city and a tower. The goal of the tower is to reach the heavens and that of the city is, perhaps, to keep them together since they seem to be afraid of being spread across all the earth. The motivation for building the city is fear of dispersion, and that is exactly what happens, so the fear of the people is an ironic foreshadowing. It should not be lost on us that the method of separating the people and forcing them out is the confusion of languages. This story not only speaks to the reason we are peoples of different nations but offers us some insight into the act of interpretation itself. The people separate based on language. We too associate with and build community with those whose speech is understood by us, which suggests communities are limited by similarity and like-mindedness.

Babel is a story about language and meaning. A people's ability to communicate gives them a false sense of power. The fact that they can understand one another makes them think they can do anything. God's response is to confuse their language. When the languages are confused, they form communities, based on the ability to communicate and understand. Babel teaches us that part of what it means to be separated from God is that we are limited in our ability to understand and to communicate—limited in speech and comprehension. The further we get from God, the more limited our ability to understand and be understood becomes. Human speech "binds lives and loosens them, builds society and isolates persons, and is both the crown and disgrace of our human existence."[12] The work of interpreting scripture is also the work of creating community as the keepers of the biblical stories have created, preserved, defended, damaged, and destroyed community in their interpretations of these words.

---

12. Michael Fishbane, *Biblical Text and Texture: A Literary Reading of Selected Texts* (Oxford: Oneworld, 1998), 36.

- Origin stories are timeless—they speak to what is most true about God and us.
- The two creation stories teach us to expect more than one perspective and look for dialogue.
- The themes relate to boundaries and separation in creation, crossing of boundaries by humans, and increased separation between God and the humans.

The Ancestors: Genesis 12–50

Genesis 12–50 is known as the ancestral narratives. The focus shifts from the larger story of humanity to a people called by God through the ancestor Abraham. Like the primeval history, the ancestral stories come to us from different sources, in the form of smaller, narrative units. The stories of Hagar and Ishmael in the wilderness, Isaac's near sacrifice, Jacob wrestling with a divine messenger, Leah and Rebekah, were told, rehearsed, and repeated before they made their way to a scroll, and even after they were written, they were still told. The recurring phrases "the God of Abraham, the God of Isaac and the God of Jacob" or "the God of your ancestors" are evidence of a refrain that existed in Israel's oral culture as a marker of identity, a liturgical proclamation or creed, and a reminder to those who used it.

The practices of the ancestors as seminomadic people, the names of the characters, are contemporaneous with names and practices of the Middle Bronze Age. However, there is no extrabiblical evidence that proves the existence of the Israelite ancestors. At issue here is the question of whether the ancestors were actual historical characters or literary constructs. The literary reading does not depend on their historicity but does not preclude it. The smaller units of the Abraham, Isaac, and Jacob cycles serve a literary function of establishing identity as people of the covenantal promise with the ancestors' god. This identity building for the Hebrew people is understood by some to demand the "unchoosing" of others. With each generation, the question of who will be the bearer of the covenantal promise arises. Will it be Ishmael, Isaac, Esau, or Jacob? The stories of these families become the stories of nations—so Esau is more than an individual. When the text approaches its final shape, Israel's relationship with Edom was long and complicated, so that the story of the Edomite's ancestor is burdened with generations of rivalry. More than Jacob's brother, Esau is the progenitor of Edom, and some of Esau's characteristics are descriptions of Edom. Thus whether the characters are historical or not, they are designed by the teller and editor to have meaning beyond the scope of the small narrative units where we encounter them. These narrative collections preserve or create a collective memory that is a foundational layer for Israel's identity. Moreover, these stories are rehearsed and adapted by subsequent generations to speak to current circumstances.

The Promise

It all begins with a covenantal promise God makes to Abraham.[13] In Genesis 12, the Lord says to Abram, *lekh, lekah.* The first word, "go" or "leave," is an imperative and the second word offers emphasis, "go you" or "get thee." Another option is "go to yourself," implying that Abraham's journey is an internal or spiritual journey as well as a physical one. There is no specific context given other than the preceding genealogy that reveals Abraham's father, Terah, started this journey to Canaan but settled in Haran (meaning crossroads). Abraham is literally and figuratively at a crossroad when he is called to leave the construct of his identity—his country, kindred, and his father's house—in exchange for a new one. The promise the Lord makes Abraham has three components:

Former Identity	Promise	Future Identity
Country	Land I will show you	Canaan
Kindred	Great nation	Descendants and renown
Father's house	Blessing	Blessed and blessing

13. Abraham is known as Abram in Genesis 12:1–17:5, where his name is changed to Abraham. The meaning of Abram is "my father is exalted," whereas Abraham means "father of a multitude." Sarai is the name of Abram's wife when she is introduced. God changes her name to Sarah. Both names mean "princess." In this section we will use Abraham and Sarah throughout.

This promise to Abraham is the core of the ancestral narratives. The patriarch risks it all, abandoning his own identity for the unknown with an unknown God. The stories of Abraham explore the questions, Will God make good on his promises? How will the promise become realized? How will God's promises stand up to the harsh realities of Abraham's life?

Each narrative cycle contains elements of the threefold promise. With Isaac's birth and survival, the crucial element of God's promise, descendants, is achieved. Jacob wrestles literally and figuratively with God and others to procure the blessing evidenced by many sons and one daughter. Joseph's actions save the known world from decimation. Thus in the Joseph story, we witness how one descendent of Abraham is used to bless "all the families of the earth" (Gen 12:3).

Mothers of Promise

Traditionally, Genesis 12–50 was titled "the Patriarchs," in part to reflect and perpetuate the emphasis on the male ancestors in the text. The culture of the Middle Bronze Age limits women to their roles in relationship to men as daughters, wives, and mothers. Women's fertility matters in the larger culture, but, specifically in the ancestral narratives, it matters because God promised Abraham many descendants. The matriarchs are the "delivery system" by which the promise of a great nation is fulfilled. Genesis 29:31–30:22 is an extended birth narrative of Jacob's sons, cast as a competition between his two wives, Leah and Rachel. Rachel, like Sarai and Rebekah before her, is barren before giving birth. In these stories, barrenness is more than a condition, it is a literary motif. The ancestral narratives introduce the motif of barrenness as the precursor to births of significant characters. The motif also comes to represent any moment of longing as individuals or a community await God's action.

Given the expectations around childbearing, it is important to note that in addition to bearing children, the matriarchs, like the men in these stories, struggle literally and figuratively with God's promise. Like the men, they name and have their names changed. They are rivals with others and they have encounters with God.

Threats to the Promise

As the matriarchs' stories of barrenness indicate, the promise of God comes under threat. In addition to barrenness, famine forces the family to migrate into foreign lands as sojourners with few, if any, rights. It is under these circumstances Sarah is taken by a foreign king twice, in Genesis 12 and 20. God's command that Abraham sacrifice his son in chapter 22 is a threat to the promise. Sibling rivalry in the Jacob and Joseph cycles result in life-threatening scenarios for heirs to God's promise.

Naming and Name Change

Naming is a powerful device in biblical narrative. God changes names of characters to mark a change in their identity. Abram's name becomes Abraham as a sign of God's promise in Genesis 17:5, and Sarai becomes Sarah (17:15). Later in the Bible, Jews in the diaspora will have their names changed by their captors as a way of changing cultural identity. In the ancestral narratives the LORD's messenger gives Hagar her son's name, Ishmael and its meaning (Gen 16:11). Sarah's long-awaited son is named Isaac, which means laughter, and Sarah gives a naming speech in 21:6-7. Leah exercises her voice through the naming of her sons.[14] Rachel, like her sister, expresses her desires and her pain in the naming of her sons. The name of her second son, Ben-oni, "son of my sorrow" is changed by his father to Benjamin, "son of my strong hand." Finally, Hagar names the God she encounters in the wilderness *El Roi,* "because she said, 'Can I still see after he saw me?' " (Gen 16:13).

Rivalry

Abraham has two wives, and each has a son. The firstborn, Ishmael, is the son of his secondary wife, the Egyptian slave Hagar. When Hagar conceives, she "no longer respected her mistress" (16:4). Hagar's "uppity" behavior elicits Sarah's feelings of "harassment" (16:5), which prompted her to treat Hagar "harshly" (16:6) so that she ran away. The

14. Ilana Pardes, *Countertraditions in the Bible: A Feminist Approach* (Cambridge, MA: Harvard University Press, 1992), 40–42.

dynamic in the household changes again when Sarah conceives a child of her own, Isaac. It is not clear in the biblical narrative that the boys were rivals (Gen 21), but Sarah felt threatened by how Ishmael's presence would have an impact on Isaac's inheritance. In the Jacob narrative cycle, we observe rivalry between Esau and his younger brother Jacob over the birthright and the blessing. Later in the story, Leah and Rachel's rivalry mirrors that of Esau and Jacob as the sister wives find themselves as rivals in procreation. The unloved firstborn and primary wife, Leah, is fertile, and Rachel, the beloved wife, is barren for a long time. As the younger siblings, Rachel and Jacob are the ideal match, bound by love and their desire to usurp their older siblings' positions and possessions. Ironically, Jacob, who suffered in a system where the older child has an advantage, perpetuates sibling rivalry among his own children by showing favor to one son over the others. Joseph suffers greatly at the hands of his brothers because he enjoys his father's favor, and because he tells them about his dreams of greatness.

Theophany

God's call and promise to Abraham in Genesis 12:1 is the orientation point of the ancestral narratives. Throughout the Abraham stories there are accounts of God speaking to Abraham, appearing to Abraham, and naming Abraham. God's presence punctuates Abraham's travel through the wilderness, reminding him that the promise is real. God's appearances serve a literary function of anchoring a series of semi-related literary units and reminding the reader along with Abraham that this story has a purpose.

Isaac's encounter with God is indirect and takes place during "the binding" (called the *Akedah* in Jewish communities). Because the story of the binding of Isaac is told from the perspective of Abraham, we can only imagine Isaac's experience of God in the story. We do know he hears his father make a claim that "God will see to it" (22:8), when he asks about the missing sacrifice. He also knows that the attempt to sacrifice him was preempted by a divine messenger who redirected his father to a ram as a substitute.

Hagar has two encounters with God—both in the exile of the desert where Sarah and Abraham sent her in Genesis 16 and 21. Both times, Hagar receives support and words of promise from God. In these moments where God appears to and cares for Hagar and Ishmael, we witness the God of Abraham in relationship with an Egyptian woman, who is other, foreign, and an outsider. These theophanies counter the bias that God's choosing of one means the exclusion of the other. If these are stories about identity, what happens between God and Hagar is of extreme importance. Hagar and Ishmael do not disappear, and they are not destroyed. They, too, are family.

Sarah doesn't realize she is in a divine encounter when she laughs at the strangers' promise of a son and then denies laughing in Genesis 18:13-15. The child who arrived later, according to the promise is named Isaac, meaning laughter. Her daughter-in-law Rebekah had an encounter with God during her pregnancy (Gen 25:22-23), which may help us understand her actions later in the narrative.

In these moments of theophany, we observe a shift from "narrative time" to an event that is not subject to time like the rest of the material. In spite of the elements of the narrative arc, the epiphany reminds the listener of a larger narrative.

One of the best-known encounter stories is found in Genesis 32. Jacob is on the move, with his father-in-law behind him, and an encounter with his estranged brother Esau before him. Anticipating that his brother will try to harm him, Jacob sends his servants ahead of him with gifts, and his family precedes him as well. "Left alone," according to 32:24, Jacob is met by a man who wrestled with him all night. The story of Jacob wresting with "an angel" (KJV) is well known. Here is what the story tells us:

- Jacob is left alone.
- A man wrestled with him "until daybreak."
- The man "tore a muscle in Jacob's thigh . . . when he saw he couldn't defeat Jacob."
- The man said, "let me go because the dawn is breaking."
- Jacob said, "I will not let you go, unless you bless me.

- The man changed Jacob's name from Jacob to Israel, "because you have struggled with God and with men and won."
- Jacob asked the man his name, but the man would not tell him.
- The man blessed him.
- Jacob named the place Peniel/Penuel,[15] "because I have seen God face to face, and my life is saved."
- Jacob limps after tearing a thigh muscle.
- For this reason, the Israelites do not eat the thigh muscle.

The brief account presents many questions. Where does the man who wrestles with Jacob come from? Why do they wrestle? How do they wrestle all night? What kind of strength does Jacob have? Why does Jacob ask for a blessing? At what point do we discern that this man is otherworldly? In addition to these questions, the text intentionally muddles identity. In Genesis 32:27, there are no proper names used, only the pronoun "he." It is not until verse 28, when "he" answers "Jacob," that we are clear on who is asking for the blessing. Interpreters have long debated the identity of the man in the story, but the suggestion is that Jacob wrestles with a supernatural force—one that displaces his hip socket with his hand and has the authority to change his name. Moreover, Jacob's naming of the place as "face of God" (or God's Presence) proves that Jacob understood the being to be divine.

For all its problems, this story arrests our imagination. This encounter with the divine is physical, and it marks Jacob physically. His new name, unlike that of his grandfather's, which speaks to his future, acknowledges his past. Unlike the other ancestors whose names were changed, the text reverts to using Israel's old name. The name Jacob has more staying power in the tradition. And in biblical poetry Jacob and Israel become a word pair, being used in parallel refrain, "the God of Jacob, the God of Israel." The theological import of this refrain is that God is present with us before and after our transformation—on all sides of our story.

Jacob's epiphany in Genesis 32 speaks to our encounter with scripture. Engaging the text is often an experience of wrestling, and like Jacob who

15. Alternate spellings of the place name indicate different traditions and sources.

asks the man's name and never learns it, we will ask questions of the text to which we will not get answers. However, every wrestling of the text transforms and changes us. Each encounter with scripture marks us, and like Jacob, we will never be the same.

Identity and Chosenness

Inherent in the stories of God's promise to Abraham is the motif of chosenness. At each turn, for every generation, one is chosen to carry the promise. The pattern we observe is that the chosen one is rarely the "likely" candidate, such as the oldest male child. In fact, none of those selected to carry the promise made to Abraham fit the bill. Isaac is Abram's second male child, and Jacob is the younger of Isaac's twins. Joseph, the one selected to help bless other nations, is the next-to-last in his family's birth order, and the promise continues through Judah the third-born. The category of oldest male child has no room for the women in the stories who literally bring forth God's promises, name them, and maneuver around and with the promise. As these narratives work to support Israel's formation of identity, the people see themselves in the gaps of the narrative as a trickster like Rebekah who uses her insider information about her sons to move Jacob into place for blessing. Israel, this underdog, like Jacob the trickster, struggles with God and man and prevails. It is no wonder that Jacob's new name, Israel, is the name for the people.

Abraham, Sarah, Hagar, Ishmael, and Isaac

The Abraham narrative cycle is introduced at the end of Genesis 11 with the genealogy of his father, Terah. We are introduced to Abraham's family; his wife Sarai and his nephew Lot. With each genealogy we observe the command to be fruitful and multiply being fulfilled. In the ancestral narratives, each genealogy brings the reader into the narrative that provides details about the family including the dynamic of rivalry between the descendants. Through whom will the story continue? Who will be selected to carry out the covenant/promise to the next generation? What will threaten the promise? With the presence of sibling rivalry, sometimes the threat to the promise comes from within the family.

Isaac's genealogy begins with the birth narrative of his twin sons, Esau and Jacob. In this story we recognize the motif of barrenness preceding an important birth. Rebekah's agony of childlessness is replaced by another agony as the two children "pushed against each other inside of her" (Gen 25:22). Her inquiry about her children results in this word from the LORD:

> Two nations are in your womb;
>   two different peoples will emerge from your body.
> One people will be stronger than the other;
>   the older will serve the younger. (Gen 25:23)

God's words about the children not only set the stage for what happens in the narrative, they also show the hand of the storytellers. Isaac's story is very brief compared to those of his father and son. In many ways, his existence is overshadowed by his father and son. The two major moments in his life—his binding (Gen 22) and the blessing of Jacob (Gen 27)—have him subjected to their actions. In many ways, Isaac is the vehicle that moves us from Abraham to Jacob. And in Jacob's story we have the nation's (Israel's) story. Esau's story is also a nation's (Edom) story. This means the characters have double duty within the narrative, and are the embodiment of "double-voiced discourse."[16] Jacob and Esau represent themselves and the nations that come from them. To what extent then is Esau's characterization telling us about the Edomites who will become the enemy of Israel, and when does Jacob's behavior speak to the people of Israel? The birth narrative sets us up for the ensuing action. The younger, Jacob, will prevail over the older and stronger sibling, who is Esau. Whether Jacob and Rebekah's behaviors are morally right or wrong, the narrator is on "team Jacob" and the audience claims Jacob as ancestor.

---

16. This term is used in dialogic criticism to describe "speech . . . expressing the author's intentions but in a refracted way" (Vice, *Introducing Bakhtin*, 19). Double-voiced discourse has a range of meanings. For more, see M. M. Bakhtin, "Discourse in the Novel," in *The Dialogic Imagination* (Austin: University of Texas Press, 1981).

For all the rivalry between these twins, it should be noted that at the end of the Jacob material, the brothers are reconciled and reunited briefly. They go their separate ways, but Esau does not disappear, nor is he destroyed. The reuniting of the brothers is reminiscent of the account of Abraham's burial. Both Ishmael and Isaac bury their father. In spite of Sarah and Hagar's differences, Ishmael and Isaac are family. In that acknowledgment, there is hope for the future of these brothers and their children.

Joseph, Asenath, Manasseh, Ephraim

Whereas the stories of Jacob and his ancestors come to us as groups of smaller narrative units grouped together, the story of Joseph stands out as a sustained narrative that is described as a "novella." The Joseph cycle is further distinguished from the other ancestral narratives by the ways God appears. Gone from this story are the theophanies in dreams or angelic visitors. Instead, Joseph has dreams and later interprets dreams. In the vicissitudes of Joseph's life, of being sold into slavery, working for Potiphar, cast into prison and seemingly forgotten, the narrator reminds us that "the LORD was with him." Near the conclusion of the story, Joseph offers a theological interpretation of his life circumstances when he forgives his brothers for what they did to him by saying, "you planned something bad for me, but God produced something good from it." Joseph is an interpreter of dreams and of God's action behind the events of his life. The story of Joseph ends with his father, Jacob, blessing all his sons before he dies. Jacob's many descendants are settled in the good land of Goshen in Egypt.

Make Sure Not to Miss . . .

- The primordial history, 1–11
- The call of Abraham, 12:1-9
- Hagar in the wilderness, 16:1-6; 21:8-21
- The binding of Isaac, 22:1-19
- Jacob gets Esau's birthright, 25:29-34, and blessing, 27:1-29
- Jacob at Bethel, 28:10-22
- Jacob at Peniel, 32:22-32
- Joseph is sold into slavery, 37
- Joseph saves his family, 41

CHAPTER 2
EXODUS

The events of history are prismatic openings to the transhistorical. . . .
The exodus became a mythos: a life teaching through which an
"objective past" recurrently gave way to . . . the present.

—Michael Fishbane, *Biblical Text and Texture*

The very first thing we are told we must know about God, the very first thing that God tells us we are to know is this: I am Adonai your god who brought you out of Egypt. God tells us that before telling us not to steal and not to kill, before telling us to observe the Sabbath day and not to worship other gods. It is as if God thinks that we need to be reminded of the great favor God did for us in order to be sure that we will reciprocate by observing the commandments. But the reminder is itself a commandment. It is the first commandment. It sounds like a simple description, but it is a commandment.

—Social Justice Seder, Agudis Achim and ASBC, 2018

Exodus is *God's signature act.* It is the point of orientation for the Israelite people, recounting how God redeemed them from bondage. Unlike the creation story, which is universal in scope, Exodus is specific. In this story God takes sides. The creation story recounts how God created the world and the exodus story explains how God formed a nation. The Hebrews are God's people, and the exodus is the story of how that happened. It is through the events and the commemoration of the exodus that the Hebrew people found a national and religious identity as Israel. Subsequent communities have made this story their own and laid claim to the God of Israel who frees the enslaved, assuming their place as God's beloved children. The exodus is justification for the legal material that takes up the remainder of the Pentateuch. Together the exodus narrative and Torah are a foundation for monotheism.

The title of the book Exodus comes from the Greek translation (the Septuagint) and means "way out" or "exit." The Hebrew Bible's name for the book, *shemot*, means "names," beginning with a genealogy that resumes the ancestral narratives in Genesis. Whereas the ancestral stories use characters to construct identity, the first fifteen chapters of Exodus form identity around an event.

Like the book of Genesis, Exodus divides easily into two large parts. Exodus chapter 1–15:21 are concerned with the events of the exodus from Egypt, and chapters 15:22–40 contain the wilderness and legal traditions. The first section includes Moses's birth and salvation, followed by Moses's exile and call. Then there is the return to Egypt, the plague narrative, and the exodus, culminating in crossing the Reed Sea. In the wilderness, the Israelites make their way to Sinai and receive the instruction (*torah*) from God. The final sections of the book are concerned with the plans for the sacred meeting tent (or tabernacle), the gold calf episode, and the building of the meeting tent. In the literary structure we observe that the exodus is the prerequisite for the giving of the instructions about how to live in the wilderness. The overriding theological meaning inherent in the shape of the book is that the goal of redemption is covenant.

God's command to celebrate, observe, and remember the exodus precedes the actual event, suggesting that the act of remembrance is a goal of the narrative. It also means that the act of remembrance serves a function in the life of the children of Israel. This remembrance works to shape identity, theology, liturgy, community, and politics.

OUTLINE	THEMES
1–15:21 The exodus	God's power of redemption God's power over Egypt and Pharaoh
15:22–40:38	God's provision in the wilderness Covenant with Israel Instruction at Sinai Community in the wilderness Worship in the wilderness

Origin Stories (Identity)

Exodus serves as the collective memory for the people of God—past, present, and future. For this reason, the story of Moses's birth and the women who surround him is far more than a singular story—it is Israel's birth story. Loosely following the shape of the hero's journey, the narrative moves from Pharaoh's edict against Hebrew baby boys to focus on the concerted effort to preserve one "healthy and beautiful" baby (Exod 2:2). The midwives, Shiprah and Puah, defy the order of Pharaoh to kill the infant boys because they fear God. Jochabed hides her baby for three months and then places him in a basket/boat and "fulfills" Pharaoh's decree by throwing him into the Nile. Pharaoh's daughter delivers him from the water, names him Moses, and makes him her own. Later in Exodus 4, Zipporah saves him from the attack of God. These actions foreshadow God's redemption of a people. The women form a network or web that protects the child, modeling God's saving acts. The governing motif in the story is "mother God": God is midwife, mother, protector, and savior for her dearly loved child.

> This is what the Lord says: Israel is my oldest son. (4:22b)

Israel's identity is rooted in deep and passionate family connections.

The Contest between Moses and Pharaoh (Theology)

God calls Moses on Mount Horeb/Sinai to serve as prophet or mouthpiece for God. YHWH is unknown to Pharaoh and he will have no incentive to meet this god's demand of freeing the Hebrews. YHWH introduces himself to Pharaoh with the plagues: the Nile turns to blood, frogs, lice, insects, blight, sores/blisters, hail and thunder, locusts, darkness, and death of the firstborn. The ten plagues allow the breadth of God's power to be displayed. The pattern in the plague narrative has Pharaoh refusing YHWH's command to let the Hebrews go. The refusal elicits a show of power from YHWH (plague), and Pharaoh capitulates temporarily. His stubborn refusal (hardening of the heart) results in another plague, and this goes on, round after round, until the final plague, death of the first-born. The ten plagues allow the God of Israel to demonstrate might and successfully compete with the gods of Egypt and the forces of nature. With each plague, YHWH builds up his resume and established himself as one worthy of respect and awe.

Why Ten Plagues?

> One possibility is that the story is employing an $x + y$ formula. This literary motif is often found in poetry and wisdom literature where there are a number of examples in the x category and only one in the y category. An example can be found in Proverbs 30:29-31, which begins, "There are three things that are excellent in their stride, four that are excellent as they walk." The emphasis is on the y, the last item in the sequence. If this model is correct, we can deduce the entire narrative is leading up to the final plague: death of the oldest male child. This argument is supported in the text by God's words to Moses before he goes into Egypt in Exodus 4:22-23:
>
> Then say to Pharaoh, "This is what the Lord says:
> Israel is my oldest son.
> I said to you, "Let my son go so he could worship me."
> But you refused to let him go.
> As a result, now I'm going to kill your oldest son."

YHWH's ongoing display of power takes place in response to the stubbornness of Pharaoh's heart. In this interaction, Pharaoh is sometimes in control of his heart, and at other times YHWH is hardening Pharaoh's heart. This raises the question of whether Pharaoh is exercising free will. The theological question here is, What would it say about God if this YHWH is manipulating Pharaoh so that the tenth plague is inevitable? What would that mean for Pharaoh and what would it mean for us? If the narrative is using an $x + y$ formula, then it is telling the story from the foregone conclusion that the tenth plague is going to happen. If that is the case, then the narrative is leading the reader to that event, and Pharaoh's behavior supports the movement of the story to the tenth plague. Another possible answer is linked to Pharaoh's role in the story. Pharaoh is a god in the Egyptian pantheon and if he is in the role of deity, then the God of Israel is in a battle with another god, and the hardening of his heart is a part of a contest between two gods. This does not necessarily mean that God would interact with humans in the same way. Another reading emphasizes Pharaoh's humanity. Both God and Pharaoh are agents of hardening in the story. God predicts in 4:21 and 7:3 that God will harden the king's heart. The promise is initially fulfilled in 9:12. Over the course of the narrative Pharaoh's stubbornness gives way to God's hardening and then in the end the stubbornness loops back to Pharaoh.[1] Any of these readings support a theology that is focused on God's preeminence, power, and might. God is powerful enough to redeem Israel, and God has the will to do so as well.

The Passover and Exodus (Liturgy)

Exodus 12–15

Exodus chapters 12–15 include the accounts of the Passover, the exodus from Egypt, and the crossing of the Reed Sea.[2] God gives specific instructions for observance of the Passover before the event takes place in Exodus 13, which means the liturgical event comes before the historical one. Moreover, the conclusion of the exodus event is marked by song. Thus liturgy is the lens through which we should read this story.[3] The attention to the commemoration of the Passover in Exodus 12 gives credence to the act of remembrance. It is an invitation to the readers and hearers of the story to enter liturgical time. The literary structure presents remembrance as a liturgical act that transforms the historical into an act of worship.

The number of verses dedicated to the actual leaving of Egypt is small in comparison to the description of the Passover and the crossing of the Reed Sea. Although the impetus for God's action is the oppression of God's

1. Terence E. Fretheim, *Exodus*, Interpretation: A Bible Commentary for Teaching and Preaching (Louisville: Westminster John Knox, 1991), 98.

2. The sea the Israelites cross in the Exodus account is *Yam Suph*. The first word, *yam* is the word for sea. *Suph* can mean "red" and "rush" or "reed." The earlier translation Red Sea has given way to more recent translations Reed Sea or Sea of Reeds, based on evidence from cognate languages.

3. Fretheim, *Exodus*, 133.

people, the literary emphasis is on God's display of power. The departure from Egypt is what happens in the space between God's mighty acts. The crossing of the sea is the metaphorical birth of the nation. The symbols of water and blood that are associated with birth are paired in these events of the blood on the doorposts and the water the Israelites must pass through. Pharaoh's final attempt to take on the God of the Hebrews results in his demise. The crossing is so significant that it comes to us in two forms, prose and poetry. The narrative crossing is followed by the "Song of the Sea." Exodus 15 is one of the oldest pieces in the Bible. Led by Miriam and Moses, the emphasis is on God, described anthropomorphically as the victor over Pharaoh, Egypt, and nature (the sea and primordial chaos) itself. In the song, YHWH's victory is more than a moment in history. It is a monument to God's ability to rescue God's people at any time under any circumstances. In its final ordering, Exodus 14 tells what happens and the poetry of Exodus 15 explains what really happens. Exodus 15 is a striking reminder that many of the Bible's most important moments are preserved in genres such as poetry, so that the event is always a point of orientation and a marker of identity.

The Wilderness and Legal Traditions (Community and Politics)

The material in Exodus after the crossing of the sea falls into the category of the wilderness and legal traditions. The narrative takes place in the wilderness, where the Israelites wander for forty years, and it is during this period that they receive the instructions that will solidify their identity as followers of YHWH. The wilderness and legal traditions take up the remainder of Exodus and Leviticus, Numbers, and Deuteronomy. The genre of the material includes instruction (both casuistic and apodictic forms of teaching), narrative, and itinerary. It is through the dialogue between the teaching material and the narrative that the reader is able to consider how Israel lives into the laws set forth by God.

The first five books of the Hebrew Bible are called the Torah. *Torah* is often translated as "law" in English versions of the Bible, though it is more accurate to describe Torah as teaching or instruction about a distinct holy way of life for God's people in an ever-changing and often hostile environment.

On the Way to Sinai: 15:22-27

On their way out of Egypt, the people are confronted with a need for water at Marah, which means bitter. In search of water, the people are led to water that they cannot drink. They complain to Moses, who calls to God, and God instructs Moses in how to "cure" the water. Once the crisis is averted, God made "a regulation and a ruling":

> If you are careful to obey the Lord your God, do what God thinks is right, pay attention to his commandments, and keep all of his regulations, then I won't bring on you any of the diseases that I brought on the Egyptians. I am the Lord who heals you. (Exod 15:26)

The narrative concludes with the people arriving at Elim, an oasis of twelve springs, where they camp. The Marah account is carefully constructed to offer a microcosm of the wilderness experience. This very short story conveys the message that freedom has its limits. The people were redeemed from Pharaoh so that they can be free to serve their new master, YHWH. Their well-being is tied to their ability to abide by God's instruction. It is a prelude to the covenant at Sinai. In this section, the people experience provision from God in the form of food (manna, Exod 16), water (Exod 17), and protection from enemies (Exod 17:8-16). In Exodus 18, Moses is reunited with his family, and in Exodus 19 the people prepare to receive the Instruction (*torah*) from God at Mount Sinai.

Sinai

> I am the LORD your God who brought you out of the land of Egypt, out of the house of slavery. (Exod 20:1)

God's provision of the Instruction at Sinai is another major moment in the overall narrative structure. Its importance is indicated by the following:

- The words of the Ten Commandments are spoken by God directly to the people.
- The Ten Commandments (Decalogue) are the introduction to the Instruction from God.
- The Ten Commandments were written by God's finger (Exod 31:18).
- They are preserved in the covenant chest (or "ark," KJV), which eventually rests within the most holy spot in the temple and is the foundation of God's throne.[4]

Scholarship in the nineteenth and twentieth centuries emphasized the resemblance between the Ten Commandments and treaties between nations in the ancient Near East. In these treaties the conquering ruler (called a suzerain) would establish stipulations with the conquered people, known as vassals. For example, the Hittite suzerain/vassal treaty and the Decalogue seem to share a few similar components:

HITTITE TREATY	DECALOGUE
Preamble	YHWH is the ruler
Prologue	Brief historical prologue
Stipulations imposed on the vassal	
Preservation and public proclamation of the covenant	Tablets placed in covenant chest
Divine witnesses to the treaty	Divine witnesses mentioned in Deut 4:26; 31:28
Blessings and curses	Blessings and curses mentioned in Deut 28

The Decalogue, when read through the lenses of a treaty with an overlord, suggests that YHWH's relationship with the Israelite people is not a legal covenant between equals. The people belong to God and are obligated to serve God in much the same way that they were obligated to serve Pharaoh in Egypt. In this reading, the emerging Israelite people

4. Patrick Miller, *The Ten Commandments,* Interpretation: A Bible Commentary for Teaching and Preaching (Louisville: Westminster John Knox, 2009), 3.

were freed from one master but purchased by another. Israel is obligated to the sovereign Lord because of God's mighty acts in the redemption of the people. The Decalogue begins with the words in Exodus 20:1, "I am the Lord [YHWH] your God who brought you out of Egypt, out of the house of slavery."

More recent insight into the origins of Israel's covenant with YHWH moved away from parallels with Hittite treaties, which were imposed between 1500 and 1200 BCE, several centuries before Israel's traditions reached written form. Covenant theology probably emerged in the eighth century BCE with the prophet Hosea, who focused on faithful love, the basis of a theological covenant, between God and the people, which deeply influenced Jeremiah and the compilers of Deuteronomy in the seventh century BCE.

Another kind of covenant that informs our understanding of the Decalogue is the marriage covenant,[5] or *ketubbah* in Hebrew. This covenant also contains mutual obligations, but the marriage covenant holds the possibility of love. The story and marriage of Ruth, which will be discussed later, is a very good example of faithful love. The Old Testament covenants lay the framework for relationship. This relationship between God and God's people has implications for how the Hebrews will interact with others, family, neighbors, and strangers.

> The Ten Commandments are a benchmark example of "apodictic" or absolute stipulations for biblical covenant. These instructions will not change over time. Absolute commandments are one of the two types of teaching we encounter in the Pentateuch. The second, larger category is known as "casuistic" or case laws. Their form conveys their function; the "if" clause contains a certain condition or set of circumstances, followed by the "then" clause which outlines the proper response: "When someone leaves a pit open or digs a pit and doesn't cover it and an ox or a donkey falls into the pit, the owner of the pit must make good on the loss. He should pay money to the ox's owner, but he may keep the dead animal" (Exod 21:33-34).

These instructions are set in a particular context and left to be interpreted contextually. A dialogue between casuistic and apodictic commandments raises the question of just how "absolute" the apodictic

5. Jon D. Levenson, *Sinai and Zion: An Entry into the Jewish Bible* (Cambridge: Harper & Row, 1987), 75–76.

requirements are. Are there circumstances that would cause us to understand these instructions differently or not? What is central about any given commandment or regulation that is not subject to shifts in time, culture, and increased knowledge?

How Israel Read the Exodus

How did the phenomenon of the exodus function in the life of Israel? To fully appreciate Exodus, we must see it as a literary construct that fuses together saga and history.[6] The literary lens that I employ will emphasize the function of the exodus narrative as a literary construct that orients and reorients the identity and purpose of its readers. Readers can observe the way the exodus serves as the point of orientation in the Bible. Several psalms make reference to the Exodus (for example, Pss 78, 80, 105, 106, 114), and the uses of these psalms ranges from liturgical to didactic. The exodus from Egypt is so pivotal that it is mentioned in all but a handful of Old Testament books, with nearly six hundred references to it in the Bible. Beyond these direct references to the exodus, Moses, Aaron, and Miriam, and God's act of salvation, there are places in scripture that make use of the narrative template for the exodus. This foundational story is intended to be told and retold, remembered and reenacted, for each generation. If you want to know who Israel is, then you listen to the story. In Deuteronomy 26:5-11 the story is part of the instructions for how one will perform the offering of the early produce:

> Then you should solemnly state before the LORD your God:
>
> "My father was a starving Aramean. He went down to Egypt, living as an immigrant there with few family members, but that is where he became a great nation, mighty and numerous. The Egyptians treated us terribly, oppressing us and forcing hard labor on us. So we cried out for help to the LORD, our ancestors' God. The LORD heard our call. God saw our misery, our trouble, and our oppression. The LORD brought us out of Egypt with a strong hand and an outstretched arm, with awesome power, and with signs and wonders. He brought us to this place and gave us this land—a land full

6. Michael A. Fishbane, *Biblical Text and Texture: A Literary Reading of Selected Texts* (Oxford: Oneworld, 1998).

> of milk and honey. So now I am bringing the early produce of the fertile ground that you, LORD, have given me."
>
> Set the produce before the LORD your God, bowing down before the LORD your God. Then celebrate all the good things the LORD your God has done for you and your family—each one of you along with the Levites and the immigrants who are among you.

This creed offers the identifying markers of the Israelites. Three moments are identified—the ancestral origins, the exodus, and the entry into the promised land. Before the exodus, the people were semi-nomads or immigrants, who as servants and slaves became a prolific population in Egypt. That multiplication, the fulfillment of God's promise to Abraham, is also the trigger for oppression by the Egyptians.

The exodus is one of the lenses through which Israel interprets its story—past, present, and future. The exile after the fall of Israel and Judah is the other primary lens. The genealogy of Jacob/Israel connects the book of Exodus with what precedes it in the ancestral narratives. Jacob's descendants are in Egypt, where they were at the end of Genesis and, true to God's promise, they are prolific. It is the evidence of God's blessing that contributes to Pharaoh's perception that Jacob's people are a threat:

> The Israelite people are now larger in number and stronger than we are. Come on, let's be smart and deal with them. Otherwise, they will only grow in number. And if war breaks out, they will join our enemies, fight against us, and then escape from the land. (Exod 1:9-10)

The Ten Commandments in Exodus begin with these words: "I am YHWH your God, who brought you out of the land of Egypt, out of the house of bondage." The overall movement of the story is bondage, redemption, and covenant. The story of God's acts of redemption explains why the Israelites are a covenant people. The freedom from slavery cannot be separated from the bonds of covenant that shape the remainder of the Pentateuch. In this narrative God moves on behalf of the enslaved and rescues them from the oppression of the Egyptian empire. The Hebrew people are incapable of freeing themselves. God frees them from Pharaoh and in so doing becomes their new master. Thus, in Exodus, freedom is not the goal so much as it is proper ownership. The teaching material about how to live in the wilderness, which follows the departure from Egypt, uses the events in the first fifteen chapters as the warrant for God's claim on God's people. Exodus is an event, narrative, paradigm, motif, and tradition. The exodus paradigm, motif, and tradition is remixed by subsequent communities and continues to shape the theological imagination of immigrant communities of faith.

African Americans and the Exodus

African captives in the United States took the story of the exodus and made it their own. They heard about the God of Israel and understood this god to be one and the same as the creator God of all the world. They therefore claimed access, as God's children, to the redemptive and liberating power of God. They were the children of Israel, Pharaoh or any oppressive force was the master, and Moses was anyone who stood in the role of liberator. The use of the narrative as an instructive motif is evident in sermons and song. "Go Down Moses" is a well-known example. Another song, "Mary Don't You Weep," has the recurring phrase, "Pharaoh's army, is drowned in the sea." The song offers a word of encouragement because the image of Pharaoh's defeated army is a reminder that God will act against the forces of evil in the world. For many of those whose history in America begins with slavery or forced labor, the book of Exodus is an identity story that takes various forms but consistently asserts the message, *We were slaves, but God . . .*

Latinx Readings of the Exodus

Latin American liberation theology starts with the context of suffering and remembers Christ's messages about the poor in the Gospels. The strong identification of Christ and Christ's presence with the oppressed supports the assertion that the Bible depicts a God who definitely has a preference for the oppressed, which in many contexts translated to a preference for the poor. The exodus is a biblical source of support for liberation theology because the story is one of slaves who found liberation "through the power of the covenant with God," and "became the people of God."

Womanist and Feminist Readings of the Exodus

When women of color read Exodus, they find themselves in the stories of the midwives, Moses's birth mother, his sister, adoptive mother, and wife. These characters are marginalized because of their gender and/or race, yet all are instrumental in Moses's and Israel's liberation. True to the definition of womanist, these characters are "committed to the survival and wholeness of entire people, male *and* female . . . traditionally capable."[7] The midwives (who may or may not have been Hebrew) defied Pharaoh's order to kill the Hebrew baby boys, and preserved life. Similarly, Moses's mother hid him and then engaged in a series of actions that led him to Pharaoh's daughter. She in turn, after discovering the baby, responded to the request of his sister Miriam, and hired a wet nurse for the baby and adopted him, placing him under her protection within Pharaoh's household.[8] Later in the narrative (Exod 5), Moses's wife Zipporah staves off an attack on Moses's life by the LORD. Individually, each of these women demonstrates aspects of God's work of liberation. Together, they make up a picture of redemption that invites readers to see themselves in the work of ending oppression. This perspective also reminds us that some saviors are not remembered in the "official narrative" because of their location in the cultural context. The irony is that there would have been no Moses without the women who did the work of redemption. Finally, it bears acknowledging that Harriet Tubman, the liberator who led hundreds of slaves to freedom on the Underground Railroad was known as "Moses."

7. Alice Walker, *In Search of Our Mothers' Gardens* (New York: Harcourt, 1983), xi.

8. The action of Pharaoh's daughter, seeing, hearing, and having compassion on the child, is a preview to God's actions. In Exodus 3, God tells Moses, "I've clearly seen my people oppressed in Egypt. I've heard their cry of injustice because of their slave masters. I know about their pain" (Exod 3:7). See "Exodus" by Judy Fentress-Williams in *The Africana Bible*, ed. Hugh Page Jr., et al. (Minneapolis: Fortress, 2010), 83.

Make Sure Not to Miss . . .

- The midwives, 1:15-21
- The call of Moses, 3:1–4:18
- The institution of the Passover, 12:1-28
- The Song of the Sea, 15
- Manna provided, 16
- The Decalogue, 20
- The Covenant Code, 20:22–23:19
- The gold calf episode, 32

Part Two

THE WILDERNESS AND LEGAL TRADITIONS

CHAPTER 3

LEVITICUS

We must remember the context or else all meaning is lost.

—W. Kamau Bell, NPR *Fresh Air* interview

Leviticus is like no other book in the wilderness/legal tradition. Unlike Numbers, which combines narrative and instruction, Leviticus is just instruction. It is not a retrospective word on the law given on the verge of entering the land of Canaan like Deuteronomy. Leviticus's instruction is rooted in ritual, sacrifice, dietary laws, and holy living. Although it is described as the "priest's manual," for its emphasis on religious rite, the book asserts that holiness is for everyone: "You must be holy, because, I, the LORD your God am holy" (Lev 19:2). Its location is the meeting tent or tabernacle (Lev 1:1), the place of encounter with God in the wilderness that is mobile. The shapers of the traditions of Leviticus are in their own wilderness of exile, recreating and imagining ritual as it had meaning in the meeting tent and as it holds meaning for them. In exile, the ritual becomes the Tent of Meeting. Ritual forms inhabitable space where the people may encounter God. Through ritual, and its "symbolic interactions," God's people have a "realistic pattern for interpreting our world, for containing our actual experiences and for enabling action and hope."[1] In this sense, the book of Leviticus is a point of orientation for a people separated from their homeland, and a repository for identity that moves with them.

1. Gordon W. Lathrop, *Holy Things: A Liturgical Theology* (Minneapolis: Fortress, 1993), 1.

This small book presents us with the question of relevance and authority because the theology of Leviticus is "embedded in the rituals."[2] The function of ritual is to recreate and maintain order, to orient and reorient the community to a shared perspective that reinforces their identity as the people of God. Leviticus, in its attempt to define holiness, establishes boundaries between clean and unclean. The categories of clean and unclean, holy and unholy, are based in part on what constitutes our material world. There are regulations that forbid the wearing of mixed fibers and eating categories of food. There are instructions for treating mold, skin irregularities, sacrifice, and sexual relations. Think about the things Leviticus addresses (for example, bodily discharges and skin diseases in Leviticus 15) and the many things that it does not (for example, in vitro fertilization to create a pregnancy or pharmaceutical birth control to prevent a pregnancy). Remember that neither modern Jews nor Christians literally sacrifice animals as a part of religious rites or worship. For these reasons, our interpretation must consider the cultural values of the ancient world as they informed a theological worldview. Leviticus reminds us that one cannot read scripture without negotiation, a process we call hermeneutics.[3] Put another way, "to say an old thing in the old way in a new situation is inevitably to distort its meaning. Authentic continuity requires responsible change.[4]

A dialogic perspective will first acknowledge the book comes from two literary sources: "P," the Priestly source, and a source we designate as "H," because it is associated with the Holiness Code. (For more about sources in the Pentateuch, see the section on the two creation stories in Genesis 1–2 on pp. 8). Second, a dialogic reading will pay attention to repetition within the book and potential dialogue between Leviticus and other books in the Torah. Third, a dialogic reading, which finds meaning in the conversation between texts and readers, will be interested in the way ritual and liturgical texts speak to its readers then and now.

2. Samuel Balentine, *Leviticus* (Louisville: Westminster John Knox, 2002), 3.

3. Ellen Davis defines hermeneutics as "the art of negotiating difficulty within the biblical tradition" in "Critical Traditioning: Seeking an Inner Biblical Hermeneutic," *Anglican Theological Review* 82, no. 4 (September 2000).

4. Lathrop, *Holy Things*, 5.

OUTLINE	THEMES
1:1–7:38 Instructions for Offerings 8:1–10:20 Rules for Priests 11:1–15:33 Purification 16 Day of Reconciliation 17:1–26:46 Holiness Code 26 Covenant Blessings and Curses 27 Sacrifice	Holiness is for everyone Sacrifice Rituals Worship Rules for holy living

The book opens with sacrifice. In the ancient Near East, sacrifice was a pervasive practice. One underlying belief in other religions was that the gods needed to eat just like humans. Apparently in parts of Mesopotamia, humans were created to feed the gods.[5] For the Israelites, God demands sacrifice, but doesn't need it (Ps 50:12-13). Sacrifice is an act of obedience and devotion, and its importance is indicated by the attention to detail in the opening chapters of Leviticus. Leviticus 1–7 provides instructions for everything from burnt flesh offerings to grain offerings, offerings of well-being, purification, freewill, ordination, sin, guilt, and reparation.

Leviticus 8–10 is concerned with the priesthood. Leviticus 11:1–15:33 provides instructions around food, purification for women after childbirth, diseases, and bodily discharges. Chapter 16 addresses the Day of Reconciliation, an observance that holds a prominent place in Jewish and Christian imaginations. The Day of Reconciliation, Yom Kippur is the most important of the Jewish holy days. It is the ritual removal of all sin that comes immediately after the celebration of the New Year, Rosh Hashanah. In the Jewish liturgical calendar, the new year is soon followed by the ability to be freed from the burden of sin.

In Christian imagination, the blood sacrifice and the sins being placed on the scapegoat as a substitution inform the theology of Christ's sacrifice for the sins of humanity, one time and for all. The priest's annual access to the most holy place in the temple (the "Holy of Holies," KJV) is evoked in the rending of the temple curtain in the Passion narratives of the Synoptic Gospels (Matt 27:51; Mark 15:38; Luke 23:45).

The Holiness Code is contained in Leviticus 17:1–26:46. Over one-third of Leviticus comes from this source, which contains material that is

5. *The Epic of Gilgamesh*.

controversial for some and central to our understanding of what it means to be God's people. The Holiness Code includes topics such as animal slaughter for sacrifice, prohibition of the eating of blood (Lev 17), sexual relations (Lev 18), ritual and moral holiness (Lev 19), forbidden spiritual practices and punishment for violating sacred instruction (Lev 20), priests, the worshipping community, and matters pertaining to worship (Lev 21–24), and the institution of the sabbatical year (every seventh year) and the Jubilee year (every fiftieth year; Lev 25). Leviticus 26 lists rewards for obedience and punishment for disobedience. The final chapter in Leviticus returns us to the Priestley writer (P), who ends the book as it began, with sacrifice.

What Is a "Detestable Practice" or "Abomination"?

The word *to'ebar* is a feminine noun in Hebrew used for "various objectionable acts," including the sacrifice of children and idolatrous practices. This term is translated into English as "abomination" in older biblical translations. Newer English translations use words like "detestable" or "abhorrent."

These are practices that are considered outside the realm of acceptable, which range from eating shellfish to sexual acts between family members.

In this center of the Torah, we come to the heart of biblical interpretation. The history of interpretation shows us a variety of patterns in determining how we will respond to the plethora of instructions, teachings, and commandments in the Bible. In addition to making a division between Old and New, or between spirit and law, our actual practice does not easily align with our proclamation. Ultimately, what communities of faith decide on current issues is secondary to the process of how we get there, because in due time, there will be another controversy. Moreover, what is the role of blood sacrifice in our contemporary world? Given that Christians and Jews, for different reasons, no longer offer sacrifices as described here, does that render an entire section of Leviticus a meaningless vestige from the past? What might a literary analysis of this peculiar book lend to our understanding of this ritual material and biblical interpretation in general? Let's consider three test cases, with dialogic (interactive) readings that broaden the interpretive lens.

Case 1: Leviticus 1:1-17

Instructions for the Entirely Burned Offering

Most readers approach the first seven chapters of Leviticus in much the same way readers approach genealogies, namely with the goal of getting to the other side! The instructions around sacrifice are offered in detail. The types of offerings begin with the entirely burned offering. It is attested in older, non-Israelite contexts and there too the goal of the sacrifice is "expiation" (purging of sin) or atonement.[6] The instructions are specific and detailed, which demonstrate that sacrifice matters greatly to the LORD, and the people's holiness is connected to their ability to carry out the protocol. The directions for sacrifice embody both apodictic (absolute) and casuistic (case) requirements. God's demand for holiness is absolute, meaning that holiness is for everyone. However, there seems to be some flexibility in how the rite is completed. In each section, provisions are made for a variety of animal sacrifices so that all the members of the community may participate, regardless of their economic status. The ritual of sacrifice functions as reconciliation, bridging the gap between humanity and God. It takes an effort. Because it is required, attention is given to the circumstances of the entire community so that no one is left out.

Inheritors of this religious tradition cannot ignore the centrality of sacrifice. Sacrifice is a ritual acknowledgment that God requires holiness. Ritual provides a way for the community to approach the holy. There may be flexibility in implementation, but the embodiment of reconciliation is required. The challenge before contemporary Judeo-Christian communities is to determine the equivalent of sacrifice to bring about reconciliation to the whole world in the present time. What rituals should inheritors of this tradition engage in that are specific and detailed while inclusive and flexible that are aimed at the world's reconciliation?

6. The English word *atonement*, which appears in the King James Version, was coined by Tyndale from three syllables: at-one-ment. Scholars continue to debate whether the biblical concept means "purging" of sin or if it means "reconciling" with God. The Hebrew term comes from a noun meaning "covering."

Case 2: Leviticus 18:22

"You must not have sexual intercourse with a man as you would with a woman; it is a detestable practice."

There has been a long and contentious dialogue in communities of faith around how or if this teaching prohibits homosexuality.[7] The prevalence of this debate must be held alongside the recognition that there are many prohibitions in Leviticus that faithful people ignore unapologetically. It is proof that some rules matter more than others, and that the hierarchy of rules may be a better indicator of our own cultural and religious context than of God's priorities.

The overarching theme of Leviticus, "holiness is for everyone," calls all people, not just priests, to holy living, which means that God's people are known not just by how they worship, but by what they abstain from, and what they do.[8] Ritual in the place of worship creates an order that imprints on the people in the form of ritualistic or ethical behavior. This perspective is reflected in the structure of Leviticus 18–20. Leviticus 18 and 20 are similar in content and appear to be intentional in structure. Both chapters begin and end with a call to obedience.[9] Leviticus 18 lists forbidden sexual practices and forbids sacrificing children to the Babylonian god Molech, followed by the negative consequences for disobeying these commands. Leviticus 20 forbids sacrifices to Molech and then lists forbidden sexual practices, followed by the positive consequences for obedience to these commands. The structure invites a dialogue between the two chapters as it draws our attention to Leviticus 19 in between them. Leviticus 19 is described as the "central summons to holiness."[10] This chapter includes elements of the Decalogue, such as keeping the Sabbath,

7. There are seven scriptures identified as potentially prohibiting homosexuality. Four are in the Old Testament: Genesis 9:20-27; 19: 1-11; Leviticus 18:22; and Leviticus 20:13. The other three references in the New Testament are Romans 1:26-27; 1 Corinthians 6:9-10; and 1 Timothy 1:10.

8. Ellen Davis, *Opening Israel's Scriptures* (Oxford: Oxford University Press, 2019).

9. Balentine, *Leviticus*, in *Interpretation: A Bible Commentary for Teaching and Preaching* (Louisville: Westminster John Knox, 1999), 151.

10. Balentine, *Leviticus*, 160.

prohibition of idols, respect for parents, no false swearing or taking God's name in vain, and not stealing and expands the definition of holiness to include a way of being in the world. In other words, holiness is defined not just by what we abstain from but by what we engage in. At the heart of the holiness code is justice and community. This structure moves from the central call to holiness outward. In other words, we first live into a model of holy living in our intimate relationships with our families and those we love and then move outward.

The prohibition in 18:22 reflects a world order that reaches back to the creation story in Genesis. The order God establishes includes the prime directive of the creation to "be fertile and multiply." In this world, procreation is an anticipated product of sexual activity. For this reason, sexual partners and occasions are regulated to optimize fertility and to protect the family unit. These regulations were issued to a male audience, which helps explain the wording of this prohibition, "with a man as you would with a woman," an idiom used for homosexual acts by heterosexuals, most likely in the family unit.[11] Thus the command that preserves an emphasis on procreation also regulates those in power in a hierarchical household from exerting power over the vulnerable—that is, women, and male and female children and slaves.

The holiness in Leviticus is not simply piety, or ritual limited to the sanctuary. To the contrary, the ethical behavior that is holiness lived in the world enables every place to be a safe space.

Case 3: Leviticus 20:10

"If a man commits adultery with a married woman, committing adultery with a neighbor's wife, both the adulterer and the adulteress must be executed."

Here the issue is not whether adultery is an offense or not, but it is concerned with the severity of the punishment, particularly when we consider the "adulteress" may have been forced or raped by the adulterer. How

11. Mary Douglas, *Leviticus as Literature* (Oxford: Oxford University Press, 1999), 238. This also explains why the prohibition does not address same-sex activity between women.

might a dialogue with other ancient Near Eastern laws broaden our understanding? When compared with laws among neighboring tribes concerning adultery, we observe that the punishments were equally severe. However, if the husband wanted mercy for his wife, he could appeal to the king and this could be granted. There was a way out. The editors of Leviticus are taking the concerns for government and community shared by their tribal neighbors and casting them differently to eliminate the role and centrality of the king.[12] In the final form of Leviticus, the law and punishment is administered by God. In the absence of the king, the inheritors of this text must decide who will interpret and administer the punishment. This is an interesting background for the account of Jesus's handling of the woman caught in adultery in John 8, where the religious leaders are ready to carry out the punishment prescribed by the law, and it is Jesus who shows mercy.

An exilic community charged with the responsibility of shaping this "priest's manual" makes clear to the audiences in exile and after that holiness is required by God, and that this life of holiness requires literal and figurative sacrifice. The communities of faith that inherit this book must determine for each generation how to live into a holiness that upholds the principles for community that are outlined in Leviticus.

Make Sure Not to Miss . . .

- Regulations for sacrifice, 1–7
- The Day of Reconciliation, 16
- Instructions for gleaning, 19:9-10; 23:22
- The command to love immigrants, 19:34

12. William W. Hallo, "Leviticus and Ancient Near Eastern Literature," in *Leviticus: A Modern Commentary* (New York: Jewish Publication Society, 1979), xxix–xxx.

CHAPTER 4
NUMBERS

The book of Numbers has two very different names. One name comes from the Latin title *Numeri*, which is derived from the Greek name *Arithmoi*. The Latin and Greek names are numerical in reference and are influenced by the census with which the book opens and closes, while the Hebrew name locates the reader in the wilderness, where Israel spends a generation. The period of forty years is the span of a generation, which means that not everyone who went into the wilderness after the exodus will survive to enter the promised land. Thus, the census at the beginning and middle of the book signals a transition from the old generation to the newer one. Many of those who eventually enter the promised land did not experience and witness God's redemption in Egypt. With the death of the old generation and birth of the new, we are aware of the importance of preserving the traditions, teachings, and narratives that form identity.[1] The Hebrew name, *bemidbar*, means "in the desert." The structure of the book takes its shape from the itinerary in the wilderness, which has three movements:

OUTLINE	THEMES
1:1–10:10 The Wilderness of Sinai 10:1–22:1 The Transjordan area 22:2–36:13 The Plains of Moab	Death of the old, birth of the new

1. Dennis Olson, *Numbers,* Interpretation: A Bible Commentary for Teaching and Preaching (Louisville: Westminster John Knox, 1996), 6.

The desert has a literal and metaphorical function in Numbers. As a historical reality, the desert is the place where the Hebrew people are confronted with the task of daily survival. They must find water, food, and shelter. Moreover, the location and experience of the desert functions as a powerful symbol. The wilderness is no-man's-land. First, it is liminal space, in between the old identity and the new. The uncertainty around the people's identity is as real as their uncertainty around how they will eat. Second, in Genesis and Exodus, we have already observed the motif of the wilderness as the place of encounter with God. Both Hagar and Abraham encountered God in the wilderness, as did Jacob, Moses, and Zipporah. Given this recurring motif, the time in the wilderness, *bemidbar*, can be seen as an intentional and ongoing encounter with YHWH. Third, we know from the Bible's composition and editing history that these texts would have been edited during the Babylonian exile, perhaps five hundred years after the exodus experience. How did the experience of exile influence the way the narrative units were assembled? How did stories about things such as blessing and inheritance speak both to a past and to a present/future?

What does it mean to be an Israelite when you were born in the desert? What is your frame of reference for someone who knows neither Egypt nor Canaan? Moreover, how does the later editing of these books during the Babylonian exile, another wilderness experience, influence the way these stories are shaped and preserved? It may be that the itinerary in Numbers is a literary device that shapes the narrative geographically, symbolically, and theologically. Just as the Israelites can document movement out of the wilderness toward the promised land, so might the community in exile read this material with an eye toward their own symbolic journey, hoping to find God's ongoing presence and provision will ring true in their own circumstances.

The census in Numbers 1 and the census in Numbers 26 can serve also as markers in the organization of the book. With each census marking a generation, one old and one new, the book can be divided between the generations.

NUMBERS 1-25: THE OLD GENERATION OF REBELLION	NUMBERS 26-36: THE NEW GENERATION OF HOPE
1: Census of 12 tribes	26: Census of 12 tribes
3: Census of the Levites	26: Census of the Levites
5: Instruction involving women	27: Instruction involving women
6: Laws concerning vows	30: Laws concerning vows
7, 15: Lists and instructions concerning offerings	28, 29: Lists and instructions concerning offerings
9: Celebration of Passover	28:16-25: Instructions for future Passovers
10:8-9: Teaching regarding the priests sounding alarm for holy war	31:6: Priests blow the trumpets to sound the alarm for holy war against Midian
13: List of spies chosen to surveil the promised land	34: List of tribal leaders from each of the 12 tribes chosen to divide the promised land
13–14: The spy story and Israel's rebellion, which led to the death of the old generation	32:6-15: The spy story of Numbers 13–14 recalled as a lesson for the new generation
10–25: Scattered geographical notations about Israel's journey in the wilderness	33: Summary of places Israel journeyed in the wilderness
18:21-32: Provisions for the Levites	35: Provisions for the Levitical cities
21:21-35: Victory over Kings Sihon and Og	32: Assignment of the land captured from Sihon and Og
25: The Midianites cause Israel to sin	31: Holy war against the Midianites

In addition to the two census accounts, the book of Numbers contains instructions, lists, itinerary, and a diverse narrative collection that includes some of the better-known stories in the Bible. In the book of Numbers, we find the accounts of Miriam's and Aaron's deaths, the bronze serpent, Balak and Balaam, the incident at Massah and Meribah, and the fateful account of the spies sent into the promised land. As the people struggle to survive physically and spiritually in the desert, there are uprisings, and challenges to Moses's authority and God's management. This diverse grouping of stories is unified by this theme of contrast between the generations. The former is characterized by disobedience and death, and the new one by obedience and hope. Each of the following stories supports this theme.

The Spies Report: 13:25-33

The spies are sent into the land to survey it. They confirm that the land is indeed prosperous and desirable, as promised. In fact, the report is mythic in proportion. The land was "actually full of milk and honey" (Num 13:27). The grape cluster was carried on a pole between two of the spies. However, there is another reality, and that is the "powerful people who live in the land" and the "huge fortifications" of the cities with the added presence of huge men, the "Nephilim," who made most of the spies see themselves "as grasshoppers." The size of the inhabitants and the fruit of the land overwhelm the Israelites. It is as if God's promise is too big, and they now must decide what kind of report they will bring. There are two narratives, or perspectives, among the spies. The majority do not believe the people can take the land, while a small minority want to move forward. The tension between competing realities forms a dialogue that pits Caleb, a representative of the new generation, against those who choose to focus on the obstacles rather than God's promise. The spies' report presents an opportunity for God's people, then and now, to decide which narrative will shape their reality. In the end, the majority prevailed by spreading a "rumor" to dissuade the people from moving forward. This narrative explains how the people came to wander in the desert for an extended period, as punishment from God for their lack of faith. God deems that "none of the men who saw my glory and the signs I did in Egypt . . . will see the land I promised to their ancestors" (Num 14:22-23).

The Daughters of Zelophehad: 27:1-11 and 36:1-12

In Numbers 27 we find the first of two stories about a challenge to Israel's inheritance tradition, which comes from women who are taken seriously. The daughters of Zelophehad challenge rules for inheritance based on gender. The daughters' objection is that their father's name will be lost because he has no sons. Moses takes the appeal to God in the meeting tent, and God's response is "Zelophehad's daughters are right" (Num 27:4). Not only does God validate their claim but the rules are changed to pass inheritance onto daughters when there is no son. Now in a later narrative unit (Num 36), the other relatives prevail on Moses to make sure that Zelophehad's daughters marry within the tribe, ensuring that property stays within the family. The second story is a reminder that patrilineal inheritance did not go away. However, the changing of the rules by God in Numbers 27 creates a precedent that laws can be adjusted and changed in new or unforeseen circumstances, and, in this instance, the change comes because the daughters came forward with their case.

Meribah: 20:1-13

The story/tradition of Massah and Meribah is found in Exodus 17, Numbers 20, and the Psalms (78, 81, 95). This event functions in tradition as a story of rebellion. The Israelites are in need of water in the wilderness. They complain to Moses (in Exodus), Moses and Aaron in Numbers, so Moses and Aaron cry out to God, who gives instructions. In Exodus, Moses is told to strike the rock and he follows directions. In Numbers, he is instructed to speak to the rock, but in this account, he strikes the rock twice. His action in Numbers has grave consequences. Moses cannot enter the promised land because of this action, which seems like a harsh punishment. When we consider the dialogue between the two accounts, we observe the overlap in the details in the two stories suggesting the Numbers account is aware of the Exodus story. In Numbers, the story takes on the book's theme of a transition from one generation to the next. That theme is further supported by the placement of the narrative after the death of Miriam and before the death of Aaron. Numbers 20 deals with the prophetic family. All will die in the wilderness. In light of the overarching theme, we can entertain the possibility that Moses's banishment from the promised land is more a consequence of belonging to his generation than of his behavior in this one moment.

Make Sure Not to Miss . . .

- Priestly benediction, 6:22-27
- Spying episode, 13
- Massah and Meribah, 20
- The bronze snake, 21:4-9
- Balaam/Balak story, 22–24
- Daughters of Zelophehad, 27:1-11; 36:1-12

CHAPTER 5
DEUTERONOMY

The English name *Deuteronomy* comes from the Greek translation of Deuteronomy 17:18, which makes reference to as "second law," and sure enough Deuteronomy reiterates a good segment of the teaching material that has already been given. On the plains of Moab, looking over into the promised land, Moses delivers a very long sermon filled with reminders of everything he's taught the people over the last forty years in the wilderness. Peppered with phrases like "remember," "take care to remember," and "don't forget," Moses gives the people his parting words, hence the Hebrew name of the book, *debarim*, or "words."

The geographical location of the book is of great significance. The vast majority of the material in the Torah takes place in the wilderness. Abraham's descendants have been living into the covenantal promise God made to their ancestor. They are now a numerous, that is, "great" nation. They have already witnessed God's blessing and have been a blessing to others. Up until this point, the promise of a homeland has eluded them. An entire generation died in the wilderness without witnessing the fulfillment of this promise, and although Moses will view the promised land, he will not enter it. Miriam and Aaron died in the wilderness with their generation except for Joshua and Caleb. Thus, Moses's words are delivered to those born in the wilderness. They have heard of God's act of deliverance, but they did not witness it. They have, however, experienced God's provision in the wilderness, and Moses wants to ensure that their identity is tied not only to the promised land but to the God who provides it. As Moses will not be joining them, these teachings are the means by which

Moses accompanies them into the promised land. The people's identity, and arguably Moses's legacy, is tied to the ability of the people to remember or keep the teaching.

The location of the book in the Torah is of equal significance. As the last book of the Torah, Deuteronomy looks forward and behind, and serves as a transition from the first division of the Hebrew Bible to the next, known as prophets or *Nevi'im*. As noted earlier, the documentary hypothesis about the composition of the Torah argues that there are four sources or literary traditions that contribute to the Torah. They are the Jahwist (J), the Elohist (E), the Priestly (P), and the Deuteronomist (D). The first four books comprise material from the first three sources. Much of Deuteronomy comes from the Deuteronomist. This D source is known as a writer/editor because scholars believe the community responsible for this book also exercised influence over the books that immediately follow it: Joshua, Judges, Samuel, and Kings. These books are known as the Deuteronomistic History by scholars who observe the same traditions that created Deuteronomy have had something to do with the theological teachings in these books. To the Deuteronomistic History and its theology we shall return later.

Unlike the book of Numbers that precedes it, Deuteronomy has little narrative material. And Moses's rehearsal of the familiar draws our attention to the role of repetition. Western writing cultures tend to be impatient with repetition. Once it is written down, the second or third occurrence of the same thing can be perceived as a waste of time. Yet, Deuteronomy has much to teach us about the power of repetition. What follows is an outline of the book:

OUTLINE	THEME
1:1–4:43 A review of Israel's history in the wilderness 4:44–28:68 Covenant instruction 29:1–32:52 Commissioning 33:1–34:12 Another covenant, Joshua's blessing and Moses's death	Remember the covenant Keep the covenant Don't forget to keep the covenant

In the opening of the book, Moses refers to Horeb (also known as Sinai) and offers a summary of Israel's history from the initial giving of the teaching in Deuteronomy 1–3. Moses's summary is set up to show that he has always given the proper direction, although Israel has not always chosen to follow it. This argument leads to Deuteronomy 4, which begins with the words "Now, Israel, in light of all that, listen to the regulations and the case laws that I am teaching you to follow, so that you may live, enter, and possess the land that the LORD, your ancestors' God, is giving to you" (Deut 4:1). The rhetorical thrust of Moses's rehearsal of the past is to make the point that he has not steered them wrong, and it would benefit the people if they listen to God's instruction that he has conveyed to them. Moses emphasizes the importance of remembering because of Israel's proclivity to forget.

The Ten Commandments (Decalogue)

Deuteronomy 5 is another account of the Decalogue. The introduction considers the audience who would not have been at the first giving of the commandments: "The LORD our God made a covenant with us at Mount Horeb. The LORD didn't make this covenant with our ancestors but with us—all of us who are here and alive right now" (Deut 5:2-3). The repetition of the Decalogue contains a powerful theological and liturgical statement. Theologically, the book makes the assertion that every generation must make the covenant their own. The new generation cannot rest on the covenant made by their parents. Thus with the repetition of the Decalogue, Moses reenacts the giving of the instruction at Sinai. This liturgical act invites subsequent generations to take on the identity as God's people. It's not enough to be born into this. They must enact it.

The centrality of each generation entering covenant with God is reinforced in the giving of the great commandment, known as the *Shema*, which is the Hebrew imperative form of the word meaning to listen or hear or obey.

The *Shema*: 6:4-5

> Israel, listen! Our God is the LORD! Only the LORD! Love the LORD your god with all your heart, all your being, and all your strength.

The great commandment begins with a claim about Israel's God, namely ownership and then primacy and/or exclusivity. The description of YHWH as "our," that is belonging to Israel, is covenantal. In other words, the relationship is contractual. Moreover, Israel's God, YHWH is *ehad*, which could mean "alone" or "one." The first possible meaning signals exclusivity of worship that is consistent with the Decalogue. There are to be no other gods. The second possible meaning for *ehad* as one is seen as a statement of monotheism.

As is the case with the Decalogue, the opening claim paves the way for the command that follows. In light of the covenantal relationship, and the nature of YHWH's being, Israel is commanded to love. The appropriate response to this sovereign being begins with love. In this formative commandment, the essence of Israel's interaction with God is rooted in the center and fullness of existence with a word that encompasses divine and human affection. Israel's God cares not just about outward behavior but inner motivation.

The verses that immediately follow (Deut 6:6-9) are about keeping God's commandments. The people are instructed to keep them, recite them to their children, talk about them, bind them on their hand and forehead, and write them on the doorposts. This teaching is to be performed, embodied, and made public. If done correctly, the Israelites will not be able to keep their identity secret. The work of repeating the instruction has as its goals both the preservation and the transformation of the tradition. Each generation makes the commandments their own, and as the example of the Decalogue in Deuteronomy demonstrates, with a different justification for keeping the Sabbath. In Exodus, the rationale for keeping the Sabbath is God's creation of the world in six days. For Deuteronomy, the keeping of the Sabbath commemorates Israel's redemption from slavery. Both traditions uphold the honoring of the Sabbath, but with the repetition we observe nuances that are unique to each generation.

Future Blessings or Curses: 28

In Deuteronomy 28, Moses offers two possible futures for God's people. One is the course of obedience, "carefully keeping all his commandments that I am giving you right now" (Deut 28:1). If the people follow that path, they will experience God's blessings detailed in 28:1-13, if they are careful not to "deviate even a bit from any of these words" (28:14). The remainder of the chapter offers an alternate future, listing the curses that will come to the people if they do not obey God's regulations. The list of curses is much longer and more detailed than the list of blessings. These verses are an example of Deuteronomistic theology, which teaches that God's blessings are awarded for obedience and God's curses are earned through disobedience. This simple equation for retribution theology is used to interpret the history of Israel throughout the period when they were ruled by kings. The destruction of the kingdoms of Israel and Judah was not the result of political and economic movements but the result of Israel's disobedience.

This perspective shapes the material that follows Deuteronomy, namely Joshua, Judges, 1 and 2 Samuel, and 1 and 2 Kings, a block of material known as the Deuteronomistic History. The books were shaped by editors in and on the other side of exile who understood the events of history to have a theological cause, and they wanted the records to reflect God's participation in those events. For this reason, readers will find occasional speeches added by these editors that reassert the teachings from Deuteronomy, with the consistent messaging that careful obedience to God and God's instruction or teaching is the way to secure stability, safety, blessing, and success.

The book of Deuteronomy is shaped in exile, which means that it is located in more than one time and space. The "there" that Moses refers to is the plains of Moab, and it is also the community in exile after the seventh or sixth centuries BCE. The result is that the individual historical moments become transhistorical experiences of a people longing to realize God's promises of an unending covenant.

Make Sure Not to Miss . . .

- The Decalogue, 5:6-21
- The *Shema*, 6:4-9
- Blessings for obedience, 28:1-14
- Curses for disobedience, 28:15-68
- The Song of Moses, 32
- Moses's blessing of the tribes, 33
- Moses's death, 34

Part Three

THE PROMISED LAND: JOSHUA AND JUDGES

The books of Joshua and Judges cover Israel's entry into the promised land up to the period before the institution of the monarchy. The old terminology for this narrative unit, "the conquest," identifies much of what is problematic with the block of material. Joshua and Judges contain stories of Israel's entrance into the land that are excessively violent, and this violence is sanctioned by God. The term *herem* is the word for *ban* that demands every living thing, including children, women, and livestock, be slaughtered. These elements have essentially been "deal breakers" for many modern readers who do not know what to do with such a deity and have a hard time connecting the God in Judges with the God who instructs us to "do justice, embrace faithful love, and walk humbly with your God," in Micah (6:8), or the one who commands the people to love the immigrants and neighbors, "as yourself" in Leviticus 19:18, 33-34, or the God described by Jesus in the New Testament.

The theological and ethical questions raised by such violence invite us to focus on genre. To what genre of literature do these writings belong and what do they claim to be? Do archaeological findings support the narrative? As a part of the Deuteronomistic History, how is the story constructed to support the overarching theme, and can we identify Israel's imagination as it works to form identity? Finally, how might a dialogic reading of the sources in Joshua assist us in navigating this text?

CHAPTER 6
JOSHUA

The book of Joshua bears the name of the new leader who replaces Moses. One of the themes of the book is to establish Joshua as the legitimate successor to the man about whom it was said, "No prophet like Moses has yet emerged in Israel; Moses knew the LORD face-to-face!" (Deut 34:10). God calls Joshua in the very first chapter of the book. In addition to promising the land of Canaan, God promises, "I will be with you in the same way I was with Moses. I won't desert you or leave you" (Josh 1:5). In the same chapter, the people respond to Joshua's instructions, "We will obey you in the same way that we obeyed Moses" (Josh 1:17). Although he is dead, Moses is mentioned in the book of Joshua over fifty times! The introduction of the book is intentionally shaped to emphasize

- God's fulfillment of the promises made to Abraham,
- the leadership of Joshua in the tradition of Moses, and
- the resolve of the people to be obedient.

Joshua paints a picture of a sweeping conquest of Canaan. The Israelites cross the Jordan River on dry ground. The crossing of the river evokes the other miraculous crossing of the Reed Sea in Exodus. Together the two crossings mark the beginning and end of the wilderness wanderings. The monument of twelve stones to commemorate the crossing is constructed for the future generations, so that they will know of God's miraculous presence. Similarly, these stories in Joshua are constructed as a monument to God's power for the Israelites.

Once in the land, the Israelites take the cities of Jericho and Ai, they make Gibeon a vassal or subordinate territory, and they engage and defeat southern kings and northern kings. The text offers summaries of the conquest:

> So Joshua took this whole land: the highlands, the whole arid southern plain, the whole land of Goshen, the lowlands, the desert plain, and both the highlands and the lowlands of Israel. He took land stretching from Mount Halak, which goes up toward Seir, as far as Baal-gad at the foot of Mount Hermon in the Lebanon Valley. He captured all their kings. He struck them down and killed them. . . . So Joshua took the whole land, exactly as the LORD had promised Moses. Joshua gave it as a legacy to Israel according to their tribal shares. Then the land had rest from war. (Josh 11:16-17, 23)

In Joshua 12 the Israelites "struck down" the kings west of the Jordan. The text portrays a stunning military victory. The victorious tone of this section portrays Joshua successfully leading the people in taking the land "exactly as the LORD had promised Moses." The language in this section and the stories of Jericho and Ai are the ones that dominate our impression of the book.

The idealistic narrative of chapter 12, in which Israel's triumph is complete, is followed with another narrative, that reveals Israel did not utterly destroy the inhabitants of the land: "Now Joshua had reached old age. The LORD said to him, ' . . . much of the land remains to be taken over" (Josh 13:1). What then was "the whole land" that Joshua took in the previous chapter? The overall structure and genre will provide lenses through which we can understand some of the motivation behind this account and the resulting shape.

OUTLINE	THEMES
1–12 Taking the land 13–22 Division of the land 23–33 Final things	Entry into the land of promise Joshua's leadership Obedience to God

Joshua and Genre

Historiography is a better term than *history* to use in reading Joshua. Historiography is historic writing, to be distinguished from history in a stricter, modern sense of the word, because although the books of Joshua and Judges appear to be dealing with history, it is unlikely that the stories in Joshua have the same goals that contemporary history writers claim to have. These very statements make assumptions about history that must be challenged. In his article "The Trouble with History," Baruch Halpern offers a description of ancient history writing that serves as a critique of modern history. Halpern reminds us that all history has an audience in mind and is meant for a purpose: "History is not how things happened, but an incomplete account, written toward a specific end, of selected developments."[1]

It is fair to say that the Israelites were not preserving the stories about the entry into Canaan for us, three thousand years in the future. So what are we to take from Joshua? One word that easily describes Joshua is *ideological*. The stories are cast to fit easily into one of two categories: One pattern is a unified and obedient nation under the leadership of the one chosen by God as Moses's successor. The second pattern involves individuals, who act alone, disobeying God and reaping the consequences. These perspectives suggest the term *propaganda*, which is the "systematic [transmission] of a doctrine or cause or of information reflecting [those] views and interests."[2] Whether the story reports victories or defeats, the story is couched in the language of obedience to God.

Another word that expresses the genre of Joshua is *testimony*. In a testimony, the storyteller recounts an event or a series of events in order to proclaim God's faithfulness, or provision or power. A testimony is an account of how God moved in the life circumstances of the storyteller in natural or supernatural ways. It includes historical events, but because the purpose of the story is to give honor to God, the storyteller may adapt

1. Baruch Halpern, "The Trouble with History," in *The First Historians* (University Park: Pennsylvania State Press, 1988), 7.

2. *The American Heritage Dictionary*, s.v. "propaganda" (New York: Houghton Mifflin Harcourt, 2020), https://ahdictionary.com/word/search.html?q=propaganda.

the chronology for maximum effect. Testimony may be structured by the goal and the obstacle, as it moves back and forth from one to the other. Some testimonies emphasize the gravity or seriousness of the state or circumstances from which the storyteller was delivered, to the point where it begins to sound as if the place of captivity is the point of orientation. As with ideological statements or propaganda, the storyteller wants to share a story of God's mighty deeds to give honor to God. The testimony also works to convince the listeners that if they are in dire circumstances God can fix their situation. When the editors of Joshua tell the story of Israel entering the promised land from the context of exile, how might their present circumstances compel them to make sure their current audience is persuaded that God is most capable of reversing their circumstances and returning them to their homeland? Surrounded by the Deuteronomistic speech, which calls for serving the LORD, and the Deuteronomistic theology, which establishes a cause-and-effect relationship between obedience to God and God's blessings, the tellers of the stories in Joshua wish to offer an encouraging and challenging testimony to those in exile.

As a test case for the genre of the book of Joshua, let's look to one of its signature stories, the destruction of Jericho, and its companion story about the city of Ai. Set in sequence, the first gives an account of a successful military engagement conducted according to God's guidance, and the second one becomes a lesson in what happens when the people do not follow God's instructions. The Jericho story is crafted to build suspense. Walled cities were virtually impenetrable by ancient weapons, and Israel's tribes are not equipped as a traditional army. God's instructions invite the people into unconventional warfare.

Holy War

Warfare, whether ancient or contemporary, almost always leads to episodes of unspeakable violence and "collateral" casualties among innocent people. In the ancient Near East, tribes and rulers fought over territory for the honor and sovereignty of their deity: for example, YHWH versus Baal (the storm god of the Canaanites) or YHWH versus Dagon (the fish god of the Philistines). The accounts of warfare edited by the Deuteronomistic Historian (in Joshua, Judges, and the books of Samuel) include a theological motivation to completely destroy all sources of idolatry that divert God's people from loyal

> covenant relationships with God and with each other. This kind of destruction is called "the ban" (see Deut 2:34; 1 Sam 15:3). This kind of tribal holy war is still evident in some regions of the world today.

Marching around a walled city would invite attack from the top of the walls. Moreover, in the divine battle plan there is no direction for what to do beyond what God has commanded: God gives instruction on a "need-to-know" basis. The soldiers and the priests, carrying the covenant chest, are to march around in silence once a day until the seventh day, when they will march around seven times while the priests blow their trumpets. Then with the long blast of the trumpet, the people will shout, and the walls will fall.

In Joshua, God is not limited to conventional warfare, which is fortuitous since Israel, the underdog nation, does not have the military prowess of the other nations, nor do they have the strategic advantage of a wall. Priests and the covenant chest on the front line are a reminder and confirmation of God's presence. The victory over Jericho is a testimony to the kind of God the Israelites are serving and to the way they should perceive the political realities of their time. Once this is understood, the second story comes into clearer focus. The people were told that "the city and everything in it is to be utterly wiped out as something reserved for the LORD. Only Rahab the prostitute is to stay alive, along with everyone with her in her house" (Josh 6:17). Achan violated "the ban" by keeping some items for himself. This is discovered when the people went to attack Ai and were defeated. Joshua consults the LORD and the LORD points out Achan's sin. Achan is discovered, and stoned to death. Only after that does the LORD give the city of Ai to the people, and this time, they could keep the plunder "as booty" (Josh 8:2).

Unlike Jericho, the destruction of Ai employs more traditional military strategy. The plan involves luring the soldiers to pursue what appeared to be a small force so that the remaining, hidden forces could go in and subdue the city. The pairing of these two stories concludes with an episode in which the covenant is renewed, which is followed by a reading of "all the words of the Instruction, both blessing and curse, in agreement with everything written in the Instruction scroll," for the "entire assembly," including "the women and small children, along with the immigrants who lived among them" (Josh 8:34-35).

Rahab

A key figure in the Jericho account is Rahab. She is introduced in an earlier passage, as the prostitute whom the spies encounter when they come into the land. In this story, Rahab takes initiative by protecting the spies from the inhabitants that search them out. She is motivated by her belief in God's power, and asks the spies to protect her and her family in exchange for her protection of them. Rahab is an example of an ideal proselyte. Her faith in YHWH results in her salvation from the destruction. In the midst of this narrative, which treats foreigners with little regard, Rahab's story is a counternarrative, one in which the Canaanite is saved and incorporated into the people and traditions of Israel.[3]

In the book of Joshua, the battle accounts are mixed with theology,[4] liturgy, and worship. Rendered in prose, they take poetic license and use a Deuteronomistic trope to make the case that possession and retention of the land is determined by obedience to YHWH. This Deuteronomistic shaping speaks to the theology and the violence in the book. In exile, Israel is without political or military power and they tell their story from the perspective of the conquered. Here we must remember the chasm between violent speech and action.[5] Powerless people often resort to violent language, especially when they are in no position to take action. The violent stories in Judges are bolstered by Israel's own sense of impotence in exile and their fervent hopes that God will visit punishment on their enemies/oppressors like or greater than that they suffered. In the stories of the enemy's destruction we discover Israel's own experiences of suffering.[6]

3. Rahab is mentioned in Jesus's genealogy in Matthew 1:5. She is also mentioned in Hebrews 11:32 and James 2:25.

4. Jerome Creech, *Joshua,* Interpretation: A Bible Commentary for Teaching and Preaching (Louisville: Westminster John Knox, 2011).

5. Ada María Isasi-Díaz, "By the Rivers of Babylon: Exile as a Way of Life," in *Reading from This Place,* ed. Fernando F. Segovia and Mary Ann Tolbert (Minneapolis: Fortress, 1995), 157.

6. Ps 137:8-9.

Joshua records the story of entry into the land in a way that supports a cultural identity of belonging to a God who can transform the circumstances at any moment if the people will be obedient. It is a story of the past that offers hope (and revenge), to a people who are defeated, exiled, and in need of hope.

Make Sure Not to Miss . . .

- Rahab and the spies, 2
- Crossing the Jordan, 3–4
- The battle for Jericho, 5:13–6:27
- The capture of Ai, 7:1–8:29
- Cities of refuge, 20
- "Choose whom you will serve . . ." 24:1-28

CHAPTER 7

JUDGES

After the unified and heroic tone of Joshua, the book of Judges would strike any reader as strange. Immediately, the reader is confronted with dual accounts of a single event. Joshua's death is referenced in 1:1 and 2:8, each account couched in a separate introduction to the book. The first introduction in 1:1–2:5 begins with the generation that was with Joshua. The second introduction includes that pattern that provides the structure to the book of Judges:

- The people did things "the LORD saw as evil," namely worshipping other gods.
- The LORD "became angry" and allowed them to be defeated by their enemies.
- The people groaned under their oppression.
- The LORD raised up leaders, "judges," who as tribal chieftains rescued them from oppression.
- Things were peaceful until the leader died (typically forty years = one generation).
- The people would go back to doing things "the LORD saw as evil."

This cycle of sin, punishment, supplication, deliverance, peace, forgetfulness, and a return to sin serves to provide both the underlying structure for the book and a theological assessment of the people. Unlike Joshua, which portrays a unified nation, the book of Judges focuses its narrative on episodes involving a specific tribe or group of tribes. Moreover, the emphasis is no longer on Joshua, Moses's successor, but on these charismatic military leaders or chieftains known as "judges" who are raised up by God. Whereas Joshua is modeled after Moses, the judges are a peculiar cast of characters. They are the embodiment of the antihero, flawed and with mixed motives. Gideon is full of doubt, Samson's rash and careless behavior leads to his own demise, Jepthah's impulsiveness costs his daughter her life. Moreover, the effectiveness of the chieftains, individual or collectively, is questionable as the people repeat the established pattern of forgetting God and returning to the worship of other gods. Their relationship with God is episodic, and there is an inability to remember from one generation to the next that worshipping other gods is counterproductive for the LORD's people.

The cycle detailed in Judges 2:11-22 is ultimately a spiral that descends into a society out of control by the end of the book, held together by the phrase "In those days there was no king in Israel. Each person did what they thought to be right." Ultimately, the book of Judges becomes the book without a king. How do these peculiar stories inform identity? If Joshua is nationalistic propaganda with an aim to build up national identity, then what is the point of Judges? What does the cycle of repeated failure say to the people about who they were and are?

OUTLINE	THEMES
1:1–2:5 Introduction to the tribes 2:6–3:6 The pattern of behavior 3:7–16:31 Stories of the Judges 17:1–21:25 The devolution of society	Israel's forgetfulness and disobedience The crisis of leadership

Judging Genre

Antiheroic is a term used to describe the charismatic leaders known as judges. Unlike Joshua, which focuses on one, united generation, Judges is a series of episodes, a patchwork of generations, tribes, and genres, held together by the pattern of forgetting, disobedience, oppression, crying out, deliverance, and forgetting again. Many deliverers are depicted as more human than we like to see in our heroes, and women have some pivotal roles to play in these stories. The theological cycle of dysfunction happens against the backdrop of the historical and political presence of the Philistines, the warring people with superior weaponry that the Israelite tribes cannot overcome. They, alongside the people's unfaithfulness, threaten the future of God's people in the promised land. In the ancestral stories of Abraham, Sarah, Hagar, and others, the recipients of God's promise encountered both external and internal threats to the promise. In Judges the threat to the promise posed by the other nations is secondary to the threat of the Israelites' own disobedience.

Many scholars categorize the short units that comprise the book of Judges as folktales, beginning with positive accounts of deliverers that then shift to complicated tales that devolve into stories that emphasize the need for a different form of leadership. Politically, Judges is a narrative that creates the justification for the monarchy, considering the glorious past under Joshua's leadership compared to the unsettled present. With Joshua's death came the end of Mosaic leadership. In the land, the reality of the Philistines demanded a strong military force to oversee and unite the tribes. Taken together, the stories in the book of Judges make a theological statement about the people and their proclivity for the sin of apostasy, which is defined as worshipping other gods. Individually, the accounts of individual judges vary in length and detail, but each one reinforces some aspect of the overall story of Israel's failure to be obedient to YHWH. These stories also bear witness to God's willingness to continue to intervene on the behalf of the people, generation after generation, failure after failure.

Case #1: Othniel, 3:7-11

Othniel is the first judge named in the book. His short story follows the pattern of Israel's behavior in 2:11-22, exactly. In response to the people's disobedience, the Lord "gave them over to King Cushan Rishathaim of Aram-naharaim." The people cried out of their oppression and God sent Othniel, younger brother of Caleb, who overpowered the foreign king and "the land was peaceful for forty years," until Othniel's death. There is wordplay in the name of the king, "Cushan of the double wickedness," that introduces the space for humor in even the shortest of stories.

Case #2: Deborah, 4:1–5:31

The unit on Deborah is noteworthy for several reasons.

1. She is the only leader in Judges who is depicted "judging" the people, that is, settling disputes under a palm tree.
2. Deborah is a woman in the role of judge.
3. The "hero" of the story isn't Barak, the military leader she summons, nor is it Deborah, but rather a woman named Jael, the wife of Heber.
4. The narrative account is followed by "the Song of Deborah," one of the oldest compositions in the Bible.

True to form, the people's disobedience leads to their oppression, and when they cry out to God, Deborah summons Barak, who is reluctant to lead the people in battle. He asks that Deborah accompany him. She responds, "I'll definitely go with you. However, the path you're taking won't bring honor to you, because the LORD will hand over Sisera to a woman" (4:9). Strangely enough, that woman is not Deborah! The Canaanite general Sisera flees the battlefield when the Israelites prevail and seeks asylum in the tent of Heber the Kenite. Heber's wife Jael invites him in and offers him shelter, and hides him under a blanket. Once Sisera falls asleep, she kills the general by driving a tent peg into his head! The victory of Israel is celebrated in the following chapter, "the Song of Deborah."

The Song of Deborah

Judges 5, known as The Song of Deborah, is one of a handful of poems set within a biblical narrative. Like the Song of the Sea in Exodus 15, Deborah's Song follows the narrative account but is believed to predate the narrative.[1] These poems in Old Testament narrative represent some of the oldest portions of the Bible. Deborah's song is a victory hymn, which emphasizes God's role in the triumph over the enemy. In verses 24-27, Jael's role in the victory is recounted. The repetition in the verses emphasizes the difference between Sisera's request for water and Jael's offering of milk (verse 25). Clearly, the thing Sisera seeks (shelter) will not be found with Jael!

Case #3: Gideon

The Gideon cycle is spread out over four chapters and two generations. Chapters 6–9 focus on Gideon, and chapter 10 follows the story of his son Abimelech. Although Gideon's story follows the pattern of disobedience, oppression, crying out, deliverance, and peace, certain elements are expanded. Of note are (1) Gideon's commissioning, (2) the way the battles are won, and (3) the Abimelech episode.

1. Gideon is an unlikely judge. God's messenger finds him threshing wheat in a winepress to hide it from the Midianites (Judg 6:11). His behavior and location make the divine messenger's greeting, "The LORD is with you, mighty warrior," ironic.
2. Gideon's unlikely calling is matched by God's military tactics. It is clear in Judges that God has a penchant for peculiar military tactics. As far as the LORD is concerned, a smaller, underequipped army is the strategy for success, and because it is the LORD's army, there is victory. Gideon's victory over Midian is among other things a reminder that God's people don't need to behave like the nations around them to be successful. This fact will matter greatly in the latter portion of the Gideon cycle, in which his son Abimelech declares himself king.
3. Abimelech's self-declared monarchy lasts three years before things fall apart. Abimelech, who used force to quell rebellions

1. Songs/poems in the Hebrew Bible include Exodus 15, the Song of the Sea; Deuteronomy 32–33, Song of Moses, Judges 5, Song of Deborah; 1 Samuel 2, Hannah's Song; 2 Samuel 22–23, David's Thanksgiving; 1 Chronicles 16:8-36, the Levites' Psalms; Isaiah 38, Hezekiah's Prayer; Daniel 2:20-23, Daniel's Praise; Luke 1:46-55, Mary's Song (Magnificat); and Luke 1:67-79, Zechariah's Blessing.

> against him and to kill all those who opposed him, finally meets his demise when an unnamed woman dropped a millstone on his head from atop the city wall.

The story of Abimelech, although brief, serves a number of functions. It may be read as a cautionary tale about unbridled power, or a warning against the dangers of the monarchy. Another element of this story is the motif of the unlikely hero/ine in the person of the woman who stops Abimelech when no one else can, using unconventional means. Gideon, himself an unlikely leader, is led into victory by YHWH, and Abimelech, who acts on his own, fails in his attempt to be king.

Case #4: Samson

The Samson story, one of the better-known stories in Judges, can be viewed as the antithesis of the Othniel account in chapter 3. Samson's story covers four chapters in contrast to the five verses devoted to Othniel, about whom we know little other than that he was the younger brother of Caleb and that he defeated the foreign king who oppressed Israel. Samson's narrative includes a birth story (Judg 13), an account of his failed marriage (Judg 14), and accounts of his encounters with the Philistines, the most powerful of Israel's enemies (Judg 15). In Judges 16, Samson is introduced to Delilah, the woman who becomes his lover and has the narrative function of "enticing" Samson to tell her the secret of his strength. After repeated failures, Delilah succeeds in getting Samson to reveal the secret of his strength to her and she, in turn, discloses the information to the Philistines so that they can subdue their enemy. Samson has a final victory when he takes down the pillars of a house, killing himself and over three thousand of his enemies.

Samson's strength is legendary, but Samson is more antihero than superhero. He makes impulsive decisions, is flagrantly disobedient, and does not seem to learn from his mistakes. In this way, he is like the people in the land who do not learn from their past experiences. Every time he tells Delilah the false secret to his strength, she calls the enemy upon him.

So, does Delilah entice or trick Samson, or is it more accurate to say that Samson either arrogantly or foolishly believes he is unconquerable, and so chooses to disclose the secret of his strength?

The women in Samson's story occupy significant space in the narrative and we should pay attention to them. His story begins with a birth narrative in which his mother is featured prominently. Like many birth accounts, Samson's begins with an introduction of the father, Manoah, and his barren wife. The LORD's messenger appeared to this barren woman and told her she would have a son who would "begin Israel's rescue from the power of the Philistines." The first woman in Samson's life participates in his creation and knows his purpose. The second woman in the Samson story is "a Philistine woman" who "caught his eye" (Judg 14:1). Samson demands and gets this woman as his wife against his parents' protests. The wedding feast sets the stage for manipulation, trickery, revenge, animal cruelty, and serious consequences for the people of Timnah and Judah. Samson's pursuit of the Philistine woman instead of a "woman among [his] own relatives," his venture into exogamy,[2] leads to devastation all around. The third woman recorded in this literary unit is a prostitute in Gaza (16:1). Word that Samson was with the prostitute spread, and a group of people from the town waited to ambush him. In a story that showcases Samson's strength, he not only eludes his would-be attackers but carries away the gateposts of the city gates on his shoulders! The final woman in the story is Delilah. The narrative describes Samson's feelings of love for Delilah, but does not reveal her feelings for him. Approached by the Philistines to betray her lover, Delilah successfully hands him over to them. She is a mysterious character. She is not a sex worker and is seemingly independent. Neither her feelings for Samson nor the Philistines are disclosed.[3]

2. Exogamy is marriage outside of tribe, family, clan, or another social unit. The danger of exogamy for the Israelites is the temptation to worship other gods instead of, or alongside, YHWH. See Exod 20:3.

3. Diana Abernathy, "Delilah," in *The CEB Women's Bible* (Nashville: Abingdon Press, 2016), 312.

Taken together, the three foreign women—his wife, the prostitute, and Delilah—contribute to Samson's demise, and to the death of many of those around him. They are described as sexually appealing and evoke the larger adultery metaphor used to describe Israel's unfaithfulness to God. Samson, like Israel, forsakes the ways of obedience (following mother's instruction = obedience to YHWH) and pursues other ways with other gods (foreign women), which results in exile. For all of Samson's strength, in the end he is captured, his eyes are gouged out, and he is imprisoned by the Philistines. His final victory is also his own demise.

The book of Judges serves the purpose of moving us from the Joshua generation to the monarchy in 1 Samuel. On the one hand, the pattern of forgetting, disobedience, oppression, crying out, deliverance, and forgetting again spirals out of control in the final chapters of Judges, so that the tribes are in chaos. That, coupled with the ongoing presence of the Philistines, makes a compelling case for the necessity of the monarchy. Also present in these accounts, as we have seen in the story of Samson, is an "exilic shadow," prefiguring the nation's downfall.

"Things Fall Apart," The End of Judges

Judges chapters 1–3 along with chapters 17–21 bracket the stories about the individual judges. The introductory chapters lay out the pattern of Israel's behavior and the concluding chapters chronicle the consequences of continuing disobedience, with the recurring phrase, "In those days there was no king in Israel."[4] Generations of forgetfulness and disobedience result in a people unmoored from their identity. It should not be lost on us that this concluding collection of horrible events begins with idolatry (17:1-6). For the Deuteronomistic Historian, this is the foundational sin, the taproot that leads to all others. What follows is war, a brutal gang-rape and murder, more war, and women captured and raped as "brides."

4. Judg 17:6; 18:1; 19:1; and 21:25.

The five chapters comprise two sections that follow a similar trajectory. They begin with individuals and move to tribes. Another way of describing the pattern is a shift from inside the "confines of a house" to a larger tribal setting.[5] The inhabitants of Canaan are not the enemy in the end. These final chapters in Judges teach that when the people forget the Lord, they become their own enemy. The story of the rape, murder, and dismemberment of the Levite's secondary wife is arguably the worst story in the Bible—one we wish we could forget because of its graphic and violent nature. It is familiar in structure to Genesis 19, the story of the strangers who come to Lot's door to assault his guests. Unlike the story in Genesis 19, however, there is no divine intervention in Judges and the woman is thrown to the crowd by her Levite husband. The crowd "raped and abused her all night long until morning" (19:25). The Levite then carries his unresponsive wife home where he cuts her into twelve pieces, to send out to the regions of Israel. Without a name or voice, the woman is denied personhood, and when she is used as a symbol she is once more violently absorbed into the story to serve the purposes of a national narrative. Brutalized in body and on the page, the secondary wife haunts us. The horrific details of the assault and the aftermath prevent us from reading this story at a safe distance. In fact, the literary function of the details may be to imprint the story upon us so that we will not forget. If we do not forget the consequences, perhaps the audience will remember that prolonged disobedience can lead to unspeakable chaos. This profoundly grotesque story concludes with these words that serve as admonition, "Has such a thing ever happened or been seen since the time when the Israelites came up from the land of Egypt until today? Think about it, decide what to do, and speak out!"

5. Johanna Van Wijk-Bos, *The End of the Beginning: Joshua and Judges* (Grand Rapids: Eerdmans, 2019), 288.

Make Sure Not to Miss . . .

- Ehud, 3:12-30
- Deborah, 4–5
- Gideon, 6–9
- Jepthah, 11:1–12:7
- Samson, 13–16
- The Levite's secondary wife, 19

Part Four

RUTH

CHAPTER 8
RUTH

In the second century before the Christian era, the Hebrew Bible was translated from Hebrew (and Aramaic) into Greek for the sake of Greek-speaking Jews. The translators, working in Egypt, decided to place the book of Ruth after the book of Judges and before the books of Samuel. This placement is based on the temporal markers at the beginning and end of the book. The small, four-chapter book opens "during the days when the judges ruled" and concludes with a genealogy for King David. When we follow this ordering, Ruth is the connective tissue between the period of the judges and that of the monarchy. The composition date for Ruth is the subject of debate among scholars. Some argue that Ruth was written around 500 BCE, during the time of Ezra and Nehemiah, who rebuilt the faith community when Israelites returned from exile in Babylon. Another group makes the case that the story of Ruth was composed earlier, around the time of the Davidic monarchy. In either case, the story addresses Israelite identity in dialogue with other narratives, events, and timelines.

Structure and Genre

Ruth is often described as a novella because it is a short, continuous narrative, like the Joseph story in Genesis. Carefully composed and beautifully written, it is treasured by faith communities as a story of loyalty and love. Attention to the overall structure of the book leads to the conclusion that Ruth is "comedic" in structure, moving from order/abundance to chaos/loss and back to order/restoration.

	OUTLINE	THEMES/SUMMARY
1	Bethlehem Moab Bethlehem	Famine comes to the prosperous family of Elimelech, Naomi, and their sons, Mahlon and Chilion. The family moves to Moab, where Elimelech dies. The sons marry Moabite women and then they too die. Naomi, now a childless widow, prepares to return to Bethlehem, now that there is food. She leaves with her daughters-in-law, but on the way gives them the opportunity to return home where they may find husbands. They both refuse at first. Eventually Orpah accepts, while Ruth refuses and insists on accompanying Naomi back to Bethlehem.
2	Bethlehem fields	Ruth becomes a gleaner (someone who gathers up what is left by harvesters). A relative of Naomi named Boaz notices her and allows her to glean with preferential treatment. She gathers enough for them to survive.
3	Bethlehem threshing floor	Following Naomi's instructions, Ruth encounters Boaz on the harvest threshing floor and asks him to be her "redeemer" (protector/husband). Boaz promised to take care of her and sends her home with a gift of grain.
4	Bethlehem city gates	At the city gates, Boaz secures the right to be her redeemer and marries her. They have a son, Obed, who is the grandfather of King David.

Comedy allows an audience to leave the known world and question the rules and mores of their society. Even though a comedy ends with things "back to normal," the characters and the audience are no longer the same. Most of this comedy consists of dialogue. The characters' interaction moves the narrative along, navigating through some of the pivotal moments in the story, allowing Ruth to function as a dialogic comedy.[1]

1. Judy Fentress-William, *Ruth*, Abingdon Old Testament Commentaries (Nashville: Abingdon Press, 2012), 18.

A Comedy about Identity

Identity in the ancient Near East is tied to family and kinship group, family name, and land. These values are conveyed in the opening verses of the book of Ruth, which introduce Elimelech by listing his homeland and family status before mentioning his name. Also named in these verses are his wife Naomi and his sons Mahlon and Chilion. If identity is tied to land, then the family's move from Israel to Moab because of the famine was a kind of death. If family name and honor is crucial to identity, then the sons' marriages to foreign women are another kind of death. In the book of Ruth, death is both real and symbolic. The famine is one kind of death or loss, followed by leaving the land, Elimelech's death, the sons' marriages, and their subsequent deaths of Elimelech and the sons. Naomi leaves home as a wife and mother, in her words "full," and returns "empty," widowed and childless, resonating with the experience of those returning to the land from exile. Like Naomi, the exiled community returned with little more than foreign wives. In the books of Ezra and Nehemiah, the issue of foreign marriages looms large as the community struggles to determine what practices are required to be the true Israel. Ironically, in the book of Ruth, it is the foreign woman who brings Naomi the Israelite new life. The Moabite offers a way forward for Elimelech's widow and the returnees from exile. Ruth demonstrates fidelity (Hebrew: *hesed*) to YHWH, her husband, and Naomi. Her faithfulness is a human example of God's faithfulness to God's people. In this dialogic comedy, it is fidelity to YHWH that determines one's family and clan.

Israelite readers who encounter this story must make a decision. Is the commandment in Leviticus and Deuteronomy to take care of the widows, orphans, and strangers in Leviticus and Deuteronomy more important than the commandment in Deuteronomy to exclude the people of Moab? Is Ruth's faithfulness to YHWH more important than her Moabite heritage? The comedy reflects the people's struggle, then and now, to determine whether God is a God of scarcity or abundance, exclusion or inclusion.

Megilloth is the Hebrew word for "scrolls" and refers to the five scrolls or books of Song of Songs/Solomon, Ruth, Lamentations, Ecclesiastes/Qoheleth and Esther. Each of these books is associated with a religious festival.

The Song of Songs/Solomon—Passover
Ruth—Pentecost
Lamentations—the Ninth of Ab
(commemoration of the destruction of the temple)
Ecclesiastes/Qoheleth—the feast of Booths
Esther—Purim

Part Five

BIRTH OF A NATION: SAMUEL AND KINGS

The 1912 sinking of the ocean liner *Titanic* on its maiden voyage from England to New York City is etched in modern Western memory. The very name, *Titanic*, is synonymous with tragedy of epic proportion. Told and retold, every account of the story concludes with the sinking of the ship. So, when director James Cameron made the 1997 film, *Titanic*, he chose to show a simulation of the iconic ship sinking at the beginning of the film. In so doing, he redirects the attention of the viewer. Now that the viewer has seen the ship sink, she can focus on the relationships, events, and stories that lead to the end. In this retelling, the story of the *Titanic* is less about the end and more about the time before and after the disaster.

The editors of the Deuteronomistic History also knew how their stories would end. The northern kingdom was destroyed by Assyria in 722 BCE, and the southern kingdom of Judah was taken by Babylon in 586 BCE. The temple in Jerusalem was razed while the city was destroyed, and many of the people were taken into exile in Babylon. The historical milestones are fixed points in the story. Everything else—the relationships, events, and stories that lead to the end and hopes for a future beyond exile—is shaped by the creative imagination of the storytellers and the theological imagination of the Deuteronomistic historians and editors. The editors of the Deuteronomistic History look over the past and engage in a theologically creative dialogue about causation. How does an understanding of what happened inform the religious, cultural, and political identity of the Jewish diaspora in exile or beyond?

CHAPTER 9

1 AND 2 SAMUEL

1 and 2 Samuel covers the rise of the monarchy and the reign of King David, and is the embodiment of "peculiar literature."[1] Israel's transition from an assembly of tribes led by charismatic leaders (judges) to a nation with a king is captured by allegory, word-play, suspense, and character development in the stories of Samuel, Eli, Saul, Jonathan, David, Michal, Abigail, Bathsheba, Uriah, Nathan and their children. These characters embody moments in the history of Israel. The beauty of the composition conceals the fact that this is a composite text with a complicated composition history. The sources for this material include a scroll attributed to Jashar,[2] a scroll containing the Acts of Solomon,[3] the official records of Israel's kings,[4] and official records of Judah's kings.[5] These sources were then shaped by the Deuteronomistic Historian, the author/editor who provides a theological explanation to the political and historical events of Israel and Judah's history . When we consider the composition history and the layers of editing, we conclude that Samuel is composed of dialogue on top of dialogue.

1. This term, used by Robert Alter, refers to the Bible's literary quality, along with its "peculiar" aims, its theological drive.

2. Josh 10:13 and 2 Sam 1:18.

3. 1 Kgs 11:41.

4. 1 Kgs 14:19.

5. 1 Kgs 14:29.

OUTLINE	THEMES
1 Samuel 1:1–7:17: The prophet Samuel 1 Samuel 8:1–15:34: Saul and the rise of the monarchy 1 Samuel 15:35–2 Samuel 5:10: David's rise to power 2 Samuel 5:11–12:31: King David 2 Samuel 13–24: The end of David's Reign	Saul and the birth of the monarchy David the ideal king The everlasting covenant

The story of Samuel begins with a man who has two wives:

> Now there was a certain man from Ramathaim, a Zuphite from the highlands of Ephraim, whose name was Elkanah. He was from the tribe of Ephraim, and he was the son of Jeroham son of Elihu son of Tohu son of Zuph. Elkanah had two wives, one named Hannah and the other named Peninnah. Peninnah had children, but Hannah didn't.

The "man with two wives" occurs frequently enough in scripture that it becomes a motif.[6] Once we recognize the motif we will expect (rightly) that the favorite wife is the one struggling with infertility and that the other, less-favored wife is the one who is able to conceive and bear. The stories of Abraham and Sarah, Jacob and Rachel, along with the stories of Rebekah and Samson's mother, have taught us to have "great expectations" for the child born to a woman, who, although loved by her husband, was previously infertile.

Against the backdrop of the annual pilgrimage to Shiloh, a story is told of sacrifice, longing, and fulfillment in the birth of a son. At this sacrifice, the size of the offering for Peninnah was commensurate with the size of her family. Hannah was childless and therefore only eligible for a single portion offering, which Elkanah enlarged in some way.[7] It was

6. See Abraham, Sarah, and Hagar in Gen 16 and following, and Jacob, Leah, and Rachel in Gen 29–30.

7. The phrase used to describe Hannah's portion, is roughly translated as "one to the face," but rendered as "double" or "worthy." The idea here is that although she was eligible for only one portion, he gave a portion that reflected his love for her.

at this annual event that Peninnah "made fun of [Hannah] mercilessly, just to bother her," causing Hannah to be so distraught that she "would cry and wouldn't eat anything" (1 Sam 1:6). Elkanah questions his wife, "Why won't you eat? Why are you so sad? Aren't I worth more to you than ten sons?" (1 Sam 1:8). The story does not include a response in words from Hannah. She does, however, act. Going to the temple, she prays to the LORD, and the priest Eli, who observes her lips moving soundlessly, assumes that she is drunk. Hannah explains to him that she is "praying out of . . . great worry and trouble" (1 Sam 1:16). When Eli understands the situation, he blesses her. Hannah goes on her way, "ate some food, and wasn't sad any longer." Then, "the LORD remembered her," and she became pregnant and had a son named Samuel, meaning, "I asked the LORD for him" (1 Sam 1:19-20).

This beautiful birth narrative, however, has a nagging problem. According to its genre, this story usually concludes with the name of the son, a name that has meaning tied to words in the narrative.[8] We are told that the child is named Samuel. However, Samuel does not mean "I have asked him of the LORD." Commentary after commentary attempts to come to terms with the discrepancy between the name and the etymology offered in the text. Samuel, *shemu'el*, means "his name is God." And the word for "asked for" in Hebrew is *sha'ul* (from the root form *sha'al*), or Saul, the name of Israel's first king.

An allegorical reading offers a way forward.[9] Hannah, the barren wife, represents the nation of Israel at the end of the period of the judges. Peninnah represents the other nations, and Elkanah is God. Peninnah (the other nations) have kings, and this is what Hannah, Israel, wants desperately. Her husband, Elkanah (which forms a sound pair with *el kana*, "jealous

8. Isaac's name means laughter and refers to the moment when Sarah laughed at the promise that she would have a son. Jacob is one of the twins born to the once-barren Rebekah. His name, "supplanter," or "heel-grabber," refers to the story of his delivery, and foreshadows his relationship with his twin, Esau.

9. Robert Polzin makes this argument in his book *Samuel and the Deuteronomist: A Literary Study of the Deuteronomistic History*, part 2, *1 Samuel* (Bloomington: Indiana University Press, 1989).

God" in Exod 20:5),[10] asks Hannah why she is upset, and asks if he is not "more" to her than "ten sons."

From this allegorical reading we can surmise Israel's desire for a king has more to do with her envy of other nations than with what God has determined she needs. God, who is a jealous God, is Israel's king. No mortal is to play that role. In 1 Samuel 8:10-22, the prophet Samuel responds to the people's outcry for a king with a warning about the potential abuses of the monarchy. Undeterred by the prophet's warning, the people insist on having a king. If their desire for a king is represented in Hannah's desperation for a son, and if this is the case, then Hannah's treatment of her son after he arrives is prescriptive for Israel once they have the king they longed for. For a woman who wants a child desperately, giving the child back to the LORD is unnatural. Yet, this is what Hannah does in the model narrative, and the word for his dedication to the LORD is also based on the root word, *sha'al*. The multiple occurrences of *sha'al* function in the following ways:

- pointing to the monarchy with the mention of Israel's first king, Saul (1 Sam 1:20);
- speaking to the people's desire and not that of God (1 Sam 1:27); and
- offering a way forward (1 Sam 1:28).

This last function of the word *sha'al/sha'ul* teaches Israel that, if she is to have a monarchy, the king, the one asked for, *sha'ul*, must be dedicated, *sha'al*, to the LORD (i.e., under the jurisdiction of the temple, perhaps). In this first chapter we observe the way the Deuteronomistic Historian shapes the narrative so that it "tells" more than one story. The first chapter is both the birth of Samuel, the birth of the monarchy, and one of the lessons about God's expectations that Israel takes from her own history.

The opening story in Samuel demonstrates the interconnectedness of the characters. The story of Saul cannot be told without Samuel, and Samuel's story is tied to Saul. The two are united in birth (Samuel's) and in

10. Judy Fentress-Williams, "What Has Happened to the Son of Kish? A Dialogic Reading of the Saul Narrative in I Samuel" (PhD diss., Yale University, 1999), 120.

death (Saul's). Saul is inextricably tied to David, and David is connected to Saul, Saul's family, and Samuel. Samuel anoints both Saul and David as king. David is Saul's servant, son-in-law, and nemesis. Moreover, Hannah's role in the story signals the role of women as a prophetic voice in the books of Samuel and Kings.

Hannah's Song

- Hannah's song follows the birth narrative in chapter 1
- Poetry following prose
- Connection to Magnificat
- Dynamic of reversals, sets the stage for the Samuel narrative arc
- Women as prophets in Samuel/Kings

Hannah's song, which follows the instructional allegory, lays the foundation for the rest of Samuel. In her psalm of praise, Hannah sets up a series of reversals, rejoicing in God's ability to strengthen the feeble and take down the mighty. The barren one has seven children in contrast to the mother of many sons who "lost them all" (2:5). The Lord lifts up the needy and brings down the lowly. The song concludes with the words,

> The Lord!
> He judges the far corners of the earth!
> May God give strength to his king
> and raise high the strength of his anointed one

Hannah's song refers to a king, the anointed (messiah), when there is none.[11] Clearly the song is proleptic, anticipating the monarchy and reminding the people that when there is a king, it is the Lord who will "judge the far corners of the earth." It also speaks to those (in other locations and times) who find themselves at the bottom of the hierarchy. The song reminds them that in that future, God will lift them up and bring down their oppressors.

The dynamic of reversals shapes the stories of Eli, Samuel, Saul, David, and Solomon. They, like the people of Israel, are raised up by God only to be brought down low for their disobedience.

11. The "Magnificat" (Luke 1:46-55) is modeled after Hannah's song.

Characterization in Samuel

Characterization is the hallmark of the Samuel narrative. In the hands of the storytellers, the kings are historical figures who, like some of the ancestral figures, serve double duty. Saul and David are more than individual kings. To some extent, they represent the nation of Israel. The characters are complex, but in the communal memory their deeds, good and bad, are seen through a particular lens. David takes on the character of what Israel got right—worship and winning. In David, she sees herself at her best. Conversely, Saul represents the nation in its disobedience and downfall. Through Saul, Israel is reminded of what it is like to be rejected by God and utterly forsaken. When Saul is told the monarchy will be taken from him, but it does not happen immediately, we are reminded of what it must have felt like for the Israelites to hear prophetic oracles of woe about God's imminent judgment, not knowing when it would happen, and perhaps understanding how Saul was given to madness. The characterization allows us to live not only through the moments of David, Samuel, and Saul, but also revisit moments in the history of the people before the whole thing ended, and identify with the challenges of trying to please this God.

The characters' assumption of different aspects of the nation's identity is not unlike the way the United States has depicted former presidents Kennedy and Nixon. Our collective memory of John F. Kennedy emphasizes the positive elements of his administration and leadership, downplaying or ignoring his mistakes and personal flaws. John Kennedy evokes the image of Camelot, and a romantic memory of this president as the embodiment of what we wanted to be as a nation. Richard Nixon's story has as its centerpiece the Watergate scandal. Our collective memory or popular opinion does not begin with his achievements in international relations. "Tricky Dick" is in our collective short-term memory, the embodiment of a president, and our nation gone bad.

1 Samuel 1–7

If he calls you, say, "Speak, Lord. Your servant is listening. (1 Sam 3:9)

Samuel, the person and the book, bridges the eras of the chieftains (judges) and the monarchy. He is more prophet than chieftain, a priest, and anointer of kings. His primary role in the narrative is that of seer or prophet whose speech is another example of "double-voiced discourse." In other words, he speaks not only to the character(s) and circumstances in the narrative, but to the audiences who eventually read the stories.

Samuel's birth narrative in chapter 1 is one of two texts that introduce the prophet. The second introduction comes in the form of a call narrative in chapter 3. The call narrative, like the birth narrative, is a genre that serves a particular literary purpose. The birth narrative establishes the character as a person of consequence in the narrative. A call narrative authenticates the prophetic vocation. In this passage, with numerous references to seeing/perception and hearing/listening, the young boy, in the Lord's service under the priest Eli, is called by God in the middle of the night. He mistakes the voice of God for that of Eli and repeatedly responds to the wrong person. Eventually, Eli discerns that the LORD is calling Samuel and tells him what to do. The prophetic word the LORD gives to Samuel is a word of judgment on Eli's house because his sons blasphemed God and Eli didn't correct them. Thus, from the beginning of his career, Samuel reinforces the rhetoric of the reversal. In concert with the dynamic of Hannah's song, Samuel's call also serves as God's announcement of punishment for the established priest, and his sons because they have forgotten the LORD.

Another narrative reversal involving Samuel occurs in chapter 16, the anointing of David as Saul's successor as the next king of Israel. God sends Samuel to the house of Jesse to anoint one of Jesse's sons as the new leader without telling Samuel which son. Samuel looks at Eliab, the oldest son, and mistakenly assumes he is the LORD's anointed, or *messiah*. God tells him,

> Have no regard for his appearance or stature, because I haven't selected him. God doesn't look at things like humans do. Humans see only what is visible to the eyes, but the LORD sees the heart. (1 Sam 16:7)

Eliab, who apparently was tall and handsome, was the obvious choice, but he was not God's choice. Nor were any of the other sons who pass by Samuel. The son he does not see is God's choice.

Through the character of the seer, the reader is invited to "see" differently, to imagine what matters to God. Through Samuel we experience God's resignation to give the people a king (1 Sam 8:7), God's disappointment in Saul (1 Sam 15:10), and God's choice of David. Although Samuel dies in chapter 25, he makes an encore appearance when his spirit is called up by the medium Saul hires. Samuel's final words in the narrative, like his first prophetic utterance to Eli, convey God's condemnation "because you didn't listen to the LORD's voice" (1 Sam 28:18).

Saul (ca. 1030–1000 BCE)

1 Samuel 9:1–31:13

Saul is depicted as a reluctant leader who is chosen by God, anointed by the prophet Samuel, and elected by the people as the first king or leader.[12] The length of his reign is unclear.[13] From the tribe of Benjamin, his home is in Gibeah.[14] His strengths as monarch resemble those of a traditional king: he is a charismatic military leader (1 Sam 11), he looks like a king (1 Sam 10:23-24), and he is decisive (1 Sam 13:8-9). Unfortunately, God isn't necessarily impressed with the things that matter to humankind (1 Sam 16:7).

12. The text is clear that Saul is chosen by God and anointed by Samuel. He is also elected by the people. Some commentators opt not to call him "king," since that term is never used to describe him. He is called *nagid*, "prince" or "leader."

13. A corrupt manuscript copy of the Masoretic Text makes it defective. The number is missing.

14. Gibeah is the location of the rape of the Levite's concubine in Judg 19, which means Saul's hometown is associated with a heinous crime.

Saul does not pursue the monarchy. It is thrust upon him. He is anointed (1 Sam 10:1), and God's spirit is upon him (1 Sam 10:1, 10). He is selected by the people (1 Sam 10:24). His reign is taken up with fighting the Philistines (1 Sam 14:47-52), and it should come as no surprise that some of the critical moments in Saul's story are connected to a battle. In the account of the battle of Michmash (1 Sam 13), we find Saul and the troops assembled, waiting for Samuel to offer the sacrifice to the LORD before going into battle. Samuel does not arrive in the appointed time, and Saul decides as king to offer the entirely burned offering himself. As soon as he is finished, Samuel appears with a condemnation, announcing that the LORD will not continue Saul's line because he didn't "keep the LORD's command." The scenario seems contrived and the punishment severe. Saul makes a mistake and loses royal succession. Given the circumstances, Saul's actions are reasonable from a military perspective. However, through the lens of the Deuteronomist, a good military decision is meaningless if making it violates God's order. Israel's first king's first mistake is the same one his people have made and will make repeatedly. They have failed to prioritize God's commandments.

The second story of Saul's rejection is in chapter 15. Again, Saul makes an executive decision as king, which makes political sense, but defies God's commandment. God commands Saul to "attack the Amalekites" and "spare no one" (1 Sam 15:3). Saul defeats the enemy but spares the king (perhaps a professional courtesy), "along with the best sheep, cattle, fattened calves, lambs, and everything of value." For sparing the choice livestock and the king, God rejects Saul from being king. Saul's rejection, however, does not result in his immediate removal. He remains in the role of king, waiting for the end to come, all the while watching the young shepherd from Bethlehem grow in popularity with the people and favor with God. The rest of Saul's story is played out in dialogue with Samuel the prophet, Jonathan his son, David his replacement, and the LORD, who eludes him. The narrator describes that divine elusiveness this way: "Now the LORD's spirit had departed from Saul, and an evil spirit from the LORD tormented him" (1 Sam 16:14).

In the latter half of his story, Saul often appears as a tragic character, one who had a quick rise and then an almost equally rapid descent. What does it mean that the LORD's spirit left Saul and what, exactly, is an evil spirit from the LORD? When did the LORD start sending evil spirits? Many interpreters of the story wrestle with whether the text is describing some type of demonic oppression or perhaps mental illness. From a literary perspective it is obvious that Saul embodies Israel and its rejection by YHWH. This king comes to represent the people in exile, utterly forsaken, desperately hoping that God will reconsider and remember them. What does it feel like to be once chosen and then rejected? Ask Saul.

Saul and His Children

Saul's children, Michal and Jonathan, love David. Both of them defy their father to save David's life (Michal in ch. 19 and Jonathan in ch. 20), even though their love and loyalty to David ultimately works against them. Michal marries David, but her marriage is childless. She is cursed with barrenness because she mocks David when he dances before the LORD. In Michal's eyes, David's ecstatic dancing is not appropriate behavior for a king, but the questionable behavior is tied to the worship of YHWH. Michal is truly Saul's daughter in this instance, because she puts the monarchy before the worship of YHWH. Her punishment of barrenness has political implications. Had Michal and David had a son, there would have been an heir who would have continued both the lines of Saul and David. Apparently, God's rejection of Saul is thorough and there is no room for compromise. Jonathan's love for David is counter-productive to his own ascent to the throne. The text describes Jonathan's love for David in this way: "Jonathan's life became bound up with David's life, and Jonathan loved David as much as himself." And then, "Jonathan and David made a covenant together because Jonathan loved David as much as himself.[15] Jonathan took off the robe he was wearing and gave it to David, along with his armor, as well as his sword, his bow and his belt"

15. Says David of Jonathan after his death, "I grieve for you my brother Jonathan! You were so dear to me! Your love was more amazing than the love of women" (2 Sam 1:26).

(1 Sam 18:1, 3-4). Jonathan literally dresses David in the crown prince's attire and figuratively names him as the heir apparent. Saul's conflicted feelings over David are exacerbated by his own children's devotion to the one who will replace him.

David, ca. 1000–960 BCE

1 Samuel 16:1–1 Kings 2:12

When God sends Samuel to anoint the new king who will succeed Saul, Samuel does not know who he is looking for. Rather than choosing one of the older sons, God has set his sights on the youngest son, who is out of sight guarding the sheep when the prophet arrives. The story of David's anointing is highly symbolic, reinforcing God's words, "Humans see only what is visible to the eyes, but the LORD sees into the heart" (1 Sam 16:7). It is an origin story fit for a legendary king, and for a nation. The word *shepherd* was often used to refer to a king. Thus, David's role as monarch is prefigured as he guards his father's sheep. With that introduction, David comes on the scene as the musician to Saul, loved by Saul's children, who goes on to slay Goliath, become king, subdue the Philistines, unite the tribes, establish Jerusalem as the capital, and bring the ark of the covenant to rest there. Under David, the nation of Israel is larger than it had ever been, taking on the territories of Moab, Ammon, and Edom. It is to this David that YHWH promises, "Your dynasty and your kingdom will be secured forever before me. Your throne will be established forever" (2 Sam 7:16). With this promise that God makes to David, God endorses the dynastic monarchy.

David is a dominant figure in Israel's corporate imagination. He is a historic figure, political maverick, military legend, icon, psalmist, and symbol. His very name means "beloved," and that he is. More importantly, he is an ideal. The monarchs in Kings are judged against David as the standard for faithfulness. His character is the embodiment of the nation as it would like to be. For the Deuteronomistic Historian, what matters most about David is that he worships and honors YHWH. However, David can also be remembered as a "sex-starved bandit."[16] Both are accurate descriptions; David the psalmist is the same David who commits murder and adultery, fails to defend his daughter, and overindulges some of his sons, which ultimately works against him. This is all part of the character of David, the man who follows after "God's own heart."[17]

Goliath and David and Bathsheba

Two defining moments in David's story come to us in the stories we know as David and Goliath (1 Sam 17), and David and Bathsheba (2 Sam 11). Characterization carries this story. David, the youngest of Jesse's sons, is cast in the role of the unlikely hero, sent on an errand to deliver food to his older brothers and their captain as the Israelite army is in a standoff against the better equipped, militarily superior Philistines. The Philistines have a champion named Goliath, and the text devotes four verses to his description. Every day the giant calls for one soldier to come forward and fight him and David accepts the challenge.

David is set apart from the other would-be champions. His very presence on the battlefield is an anomaly. He is not a trained soldier. His brothers see him as a nuisance who is "arrogant" and "devious." The armor of the king is too big and unwieldy for him. Yet armed with "the name of the LORD of heavenly forces, the God of Israel's army" (1 Sam 17:45), a slingshot, and five smooth stones, David is victorious.

Dialogue is just as important as the action in this story. David is motivated to fight because the "uncircumcised Philistine" has *insulted* "the army of the living God." Goliath's taunting and treatment of Israel are an affront to their God; thus, God's name is on the line. David's confidence in his ability to take on the giant comes from his testimony, when he recounts how God enabled him to overcome danger when he watched the sheep. Unencumbered by the "stuff" of the army or the monarchy, this is

16. Walter Brueggemann, *David's Truth in Israel's Imagination and Memory* (Minneapolis: Fortress, 2003), 4.

17. This much-used description of David is based on 1 Sam 13:13-14. The prophet Samuel tells Saul that God will end his rule and will search for a man "following the Lord's own heart."

David "unplugged" and available for God to use. The army of Israel follows David's lead. His triumph over Goliath emboldens the Israelite forces to pursue, defeat, and plunder their enemies. At the end of the account, King Saul asks his general Abner, "Whose son is that boy?" and has David brought to him and taken into the king's service.

King Saul's question about who David is at the end of 1 Samuel 17 comes to mind in the story of David and Bathsheba in 2 Samuel 11, with David's inquiry about the woman he sees (2 Sam 11:13). David is now established as warrior and king. Whereas he was set apart from his brothers in the previous story because of inexperience and youth, he is set apart from the rest of the army in this second story because of his privilege. Second Samuel 11:1 says that "in the spring, when kings go off to war, David sent Joab." Young David inserts himself into the scenario in the previous story; here the established David absents himself. King David is the ultimate insider and his behavior is informed by his position of power and privilege.

In 2 Samuel 11, the verb "send" is used repeatedly, primarily applying to David. It is a common verb; however, its repetition emphasizes David's position as king. David "sent" Joab. He "sent and inquired" about the woman he saw. He "sent" messengers to take her. Then, Bathsheba "sent" word to David that she was pregnant, and David "sent" a message to Joab, "*Send* me Uriah the Hittite," Bathsheba's husband. When David told Uriah to go home, a gift was "sent" from the king. When Uriah does not go home to sleep with his wife, out of respect for the Lord's army, David "sent" him back with a letter for Joab that contained instructions for Uriah's death. After Uriah's death, Joab, David's officer, "sent" a report. When Bathsheba completed the time of mourning for her husband, David "sent" for her and married her. In an uncharacteristic move, the narrator reports, "But what David had done was evil in the LORD's eyes," and then the LORD "sent" the prophet Nathan to bring a word of judgment to David. The narrator's commentary reminds the audience that David is not the highest authority. From a literary perspective, all of David's "sending" and all of the power associated with it is trumped by God's power when God "sends" the prophet to bring a word of condemnation to the king.

The same God whom David recognizes and honors in 1 Samuel 17 enters into the narrative in 2 Samuel 11 and 12, and in both instances has the last word. When we place these two stories in dialogue, paying attention to the characterization, a pattern emerges:

DAVID AND GOLIATH	DAVID AND BATHSHEBA
David is the outsider because of youth and inexperience.	David is the outsider because of privilege.
Goliath demonstrates his power by taunting and challenging the Israelite army.	David exercises power by "sending" for people, including Uriah, a member of the Israelite army.
David is moved to action in order to defend the Lord's name and reputation.	Uriah the Hittite does not act (sleep with his wife) out of respect for the Lord's army.
Goliath's defeat is a surprise.	Nathan's parable and its meaning take David by surprise.
Repercussions of David's victory encourage and embolden the army.	Repercussions of David's actions trickle down to his children (Amnon, Tamar, and Absalom).

In one story, David reminds us that God lifts up and empowers the lowly and, in another story, David reminds us that God brings down the mighty. Both moments are captured in Hannah's song, in David's life, and in the nation's identity.

David and Amnon and Tamar

Amnon's rape of his sister Tamar is a remix of the David and Bathsheba account. A remix is a story or image or song that incorporates elements of a preexisting one. In a fundamental sense, "everything is a remix."[18] Every storyteller, songwriter, or visual artist is influenced by the work of others to which they are exposed and ultimately inspired by. This particular remix takes the elements of power, action, surprise, and the repercussions from the story in 2 Samuel 11 and uses them in 2 Samuel 13. Amnon,

18. "Everything Is a Remix" is the title of Kirby Ferguson's YouTube series, found at https://www.youtube.com/c/KirbyFerguson/videos.

fueled by lust, is the protagonist at first, exercising power over his sister Tamar. His lust overrides any consideration of his sister, or the morality or ethics of his plan. All he can think about is how he cannot "do anything to her." Amnon is depicted as obsessed, conniving, violent, and cruel. His desires are the only ones that matter. In the story, he is joined by a "yes man," who does not challenge him in his quest to rape and "insult" (reminiscent of Goliath insulting Israel) Tamar. Tamar's words to her brother are haunting:

> No, my brother! Don't rape me. Such a thing shouldn't be done in Israel. Don't do this horrible thing. Think about me—where could I hide my shame? And you—you would become like some fool in Israel! Please, just talk to the king! He won't keep me from marrying you. (2 Sam 13:12-13)

Her plea to her brother reminds the reader that we have no record of what Bathsheba might have said to David. In that sense, Tamar speaks for Bathsheba and for those others who are silenced in the tradition. The horror of this story is exacerbated by David's subsequent lack of action. When David was told, "he got very angry, but he refused to punish his son Amnon because he loved him as his oldest child" (2 Sam 13:21). A father's dereliction of responsibility in correcting his son is an ongoing motif in Samuel. Eli failed to discipline his sons, and Samuel's sons were wayward as well. In this account, David's failure to act against his son results in the betrayal of his daughter. The position of privilege that protects Amnon from David leaves Tamar exposed. Her brother Absalom, who is supposedly on her side, instructs her, "Keep quiet about it for now, sister; he's your brother. Don't let it bother you" (2 Sam 13:20). Tamar is a victim of rape who is further victimized by her father and brother, who are influenced by and participate in "rape culture." The narrator takes the reader within David's family unit. There we observe a dysfunction that is symbolic of the nation's malaise. If David cannot treat all of his family members justly, then his worship has become a form of empty piety. When David fails to punish Amnon, Absalom takes matters into his own hands by killing his brother.

The remainder of David's story in 2 Samuel 13–1 Kings 2 is turbulent and tragic. David restores Absalom and Absalom returns the favor by rebelling against his father, forcing David to flee for his life. Absalom dies, and David mourns and returns to Jerusalem. A man named Sheba attempts a second rebellion upon David's return. The remaining material, the "throne succession narrative," depicts an aging king and the struggle to name his successor, a psalm of thanksgiving, last words, and David's death.

Throne Succession Narrative

2 Samuel 9–1 Kings 2 is a unit of material deemed the throne succession narrative. In these chapters we follow the story of struggle that determines who will succeed David on the throne. In this literary unit, the political maneuverings of David's sons come first, and it is not until the end that we see how the unlikely son, Solomon, will become king in his father's stead. We recognize this theme of the younger, unlikely child being chosen in the story of David's anointing.

David and the Covenant

A pivotal moment in the book of Samuel comes when God makes a covenant with David and his descendants, what we know as "the house of David." Literary artistry is evident in the wordplay around the word *bayit,* "house." David is "settled" in his house of cedar, and laments the fact that the covenant chest (ark) is in a meeting tent (the tabernacle). The prophet Nathan encourages David to move forward with his plan to build the temple, but God appears to the prophet and reverses the plans. God first states, (1) David is not the one to build a temple, (2) God did not ask for a "house," and (3) instead, God will build a "house"/dynasty for David that is "established . . . forever" (2 Sam 7:13). Here we have, for the first time, a dynastic succession, and it is conveyed through the metaphor of adoption. God can endorse the monarchy when it becomes God's family. From a theological perspective, much of what we have encountered has not been in support of succession. Samuel's sons, Eli's sons, and even Saul's son Jonathan are not God's choice. Up until this time, God has preferred choosing from more than one family. Now God's commitment to the line of David is facilitated through adoption. For all of its permanence, the covenant God makes with David, true to Deuteronomistic theology, is conditional. If David or his descendants disobey God, they will be punished, but the people's disobedience cannot overturn the covenantal relationship—the covenant is "established forever." In other words, God's commitment to the people is greater than the people's commitment to God. God will not take God's lovingkindness away . . . and those in exile hear these words from the past as words of assurance and promise. No matter how bad things get, God will "never take away my faithful love . . . your dynasty and your kingdom will be secured forever before me" (2 Sam 7:15-16).

Make Sure Not to Miss . . .

- Hannah's song, 1 Sam 2
- Samuel's call narrative, 1 Sam 3
- Saul anointed as king, 1 Sam 9:1–10:8
- David anointed as king, 1 Sam 16:1-13
- David and Goliath, 1 Sam 17
- Jonathan's covenant with David, 1 Sam 18:1-5
- David's lament over Saul and Jonathan, 2 Sam 1:17-27

CHAPTER 10
1 AND 2 KINGS

The opening chapters of Kings are a continuation of the David story. Chapters 1–2 complete the unit known as the throne succession narrative (2 Sam 9–1 Kgs 2), and the next block of material about Solomon (2 Kgs 3–11) resembles the character-driven narrative we encountered in Samuel. The remainder of 1 and 2 Kings is a collection of smaller units that take us through the nation's division into the two kingdoms of Israel and Judah, and a summary of the reigns of the kings in both kingdoms until the destruction of the north (Israel) in 722 BCE, and the demise and exile of the south (Judah) in 586 BCE.[1] Originally grouped along with Samuel, Kings would have been books 3 and 4 of the books of "Kings" or "Reigns," and Kings makes reference to other sources, such as the "official records of Judah's kings," official records of Israel's kings," "the Acts of Solomon," which contribute to the history of the monarchies in Israel and then Israel/Judah. The first "draft" of Kings was compiled from these sources after the fall of the northern kingdom, Israel. It was then subject to rounds of editing after the fall of the southern kingdom of Judah by the author(s)/editor(s) described as the Deuteronomistic Historian.[2]

In its final redacted form, the book of Kings is a journey to the Babylonian exile. The story of the united and divided kingdom has a known destination. Every narrative strand, every episode, every monarch and all the prophets have a role to play in the inevitable conclusion. For the

1. Michael D. Coogan, *The Old Testament: A Historical and Literary Introduction to the Hebrew Scriptures*, 3rd ed. (Oxford: Oxford University Press, 2013), 290–91.

2. Coogan, *The Old Testament*, 291.

writers of Kings, these historical events were inextricably tied to Israel's relationship with God. For the Deuteronomist, the matters of obedience to God's commandments and proper worship matter most. The history in Kings is "preached history," meaning the events are shaped by theology and literary artistry.[3]

Structure and Placement in Kings

Whereas the Samuel narrative is driven by characterization, Kings is directed by a historiographic theology. The series of events that led up to the ends of both kingdoms provides a loose framework for the narrative units. This framework is tempered by the overall theological message of the disobedience that led to the nations' demise. The interplay between historiography and theology means that the placement and overall structure of smaller units is a literary tool employed by the author/editor to create meaning; for example, the story of the monarchy after Solomon moves from northern monarch to southern monarch so that there is a sense of unity alongside the reality of political separation. Another example of this intentional shaping is observed in the formulaic introductions and conclusions that frame the material on each of the monarchs. The formula includes the date the reign begins, the length of the reign, and, for Judean kings, the age at accession and the queen mother's name.[4] What follows in the introduction is the evaluation of the king by the Deuteronomistic author/editor. The kings either worshipped YHWH exclusively or they did not. The northern kings who sinned were said to follow in the way of Jeroboam, the non-Davidic ruler who preceded them. Southern kings were held against the standard of their father, David, the model of proper YHWH worship. Whether the material between the opening and concluding material on the king is brief or lengthy and rich with detail, the

3. Richard D. Nelson, *Kings,* Interpretation: A Bible Commentary for Teaching and Preaching (Louisville: Westminster John Knox, 1987), 2.

4. Robert R. Wilson, "Introduction to 1 Kings," in *The Harper Collins Study Bible* (New York: HarperOne, 2017), 475.

reader has the essential information in the introduction, according to the Deuteronomistic perspective. Did the king worship YHWH or not?

OUTLINE	THEMES
1 Kings 1–2: Conclusion of the throne succession narrative 1 Kings 3–11: Solomon's reign 1 Kings 12: A nation divided 1 Kings 12–2 Kings 17: Northern kingdom comes to an end 2 Kings 18–25: Judah's last days	The Golden Age of Solomon's reign Sin of Solomon Sin of Jereboam Recurring apostasy of king and people in Israel and Judah Incidents of repentance and reform in Judah Consequences of Apostasy God acts in history

Solomon ca. 960–930
1 Kings 1–11

Solomon is introduced at the end of the David/Bathsheba/Uriah story, thus making it, among other things, a birth narrative.[5] Solomon is the child born to David and Bathsheba after the tragic death of their first baby.[6]

> Then David comforted his wife Bathsheba. He went to her and had sex with her. She gave birth to a son and named him Solomon. The LORD loved him and sent word by the prophet Nathan to name him Jedidiah because of the LORD's grace. (2 Sam 12:24-25)

The name Solomon is derived from "peace." Jedidiah, which means "loved by the LORD," is a variation of his father's name, David, which means "beloved."[7] Like his father, Solomon is beloved and favored. A younger son, he was not the obvious heir to the throne, but he was the

5. The birth narrative is a motif in the Bible used to introduce a major character into a narrative. Usually the child is born to a previously barren mother, or some other difficult circumstance, and the naming of the child is some type of foreshadowing for the narrative arc.

6. The first child of David and Bathsheba was the product of the adulterous relationship David initiated. According to the Deuteronomist, that child died as divine punishment for David's sin (2 Sam 12:15-25).

7. Another possible etymological meaning is "friend" for David and "friend of God" for Solomon.

one God selected. Once appointed king, God appeared to him saying, "Ask whatever you wish, and I'll give it to you" (1 Kgs 3:5). Not only is Solomon favored, but he asks for the right thing, "a discerning mind" (1 Kgs 3:9). Solomon's request for wisdom brings with it riches and notoriety. God promises Solomon "there won't be a king like you as long as you live" (1 Kgs 3:13). God's appearance to Solomon in chapter 3 is one of three epiphanies in this block of material, each at a pivotal moment. The first appearance is the narrative with Solomon's request for and receipt of wisdom. The placement of this epiphany early on confirms Solomon as the legitimate king. The Davidic covenant is in effect.

If the characterization of David in the Deuteronomistic History reflects Israel as obedient and if Saul is Israel in its disobedience, then King Solomon depicts the nation in its glory. Solomon is a legend in his own right, known for wisdom and wealth. It is under Solomon's reign that the nation shifts from military independence (achieved by David) to building projects. Solomon is credited with building the temple, his own palace, and one for his wife, the Egyptian princess. His building projects include the wall of Jerusalem, and the cities of Hazor, Megiddo, and Gezer. The narrator's description of his possessions contributes to the legendary nature of the Solomon story and it supports the theological promise that riches and honor are in fact the fruits of wisdom. Solomon's wealth, according to the Deuteronomistic Historian, is the by-product of obedience. Solomon's reported wealth is not the only way in which his wisdom is evidenced. The narrative employs three women in two legends to test and prove Solomon's wisdom.

Test 1: Two Prostitutes and a Baby

This first account is placed right after the story of Solomon's dream, in which God grants him wisdom. The setting is the royal court. Two women come before the king for judgment with a complaint that is presented like a riddle. They are both prostitutes and mothers of boys of the same age. They live in the same house, and during the night one of the babies died. Both women claim the living child. For all they have in common, the challenge before the king is to see past what is before him so he can identify the mother. Solomon responds to the test by testing the plaintiffs. The test is not designed to determine the truth, but to identify love. The heart of the true mother would rather surrender custody than see her child die. Solomon's "test" proves his wisdom.[8]

Test 2: The Queen of Sheba

Solomon's second "test" comes from a woman of wealth, wisdom, and renown, the Queen of Sheba (modern-day Ethiopia, Eritrea, or Yemen).[9] Her visit is affirmation by the outside world that this small, young nation was worthy of recognition. The queen is portrayed as Solomon's equal not only in wealth but also in wisdom. In fact, she is presented as an embodiment of wisdom. Having heard of Israel's king, she comes to "test him with riddles." Solomon, in turn, "answered all her questions; nothing was too difficult for him to answer." In fact, the king's wealth and wisdom "took her breath away" (1 Kgs 10:5), and the exchange between Sheba and Solomon results in her acclaim for "the LORD your God" (1 Kgs 10:9). This is the model for interaction with foreign women and it is in direct opposition to what happens with Solomon later on with his foreign wives.

In addition to the exchange of wisdom there is an exchange of wealth that evokes the royal or political marriage and the language about the exchange of goods is suggestive. Although the text is silent on the subject, the extant traditions around Solomon and the queen imagine a sexual relationship.[10] The placement of the story right before the section that describes Solomon's love of foreign women is telling.

Narrative placement is one of the ways a writer or editor shapes meaning. With the stories of the two prostitutes and the Queen of Sheba we observe two types of dialogue. First, the two legends form a dialogue that

8. The book of Proverbs teaches that a wise young man must be able to choose Lady Wisdom over Lady Folly. In Solomon's first test he uses wisdom to choose the woman who spoke the truth.

9. Stephen Breck Reid, "1–2 Kings," in *The Africana Bible*, ed. Hugh Page Jr. (Minneapolis: Fortress, 2010), 131.

10. Marina Warner, "In and Out of the Fold: Wisdom, Danger and Glamour in the Tale of the Queen of Sheba," in *Out of the Garden*, edited by Christina Büchmann and Celina Spiegel (New York: Ballantine, 1995), 153.

confirms Solomon's wisdom at home and abroad, which had an impact on those of high and low estate. A second dialogue is created by the placement of these two legends. The story of the two prostitutes precedes the section on Solomon's administration and building projects in chapters 4–9, and the Queen of Sheba account follows it. The two legends surround and set the tone for the details about the projects' materials, the builders, the workers, and the length of time. In the first legend, Solomon's wisdom is used for domestic matters and his attention is focused inwardly. The prayer of dedication for the temple requests God's ongoing presence and protection:

> May the Lord our God be with us, just as he was with our ancestors. May he never leave or abandon us. May he draw our hearts to him to walk in all his ways and observe his commands, his laws and his judgments that he gave our ancestors. (1 Kgs 8:57-58)

God appears to Solomon a second time in the chapter that follows the temple's dedication. Here God affirms and reassures Solomon that he has heard the king's prayer: "I have set apart this temple that you built, to put my name there forever. My eyes and my heart will always be there" (1 Kgs 9:3). God's unfailing presence requires that Solomon "do all that I have commanded, and keep my regulations . . . then I will establish your royal throne forever, just as I promised your father David" (1 Kgs 9:4-5). If Solomon is truly wise, he will continue to keep God's commandments. The divine visit is followed by Sheba's visit, in which Solomon's wisdom captures the attention of the outside world. This second legend serves as a transition to focus on Solomon's intermarriage with foreign women.

God's third appearance to Solomon comes right after the account of the Queen of Sheba's visit and is directly related to his entanglements with foreign women. Solomon had seven hundred wives and three hundred secondary wives, and over time, "they turned his heart after other gods." God confronts Solomon with a word of judgment:

> Because you have done all this instead of keeping my covenant . . . I will most certainly tear the kingdom from you and give it to your servant. Even so, on account of your father David, I won't do it in your lifetime. I will

> tear the kingdom out of your son's hands. Moreover, I won't tear away the entire kingdom. I will give one tribe to your son on account of my servant David and on account of Jerusalem, which I have chosen. (1 Kgs 11:11-13)

Solomon's story is structured by the Deuteronomist to depict him choosing the way of wisdom at the beginning of his reign. He asks for wisdom and receives it, but wisdom is a "way," a practice, that requires keeping God's commandments continuously. The marriage imagery is pervasive in the story and is used to demonstrate Solomon's inability to be faithful to those commandments. Solomon's affinity for foreign women and resulting dalliance with other gods led to the destruction of his primary relationship with YHWH. Ultimately, it is YHWH's faithfulness to the promise with David that spares Solomon and the people from utter destruction.

The literary and theological depictions of Solomon explain a political reality, namely that the tribes united under David did not hold together for long. Solomon was not the warrior that his father was, and he negotiated political marriages to keep Israel's territories from shrinking. At the end of Solomon's reign is the story of two men, Jeroboam and Rehoboam. Jeroboam was a servant of Solomon, "a strong and honorable man," who encountered the prophet Ahijah, who performed a "sign-act" by tearing his garment into twelve pieces and instructing him to take ten, "because Israel's God, the LORD, has said, 'Look, I am about to tear the kingdom from Solomon's hand. I will give you ten tribes. But I will leave him one tribe on account of my servant David and on account of Jerusalem" (1 Kgs 11:31-32). Solomon tried to kill Jeroboam, and Jeroboam went to Egypt until Solomon's death. The end of Solomon's reign uses tropes from the Saul and David story. Solomon, like Saul, tries to kill the one over whom God has made a promise, and, like Saul, Solomon learns he cannot stop God's promise. Solomon dies and his son Rehoboam takes the throne but makes a poor decision of taking advice from his peers and not the elders. The people rebelled and Jeroboam was made king over the ten northern tribes, leaving Judah and Benjamin for Rehoboam. In the division of the nation we observe the tension between God's proclivity not to be bound by human constraints of dynastic succession and God's commitment to David. With the division of the kingdom, both ideals are served. However, neither the north nor the south is able to adhere to God's commandments.

The North and the Sin of Jeroboam

One of King Jeroboam's first acts is to establish a capital for the northern kingdom, which was in Shechem, and his next act was to address the issue of worship. Even though the nation is now divided into two kingdoms with different rulers, the temple in Jerusalem was still the sole place where worship took place, and the people of the north would still travel to the south to sacrifice and to worship there. Jeroboam made a political decision to offer alternative worship sites. He erected two golden calves, and placed one in Bethel and one in Dan, the southern and northern poles of the new nation. The calf was a symbol associated with fertility and strength in the ancient Near East. It was the image selected to represent El, the head of the Canaanite pantheon, and it also represented Baal the storm god and son of El. It is possible that the bull also represented some earlier form of YHWH worship, in which case Jeroboam was attempting to offer an alternative to worshipping at the Jerusalem temple by reviving liturgy from the people's past. However, the return to the older form of worship was a violation of God's prohibition against idol worship. In further violation of God's commands, Jeroboam appointed priests who were not from the house of Levi. Thus, the decision that was politically wise cast a shadow over Jeroboam's reign and the northern kingdom and became the standard of apostasy against which all disobedient kings were measured.

With the division of the nation of Israel into two there is a shift from longer to shorter units shaped by an evaluative formula imposed by the Deuteronomistic editor:

- Name of king
- Year monarch assumes the throne

- Number of years served
- Name of queen mother
- Theological assessment of the reign—did the king do what was "right in the eyes of the Lord," following after David, or did the king do "evil in the sight of the Lord, walking in the way of his ancestor [Jeroboam] and in the sin that he caused Israel to commit"?

Deuteronomistic Editing of Kings

Much scholarly attention has been given to the editing of Kings. The book in its final form reflects editing that is exilic and possibly postexilic, which introduces questions around the theological perspectives of the editors, and the messages conveyed by the Deuteronomistic theologian. A consistent theme of the Deuteronomist is that God punished the northern and southern kingdoms for their sin of apostasy (worshipping other gods) through the assaults of the surrounding superpowers, like Assyria and Babylon. These political and military incursions were actually brought about by God. Scholars also identify a theme of hope in the books of Samuel and Kings.

The southern kingdom of Judah was smaller (comprising only two tribes) and had less political power than the northern kingdom of Israel, which had the larger population and the advantage of geography for defenses and commerce. The principal advantage of the south was Jerusalem and the temple. For all of its political advantages, the northern monarchy was characterized by volatility and instability. The exception was the Omride Dynasty, which lasted over one hundred years. King Omri purchased and made Samaria his capital city, replacing Shechem. He captured the Moabite territory and his name appears in extrabiblical sources. He is also the father of Ahab who "did evil in the LORD's eyes, more than anyone who preceded him (1 Kgs 16:30). The introduction of Ahab into the story is also the introduction of Elijah into the story.

KINGS OF ISRAEL AND JUDAH			
ca. 1020–1000 BCE	King Saul		
ca. 1000–960 BCE	King David		
ca. 960–930 BCE	King Solomon		
ca. 930–922 BCE DIVISION OF THE KINGDOM			
Kings of Judah		**Kings of Israel**	
922–915	Rehoboam	922–901	Jeroboam I
915–913	Abijam		
913–873	Asa		
		901–900	Nadab
		900–877	Baasha
		877–876	Elah
		876	Zimri
		876–872	Tibni
		876–869	Omri
873–849	Jehoshaphat		
		869–850	Ahab
		850–849	Ahazia h
849–843	Jehoram	849–843	Joram
843–842	Ahaziah	843–815	Jehu
842–837	Athaliah		
837–800	Jehoash		
		815–802	Jehoahaz
800–783	Amaziah	802–786	Joash
		786–746	Jeroboam II
783–742	Azariah/Uzziah		
		746–745	Zechariah
		745	Shallum
		745–737	Menahem
742–735	Jotham		
		737–736	Pekahiah
735–715	Ahaz	736–732	Pekah
		732–722	Hoshea
		722 BCE	Fall of Samaria (the Northern Kingdom) to Assyria
715–687	Hezekiah		
687–642	Manasseh		
642–640	Amon		
640–609	Josiah		
609	Jehoahaz		
609–598	Jehoiakim		
598–597	Jehoiachin		
597–587	Zedekiah		

Elijah and Elisha: "The Dynamic Duo"

Another element in Kings that makes it a "peculiar" history is the Elijah-Elisha cycle. Prophets are no strangers to biblical narrative. In 1 Samuel we have witnessed the role of Nathan functioning as a prophet in the royal court, speaking God's word to the king. Elijah and Elisha are different. Their actions upstage their words. They take the miraculous to a new level, and in contrast to the other prophets in this block of material, they are not just supporting cast—they are often the main characters in stories that resemble hagiography in form.[11] The Elijah and Elisha material forms its own cycle, which exists at times apart from the world of the kings, and at other times intersects directly with the workings of the monarchy. When Elijah and Elisha come before the king, there is the obvious intersection between the world of the sacred and that of the profane. In the historiography, the prophets are a reminder that the kings of Israel are not to behave like the kings of other nations. The presence of the prophets and their miracles reminds the reader this is no ordinary history. What happens in the affairs of the kingdoms is directly related to the kings' abilities to be obedient to the first and second commandments of the Decalogue.

Elijah and Jezebel: "The Odd Couple"[12]

Elijah is a major figure in the Bible and Jewish tradition. He is one of the two figures (along with Moses) who appears beside Jesus in the Gospel accounts of his transfiguration. A seat is saved for Elijah in the Seder and Elijah is one of the two biblical characters who does not die. Rather, he is "taken up" in a chariot of fire. Elijah raises the dead and takes on the prophets of Baal at Mount Carmel. Elijah defied the northern King Ahab

11. John Gray, *I & II Kings*, Old Testament Library (London: SCM Press, 1964), 335.

12. "The Odd Couple" comes from Phyllis Trible's article, "The Odd Couple: Elijah and Jezebel," in *Out of the Garden, Women Writers on the Bible*, ed. Christian Büchmann and Celina Spiegel.

from the Omride Dynasty,[13] who constantly disobeys God. But by all accounts, Elijah's most formidable opponent is Ahab's wife, Jezebel. Jezebel's notoriety rivals Elijah's reputation. She is as passionate for her gods as Elijah is for his. The confrontation between Elijah and the prophets of Baal is a confrontation between Elijah and the Phoenician princess made queen of Israel, and in a literary sense may evoke a battle between YHWH and Asherah.[14] In this story we confront one challenge of monotheism. If there is one god, a single gender is assigned because the human construct is saddled with gender. In a pantheon, there is room for both genders. In a monotheism, when YHWH wins, so does patriarchy.

Kings of the South: Hezekiah and Josiah

The cycle of disobedience and the destabilizing volatility of the movement from one dynasty to the next in the northern kingdom finally ends in its destruction. The southern kingdom, ruled by the descendants of David, had more stability than the north, which experienced quite a bit of volatility going from one dynasty to the next. However not every southern king followed in David's footsteps. In the southern kingdom, there are two kings who, according to the Deuteronomist, stand out above the rest in that regard: Hezekiah and Josiah. Hezekiah's story appears in 2 Kings 18–20, and the narrator's evaluation of him is as follows:

> There was no one like him among all the kings of Judah after him, or among those who were before him. For he held fast to the LORD; he did not depart from following him but kept the commandments that the LORD commanded Moses. (2 Kgs 18:5-6 NRSV)

The Hezekiah cycle is a reminder to trust God in spite of what is happening in the political realm. Besieged by Assyria, the small nation of Judah is running out of tribute and options. The prophet Isaiah proclaims

13. The northern kingdom of Israel was characterized by instability in leadership. King Omri was one of two dynasties. His lasted approximately thirty-three years with his son Ahab and his grandsons Ahaziah and Joram.

14. Asherah is a Canaanite goddess, a consort to El (the head of the pantheon) and mother of the gods.

God's ability to deliver God's own, and deliverance does, in fact, happen miraculously. In another account, one of Hezekiah's illness and healing, God extends the king's life, but also sends a word of woe, predicting the destruction of Jerusalem and the deportation of the people. Although Hezekiah's son Manasseh "did what was evil in the LORD's eyes," his grandson Josiah was described in superlatives: "There's never been a king like Josiah, whether before or after him, who turned to the LORD with all his heart, all his being, and all his strength, in agreement with everything in the Instruction from Moses" (2 Kgs 23:25).

The young king is remembered for the religious reform he brought to Judah. Josiah orders that the temple be repaired (2 Kgs 22), and in the course of this work, a "book of the law" is discovered, and read to the king. Upon hearing the contents of the book, "he tore his clothes." In the absence of this instruction, the people had gone far afield of God's teaching. Josiah instructs the temple officials to "inquire of the Lord," and the priests go to Huldah, a prophetess, who confirms that the people have incurred God's wrath because of their disobedience. The doom includes a bit of promise, in the word that Josiah will not live to see the disaster and that he will die "in peace." Josiah's reform goes into effect because of what is read, and the details of the reform, such as getting rid of defiled shrines (see a complete list of the details of the reform in 2 Kgs 23), lead many scholars to the conclusion that the rediscovered instruction book is in fact Deuteronomy.

Josiah dies in battle (not the peaceful death promised) and his son Jehoahaz assumes the throne. Josiah's son does not follow in the ways of his father and is captured by Pharaoh who places his own person, Eliakim, also known as Jehoiakim, on the throne. Eventually Jehoiakim rebels against Pharaoh just as Babylon is coming to attack. Jehoiakim dies and is succeeded by his son Jehoiachin. Again, a foreign power places a puppet king, this time Zedekiah, on the throne. Zedekiah, like the kings before him, rebels against the nations that oppressed him. This rebellion results in Nebuchadnezzar's destruction of the temple and removal of the people of Judah into exile.

The exodus and the exile are the two poles upon which the history of Israel hangs. It is in the exodus that God establishes a community of tribes descended from Abraham into a nation, and the exile is the loss of these markers of identity that enabled them to declare themselves as a people set apart.

Make Sure Not to Miss . . .

- Solomon succeeds David, 1 Kings 1:1–2:46
- Solomon's prayer for wisdom, and the test, 1 Kings 3
- The dedication of the temple, 1 Kings 8
- The Queen of Sheba visits, 1 Kings 10:1-13
- Solomon's death, two kingdoms, and the golden calves, 1 Kings 11:1–12:33
- Elijah, the prophets of Baal, and Elisha, 1 Kings 18:20–19:21
- Elijah is taken up into heaven, 2 Kings 2:1-18
- Athaliah, the only female ruling monarch, 2 Kings 11
- The northern kingdom (Israel) comes to an end, 2 Kings 15:8-31; 17:1-41
- The fall of Judah, 2 Kings 24:1–25:21

Part Six

CHRONICLES, EZRA, NEHEMIAH, AND ESTHER

The books of Chronicles, Ezra, and Nehemiah are associated with the "postexilic" period, the time of the return and restoration. The Persian king, Cyrus, allows the Jews to return to their homeland. The long-awaited hope for and the reality of the return are two very different things. Ezra and Nehemiah describe the return to the land and the construction of the city wall around Jerusalem and the temple. As difficult as these tasks may have been, the real heavy lifting comes in the restoration of Jewish identity. What does it mean to be the people of God in a postexilic world where so much has changed? Ezra and Nehemiah construct an identity with secular and sacred space, establishing the Mosaic law as the point of orientation. Chronicles looks back on the story of the monarchy and tells it anew, this time with the purpose not so much of explaining the exile so much as of finding a way forward. Chronicles is the last book in the ordering of the Hebrew Bible. The last words of the Hebrew Bible describe Cyrus's decree that the people should return to the land and rebuild the temple and conclude with the command that the people should "go up," conveying hope. The last word in a dialogic text is never the last word. As Chronicles clearly demonstrates, the traditions are available for interpretation and reinterpretation.

CHAPTER 11

1 AND 2 CHRONICLES

All right, people, let's do this one last time.

—Peter Parker in *Spiderman: Into the Spider-Verse*

In 2002, Marvel released the movie *Spiderman*, about Peter Parker, an adolescent transformed into a superhero by a radioactive spider bite. The well-known origin story has been told and retold in subsequent movies in 2004, 2007, 2012, 2014, 2018, and 2019.[1] Each movie has its own cast and distinct director's vision. The success of the Spiderman franchise speaks to the willingness, or perhaps desire, of audiences to have a familiar story told and retold at different moments in time. While foundational elements remain the same, each telling offers a unique lens into Peter Parker's identity, and by extension that of the audience.

A similar dynamic is at work in the books of 1–2 Kings and 1–2 Chronicles. First and Second Kings begins with the reign of Solomon and then moves through the history of the divided monarchy until the destruction of the northern kingdom of Israel, and then the southern nation of Judah. First and Second Chronicles cover the time of the united monarchy (Saul, David, and Solomon), and then follows the timeline of the divided kingdoms until the destruction of Israel in the north and Judah in the south. The composition date for Chronicles (fourth century BCE) is later than that of Kings (sixth century BCE for final editing). The Chroni-

1. *Spiderman 2*, 2004; *Spiderman 3*, 2007; *The Amazing Spiderman*, 2012; *The Amazing Spiderman 2*, 2014; *Spiderman: Homecoming*, 2017; *Spiderman: Into the Spider-Verse*, 2018; *Spiderman: Far from Home*, 2019.

cler looks at the time of the monarchy from a greater distance. Reflecting its late composition, Chronicles is the very last book in the Hebrew Bible. However, in the ordering of the Old Testament, 1–2 Chronicles follows 1–2 Kings because it covers the same material. The reader is advised not to let this placement of the books suggest that they share a similar perspective. Chronicles is its own franchise.

In the Chronicler's account, the high points of the history would be creation, the establishment of the Davidic monarchy, and the moment of return to the land. The sweeping strokes of this account led one scholar to claim the Chronicler "reworked, altered and falsified" his sources (which include Kings), to support his "dogmatic frame of reference," rendering it useless as a historical source.[2] Such a commentary reflects an expectation that the text be "historically accurate," that it render an unbiased account of what happened.

Chronicles' intentional shaping of the tradition is a reminder to us that all history is about some things and not others; that all history is abridged, starting at one place and ending at another. Moreover, all history is "an incomplete account, written toward a specific end, of selected developments."[3] In this sense, then, Kings is not a historical measure for Chronicles; rather Chronicles is a remix of Samuel and Kings, reminding us to ask, What is the specific end of the writers of both Kings and Chronicles?

Chronicles reminds us that the shapers of these traditions are responding to a particular set of circumstances by recruiting the past to shape identity in their time. A more useful description of Chronicles is diaspora literature or protest literature. This is writing by an oppressed people that seeks to explain how they found themselves in exile, and more importantly, how they might find a way forward.[4]

Chronicles can be divided into three main sections.

2. Brevard Childs, *Introduction to the Old Testament as Scripture* (Philadelphia: Fortress, 1979), 642.

3. Baruch Halpern, *The First Historians* (University Park: Pennsylvania State Press, 1988), 7.

4. Renita Weems, "1–2 Chronicles," in *The Africana Bible*, ed. Hugh Page Jr., et al. (Minneapolis: Fortress, 2010), 287–88.

OUTLINE	THEMES
1 Chronicles 1–9: Genealogy from Adam to Saul 1 Chronicles 10–2 Chronicles 9: Saul, David, Solomon 2 Chronicles 10–36: Judah and exile	The Davidic Monarchy

As diaspora literature, Chronicles begins with a genealogy that reaches back to Adam, offering a broad scope of history. The second section of the book offers a summary of the united monarchy under the first three kings (Saul, David, and Solomon), and then gives an account for the nation of Israel and the nation of Judah until the Babylonian exile. The Chronicler organizes its sources using typology, shaping the narrative units into patterns that teach us about cause and effect. Disobedience will have its consequences as will obedience. This type of ordering demands that some elements be glossed over or flattened out to support the pattern.[5] In the Chronicler's story David is legendary—the ideal standard of righteousness. The typological lens has no room for David's full humanity.

Chronicles' intentional shaping of the tradition is a reminder to us that all history is about some things and not others—that all history is abridged, starting at one place and ending at another. Moreover, all history is "an incomplete account, written toward a specific end, of selected developments."[6] In this sense, then, Kings is not a historical measure for Chronicles; rather Chronicles is the corrective to Samuel and Kings, reminding us to ask what the specific end is of the writers of both Kings and Chronicles. Moreover, what type of communal identity was being promoted by Kings versus Chronicles? What historical differences at the time of composition directed the shaping of the narrative? Chronicles reminds us that the shapers of both these traditions are responding to particular sets of circumstances as they reflect on the past to shape identity.

5. Childs, *Introduction to the Old Testament as Scripture*, 648–52.

6. Halpern, *The First Historians*, 7.

Genealogy

Genealogies are the unsung workhorses of biblical literature. Always more than a list of names, storytellers use different genealogical formats that are tied to their functions. The Chronicler uses genealogy to tie the community to the past, affirm its place in the ancestry, and move to the elements of the story that it wants to focus on. It begins with genealogical lists in the primeval history, moving from Adam to Noah and Abraham and the ancestral patriarchs. All of Jacob's sons are listed in 1 Chronicles 2:1-2, but there is an emphasis on the southern tribes of Benjamin and Judah. Judah, the tribe of David, is the central point. In this journey from Adam to David, the genealogies spend some time on the tribe of Levi, revealing an interest in the priestly line and offices. This focus no doubt reflects an emphasis on the role the Levites will play in the reestablishment of the religious life and identity of the people. The "unbroken succession" of the tribe of Levi also points to God's ongoing presence and favor.[7]

The Monarchy United

In the second section of the work, the Chronicler begins with Saul's death: "So Saul died for his unfaithfulness . . . and [the LORD] turned the kingdom over to David son of Jesse" (1 Chr 10:13-14), indicating an emphasis on David and the Davidic monarchy. The fourteen verses devoted to Saul's reign function as an introduction to the David narrative, which resembles a "highlight reel": David is anointed, he captures Jerusalem, brings the covenant chest (ark) to Jerusalem, defeats the Philistines, establishes worship, and enters into an eternal covenant with God. David's career as a mercenary for the Philistines, his violation of Bathsheba and murder of Uriah, the rape of his daughter Tamar, Absalom's rebellion, and other less-flattering parts of his story end up on the cutting-room floor of the Chronicler's history. The Chronicler's goal as a purveyor of the tradition is to create a counter-narrative that can withstand the damage of the exile and the ongoing demoralization of the diaspora experience. David is

7. Melody Knowles, "Genealogy for a Purpose," in *The CEB Women's Bible* (Nashville: Abingdon Press, 2016), 490.

not only the chosen king with an eternal covenant, but he is an icon for a people who need a glorious past as a point of orientation.

Judah's Past and Future

The last section of Chronicles follows the events of the southern kingdom to the inevitable end in defeat and exile. Now, however, the lens of a typological reading reassures the audience that the same God who "brought the Babylonian king against them" (2 Chr 36:17) is the God who took a lowly David and lifted him up, promising an eternal covenant. The audience is the inheritor of the covenant and there is still hope in the covenant. Here we observe the confessional use of the Bible is fundamentally antihistorical, making of scripture a sort of map, a single, synchronic system in which the part illuminates the whole, in which it does not matter that different parts of the map come from divergent perspectives and different periods.[8] This shaping of history, while effective in shoring up identity, creates a flattened narrative that has theological implications. Without the nuance of a fuller narrative, there is the potential for a strident religion.

Make Sure Not to Miss . . .

- Genealogy from Adam to Saul

8. Halpern, "The Trouble with History," in *The First Historians.*

CHAPTER 12

EZRA AND NEHEMIAH

Identity Reconstructed

Ezra and Nehemiah, separate books in the Old Testament, were considered one book in the Hebrew Bible, and so it makes good sense to consider them together. They are both concerned with the business of returning to the land and reestablishing identity, marking the beginning of the postexilic period. In Ezra, sacrifice is reestablished and the foundation of the temple is laid. In Nehemiah, the wall around Jerusalem is built. The language describing the building projects is appropriate to the task—it is detailed and metaphorical, specific and idealistic. This presentation of the practical work of building the temple and the walls of a city is easily understood as the reconstruction of a people. How does one rebuild something that has been lost for a long time? The challenge of rebuilding is that the context is always different, and for the most part, so are the builders. The memories of the past must guide what happens but they can also limit what must happen.

The building of the temple is central to Israelite/Jewish identity. In addition, there is the practice of sacrifice and the observance of holy days to be re-instituted. The Israelite priesthood must be re-established to teach the people about what to eat, how to deal with diseases, and how to perform rituals for approaching God through worship. In the absence of these identity markers in practice, the people's memory of them can become nostalgic and idealized. These are the internal concerns.

Ezra and Nehemiah remind God's people that there are also external challenges. There are "enemies" whose interests will not be served by the rebuilding of a temple and wall. Moreover, what about the people who had been left behind in the land—those who were not driven into exile? The people left behind were of less consequence to the Babylonians than those taken. But they were, nonetheless, Israelites. During the seventy years of exile, the debate about the identity of the "true" Israel escalated, whether God's people were those in the land or those in exile.

Ezra and Nehemiah cover a period of about one hundred years from the time of Cyrus's edict (beginning in 539 BCE through the completion of the temple in 516/515 BCE) to the restoration of the walls around Jerusalem in 445/444 BCE. The books follow this trajectory:

OUTLINE	THEMES
Ezra 1–6: Worship re-established; temple rebuilt Ezra 7–10: Torah re-established Nehemiah 1–7:73a : Wall rebuilt Nehemiah 7:73b–10:39: Ezra reads the law Nehemiah 11–13: Building projects completed	Worship renewed Temple and wall reconstructed Identity restored

Celebration with a Public Reading of Torah: Nehemiah 8–13

The books of Ezra and Nehemiah identify the elements that were central to the identity of the returnees. In Ezra, Cyrus's edict to return to the land is followed by a census: a list of names and numbers. After the return, sacrifice happens first, and the Festival of Booths is observed, followed by the building of the temple. The temple is not built without opposition but it ultimately proceeds. Ezra, known as the father of rabbinic Judaism, plays a major role in the next section as a scribe who is entrusted with the Torah and its instruction. The prohibition against intermarriage with foreign wives takes center stage at the conclusion of the book as the people must decide how to be followers of the Torah in light of their current situation. As a sign of their adherence to YHWH, they "promised to send their wives away" (Ezra 10:19). What is peculiar here is that there are no details as to what exactly took place, or how or when this spousal exodus occurred. Of all the potential violations of their identity that people would have recognized, why this one? Does it have anything to do with the symbolism of intermarriage in the prophetic tradition? There is a similar trajectory in Nehemiah. Nehemiah is the cupbearer to the king who secures permission to return and oversee the building of the walls around Jerusalem. The rebuilding of the walls invites opposition. After the wall is complete, Nehemiah registers the families. Then Ezra reads the Instruction from Moses, and again there is an account of the Festival of Booths, followed by a "psalm" by the Levites that rehearses the history of the people. After this, there is a commitment ceremony, dedication of the wall, and the work of restoring the temple and adherence to the law, with emphasis on keeping the Sabbath and condemnation of mixed marriage.

Through the books of Ezra and Nehemiah, we encounter the elements that shape the identity of God's people in the postexilic period. Markers of this early Jewish identity that become a distinct culture include Jerusalem, the temple, the Torah, and separateness (the wall and no intermarriage). These elements become characteristics of Rabbinic Judaism.

CHAPTER 13
ESTHER

Every fairy tale had a bloody lining. Every one had teeth and claws.

—Alice Hoffman, *The Ice Queen*

Set in the Persian court of the fifth century BCE, the story of the beautiful, orphaned Jewish girl who becomes queen is often cast as a type of fairy tale. Against all odds, Esther finds herself selected as queen to Ahasuerus (Xerxes), but no one in the court knows her true Jewish identity. Her privileged existence is challenged when her cousin Mordecai calls her to go to the king on behalf of the Jews who face genocide at the hands of Haman, the king's highest-ranking official. Esther risks her life to plead for her people and wins them the right to defend themselves. Haman and the other enemies of the Jews are defeated, and the victory is commemorated with the festival that came to be known as Purim. Like a fairy tale, the book of Esther has very good and very bad characters. Haman is depicted as a man obsessed with annihilating the Jewish community in Persia. Mordecai is a model righteous character. Esther, the book's namesake, is the unlikely hero who risks it all to successfully save her people. There is even a "happily ever after" celebration, but in Esther, it comes on the other side of a bloodbath where the would-be victims of the story killed over 75,000 people: "The Jews put down all their enemies with sword blows, killing and destruction. They did whatever they wanted to those who hated them" (Esth 9:5).

Beneath the facade of a fairy tale is a survival story in the form of a court narrative or diaspora tale. The *court narrative* is the term used for a story about Jews of the diaspora in a foreign court, subject to the whims of a foreign ruler. It is rooted in the trauma of the constant threat of genocide and the dance that the people in the diaspora must do to survive. The other examples of this genre are the Joseph story in Genesis 37–50, and the tales of Daniel, Shadrach, Meschach, and Abednego in Daniel 1–6. Each survival story is a communal memory that informs one's sense of identity. Assimilation is required for survival in a foreign court, but too much assimilation is death to the Israelite identity. The right balance must be attained in the stories so that the characters adjust enough to survive, but resist practices and beliefs that undermine their identity as God's people. In the court tales of Daniel and his countrymen, the exiled Israelites risk their lives to preserve their religious identity. In the Joseph story, Joseph operates within a foreign power to save many people, including his own, from the ravages of famine. In Esther, the Jewish diaspora in Persia is confronted with the threat of genocide. Although different in setting and style, all of the court tales address the challenge of survival, both physical and religious.

OUTLINE	THEMES
1:1–2:18 Esther becomes queen 2:19–8:3 Mordecai and Haman 8:4–10:3 The revenge of the Jews	Reversals, divine and otherwise Triumph of the Jews

Esther is a type of comedy called carnivalesque. With the term *comedy*, I refer to the overall *u* shape of the plot. The story begins with an ordered world that is plunged into chaos and eventually restored to order. Carnivalesque is a type of comedy that emphasizes the reversal of power structures in a way that emphasizes humor, satire, and the grotesque.[1] It is a literary form that mimics the cultural event of carnival (think Mardi Gras in New Orleans or Carnival in Rio de Janeiro), with reversals and cultural satire. Additional elements in carnivalesque include:

1. Kenneth Craig, *Reading Esther: A Case for the Literary Carnivalesque* (Minneapolis: Fortress, 1995), 32.

- a sense of the "great city";
- laughter directed toward exalted objects;
- unusual combinations between the sacred and profane, high and low, wise and foolish;
- a whole system of debasing, bringing down to earth; and
- death and renewal.[2]

The book of Esther begins with a description of the great city of Susa, the capital of Persia, ruled by a mighty king who is so controlled by his advisors that he is at moments laughable. The Jews, who are of little value to the Persians, infiltrate the highest realms of power via Esther, the queen. Haman, the king's trusted officer, is removed from office and Mordecai, the Jew, is exalted. The reversal of the power structure is demonstrated through the story elements of "the banquet," gender, and violence and revenge.

The Banquet and Gender

The banquet in the book of Esther is central to the structure of the story. In chapter 1, Ahasuerus gives a banquet for his officials and all the men of Susa. Vashti, the queen, also hosts a banquet in the first chapter. In chapter 2 there is a banquet, this one to celebrate the enthronement of the new queen, Esther. In chapter 3, Haman and the king have a drink after the order to exterminate the Jews is sent out. In chapter 5 and then again in chapter 7, Queen Esther hosts a banquet for the king and for Haman, and it is during the second banquet that she reveals her identity and pleads for the lives of her people. A banquet is held by the Jews in chapter 8 to celebrate Moredecai's promotion and the ruling that allows the Jews to defend themselves. Finally, there is the institution of Purim recorded in chapter 9. Almost all of the decisive actions in the book are connected to a banquet, or the antithesis of a banquet, like Esther's decision to fast in 4:16.

2. Sue Vice, *Introducing Bakhtin* (Manchester: Manchester University Press, 1998), 152–53.

It is against the backdrop of the banquet that some of the issues of gender are introduced. The women and men exist in separate realms, except when women are invited into the realm of the men. Ahasuerus sends for Vashti (1:10), and Esther is not supposed to come to the king unless he calls for her (4:11). In the first set of banquets, Vashti's refusal to come when summoned is a real challenge to the king's power. He uses his power to depose Queen Vashti because she defies his order to appear before him and his guests. Shortly thereafter, he regrets his decision, but it cannot be reversed (1:19). For all of his power, Vashti's refusal to obey his command forces him into an untenable situation. Esther's violation of the rules in 5:2 forces him into another untenable situation. With Esther, he decides to ignore his own ruling and make an exception for his queen. Both women, who in the larger cultural narrative are possessions and objects, in their own ways exercise power from the margins of the women's realm that change the course of history. Fitting with the genre of comedy or carnivalesque, gender is used to create a reversal.

There is a correspondence between the opening banquet(s) hosted in the palace and the last banquet, Purim, which form an envelope structure for the book. The opening banquets in chapter 1 begin with the king's banquet, which has three parts. There is a banquet for the king's officials and courtiers that lasted six months. This is followed by a seven-day feast for "everyone in the fortified part of Susa . . . important . . . or not." The language is elaborate and detailed, emphasizing the wealth and power of Ahasuerus, who ruled "from India to Cush—one hundred twenty-seven provinces in all" (Esth 1:5, 1). The banquets at the end of the book document the establishment of the Festival of Purim, where the Jews celebrate their survival and triumph over their enemies. If the first banquet demonstrates the power of the king, the last banquet is the triumph of the besieged Jews, another reversal.

Violence and Revenge

Although the court tales in Genesis and Daniel include elements of reversal or revenge, Esther takes revenge to a new level. Haman is intent on genocide because one Jew, Mordecai (in accordance with Jewish law), publicly refuses to bow down to him. If Mordecai is the only Jew defying the edict, then the other Jews are in compliance. Haman's extermination plan takes time, money, and effort. It is a sustained effort that is fueled by fear, fueled by the action of one person. In the same way that Vashti's noncompliance with the king's command gives rise to fear about all wives rebelling, so does Mordecai's refusal to bow to Haman. This fear of the Jewish "other" is reflected in his wife's statement about Mordecai, "If he is of Jewish birth, you'll not be able to win against him" (6:13). He plans a violent and cruel execution for the Jews, immolation. The reversal in this story allows for Haman to be killed by the device he installed for Mordecai. Moreover, the Jews are allowed to defend themselves and their property. However, the self-defense is exaggerated to the point of a bloodbath, as tens of thousands are killed. The account of the Jews defending themselves resembles revenge fantasy—an account that gives voice to the suppressed anxieties and fears of a people who feel powerless in a foreign nation. The scale of the killing invokes the excess of carnival. Pulsating beneath the carnival is the interaction between sex and death. Esther begins with celebration, which shifts in emphasis to sexuality, namely the king sleeping with all the beautiful virgins of the land, and ends with a death orgy and feast. The genre gives shape to the survival story. The opening banquet is "over the top," as is the procurement of the new queen, and Haman's plan of genocide and the Jews' revenge on their enemies.

Theology and Identity

All of these reversals and the revenge fantasy episode happen in a book that doesn't mention God. How does the book of Esther form and inform identity for Jews in the diaspora? One possible answer is tied to the genre of carnival itself. The Festival of Purim takes place within the construct of religious practice. God is all around the story, but if it is to truly be carnival, perhaps this is the space where the name of the divine one is not mentioned. The greatest reversal of all would be a world without God.

Another possible answer comes from the dialogue between Mordecai's "Jewishness" and that of Esther. Mordecai represents the figures that we are familiar with from the Daniel court tales. His Jewishness is obvious and it is a catalyst for anti-Semites. Esther embodies a different way. Her assimilation enables her to occupy a place of (relative) power, and from that place she acts to save her people, when prompted by her older, more devout cousin. The two characters work together to save the Jews in a world where Jewish identity is underground perhaps out of necessity and perhaps out of choice.

Part Seven

HEBREW POETRY: PSALMS, LAMENTATIONS, AND SONG OF SONGS (SOLOMON)

The LORD is my shepherd, I shall not want.
He maketh me to lie down in green pastures: he leadeth me beside the still waters.
He restoreth my soul: he leadeth me in the paths of righteousness for his name's sake.
Yea though I walk through the valley of the shadow of death, I will fear no evil: for thou art with me; thy rod and thy staff, they comfort me.
Thou preparest a table before me in the presence of mine enemies: thou anointest my head with oil; my cup runneth over.
Surely goodness and mercy shall follow me all the days of my life: and I will dwell in the house of the LORD forever.

—Psalm 23 (KJV)

The beloved and well-known King James Version of the Twenty-third Psalm is both artifact and experience, art and muse. Drawing on the age-old imagery of a sheep with a shepherd, the psalm takes the reader on a journey through abundance and desolation to arrive safely "home," a journey that rings true for modern as well as ancient audiences. There is such an immediacy and relevance to the psalm that generations of readers continue to use it in worship and devotion. Moreover, this psalm has inspired countless musicians and artists whose responses to it give expression to some of our most difficult and delightful experiences. It is referenced in music by Coolio, Puff Daddy and Notorious B.I.G., Grateful Dead, and U2, and in movies such as *Jarhead, We Were Soldiers,* and *Titanic.*

The pervasiveness of Psalm 23 is an example of how psalms transcend a specific time and context to speak to a universal human experience. The ancient texts are surprisingly immediate. They are, to borrow from Stevie Wonder, *Songs in the Key of Life*.[1] The book of Psalms, along with Lamentations and the Song of Solomon, also known as the Song of Songs, are collections of poetry in the Hebrew Bible.

1. Title of Stevie Wonder's album released September 28, 1976.

CHAPTER 14

PSALMS

The title comes from the term *psalmoi,* for "instrumental music," which is the Greek translation of the Hebrew word *tehillim,* "praises." This large collection is divided into five sections or books, perhaps on analogy with the five books of the Torah: Psalms 1–41, 42–72, 73–89, 90–106, and 107–50. The psalms range in length from the two verses (Ps 117), to Psalm 119 with 176 verses. They are hymns, laments, thanksgivings, and praises. Some are associated with a specific historical event, like the destruction of Jerusalem (79) or the exile (137). Others were sung on pilgrimage (120–34) and others simply praise God (150).

A literary approach to the Psalms focuses on parallelism, genre, and rhetorical function. Literary studies of the Psalms assume that the message of the psalm cannot be separated from its form and is interested in how the literary elements and form of psalms work to create meaning and memory.

OUTLINE	THEMES
1–41	Psalms of David
42–72	Psalms of David, Korah, and Asaph
73–89	Psalms of Korah and Asaph
90–106	Untitled Psalms
107–51	Psalms for Liturgies and Festivals

Parallelism

Whereas biblical readers and interpreters often neglect the literary qualities of narrative scripture in their search for its meaning, this is not easily done with the psalms. Psalms are poetry—they demand attention from the reader. The language is terse, and the vocabulary is peculiar. The shorter lines of Hebrew verse mean that the very layout on the page is different:

> Just like a deer that craves streams of water,
> my whole being craves you, God. (Ps 42:1)

Psalms are unapologetically metaphorical and symbolic in expressing their theology. With the Psalms we cannot fool ourselves into thinking that we can separate the meaning from the form. "To know the psalms are poetic is not to forget they are scripture. To read and hear them as scripture requires that one receive them also as poetry."[1]

In the English language, we distinguish poetry from prose according to a set of characteristics that includes terseness, line length, rhyme, verse, and meter. Poetry in biblical Hebrew is harder to characterize. Scholars have not been successful in clearly identifying meter, and rhyme is elusive although wordplay and homophones (words that sound similar) are sometimes apparent. Two elements that are readily detectable in Hebrew poetry are parallelism and metaphor.

Parallelism is defined as "the correspondence of two parts" through "syntax, morphology and meaning."[2] Ideas in Hebrew poetry come in the form of two lines that can be considered a unit.[3] Put another way, parallelism is a form of intentional repetition that is meaningful.

> Heaven is declaring God's glory;
> the sky is proclaiming his handiwork. (Ps 19:1)

The first line (a) makes an assertion and the second line (b) is a response of some type. The second line can affirm, expand, challenge, or explain the first. In Psalm 19:1, the first subject, "heaven," becomes more specific with the second subject, "the sky." The verb in the second line, "proclaiming," is not just more specific than the verb "declaring." It is louder, broader, and bigger. And the direct object in the "a" line, God's glory, is specified somewhat with the word choice of "handiwork" in line "b." The second line, "line b . . . supports" the first line, and "carries it further, backs it up, completes

1. Patrick D. Miller, *Interpreting the Psalms* (Philadelphia: Fortress, 1986), 17.

2. James Kugel, *The Idea of Biblical Poetry: Parallelism and Its History* (New Haven, CT: Yale University Press, 1981), 2.

3. Parallelism exists between two, sometimes three lines.

it, goes beyond it."[4] This sense of the "b" line resounding, seconding, and expanding the first is expressed in the phrase "a and what's more b."[5] This concept of seconding means that parallelism is about more than simple repetition and that every line in Hebrew poetry matters. Parallel lines, regardless of their categorization, form a dialogue in intensity of meaning, supported by grammar and linguistics (phonology, morphology, form), syntax (word order), and lexicography (definition).[6] Thus Hebrew poetry by design creates a sense of anticipation in the reader to look for more.

Metaphor

The Psalms' ability to captivate and shape our imagination, to not only describe but to recast our theological vision, is achieved through metaphor. Distinguished from simile, which employs the word *like* to establish a comparison, metaphor creates a new reality by joining concepts heretofore uncombined. In this way, metaphor uses what is known to express the unknown:

> The LORD is my light and my salvation;
> Should I fear anyone? (Ps 27:1)

> The LORD is my solid rock, my fortress, my rescuer. (Ps 18:2a)

Metaphor uses the familiar to transport the listener to what has not been experienced. In so doing it transgresses categories in language, forming new dialogues between images and concepts and recasting our imagination. It should not be lost on us that the making of images is forbidden in the second of the Ten Commandments. Israel's poetry creates images, serving as its own "verbal iconography," which allows us to imagine God in new ways.[7]

Because the brain is wired to make sense of things, metaphor triggers that impulse in the brain by inviting it to make sense of two things that do not ordinarily form a natural association. There is a tension in metaphor, an

4. James Kugel, *The Idea of Biblical Poetry: Parallelism and Its History* (Baltimore: Johns Hopkins University Press, 1981), 52.

5. Kugel, *The Idea of Biblical Poetry*, 13.

6. Adele Berlin, *The Dynamics of Biblical Parallelism* (Bloomington: Indiana University Press, 1992), 17.

7. William P. Brown, *Seeing the Psalms: A Theology of Metaphor* (Louisville: Westminster John Knox, 2002), 4.

"is" and an "is not,"[8] as it creates a meaning that only inhabits the metaphor itself. One of the reasons that the Psalms have long had appeal is tied to the power of metaphor to transcend a single historical moment and create a metaphorical space that transcends time. Moreover, parallelism and metaphor work together as an ongoing invitation to the audience to think of God differently, to imagine God anew.

Genre

Within the large collection of the Psalms, a number of types can be identified along with the defining characteristics. Early genre study of the Psalms focused on categories and their elements:

Thanksgiving Psalms
Hymns
Wisdom Psalms
Creation Psalms
Liturgical Psalms
Praise (individual and communal)
Lament (individual and communal)

All of these categories can be organized under the broad classifications of praise and lament.[9] In spite of the title of the collection, *tehillim* or praises, laments occur more frequently than any other type of psalm. Additionally, individual laments outnumber communal laments. This is because creating a communal lament requires that an event must be catastrophic enough to bring the entire community to the place of lamentation. An individual's pain or loss is sufficient justification. For this reason, the communal laments are associated with historical events, like the destruction of Jerusalem, Psalm 79, or the exile, Psalm 137. What are we to make of the fact that the dominant type in the collection of "praises" is lament?

Function

Understanding the presence of the lament may come from understanding its function. The lament is a call to action wherein the psalmist describes a crisis, illness, traumatic event, or some type of suffering that is too great

8. Sallie McFague, *Metaphorical Theology* (Philadelphia: Fortress, 1982), 13.

9. Claus Westermann, *Praise and Lament in the Psalms* (Atlanta: John Knox, 1981), 18.

to adjudicate. The tendency of the lament to describe the suffering is not solely for the purpose of complaining, but to make sure God understands the extent and the immediacy of the situation:

> LORD, I have so many enemies!
> So many are standing against me.
> So many are talking about me:
> "Even God won't help him." *Selah*
> But you, LORD, are my shield!
> You are my glory!
> You are the one who restores me. (Ps 3:1-3)

> How long will you forget me, LORD? Forever?
> How long will you hide your face from me?
> How long will I be left to my own wits,
> agony filling my heart? Daily?
> How long will my enemy keep defeating me? (Ps 13:1-2)

> My God! My God,
> why have you left me all alone?
> Why are you so far from saving me—
> so far from my anguished groans? (Ps 22:1)

The lament betrays the psalmist's assumption that YHWH, the LORD, is the only one who can help. It also reflects the identity of an oppressed people:

> Some people trust in chariots, others in horses;
> but we praise the LORD's name. (Ps 20:7)

When we remember Israel's history in the wilderness, and then as a marginalized community in Canaan, and finally, albeit briefly, a stand-alone nation before exile, it is likely that her passionate dependence on God over chariots and horses is just as much out of necessity as it is faith. A chronically oppressed people's faith is formed by their experience. In the Psalms we can observe a response to suffering that cries out to God and in so doing recasts the situation. When God is introduced, the psalmist is intentionally shifting the power dynamic to focus not on just the circumstances but the God who has power over them. The lament then "offers a selective view of an Israelite ethos, born in crisis, that is dynamic, creative, pluriform, polyphonic and transgressive." It is "poetry of resistance."[10]

The function of the lament psalm is to move the individual or community from one state to another. The lament begins by calling out to God and

10. Hugh R. Page Jr., *Israel's Poetry of Resistance* (Minneapolis: Fortress, 2013), 17.

naming the problem(s), giving language to suffering, and articulating grief. Laments are not polite or civilized. The crying out is not metaphorical, even if metaphors are used to express it. Laments are not dignified, nor are they bashful in asking God to answer. In the genre of psalm there is no avoiding the intimacy of this relationship between the one who suffers and the one who can save. The psalmist is vulnerable and the need is laid bare. There is often a sense in the lament that this is the last chance. And then the lament shifts from the petition to God to either a promise or vow to praise, or immediate praise.

The transition from lament to praise has long held the interest and curiosity of biblical interpreters; however, if we remember that the genre of psalm includes prayer, then here is a dialogue that directly requests an intervention or answer from God, a central element of prayer. Perhaps the praise or response to praise happens because of the way that prayer works. The supplicant pours out the lament, and in emptying themselves, makes room for a response. The dire circumstances are a part of the psalmist's community as a people who have a history of laments that describe and inform their identity. The exercise of lament also calls to mind God's faithfulness in the past, which leaves the psalmist no choice other than to enter into praise. Lament is part of a particular arc that moves from lament and petition to praise.

Sorrow Songs in the Negro Spirituals

In his book, *The Souls of Black Folk*, W. E. B. DuBois discusses "sorrow songs," music created by African captives, exiled in America. The songs are laments, prayers sung to God as a form of protest and supplication, looking for justice from a righteous God. This original American music conveys "soul-hunger" and "restlessness,"[11] "unvoiced longing toward a truer world."[12] The music also carries "hope—a faith in the final justice of things."[13] In the sorrow songs we have a window into the identities of an oppressed people and their belief in a God who saw them and would remember them. In the music they wrestled with "good and evil, suffering and pain."[14] Their laments, like those in the psalms, created sacred space, a sanctuary for the soul.

11. W. E. B. DuBois, *The Souls of Black Folk* (New York: Penguin, 1982), 271.

12. DuBois, *The Souls of Black Folk*, 267.

13. DuBois, *The Souls of Black Folk*, 274.

14. Cheryl A. Kirk-Duggan, *Exorcising Evil: A Womanist Perspective on the Spirituals* (New York: Orbis, 1997), xiv.

CHAPTER 15
LAMENTATIONS

OUTLINE	THEMES
1	Jerusalem bereft
2	The wake of God's wrath
3	Plea for restoration
4	
5	

The dynamic of lament is observed in the five chapters of Lamentations, a series of laments that are associated with the destruction of Jerusalem and the temple in 586 BCE. It is hard to miss the intentionality in the form of these prayers. Chapters 1, 2, and 4 begin with the words, "Oh no!" The first four chapters are acrostic—each verse begins with successive letters of the alphabet, so chapters 1, 2, and 4 have twenty-two verses, corresponding to the letters in the Hebrew alphabet. Chapter 3, the center of the book, has three verses for each letter for a total of sixty-six verses. The use of the acrostic allows for everything from "A to Z" to be said. A number of the lines in Lamentations consist of a longer "a" line followed by a shorter "b" line. Some have designated this three/two pattern as "Qinah" meter, associated with mourning. The fifth chapter is not an acrostic but does, like chapters 1, 2, and 4, have twenty-two verses. Lamentations is one of the five books in the festival scroll, or *megillot,* and is associated with the Ninth of Ab.[15] The form of the laments in Lamentations and the overall shaping of the book carries meaning. Lamentations stands as a witness, as testimony to the trauma of Jerusalem's destruction. It gives voice

15. The Ninth of Ab commemorates the destruction of Solomon's and the Second Temple.

to the city personified as a woman, "Daughter of Zion," who is the victim of the devastation inflicted by God. That devastation is expressed through the images of a widow, slave, homeless person, and orphan. The detail of the images works with the acrostic pattern to offer a substantial testimony to the destruction of the city at God's hand. One part of the trauma of Jerusalem's destruction is tied to the belief that it came from God:

> The LORD did what he had planned. He accomplished the word that he had commanded long ago. He ripped down, showing no compassion. He made the enemy rejoice over you; he raised up your adversaries' horn. (Lam 2:17)

How does a lament function when the God who is usually in the role of deliverer is the one inflicting the wounds? With this question we observe that Lamentations is no ordinary lament. It is even more tormented as it seeks respite from the very one who is causing the suffering. The theology implicit in Lamentations is rooted in God's sovereignty. God who has the power to bring about the destruction of Jerusalem is the only one who can restore the people and the land.

Thus while Lamentations is grounded in the confidence in the Lord's ability to hear and answer prayer, it is also riddled by the fear that the Lord may not be willing to hear and answer the prayers of the people this time. Perhaps this is why it concludes with a question instead of confidence. Laments in the Psalms usually move from lament and supplication to praise, but the book of Lamentations ends with uncertainty:

> But you, LORD, will rule forever;
> your throne lasts from one generation to the next.
> Why do you forget us continually;
> why do you abandon us for such a long time?
> Return us, LORD, to yourself. Please let us return!
> Give us new days, like those long ago—
> unless you have completely rejected us,
> Or have become too angry with us. (Lam 5:19-22)

Note that the passage begins with an expression of confidence in God's power, which is a feature in many of the psalms. However the context that gives rise to Lamentations challenges that easy confidence. The destruction of Jerusalem and its aftermath of ongoing devastation and suffering cause the lamenters to ask the most terrifying question of all—has God "completely rejected us"?

The witness to God's faithfulness shows up in the middle of the book in chapter 3:

> Certainly the faithful love of the LORD hasn't ended; certainly God's compassion isn't through!
> They are renewed every morning. Great is your faithfulness.
> I think: the LORD is my portion! Therefore, I'll wait for him.
> (Lam 3:22-24)

The structure of this lament offers a space for hope while remaining present to the experience of those in the midst of suffering. It offers a dialogic response to the structure of the laments in the psalms that reflects the anxiety, frustration, and uncertainty of waiting for God, and hoping that once again, God will be faithful.

CHAPTER 16

SONG OF SOLOMON/SONGS

The title of this poetry collection is a superlative. "Song of Songs" is the greatest or the best song ever; it is "the most excellent of songs!"[1] The superscription (1:1a) attributes the composition to Solomon, hence the English title, Song of Solomon, and the date for the composition ranges from the time of Solomon to the Hellenistic period, the fourth to second century BCE.[2] The imagery is lush and at times overwhelming, inviting a sense of intoxication as all of the senses are brought to bear in this poetry. This song is full of longing and desire—the kind that is so powerful it is all-consuming. If this is chaste love, it certainly doesn't want to be!

OUTLINE	THEMES
1:1 Superscription 1:2-4 Desire 1:5–2:7 Love's dialogue 2:8–3:11 The woman speaks 4:1–5:1 The man speaks 5:2–6:3 The woman speaks 6:4–7:9 The man speaks 7:10-13 The woman speaks 8:1-14 Love's dialogue	Love is everything Seeking and finding love Longing and desire The garden

1. Renita J. Weems, "Song of Songs," in *The Women's Bible Commentary,* ed. Carol Newsom, Sharon Ringe, and Jacqueline Lapsley (Louisville: Westminster John Knox, 1998), 156.

2. J. Cheryl Exum, *Song of Songs: A Commentary*, Old Testament Library (Louisville: Westminster John Knox, 2005), 66.

Everything comes to us through the dialogue of the lovers. From them we learn about the nature, power, agony, and exhilaration of love.[3] Song of Songs reminds us of why poetry matters so much: some things can be best expressed metaphorically because our language fails us when we try to describe them. Things that matter most to us are often introduced with these phrases, "it's like . . ." or "it reminds me of . . ." and so forth. Metaphor is used to point toward passion and desire, gateways to the most powerful aspects of our existence—the potential for intimacy and the transformative nature of love.

Geographic locations, including Jerusalem, Lebanon, Mount Carmel, and Sharon are referenced, but it is not always clear that they are being used accurately. The loose geography is indicative of imagination extending beyond that of a current reality to reach back to the past and redeem it. Similarly, the garden in the Song of Songs has multiple meanings. It refers to a literal, walled garden, and it is also the woman. The woman is in a garden and she is a garden. The garden references in the song facilitate a dialogue with the woman and man in the garden of Eden. Through the use of a holy imagination, the poets of the Song of Songs resurrect the themes of the garden of Eden. When expelled from the garden of delights, Adam and Eve are ashamed of their nakedness, and the woman's punishment muddles desire with hierarchy. In this revision of Eden, there is mutuality between the lovers, who enjoy "love for love's sake."[4] There is no mention of marriage and no reference to procreation. The song begins and ends with the woman's voice and in both cases her attention is focused on her lover who is her equal. The equality between the woman and man is a reminder of what we perhaps were originally made to be—fully embodied, "naked," but not "embarrassed."[5]

These love poems have long intrigued and puzzled religious communities, unsure of how to respond to the sensual nature of the poetry, attempting to mine it for religious significance. In Christian tradition, the song is used as a lens to describe the relationship between Christ and the

3. Exum, *Song of Songs*, 62.

4. Brevard S. Childs, *Biblical Theology in Crisis* (Philadelphia: Westminster, 1970), 192.

5. Gen 2:25.

church. In Jewish tradition, the Song of Songs is a liturgical text, connected to the celebration of Passover. When Israel passed through the Sea of Reeds, the Song of Songs is what the LORD sang to her. This image of intimacy and desire at the moment the people become a nation is arresting for all of the potential and hope that it holds. Used liturgically, it is an invitation for God's people to remember themselves as God's beloved as their initial point of orientation.

Part Eight

WISDOM LITERATURE

A baby on its mother's back does not know that the way is long.[1]

The universality of Proverbs is made evident in this Ibo proverb. The word-image of a woman carrying a baby creates worlds of meaning that ring true for mothers and everyone else, irrespective of their experience in carrying babies on their backs. The short saying makes an immediate and powerful impact. It should come as no surprise that every culture has proverbs. These short, pithy statements sometimes rhyme. Some use imagery or alliteration. All are intentionally oral so that you can say and remember them. In this way they are portable, wisdom you can take with you. Proverbs, along with Job and Qohelet/Ecclesiastes, are some of the better-known forms of the wisdom material in the Bible.

Proverbs often espouse common sense, providing guidelines for navigating the world. Yet, for all their practicality, biblical proverbs are not simply "folk wisdom." The proverbs are couched in a broader understanding of wisdom as a way of life, a practice that is rooted in creation and the observance of Torah, God's law. Wisdom is the tradition that orients the audience to live in their proper place, in harmony with the rest of the created order. In the book of Proverbs we learn, "Wisdom begins with the fear of the Lord, but fools despise wisdom and instruction" (Prov 1:7). When the first humans were evicted from the garden of Eden, they lost

1. Chinua Achebe, *Things Fall Apart* (New York: Penguin, 1959), 101.

access to the tree of life, and eternal life. Wisdom is the "tree of life" (Prov 3:18), the means by which practitioners can lengthen their days. Death is inevitable, but wisdom is the path to a longer and meaningful life.[2]

Proverbs' presentation of wisdom forms a dialogue with the book of Job, a series of monologues and dialogues around what can be known and understood about God and ourselves in the midst of suffering. The dialogues are framed by an iconic tale about a righteous man named Job who suffers greatly and seeks understanding out of his anguish. Job, his wife, and his friends struggle to find meaning in response to trauma that threatens to undermine both everything once believed about God, and the order of the world espoused in Proverbs. Job longs for answers from God so that he can resolve the tension between his beliefs and his suffering.

In the book of Qohelet/Ecclesiastes, we encounter musings on the nature of wisdom. The teacher, Qohelet, offers observations about wisdom based on his lifetime of searching and seeking. The character is associated with Solomon and is in the latter years of life. His assertions about wisdom offer a far less rosy picture of wisdom than Proverbs does. Taken together, these three books take the reader on a journey that espouses and then challenges the way of wisdom.

2. Roland E. Murphy, *The Tree of Life: An Exploration of Biblical Wisdom Literature* (Grand Rapids: Eerdmans, 2002), ix–x.

CHAPTER 17

PROVERBS

Wisdom begins with the fear of the Lord . . .
Get wisdom! Get understanding before anything else. (Prov 1:7; 4:7)

OUTLINE	THEMES
1–9 Discourses from father to son 10–29 Proverbs of Solomon 30 Words of Agur 31 Words of King Lemuel	The fear of the Lord Wisdom gives life Wisdom is a path, a way

The thirty-one chapters in Proverbs are a compilation of material from different times and places. Some are originally written and some oral. The vast majority are associated with Solomon, son of King David; chapter 30 is attributed to Agur and 31 to King Lemuel. The term *proverb* comes from the word *mashal*, which means wise saying or parable. A parable is a metaphor of types—it sets two things alongside one another and invites us to make sense of their juxtaposition. The preferred combination is of opposites, making the desired conclusion clear: "Hate stirs up conflict, but love covers all offenses" (Prov 10:12) or "laziness brings poverty; hard work makes one rich" (10:4). When one sees the consequences of choosing wisdom versus going the way of folly, only a fool would not pursue wisdom. Thus, the goal of the proverb is instruction, and the primary method of teaching is didactic.

This moral instruction presumes a young, male audience. There is some urgency in the message, perhaps to stave off the lasting consequences of choosing the wrong path. The teachers in Proverbs are parents, a father and mother (representatives of wisdom teachers), who offer wise words and advice on navigating the world. Some proverbs are straightforward and others are deceptive in their simplicity. Proverbs 26:4 appears to be straightforward:

> Don't answer fools according to their folly
> Or you will become like them yourself

until we come to the following verse:

> Answer fools according to their folly,
> Or they will deem themselves wise.

Placed in succession, these two proverbs demonstrate that wisdom is more than a set of prescribed rules. Rather, the way of wisdom is an ability to navigate the world so that one knows when to answer fools and when to refrain from answering fools.

Observing nature is another method of learning the way of wisdom. The created order has much to teach those who would listen, and in Proverbs, the audience is invited again and again to find the wisdom in the natural world (Prov 6:6-8). Indeed, wisdom is in the very fabric of the world: "The LORD laid the foundations of the earth with wisdom, establishing the heavens with understanding" (Prov 3:19).

Woman Wisdom

Wisdom, personified as a woman, speaks for herself in the early chapters of Proverbs. She cries out in chapter 1 to an audience that she describes as "clueless." She addresses the young men directly, calling them to follow her and avoid the way of fools. In chapter 8, she offers her credentials.

> The LORD created me at the beginning of his way,
> before his deeds long in the past
> I was formed in ancient times,
> at the beginning, before the earth was.
> (Prov 8:22-23)

Wisdom has been since the beginning or creation, and was "beside him, as a master of crafts . . . delighting in the human race" (8:30-31). Just as wisdom is not easily attained, Woman Wisdom's origins, though clearly stated, are also mysterious. The metaphors used in her self-revelation, "birthing, acquiring, anointing, creating—point variously to what is otherwise inexpressible."[1] Wisdom is created and possibly co-creator. Wisdom's personification is reminiscent of goddesses in the ancient Near East for many interpreters, while others think of her as an "independent expression of God's wisdom."[2] Others argue she is a literary construct, another metaphorical voice that stands in contrast to the personification of the choices the young man is to avoid, the "strange woman" and the "foolish woman." What is certain is Wisdom's preeminence, her ongoing presence in the created order. It is from this position of authority that Wisdom addresses her audience as "children," and calls them to follow in her ways.

Proverbs offers a "traditional piety": one that is certain of a moral order that rewards appropriate behavior and punishes divergence.[3] The didactic *mashalim* found in Proverbs leads to the conclusion that although wisdom may be elusive, when one walks in that way, theirs will be the riches, glory, and honor (Prov 3:16). This simple equation is disrupted in the remaining books that belong to the wisdom tradition. In Job, we have a story about a wise man whose suffering is iconic. Qohelet/Ecclesiastes is a collection of musings about life from the perspective of an individual whose experiences do not support the worldview created in Proverbs.

1. Christine Yoder, "Proverbs," in *The Women's Bible Commentary*, ed. Carol Newsom, Sharon Ringe, and Jacqueline Lapsley (Louisville: Westminster John Knox, 2012), 236.

2. Yoder, "Proverbs," 237.

3. Robert Alter, introduction to "Proverbs," in *The Hebrew Bible: A Translation with Commentary* (New York: W. W. Norton and Company, 2019), 345.

CHAPTER 18
JOB

The name and the suffering of Job are well known in many circles. Job's story has been the inspiration for artists and a focal point for theologians. Our fascination with this iconic biblical character is rooted in the didactic tale that is the prologue in the first two chapters, and the epilogue found in 42:7-17. However, the majority of the book is not narrative but poetry, an extended series of monologues and dialogues that constitute an extended conversation about suffering. The tale on either side of the poetry is formulaic in some ways: the pious man endures unimaginable suffering, and does not sin, and is rewarded. On its own, readers are presented with a universe where those who are pious are rewarded for their righteous behavior, even when suffering seems to come out of nowhere. It encourages a kind of blind obedience and ritualistic piety. The poetic material interrupts that carefully constructed world, daring to ask questions and wrestle with a universe that does not make sense. In this universe, Job's friends opine on the reasons for and the nature of suffering, and Job finally gets an audience with God.

OUTLINE	THEMES
1–2 Prologue 3–37 Poetic Section 38–41 God's response 42:1-6 Job's response 42:1-17 Epilogue	Unexplained suffering Creation Wisdom God's sovereignty

Interpreters of the book of Job approach the didactic tale and the poems as a means of engaging theological issues around suffering, justice, and God's nature, many of which are subsumed under the term *theodicy*, which seeks a divine solution or answer to the problem of evil and suffering. For the purposes of our exploration, I will focus less on answers and emphasize questions. Specifically, there are questions in the book of Job that reach beyond the lips of the characters and the context of the story and become either questions that we ourselves would ask, or questions that seem to speak to the reader, challenging belief systems. These questions originate in the chronotope, or "time-space," of Job's story, and they extend to invite us, either voluntarily or involuntarily, into Job's abyss. Three questions in particular are worthy of our consideration.

"Does Job Revere God for Nothing?"

The prologue centers around a conversation between the LORD and the Adversary regarding Job's righteousness. The story has the divine beings "present themselves" before the LORD. With them is the Adversary, with whom the LORD initiates a dialogue that begins with a question: "Where did you come from?" The question answered, the LORD asks another question, "Have you thought about my servant Job?" praising him and calling attention to Job's "absolute integrity," to which the Adversary offers a challenge in the form of a question:

> Does Job revere God for nothing? Haven't you fenced him in—his house and all he has—and blessed the work of his hands so that his possessions extend throughout the earth? But stretch out your hand and strike all he has. He will certainly curse you to your face. (Job 1:6, 8, 9-11)

The Adversary's questions are good ones. Does Job revere God because of the benefits of fearing God? Would he be faithful if he didn't have the benefits of wisdom? Can we separate the practice of piety from its rewards? For reasons that vex generations of readers, YHWH appears to take the

Adversary's bait and accepts the challenge (on Job's behalf). YHWH gives the Adversary permission to "strike all that he has," to see if Job will in fact "curse you [God] to your face." Presented in a dramatic literary style, "while this messenger was speaking another arrived" (1:18), a series of messengers bring Job catastrophic news of loss upon loss. After losing all his children and his possessions, Job passes the test: he "didn't sin or blame God" (1:22).

"Are You Still Clinging to Your Integrity?"

In the second round of dialogue between God and the Adversary, God insists on Job's steadfastness: "He still holds on to his integrity, even though you incited me to ruin him for no reason." The Adversary's response is to up the ante and gain permission to attack Job's body, arguing, "People will give up everything they have in exchange for their lives" (2:3, 4). God permits the Adversary to afflict, but not kill Job. This results in the "severe sores." In Job's dismal state, his wife, who prior to this moment has been invisible and silent, shows up in the narrative this one time to ask the question, "Are you still clinging to your integrity? Curse God and die." Historically, interpreters have followed Job's lead in their response to her question. "You're talking like a foolish woman." Job's wife is often seen as a foil to Job's integrity, an example of one who lacks faith. However, another understanding of Job's wife's question can be obtained from our understanding of the word *integrity*. What exactly is she asking him? One compelling possibility is that she is challenging his outward piety, questioning its depth. Job's wife takes issue with his external behavior and invites him to be authentic, own his anger, and rail against God. Perhaps her challenge comes to those whose behavior is pious, but whose spirits are in turmoil. The irony in this exchange is that Job rebukes her in chapter 2, but in chapter 3, comes very close to what she suggested, not by cursing God, but by cursing the day he was born (3:1). Job's wife invites her husband and us to give up pious outward behavior for an authentic exchange with our creator.

"Will We Receive Good from God but Not also Receive Bad?"

Job's reprimand of his wife, "You're talking like a foolish woman," is followed by another question, which although posited in the folktale also stands alone: "Will we receive good from God but not also receive bad?" Job's question challenges the very assumptions behind the problem of suffering. Part of the problem of suffering is the assumption that we are not supposed to suffer, or that if we suffer we must be able to understand why.

According to the narrative, with these words, Job passes the test, because he did not "sin with his lips" (2:10). From here the story shifts in focus to Job's friends who come to comfort him and serve the literary function of introducing the larger, poetic section of the book. After a seven-day silence, Job begins by lamenting his birth, and "cursing" the day he was born.

Poetic Section: 3–37

The central portion of the book opens with Job's lament, which begins with "Perish the day I was born." This is followed, in chapters 3–31, with a series of speeches by Job's friends, Eliphaz, Bildad, and Zophar, and Job's responses. After each friend's speech, Job issues his debate-like response and the cycle repeats itself. Eliphaz and Bildad speak three times and Zophar twice, with Job's responses, in chapters 3–31. Job continues to profess his innocence, and then in chapters 32–37, a new voice in the person of Elihu speaks. Elihu's speeches seem to interrupt the conversation cycle and his words are followed by the greatly anticipated response from God.

God Answers . . . in the Form of a Question: 38–41

After chapters of anguished and agonized reflection, God finally answers Job in chapter 38. However, this appearance is probably not what Job had hoped for. Instead of answering questions, God appears for the purpose of interrogating Job. The opening question, "Where were you when I laid the earth's foundations? Tell me if you know," sets the tone. What follows is a series of unanswerable questions, phrased more as riddles, that Job cannot answer because Job's knowledge and experience are limited to his existence. He can only know what he knows. The questions begin with the work of creation itself and then move on to elements of the created order. As creator, God knows and understands the ways of all the earth, and everything in it. God's questions alert the reader and Job to the vastness of the created world, in a way that amazes and decenters the experience of this one human being. Job's ability to question and wonder does not grant him the authority or privilege of the creator. The questions go on and on (38:1–40:2) and finally Job responds:

> Look, I'm of little worth.
> What can I answer you?
> I'll put my hand over my mouth.
> I have spoken once, I won't answer;
> twice, I won't do it again. (40:4-5)

In 40:6, God resumes speaking with another round of questions, this time focusing on Behemoth (literally beast) and the Leviathan. Elements of the descriptions of these creatures resemble the hippopotamus and the crocodile, but their descriptions become mythical in proportion, evoking creatures from Canaanite mythology.

Job's Response: "You Win": 42:1-6

Job then replies, beginning with an acknowledgment of God's power and his own limitations:

> My ears had heard about you,
> but now my eyes have seen you.
> Therefore, I relent and find comfort
> on dust and ashes. (42:5-6)

It is from God's divine disclosure that Job is able to understand "the incommensurability between his human notions of right and wrong and the structure of reality."[1] Job's quest for answers leads to something else—in acknowledging his limitations he also can recognize he has a place in the created order with the creator and perhaps find some comfort in the unknowability of our existence. Sometimes our only option is to choose the relationship over knowledge.

Epilogue: 42:7-17

In the epilogue, "the LORD acted favorably toward Job . . . doubled all Job's earlier possessions . . . blessed Job's latter days more that his former ones . . . seven sons and three daughters . . . no women in all the land were as beautiful as Job's daughters . . . then Job died old and satisfied." Yay? The "restoration" in the epilogue seems trite in light of all that Job has experienced. These new children do not replace those he lost. In some ways the epilogue seems as out of place as if the book is trying to return to a model of traditional piety that we now know is not sustainable.

The dialogues of Job continue to call us to wrestle with our limitations to understand elements of our existence, the existence of pain and suffering that we do not understand, and our mistaken assumption that if we understood why there was suffering that we would be better able to bear it. In Job, we discover that, as a part of the created order, our hope is in our relationship with God.

1. Robert Alter notes in *The Hebrew Bible: A Translation with Commentary* (New York: W. W. Norton and Company, 2019), 577.

CHAPTER 19
QOHELET/ECCLESIASTES

The title *qohelet* means "collector" or "one who gathers" or "assembles" a crowd, so that the word comes to be associated with a preacher or teacher—one who brings a crowd together for instruction. Following the lead of the superscription, "David's son, king in Jerusalem," Jewish and Christian traditions attribute Qohelet to an older Solomon, as a literary bookend with Proverbs, which is associated with Solomon at the prime of his life.

OUTLINE	THEME
1:1-11 Introductory musings 1:12–11:6 The Teacher's search 11:7–12:14 The end of the matter	Death is inevitable Limits to what can be known

"Perfectly pointless, says the Teacher, perfectly pointless. Everything is pointless." Qoheleth opens with this arresting assertion. Gone is the optimism of Proverbs, or the dogged faithfulness in Job. Ecclesiastes begins from a place of despair and ends in one of resignation. The root of the word for pointless is *hebel*, which means "breath" or "puff." It is the opposite of *ruah*, the breath of life.[1] The writer begins this collection of wisdom by pointing to the ephemeral and transitory state of life. If nothing lasts forever, and we are all going to die, what's the point? The community represented in this text did not believe in an afterlife, and the inevitability of death, accompanied by the reality of suffering, led the writer on a search.

1. Robert Alter, notes in *The Hebrew Bible: A Translation with Commentary* (New York: W. W. Norton and Company, 2019), 675.

Two words are used to describe the writer's journey. One is *darash,* which means to search, and the other is *tur*, which means to seek out, spy out, explore. In other words, the writer searched and searched. His experience has taught him what Job already learned—that the righteous suffer and many wicked people appear to be doing just fine:

> I also observed under the sun that the race doesn't always go to the swift, nor the battle to the mighty, nor food to the wise, nor wealth to the intelligent, nor favor to the knowledgeable, because accidents can happen to anyone. People most definitely don't know when their time will come. (Eccl 9:11-12)

Unlike Job who finally does have an encounter with God (Job 38–41), the writer of Ecclesiastes is left to his own musings and attempts to create order. In the face of these limitations, the best the teacher has to offer is the admonition to "remember your creator in your prime," and to enjoy the life you have. "Whatever you are capable of doing, do with all your might because there's no work, thought, or wisdom in the grave, which is where you are headed" (Eccl 9:10).

There is a difference between the pursuit of wisdom described in Proverbs and the search for meaning in Qohelet. The differences between the books are those of perspective, experience, and theology. The resolution that comes at the end of the book is the resolution of someone who is wearied by the experiences of life. Qohelet has come to respect the limitations of human experience, even as we try to find our ways into wisdom.

> So this is the end of the matter; all has been heard. Worship God and keep God's commandments because this is what everyone must do. God will definitely bring every deed to judgment including every hidden thing, whether good or bad. (Eccl 12:13-14)

Qohelet is a person of faith, but his is not a naive or simplistic belief. God is real, but our ability to define and understand God is limited. That is all we can know in this life.

Part Nine

PROPHETS

I've been to the mountaintop and I've seen the other side.

—Martin Luther King Jr.

When Martin Luther King Jr. uttered these well-known words, he evoked an image familiar to his audience, that of the prophet Moses, who stood on Mount Nebo and looked over into Canaan, the promised land. The people of Israel were about to go into the land, but Moses would not accompany them. He offered words of encouragement based on what he had seen. The familiar image of Moses provided interpretive clues for King's audience. Just as the Israelites finally found their way to the promised land, so too would those in the fight for civil rights during the 1960s. The impact of the prophetic event was reinterpreted and had deeper meaning in the wake of King's assassination. The words had meaning when they were offered, had more meaning after his death, and continue to be gleaned for meaning in our current context. Prophetic words create an image for the audience that are open to reinterpretation again and again.

There are three different words in the Old Testament for a prophet: the first two words, *ro'eh* and *hozeh*, are translated as "seer" and "visionary," respectively. The visual nature of these words is not to be overlooked. The prophet's work can be understood as reporting from a vantage point that the community does not have and being able to see more than they can, like Moses and MLK on the mountaintop. The prophet is exposed to God's words, God's vision, and perspective.

The third word, *navi'*, speaks to the office of prophet. In simple terms, the prophet speaks on God's behalf. The message of the prophet is best described as "forth-telling" as opposed to "foretelling." God conveys messages to the people in order to affirm or correct identity. If the people have lost their way, the prophet issues an oracle of woe, which could be a warning or an announcement of punishment. The prophet may give a word of comfort or an oracle of promise that provides the people with an image of what God has in store for them.

In the Bible, prophets operate in different spheres. In the Pentateuch, Moses, Aaron, and Miriam are a family of prophets. In Samuel, Nathan and Isaiah are "court prophets," operating in service to the royal court. There are prophets who are "free agents," operating on the periphery of society but always with a support group. Some prophets are classified as "writing" prophets. For these prophets we have books, unlike prophets like Elijah and Elisha who are known for their actions more than their oracles.

In the Old Testament there are three Major Prophets, Isaiah, Jeremiah, and Ezekiel. The Book of the Twelve consists of the twelve so-called Minor Prophets. The division of Major and Minor Prophets has to do with length. Isaiah, Jeremiah, and Ezekiel are 1,291, 1,364, and 1,271 verses long, respectively; each is long enough to be on a single scroll. The Minor Prophets combined are a total of 1,050 verses, and fit on one scroll. The Major and Minor Prophets spoke in the north and the south for approximately three centuries, from the eighth century BCE to the postexilic fifth century BCE. Their messages are informed by distinct theologies or understandings of how God works in the world.

The Call Narrative

Jarena Lee, Zilpha Elaw, and Julia Foote were three African American women evangelists and preachers in the antebellum United States. They risked physical harassment and harm. They did not enjoy the support or endorsement from their communities of faith with any regularity if at all. They made sacrifices in their personal lives and with their families. Zilpha Elaw traveled into the South to proclaim the good news where she risked being kidnapped and forced into slavery. They were willing to endure all of these hardships because God called them to preach. Their actions and decisions were ruled by a powerful encounter that changed them forever. In fact, their autobiographies can be construed as extended call narratives. Everything that was accomplished resulted from the supernatural and overwhelming encounter with the divine presence of God that commissioned each one to speak for the Lord. The call narrative is the origin story for these prophetic preachers.

The call narratives of Jarena Lee, Zilpha Elaw, and Julia Foote help us as we encounter the call narratives in the Major Prophets. The call narrative is where the prophetic vocation begins. It is the motivation and justification for a vocation that is not dependent on the sanction of official religious organizations. It is an origin story that explains the prophet's motivation and mission. Moreover, the call narrative establishes the prophet's God-given authority to speak on God's behalf. It may include the themes and theological perspective that will inform the work of the speaker/seer. In this work about the holy imagination of biblical writings, we will explore the call narratives of the Major Prophets to highlight those themes and theologies.

CHAPTER 20
ISAIAH

Isaiah is very important for Jewish and Christian communities. For Jews, this book speaks comforting words of promise about Israel's restoration. For the early Christians, these prophetic words illuminate the birth, death, and resurrection of Jesus Christ. It is the second most frequently quoted Old Testament book in the New Testament.[1] The book is sixty-six chapters long, and most scholars agree that it divides into at least two parts, chapters 1–39 and chapters 40–66. Some identify the last ten chapters, 56–66, as a separate unit. Whether two divisions or three, there is agreement that the Isaiah scroll represents more than one voice over a period of time that spans from the eighth century Syro-Ephraimitic war, circa 734 BCE, through the sixth century fall of Judah to Babylon in 586 BCE to some unspecified time after that. The prophecies of Isaiah inform Israel's identity at a range of different moments in history. First Isaiah, chapters 1–39, is associated with the period of Assyrian dominance in the eighth century BCE. In this segment, the prophet speaks to a people who have lost their identity, evidenced through their lack of ability to comprehend and recognize. Second Isaiah, chapters 40–55, is associated with the end of Babylon's dominance and the end of Judah's exile in Babylon. In these chapters, the prophet utters words of comfort to a people or to a remnant of the people who call them back into an identity as "a light to the nations." The last section of Isaiah, chapters 56–66, can be associated with the time of Persian political dominance, where the idea of an identity with

1. The Psalms are referenced sixty-eight times in the NT and Isaiah is quoted fifty-five times.

a universal impact is expanded. These themes, spread across centuries and communities, are held together by the themes of God's holiness and majesty. They are present in the call narrative of the prophet Isaiah. However, unlike other prophetic books, Isaiah does not begin with a call narrative but with a covenant disputation.

The Covenant Dispute

Instead of the anticipated call narrative, which comes in chapter 6, the Isaiah collection begins with a covenant dispute, in which the characters or grieved parties are God and God's people, among the heavens and the earth. The dispute is the result of a broken covenant. In the event that a covenant is broken by unfaithfulness or disloyal love for false gods, the Lord complains to the witnesses (the divine assembly) about the unfaithfulness of the people.

> Hear you heavens, and listen earth,
> for the LORD has spoken:
> I have reared children; I raised them,
> and they have turned against me! (Isa 1:2)

These words introduce us to a series of prophetic oracles that employ the imagery of family (the most fundamental human relationship), and the variety of ways in which Judah's inhabitants have broken their bonds. The oracles include words of doom primarily with some hope for restoration. Throughout these early chapters, whether God is the metaphorical midwife, husband, father, or gardener,[2] it is clear that God has done far more than fulfill an obligation to the wife, child, or vine. Moreover, God loves the people but in return has been forsaken and betrayed. The cry for justice concerning this broken covenant is the prelude to the prophet's call. Unlike the call narratives of Jeremiah and Ezekiel, which provide a geopolitical context, Isaiah's call prefaces the political context with the spiritual situation. The ordering of these chapters conveys the message that

2. Patricia Tull, *Women's Bible Commentary*, ed. Carol Newsom, Sharon Ringe and Jacqueline Lapsley (Louisville: Westminster John Knox, 2012).

the spiritual realm is more important than the political one (theopolitics).[3] With the oracles of Isaiah, we are reminded that the prophet is not an evangelist. Rather, the prophet addresses a people who are presumably already in a relationship, albeit tenuous, with God.

The Call of Isaiah

I volunteer! I volunteer as tribute!

—Katniss Everdeen[4]

> In the year of King Uzziah's death, I saw the Lord sitting on a high and exalted throne, the edges of his robe filling the temple. Winged creatures were stationed around him. Each had six wings: with two they veiled their faces, with two their feet, and with two they flew about. They shouted to each other, saying:
>
> "Holy, holy, holy is the LORD of heavenly forces!
> All the earth is filled with God's glory!"
>
> The doorframe shook at the sound of their shouting, and the house was filled with smoke.
>
> I said, "Mourn for me; I'm ruined! I'm a man with unclean lips, and I live among a people with unclean lips. Yet I've seen the king, the Lord of heavenly forces!"
>
> Then one of the winged creatures flew to me, holding a glowing coal that he had taken from the altar with tongs. He touched my mouth and said, "See, this has touched your lips. Your guilt has departed and your sin is removed." Then I heard the Lord's voice saying, "Whom should I send, and who will go for us?" I said, "I'm here; send me." (Isa 6:1-8)

3. Theopolitics describes the dynamic between king and prophet in the eighth century. Should the king's behavior be governed by what makes sense politically or militarily or by what God says through the prophet? Isaiah urges the kings to acknowledge God's sovereignty not only in their worship but in the political realm.

4. Gary Ross, *The Hunger Games* (Lionsgate, 2012).

In the Year of King Uzziah's Death . . .

Isaiah's call begins with and is tied to a historical moment. The northern kingdom was in a state of instability and ongoing conflict, attempting alliances with other powers to stand against the Assyrian empire. The southern kingdom was able to stay out of this turmoil during the reign of King Uzziah. In fact, Judah enjoyed stability and strength during his reign. His death coincided with the rise of a new Assyrian leader, Tiglath Pilesar, and Judah would no longer be able to remain unnoticed. Now Judah was thrust into the political turmoil that the northern kingdom had been struggling with.

Three Major Crises in Judah's History

The Syro-Ephraimitic War, 734 BCE: The kings of Israel and Damascus formed an alliance to resist Assyria. They pressured other nations to join them.

The Ashdod Rebellion, 714–711 BCE

The Revolt of the Western Coalition and the Sennacharib Invasion, 705–701 BCE

The call of Isaiah is tied to the beginning of this period.

In contrast to the specific historical stamp is the otherworldly vision that invades the temple. The image is of God's throne, superimposed upon the temple. Fiery creatures called seraphs (or seraphim) proclaim God's holiness. The sensory spectacle—sight, sound, and touch—saturates the prophet's vision as he sees, hears, and feels the vibration. The overwhelming sensation, however, when confronted with this revelation, is a profound awareness of his inadequacy.

> I said, "mourn for me; I'm ruined! I'm a man with unclean lips, and I live among a people with unclean lips. Yet I've seen the king, the Lord of heavenly forces!" (6:5)

The seraph responds,

> Then one of the winged creatures flew to me, holding a glowing coal that he had taken from the altar with tongs. He touched my mouth and said, "See, this has touched your lips. Your guilt has departed and your sin is removed." (6:7)

What follows is the call and a response:

> Then I heard the Lord's voice saying, "Whom should I send, and who will go for us?" I said, "I'm here; send me." (6:8)

Overcome by God's holiness and majesty, Isaiah has little choice but to first repent and then volunteer to serve as God's spokesperson. This theme of God's holiness is pervasive in all of Isaiah. In Isaiah's call narrative, God's holiness overwhelms the temple itself. The call narrative establishes a major theme for the book of Isaiah: God's holiness is bigger than everything—even the nations of Assyria, Egypt, and Babylon. Therefore, it does not fit into the world of politics and nations. Rather, it overrules and contradicts them. But, if God's holiness is so great, one must wonder how it is that the people of the southern and northern kingdoms of Judah and Israel seem to be so lost. According to the prophet Isaiah, they have forgotten their true identity:

> Hear you heavens, and listen earth,
> for the LORD has spoken:
> I reared children; I raised them,
> and they turned against me!
> An ox knows its owner
> and a donkey its master's feeding trough
> But Israel doesn't know;
> my people don't behave intelligently. (Isa 1:2-3)

Perhaps this is why the message Isaiah is given in the call narrative is as follows:

> God said, "Go and say to this people:
> Listen intently, but don't understand;
> Look carefully, but don't comprehend.
> Make the minds of this people dull.
> Make their ears deaf and their eyes blind,
> so they can't see with their eyes

> or hear with their ears,
> or understand with their minds,
> and turn, and be healed." (6:9–10)

In response to this, the prophet asks,

> "How long, Lord?" And God said, "Until cities lie ruined with no one living in them, until there are houses without people and the land is left devasted. The LORD will send the people far away, and the land will be completely abandoned. Even if one-tenth remain there, they will be burned again, like a terebinth or an oak, which when it is cut down leaves a stump. Its stump is a holy seed." (6:11-13)

Isaiah's call narrative exposes us to the holiness of God and the fate of the people. In the same way that God's holiness immediately exposes Isaiah's sin, so too does the display of God's holiness shine a light on the people's inadequacies.

OUTLINE	THEMES
Oracles of woe for doomed people: 1–39	Punishment is inevitable
Comfort and promise after punishment: 40–55	Redemptive suffering A remnant A new thing
Hope for the future in the love above: 56–66	The true Israel

First Isaiah: Identity Lost

First Isaiah, chapters 1–39, is consistent with the theme in the last part of Isaiah's call narrative. God is definitely going to punish the people and prophetic intervention will not keep it from happening. The task of the prophet is not to facilitate a change in the course of events, but rather to prepare the audience for impending doom and provide hope in the promise of the small part that will remain. The one-tenth, or the stump referred to in the passage, is the source of hope for the community of faith.

This small remainder comes to be known as the remnant, the seed from which God will start again.

The significance of this message cannot be separated from the identity of the people. Isaiah's audience was shaped by a "Jerusalemite," "Davidic," or "Zion" theology. God's promise to David in 2 Samuel 7 that David's line would be established forever led to an understanding that no harm would ever come to Judah since David's line was "forever" established there. This thinking was tied to the temple, the place where God's spirit abided. Nothing would happen to the temple, the home of the ark of the covenant, and nothing would happen to Jerusalem, the city that housed the temple. Nothing would happen to the Davidic monarchy. Isaiah's prophecies in chapters 1–39 overturn this theological perspective. Punishment is inevitable because of God's holiness and the people's failures, and God keeps the promise to David through the remnant.

Jerusalem and Zion

Jerusalem is the capital city of Judah. It is the city captured by David where Solomon's temple is located. The term *Zion* refers to the "heavenly Jerusalem." It is the mythical cosmic mountain, the place of God's dwelling. Like the Davidic covenant, Zion is eternal, and as sacred space, it exists out of space and time. In the aftermath of Jerusalem's destruction, the concept and motif of Zion become even more important for the people of Judah as a means of connecting to their identity and remembering God's promise to David.[5]

Second Isaiah: Identity Restored

Isaiah chapters 40–66 make up what is known as Second Isaiah. After thirty-nine chapters of judgment, this section opens with the following words:

Comfort, comfort my people!
  says your God.
Speak compassionately to Jerusalem,

5. For more on this, see Jon D. Levenson, *Sinai and Zion: An Entry into the Jewish Bible* (Cambridge: Harper & Row, 1987).

and proclaim to her that her compulsory service has ended,
that her penalty has been paid,
that she has received from the LORD's hand double for all her sins! (40:1-2)

The reassurance and comfort of the second part of Isaiah speaks to a community in exile. It appears to stand in stark contrast to the words of impending doom that precede it, when in fact it is a continuation of God's work in the world. The holiness of God cannot be separated from God's sovereignty, which means that there was always a plan behind the punishment. Now that the time of punishment is complete, God comforts the people and the work of God goes on. The identity of the southern kingdom that was previously tied to the physical locations and places of Jerusalem and the temple is restored to an identity that stems from a Holy and Sovereign God. These themes are demonstrated in the following passage(s):

Exodus: The Remix

The LORD your redeemer,
the holy one of Israel says,
For your sake, I have sent an army to Babylon,
and brought down all the bars,
turning the Chaldeans' singing into a lament.
I am the LORD, your holy one,
Israel's creator, your king!
The LORD says—who makes a way in the sea
and a path in the mighty waters,
who brings out chariot and horse,
army and battalion;
they will lie down together and will not rise;
they will be extinguished, extinguished like a wick.
Don't remember the prior things;
don't ponder ancient history.
Look! I'm doing a new thing;
now it sprouts up; don't you recognize it?
I'm making a way in the desert,
paths in the wilderness.
The beasts of the field,
the jackals and ostriches, will honor me,

> because I have put water in the desert
> and streams in the wilderness
> to give water to my people,
> my chosen ones,
> this people whom I formed for myself,
> who will recount my praise. (Isa 43:14-21)

The exodus is the imaginative lens through which Israel understands its relationship with God. God redeemed the people with "a strong hand and outstretched arm" (Deut 26:8). They were led through the sea on dry land (Neh 9:11) while Pharaoh's "horse and rider drowned in the sea" (Exod 15:1). If the exodus is God's "signature act," then the exile is the "anti-exodus," the undoing of what God did to make Israel God's own. For this reason, there is with the exile the question of Israel's identity. Were they still God's people? The reassuring answer to this question in Second Isaiah uses the imagery and language of the exodus to overturn the "anti-exodus." The imagery draws on the past and then commands, "Don't remember the prior things: don't ponder ancient history." Is the ancient history the exile or the exodus? The images after the command, "Don't remember . . . don't ponder," are images of the wilderness, the place where God's people dwelled after their release from Egypt. The harsh reality of the wilderness is transformed in Isaiah's prophetic oracle. Just as God made paths through the chaos of the sea, so will God make paths in chaos of the wilderness. Moreover, God transforms the chaotic wilderness with water and streams. By using the familiar tropes of crossing the sea and the wilderness, the prophet creates a new understanding of God's redemptive work that does not simply move people from or through a trial, but transforms the very terrain of the oppressive or dangerous place. The community in exile is invited to imagine God's redemptive work on their behalf as a work of transforming the space they occupy because they are the "people . . . formed for myself." The word here for "formed" evokes God's work of creation in Genesis 2, where God "formed" the *adam*/human from the dust of the ground. God will make a garden in the desert place of exile, and in so doing, confirm that the people of Israel do belong to God. The work of salvation that occurs in the second exodus goes beyond the people of Israel. In 2 Isaiah, we observe a shift to salvation made available to the world. The anointed one, the *messiah*, will reinterpret Israel's understanding of king and expand the purpose of God's promise to David.

The Servant Songs

Four "songs" about the servant of YHWH in Second Isaiah are known as the "Servant Songs": 42:1-4; 49:1-6; 50:4-11; and 52:13–53:12. In the first song, the servant is called the chosen one, to whom YHWH has given his spirit to establish justice. In the second and third songs, the servant speaks for himself. The fourth song's unidentified speaker presents an image of a suffering servant, one who is likened to "a lamb being brought to slaughter." This servant suffers on behalf of the people. Some scholars consider these songs as a separate literary unit. As a unit, there is some pressure to identify a single servant. However, the individual songs seem to resist such an assignment. The songs seem to be driven by what the servant does. It is possible then that the identity of the servant is tied to the work of the servant. In addition to the theme of redemptive suffering the servant songs expand the scope of God's work redemption in the world beyond the restoration of Judah.

Third Isaiah: Identity Expanded

The presumed setting for the last eleven chapters of Isaiah, referred to by some scholars as Third Isaiah, is Jerusalem on the other side of exile. The literary function of these last chapters is to support the overall unity of the book with "a reuse, reordering and reinterpretation of Second and Third Isaiah." In Third Isaiah, the image of Zion assists the adjustment to a homeland that pales in comparison to her past glory. In chapters 65 and 66, specifically, the closing chapters, Zion is cast as a mother who labors, births, and nurses her children. The suffering of the nation is recast as labor for new life, prosperity, and sustenance. The nurturing image of God in 66:11-14a sits in contrast to the image of punishment for the Lord's enemies. This salvation may be available to all, but those who do not receive it will not occupy neutral space.

The final image in Isaiah is of the nations being gathered "to my holy mountain Jerusalem." The salvation of the Lord goes out to "distant coastlands that haven't heard of my fame or seen my glory" (66:19). The expansiveness of this image of salvation is by the final image of the enduring punishment for those who rebel against God. The theological lenses of Isaiah interpret ancient and future historical events to offer meaning not only to soothe Judah's suffering but to affirm an identity rooted in God's holiness.

Make Sure Not to Miss . . .

- The song of the vineyard, 5
- Isaiah's call narrative, 6:1-13
- The sign of Immanuel, 7:10-25
- The celebration of the Davidic king, 9:1-7
- Ideal Davidic rule, 11:1-9
- Comfort for God's people, 40
- The Servant Songs, 42:1-9; 49:1-6; 50:4-11; 52:13–53:12

CHAPTER 21
JEREMIAH

If the imagery of Isaiah supports the concept of God as holy and sovereign, then the language of Jeremiah creates images of God as intimate and interrelated. Jeremiah exposes the inner life of the prophet who stands in the liminal space between God and God's people. Through the poetry and prose of Jeremiah, we experience the relationship between God and God's people as complicated, passionate, and messy. Jeremiah is, for the most part, rejected by his people, and he has a tormented relationship with the God who called him. For these reasons, Jeremiah is not an easy read. In addition, the book, laden with emotionally heavy rhetoric, lacks an obvious structure and chronological order. "Its plethora of genres, speakers, and competing theological claims present a formidable challenge to anyone."[1] Emotionally heavy, this is not a book that makes logical sense. However, a case can be made that Jeremiah makes sense dialogically. That is to say, the many "genres, speakers, and competing theological claims"[2] form a dialogue, albeit an anguished one, that bears witness to and makes meaning out of the trauma of exile.

The Call of Jeremiah

> These are the words of Jeremiah, Hilkiah's son, who was one of the priests from Anathoth in the land of Benjamin. The LORD's word came to Jeremiah

1. Louis Stulman, *Jeremiah,* Abingdon Old Testament Commentaries (Nashville: Abingdon Press, 2005), 11.

2. Stulman, *Jeremiah*, 11.

in the thirteenth year of Judah's King Josiah, Amon's son, and throughout the rule of Judah's King Jehoiakim, Josiah's son, until the fifth month of the eleventh year of King Zedekiah, Josiah's son, when the people of Jerusalem were taken into exile.

The LORD's word came to me:
"Before I created you in the womb I knew you;
Before you were born I set you apart;
I made you a prophet to the nations."
"Ah, LORD God," I said, "I don't know how to speak
because I'm only a child."
The LORD responded,
"Don't say, 'I'm only a child.'
Where I send you, you must go;
what I tell you, you must say.
Don't be afraid of them,
because I'm with you to rescue you,"
declares the LORD.
Then the LORD stretched out his hand,
touched my mouth, and said to me,
"I'm putting my words in your mouth.
This very day I appoint you over nations and empires,
to dig up and pull down,
to destroy and demolish,
to build and plant." (1:1-10)

Context for the Call

. . . in the thirteenth year . . . and throughout . . . until . . . when . . .

Jeremiah's prophetic career is set within a specific historical context, the forty years between 627 to 587/6 BCE. This means that Jeremiah's prophecies are attached to a period of time nearly one hundred years after the northern kingdom of Israel had been defeated by the Assyrians. The Assyrian Empire's power is beginning to wane and smaller nations like Judah are trying to regain power and reassert independence. Under Josiah, Judah experienced a religious renewal and regained independence. Eventually, Babylon defeats Assyria and the small nations try to take advantage of the transition of power by forming coalitions of smaller nations that would rebel against the superpower, just as they had done with Assyria. Babylon responds with blunt force and subdues these smaller nations with deportation and destruction, and Judah did not escape this fate. Babylon deported inhabitants of Judah in 597 BCE, finally destroying the city of Jerusalem and the temple in 587/6 BCE.[3] Jeremiah was called to proclaim God's messages to God's people before and after the devastation of exile, and while they waited to see if God would, in fact, restore them. The prepositions in the time stamp—*in*, *throughout*, and *until*—convey not only a span of time but a sense of the experience of time. In retrospect, we can organize events based on our understanding of causality and eventuality. The introduction is leading up to the "when" of the exile. We know from the very beginning that the exile is the event through which other events, past and present, will be interpreted.

Before I created you in the womb . . .

The time stamps that are used to set the stage for Jeremiah's call, "in, throughout, until, when," are set into dialogue with two prepositions in God's call to Jeremiah, "before," and "before." God's word begins with an alternate timeline, before and before. With these words, another dimension is brought to our consideration and that perspective goes back to a time that predates Jeremiah's existence. The depiction of God as creator in Genesis is intimate and just beyond our imagination. On the one hand, God refers to creating Jeremiah in the womb, which is wondrous in its own right. God's ultimate claim in the opening words of the call, however, is knowledge of Jeremiah before he was formed in the womb. What was Jeremiah before he was formed in the womb? Whereas in Isaiah, God claims authority with a big show of holiness, God claims authority by referring to realms of existence and intimacy beyond our understanding. Jeremiah's depiction of God offers another image of authority, and it is intimate and maternal. God's knowledge of the prophet before creation and

3. Citizens (prominent and wealthy ones) were deported with each of these incursions in 597, 587, and 582 BCE.

before birth sets up an imbalance in knowing. What God knows is already beyond the prophet's ability to know, so in spite of his protestations, "I'm only a child," Jeremiah has no choice but to comply.

Jeremiah's resistance of God's commission evokes the call of the prophet Moses in Exodus 3. In response to God's call, Moses had legitimate and logical reasons to question God's choice. Unfortunately for him, God had a response for each one of Moses's protestations. In the tradition of prophets, Moses is set apart: "No prophet like Moses has yet emerged in Israel; Moses knew the LORD face-to-face!" Jeremiah's likeness to Moses comes both from his resistance to God's call and from his theological orientation. Like Moses, Jeremiah ascribed to a Deuteronomistic theology. This perspective understands the covenant of God to be conditional. God and the people both have an obligation, and if the people do not uphold their solemn promise to keep the covenant, God is not obligated to uphold the sacred promise. Moses led the people out of Egypt and guided them through the wilderness for forty years into the promised land. Jeremiah prophesied for a period of forty years and presided over the journey out of the promised land, the "anti-exodus," and then ended up in Egypt.

God's response to Jeremiah's objections is twofold. First, God speaks to the prophet, reinforcing both God's authority and presence. Next, God touches the prophet's mouth, placing "my words in your mouth" (1:9). Now the prophet is prepared and appointed to "dig up and pull down, to destroy and demolish, to build and plant" (1:10). The first four verbs in this last section connote destruction and the last two are for rebuilding. These verbs of destroying and restoring correspond to the overall dialogic structure of the book:

OUTLINE	THEMES
1–25 Uprooting 26–29 Narratives about the prophet 30–33 Scroll of Comfort 34–45 Narratives about the prophet 46–51 Oracles against the nations 52 Epilogue	Destruction, chaos, and trauma The agony of the prophet Hope for a new future

Two visions: The almond branch and the pot boiling. The next part of Jeremiah's call comes in the form of two visions, one of an almond tree and one of a pot boiling over from the north. Both times the prophet is first asked, "What do you see?" After he answers, the LORD explains the meaning or the significance of the vision. The issue of interpretation is imbedded in Jeremiah's call. In addition to the work of seeing, the prophet my receive an interpretation. The first vision's meaning is in the words. The word for almond, *shaqed,* is an intentional wordplay with God's message, "I am watching *over/shoqed* my word until it is fulfilled. In the case of the second, Jeremiah's vision confirms that something bad is coming from the north.

Jeremiah is a collection of prophetic oracles conditioned and oriented by the reality of the Babylonian exile. The destruction of Jerusalem and the temple is the self-understood death of the nation as it was known. One of the primary metaphors used to communicate this movement from death to new life is that of the family. In Jeremiah, we observe a family that is broken and then grieves and struggles to re-establish itself.[4]

A Marriage of Metaphor

You without me: like cornflake without the milk
It's my world—you just a squirrel, tryin' to get a nut

—"The Rain" by Oran Juice Jones

Metaphor is one of the dominant tools used in biblical literature. One of the most well-known metaphors, "The LORD is my shepherd," uses the known vocation of a shepherd to help the audience gain a greater understanding of the LORD's purpose or identity. Ancient Near Eastern deities were generally not known as caretakers. The metaphor is by definition radical because it combines ways of thinking that did not formerly coexist. Similarly, the metaphor of family that is used to describe God's relationship with God's people is familiar yet unexpected. People and priests in Judah had a clear understanding of how families worked, so when the prophet (Hosea in the north, and then Jeremiah in the south) describes Judah's relationship with God as that of an unfaithful wife, several things

4. Kathleen O'Connor explores the motif of family in chapter 5 of her book *Jeremiah: Pain and Promise* (Minneapolis: Fortress, 2011).

became clear. First of all, in a patriarchal social hierarchy, the family relationship was not between equals. The husband wields the authority and power over the assets in the family. Thus the family metaphor triggers expectations around the wife's fidelity, rooted in shame/honor culture. Women could bring honor or shame to the family, and Judah's disobedience has brought shame on her husband, YHWH, who responds with judgment couched in regret.

"I remember your first love"

With this imagery, the prophet begins by describing the good old days in Jeremiah 2:2:

> I remember your first love,
> your devotion as a young bride,
> how you followed me in the wilderness,
> in an unplanted land.

God describes the time that Israel wandered in the wilderness as a "honeymoon," a time when Israel was devoted to "her man." The metaphor is telling. YHWH's experience of the wilderness may not readily jibe with that of the people. An entire generation died in the wilderness. It was a time of wandering and wondering, murmuring and regulation. From the perspective of the people, the wilderness may evoke any number of images, but "honeymoon" would not top the list. The metaphor betrays God's hand. God is interested in a people who are totally devoted, even if it is because they have no other options. The prophetic oracles detail that God found Israel, cleaned her up, and provided for her. Everything she has comes from God (Jer 2:20a, 22a). Israel in the desert had no choice but to be completely dependent upon God. This early oracle suggests that this is the way God likes things to be.

Unfortunately, YHWH's wife is not very good at faithfulness. Judah's sin of worshipping other gods is equated with adultery in the family metaphor. The family metaphor is used to depict Judah as a bride turned adulteress and prostitute. The descriptions of the unfaithful wife are disrespectful, condescending, and offensive:

You are like a frenzied young camel,
racing around,
a wild donkey in the wilderness,
lustfully sniffing the wind.
Who can restrain such passion?
Those who desire her need not give up;
with little effort they will find her in heat. (Jer 2:23-24)

This description of Judah's behavior is demeaning and disparaging, suggesting this behavior is simply her nature. Judah is no better than an animal, unable to control her primal lust for other gods. God sounds like an angry lover, and at some point, God's passionate anger crosses a line. The powerful, albeit problematic language effectively carries the weight of God's sense of betrayal. But the family metaphor is messy. God's role of husband/father cannot be separated from the cultural influences that define the role. That in part is what makes the metaphor meaningful. The expectations around family roles is what makes the metaphor work. It is also what makes the metaphor problematic. The audience already understands the obligations of a husband and wife. Judah has failed to honor her commitment in seeking after other gods. Any husband would understandably seek justice and would be within his rights to punish his wife. The use of the family metaphor helps to explain the gravity of Judah's apostasy and God's right to punish the offender. Alternately, and perhaps unintentionally, the use of the family metaphor reinforces some of the cultural expectations about family roles, rooted in a system where the husband has power and authority over the wife. The wife is obligated to obey and follow. What works in the metaphor does not translate well into earthly matters. In earthly marriages, the husband/father is not to be equated with God. Moreover, the justification of God's anger and punishment of his wayward wife runs the risk of appearing to condone domestic violence. Within the confines of the metaphorical world, God's anger raises a number of questions. How far is God willing to go to make a point? Will God's pain overrule God's propensity for mercy? Will God put Judah aside forever? Has not the trauma of the exile been enough? The metaphor of marriage effectively contains the dysfunction of the covenant relationship between Judah and YHWH. However, the components of the metaphor are themselves dysfunctional.

The metaphor of marriage in the prophetic oracle is addressed to an audience who is entirely or mostly male.[5] The target audience is invested in the value system of a shame/honor culture. They are comfortable with the assumptions about a wife's role and behavior. They support an environment where punishment keeps everyone in their respective place. The rhetorical power of such a metaphor is that it first gains buy-in from the male audience in support of punishing an adulterous wife—and then startles the men because they are the whoring wife. The prophet uses a broken system to highlight another broken system.[6]

The Scroll of Comfort

Four chapters nestled in the collection of Jeremiah are rightly described as the scroll of comfort or book of consolation. The hope expressed in this section is not generic. Rather, the images and words of hope are specifically derived from the trauma of exile. Recovery from trauma requires remembering and not suppressing the events—the scroll of comfort is intentionally therapeutic in its movement back through the devastation, horror, and loss of the exile. In chapter 31 God promises, "The one who scattered Israel will gather them" (31:10), "I will turn their mourning into laughter and their sadness into joy" (31:13), and "There's hope for your future, declares the LORD" (31:17). The dialogue in Jeremiah is one between the prophet and the God who called him. There is also a dialogue between the prophet and the other prophets of his day. Additionally, there is a dialogue between the different theological understandings of what God is doing and how that changes Judah's identity. These dialogues contribute to a conversation about God's actions in history. In the scroll of comfort, the hope of God's restoration takes on the trauma of the past and the painful reality not only of the exile but what led up to it. This section

5. Renita Weems, *Battered Love, Marriage, Sex and Violence in the Hebrew Prophets* (Minneapolis: Augsburg Fortress, 1995), 41.

6. Weems, *Battered Love*, 51–52.

affirms a God who will ultimately relent and restore, and create again with a new covenant, written on the hearts of the people.

Jeremiah is a composite of genres, speakers, and competing theological claims[7] that form dialogues around the trauma of the exile and its repercussions. The prophet's scribes and editors use their grounding in Deuteronomistic theology to explore why the exile occurred and to find hope for the future. The metaphor of marriage imagines into the inner workings of an intimate relationship that must pass the litmus test of piety and devotion. The scroll of comfort offers a counter-narrative that expands a theology beyond the broken covenant. Jeremiah's internal and external words remind us that this covenantal relationship with God is a living and breathing work in progress. The Judahite community in exile cannot escape the reality of the broken covenant. However, that covenant comes from a God whose knowledge exceeds that of the people in exile. The God who knows the spaces before we were formed in our mother's womb will find a way to enact a new covenant and bring a new creation to the fatigued and battle-weary community in exile.

7. Stulman, *Jeremiah*, 11.

Make Sure Not to Miss . . .

- The potter's wheel, 18:1-12
- Jeremiah's lament, 20:7-13, 14-18
- True vs. false prophets, 28:1-17
- Seek the peace of the city, 29:1-32
- The new covenant, 31:31-34

CHAPTER 22
EZEKIEL

There are three things that matter in property: Location, location, location.

—Real Estate Agents' Mantra

OUTLINE	THEMES
1–24 Oracles against Judah and Jerusalem 25–32 Oracles against the nations 33–39 Restoration for Israel; judgment for the nations	God's presence and God's absence

The trajectory of Israel's identity narrative is that God called the people, redeemed them, and brought them through the wilderness of "dangers seen and unseen" to establish them in the "promised land" full of milk and honey. The whole point of the story is to end up in the land, but the event of the exile overturns everything and raises questions about who/what Israel is. The destruction of Judah and temple in Jerusalem, and the Babylonian exile is the cognitive dissonance inducing trauma that forever changes the identity and religion of the small nation. The experience of exile was overwhelming, yet so was Ezekiel's experience of God. The very first verse of the book alerts the reader that "we are not in Kansas anymore." In fact, the messages in Ezekiel are both tied to location and test the limits of location. The theology that contributes to Israel's identity as a people is location specific. The legitimate worship of God takes place in the temple of Jerusalem and God's people understood themselves as tied to and protected by this location, now lost. This is the context for Ezekiel's call and ministry.

Ezekiel has a highly distinctive style. The writing is more prosaic than poetic, and he "exhibits a weakness for repetition."[1] Nonetheless, the images are dramatic, exploiting the limits of metaphor or hyperbole.[2] Ezekiel's language and actions take our understanding of prophecy to a new level. He travels by divine teleportation. There are more sign-acts[3] in Ezekiel than any other prophetic book. This younger contemporary of Jeremiah doesn't speak after receiving his prophetic commission until after the exile (wait, what?). He lies on his left side for 390 days and on his right for 40. He cuts his hair and burns one-third, strikes one-third with a blade, and scatters the remaining third to the wind. And, Ezekiel does what no one is supposed to do. He *sees* God. One is left to wonder, which element is more controversial—the fact that Ezekiel sees God, or that he sees God by the Chebar River in Babylonian territory?

The ordering of the three Major Prophets Isaiah, Jeremiah, and Ezekiel in the canon is chronological. The prophet Isaiah was active during the eighth century BCE, and Jeremiah's prophetic work took place in the seventh century BCE. Ezekiel was a younger contemporary of Jeremiah who was a part of the first group deported to Babylon in 597 BCE. Ezekiel was a Zadokite priest who prophesied from 593 to 573 BCE, a period of at least twenty years.

Ezekiel can be divided into three parts (see outline above). For the purposes of this chapter, we will examine identity in Ezekiel based on three of his visions, through the lens of location, that is, through divine presence and absence. What identity can the Babylonian exiles have away from the land? Are they still the people of God, and if so, where is their God?

---

1. Robert Alter, introduction to "Ezekiel," in *The Hebrew Bible: A Translation with Commentary* (New York: W. W. Norton and Company, 2019), 1049.

2. Ellen Davis, *Swallowing the Scroll: Textuality and the Dynamics of Discourse in Ezekiel's Prophecy* (Sheffield, UK: Sheffield Academic, 2009).

3. A sign-act is a nonverbal prophetic tool that conveys a message from God. The sign-act is often followed by an explanatory oracle.

Location 1: By the Rivers of Babylon

Ezekiel's call is much longer than the call narratives we have seen in Isaiah and Jeremiah. Moreover, the genre is consistently prosaic, whereas the calls of Jeremiah and Isaiah are poetry interspersed with prose. Chapter 1 is Ezekiel's vision, followed by his commission in chapters 2 and 3.

> In the thirtieth year, on the fifth day of the fourth month, I was with the exiles at the Chebar River when the heavens opened and I saw visions of God. (It happened on the fifth day of the month, in the fifth year after King Jehoiachin's deportation. The Lord's word burst in on the priest Ezekiel, Buzi's son, in the land of Babylon at the Chebar River. There the Lord's power overcame him.)
>
> As I watched, suddenly a driving storm came out of the north, a great cloud flashing fire, with brightness all around. At its center, in the middle of the fire, there was something like gleaming amber. And inside that were forms of four living creatures. This was what they looked like: Each had the form of a human being, though each had four faces and four wings. Their feet looked like proper feet, but the soles of their feet were like calves' hooves, and they shone like burnished bronze. Human hands were under their wings on all four sides.
>
> All four creatures had faces and wings, and their wings touched each other's wings. When they moved, they each went straight ahead without turning. As for the form of their faces: each of the four had a human face, with a lion's face on the right and a bull's face on the left, and also an eagle's face. The pairs of wings that stretched out overhead touched each other, while the other pairs covered their bodies. Each moved straight ahead wherever the wind propelled them; they moved without turning. Regarding the creatures' forms: they looked like blazing coals, like torches. Fire darted about between the creatures and illuminated them, and lightning flashed from the fire. The creatures looked like lightning streaking back and forth.
>
> As I looked at the creatures, suddenly there was a wheel on the earth corresponding to all four faces of the creatures. The appearance and composition of the wheels were like sparkling topaz. There was one shape for all four of them, as if one wheel were inside another. When they moved in any of the four directions, they moved without swerving. Their rims were tall and terrifying, because all four of them were filled with eyes all around. When the

> creatures moved, the wheels moved next to them. Whenever the creatures rose above the earth, the wheels also rose up. Wherever the wind would appear to go, the wind would make them go there too. The wheels rose up beside them, because the spirit of the creatures was in the wheels. When they moved, the wheels moved; when they stood still, the wheels stood still; and when they rose above the earth, the wheels rose up along with them, because the spirit of the creatures was in the wheels. The shape above the heads of the creatures was a dome; it was like glittering ice stretched out over their heads. Just below the dome, their outstretched wings touched each other. They each also had two wings to cover their bodies. Then I heard the sound of their wings when they moved forward. It was like the sound of mighty waters, like the sound of the Almighty, like the sound of tumult or the sound of an army camp. When they stood still, their wings came to rest. Then there was a sound from above the dome over their heads. They stood still, and their wings came to rest. Above the dome over their heads, there appeared something like lapis lazuli in the form of a throne. Above the form of the throne there was a form that looked like a human being. Above what looked like his waist, I saw something like gleaming amber, something like fire enclosing it all around. Below what looked like his waist, I saw something that appeared to be fire. Its brightness shone all around. Just as a rainbow lights up a cloud on a rainy day, so its brightness shone all around. This was how the form of the LORD's glory appeared. When I saw it, I fell on my face. I heard the sound of someone speaking. (1:1-28)

Ezekiel's call narrative begins, at a particular time, and in a particular place, namely "with the exiles at the Chebar river." The location of the call is Babylonian exile. In that place of utter desolation that is foreign soil, Ezekiel had "visions of God." The opening words of the call narrative make a profound theological claim, namely that God's presence is not only not limited to the Jerusalem site, but that it can also be found in the land of the Babylonians. God will show up in the most unlikely of places, and in the case of Ezekiel's vision, God not only shows up, but "shows out!"

Ezekiel's location is clear. The site of the vision is less so, and the nature of the vision stretches our abilities to comprehend. More than a few people have described Ezekiel's vision as a whole as surreal, even psychedelic or drug-induced. What we can affirm is that what Ezekiel describes here is extraordinary and supernatural. The description is detailed and defies logic. When something has four faces, one in each direction, what does it mean to move straight ahead? What are we to make of eye-rimmed wheels, and what exactly is a wheel in the middle of a wheel? The vision is not only overwhelming in terms of its content, but its force. The LORD's word "burst in on" him and the LORD's power "overcame him" (1:3). The event of the vision and call/commission is equal if not greater in scope than the exile. Ezekiel is tossed from the overwhelming event of exile to an overpowering encounter with God.

In this vision, known as the throne-chariot vision,[4] Ezekiel is describing a throne with wheels, a mobile seat. Whereas Isaiah in his call narrative gives a description of the seraphim, these four-faced, winged creatures Ezekiel describes may be cherubim guardians of the divine sanctuary. Ezekiel's experience is breathtaking not only because of what he beholds, but because of the implications. No one is permitted to see God, and this vision report is one of the reasons that Ezekiel's inclusion in the canon was debated. The description of the throne chariot is both powerful and tentative. "Something like," "looked like," and "like" are recurring phrases. The description of the vision concludes, "This is how the form of the LORD's glory appeared" (1:28). And the glory comes to an exile by the Chebar River. The first vision is clear on this thing—God is present, and this presence is so meaningful because the recipient of the vision is in a place of exile.

Ezekiel's commission comes after the overwhelming experience of the vision:

> The voice said to me: Human one, stand on your feet, and I'll speak to you. As he spoke to me, a wind came to me and stood me on my feet, and I heard someone addressing me. He said to me: Human one, I'm sending you to the Israelites, a traitorous and rebellious people. They and their ancestors have been rebelling against me to this very day. I'm sending you to their hard-headed and hard-hearted descendants, and you will say to them: The LORD God proclaims. Whether they listen or whether they refuse, since they are a household of rebels, they will know that a prophet has been among them. And as for you, human one, don't be afraid of them or their words. Don't be afraid! You possess thistles and thorns that subdue scorpions. Don't be afraid of their words or shrink from their presence, because they are a household of rebels. You'll speak my words to them whether they listen or whether

4. The throne chariot appears in the vision in Ezekiel 8–11.

> they refuse. They are just a household of rebels! As for you, human one, listen to what I say to you. Don't become rebellious like that household of rebels. Open your mouth and eat what I give you. Then I looked, and there in a hand stretched out to me was a scroll. He spread it open in front of me, and it was filled with writing on both sides, songs of mourning, lamentation, and doom. (2:1-10)

The voice addresses Ezekiel as "human one," from the Hebrew phrase, *ben adam.* The terminology makes a clear distinction between the glory of God and the human who experiences it. Ezekiel, the "human one," is called to prophesy to his people, described as a "household of rebels," "rebellious ones," "hardheaded," and "hard-hearted."

> Then he said to me: Human one, eat this thing that you've found. Eat this scroll and go, speak to the house of Israel. So I opened my mouth, and he fed me the scroll. He said to me: Human one, feed your belly and fill your stomach with this scroll that I give you. So I ate it, and in my mouth it became as sweet as honey. Then he said to me: Human one, go! Go to the house of Israel and speak my words to them. You aren't being sent to a people whose language and speech are difficult and obscure but to the house of Israel. No, not to many peoples who speak difficult and obscure languages, whose words you wouldn't understand. If I did send you to them, they would listen to you. But the house of Israel—they will refuse to listen to you because they refuse to listen to me. The whole house of Israel is hardheaded and hard-hearted too. I've now hardened your face so that you can meet them head-on. I've made your forehead like a diamond, harder than stone. Don't be afraid of them or shrink away from them, because they are a household of rebels. He said to me: Human one, listen closely, and take to heart every word I say to you. Then go to the exiles, to your people's children. Whether they listen or not, speak to them and say: The LORD God proclaims! Then a wind lifted me up, and I heard behind me a great quaking sound from his place. Blessed is the LORD's glory! The sound was the creatures' wings beating against each other and the sound of the wheels beside them; it was a great rumbling noise. Then the wind picked me up and took me away. With the LORD's power pressing down against me I went away, bitter and deeply angry, and I came to the exiles who lived

> beside the Chebar River at Tel-abib. I stayed there among them for seven desolate days. (3:1-15)

The call narrative depicts a God whose glory is beyond our ability to describe. It also describes humanity as rebellious and "hard" of heart and head. Ezekiel is called to bring a word to these people who may not listen. His call offers a message about God's presence that immediately offers hope to those who understood God's presence and glory to be limited to the temple. The priestly devotion to the holy mountain of Jerusalem was a limited understanding of God's glory. Similarly, the people have underestimated the scope of God's holiness and the size of the gap between them and God. This God moves from one place to another, from "glory to glory."

Eating the Scroll

Ezekiel is presented with a scroll that he is instructed to eat. Even though the message God has for the people is one of condemnation, he finds the scroll "sweet." Please note that, like Isaiah and Jeremiah, Ezekiel's call narrative includes some contact with the mouth—a type of consecration of prophetic speech. Ezekiel's consumption of the scroll is metaphorical for taking in God's word. The metaphor of the scroll also indicates the form of the word. Unlike the other major prophets, Ezekiel's word comes first in written form. The written form is still dialogic. It includes more than one perspective and is ongoing.

Thus, one way to navigate the book of Ezekiel is the theme of the presence and absence of God. The elements of presence and place are evident in Ezekiel's call narrative and in two other visions in the book; the vision of temple in chapter 8 and the vision of restoration in chapters 40–48.

Location 2: God's Glory Departs the Temple (8–11)

The second vision about God's presence takes place in Jerusalem the holy city, and in this vision, the familiar elements of the throne chariot return. In this second vision, the abominations of the Jerusalem temple are not only an indictment against the people, they are the reason that God's presence cannot remain. The sins of the people force God's presence to depart and it is the absence of God's presence that makes the temple and the city vulnerable. In this vision, the presence of God moves in stages away from the temple and then from the city of Jerusalem. This second vision is key to the theological stability of the book. If Ezekiel's theology claims that the temple cannot be destroyed because of God's spirit, the vision in chapters 8–11 explains the action that preceded the temple's destruction in a way that corresponds to the Jerusalemite theology. The temple is able to be destroyed because God's spirit is no longer there and God's spirit was forced to depart because the sin of the people was so great. The mobility of the presence also provides hope to the displaced community, reinforcing the concept in the first vision, that God's presence can be experienced in other spaces.

Location 3: Jerusalem Restored (40–48)

Ezekiel ends, as it begins, with an extended vision. This final vision frames the book with the hope of return and restoration. God's divine presence returns to the temple—a new, heavenly temple. The passage is clearly in dialogue with the previous visions in chapter 1 and chapters 8–11:

> Then he led me to the east gate, where the glory of Israel's God was coming in from the east. Its sound was like the sound of a mighty flood, and the earth was lit up with his glory. What appeared when I looked was like what I had seen when he came to destroy the city, and also like what I saw at the Chebar River, and I fell on my face. Then the LORD's glory came into the temple by way of the east gate. A wind picked me up and brought me to the inner courtyard, and there the LORD's glory filled the temple. A man was standing next to me, but the voice that I heard came from inside the temple. He said to me, Human one, this is the place for my throne and the place for the soles of my feet, where I will dwell among the Israelites forever. The house of Israel will never again defile my holy name, neither they nor their kings, with their disloyalties and with their kings' corpses at the shrines. When they set their plazas with mine and their doorposts next to mine, the wall was between us. They defiled my holy name with their detestable

practices, so I consumed them in my anger. Now let them remove their disloyalties and their kings' corpses from me, and I will dwell among them forever. (Ezek 43:1-9)

The final vision's dialogue is not limited to the Ezekiel corpus. As prophetic literature is meant to be interpreted and reinterpreted, this third vision of the temple is both detailed and symbolic. Founded on the concept of heavenly prototypes for earthly cities, the vision reverberates throughout Jewish traditions and Christian (even in John's vision of a new heaven and earth in Revelation). God's mobility in the book's opening vision has new meaning in the broader context of the concluding vision. God's ability to transcend the limits of time and space comes from the broader context of a heavenly plane that supersedes the plane of human existence. The exiled community will know God's presence even as they hope for a return to a restored Jerusalem. The God who oversees the destruction is the same God who will restore.

The Valley of Dry Bones

Easily one of the most iconic passages in the Bible, the prophet Ezekiel is teleported to a valley of dry bones and asked by God, "Human one, can these bones live again?" (Ezek 37:3). The location is fraught with meaning. Burial codes in Judah would demand that bodies be buried immediately. A valley of dry bones is a site of devastation. Not only were many people slaughtered but there was no one to bury the dead (see Psalm 79:3). Ezekiel's response is the only true response to such a question. God does something that evokes creation, but is not that—it is restoration. Instead of creating new life, God restores life to that which is clearly lifeless. The description of the process, sinew, muscle, and flesh is intentional in depicting a God who knows how to restore because God is the creator. No one knows how to restore better than the creator!

This passage is a part of the Easter Vigil in some Christian traditions, as a resurrection story.

Ezekiel tests our understanding of space and time. His vision stretches our understanding of reality, and indeed, God's people will have to imagine differently if they will survive the torment of exile. They will need to imagine outside of their current understandings of space and time.

Make Sure Not to Miss . . .

- Ezekiel's call narrative, 1:1–3:27
- The Spirit abandons the temple, 8–11:25
- The Valley of Dry Bones, 37:1-14

CHAPTER 23
DANIEL

Didn't my Lord deliver Daniel? Then why not every man?

—Negro spiritual

The Negro spiritual "Didn't My Lord Deliver Daniel?" forms a dialogue between the account of Daniel's miraculous deliverance from the lion's den, and the African slaves' longing for their own liberation. The creators of the spirituals saw themselves as inheritors of the biblical narratives and traditions of liberation. Daniel's experience in the lion's den is a testimony to God's saving power and as such, it is both a source of hope and frustration. If God did it then, why isn't it happening now? "Why not every man?" Similarly, the book of Daniel represents two different communities; one that proclaims God's ability to deliver the exiles from the oppressive power of the king, and another that waits for deliverance from the evil empire.

Daniel is a strange composite of a book. It represents two different time periods, the first part comes from the fourth or third century BCE and the latter part is tied to the second century BCE, also known as the Second Temple Period.[1] It is written in two languages, Hebrew and Aramaic,[2] and it has two genres: court/diaspora tales (chapters 1–6) and apocalyptic literature (chapters 7–12). For all of its differences, the two parts of the book are unified through the character of Daniel, and by

1. 516 BCE to 70 CE.

2. Aramaic is closely related to Hebrew. In the ancient world, Aramaic was more widely used than Hebrew and was a major language that had widespread usage.

the dialogue between these diaspora communities over time. The first six chapters, like other court tales, celebrate and preserve stories of survival in the known world, whereas the second half of the book responds to the increasingly difficult context of the diaspora with an alternate reality. The book's composition date is somewhere around 165 BCE, making it the last book of the Hebrew Bible chronologically, and the second part of the book, the apocalyptic piece, most closely resembles material from the Dead Sea Scrolls or the Apocrypha.

OUTLINE	THEMES
1–6 The court tales 7–12 The apocalyptic imagination	YHWH is God, even in Babylon Danger of empire God's realm and God's reign is everywhere

The Imaginative World of the Court Tale

A biblical court/diaspora tale is a story about Jews in a foreign court where the hero overcomes a life-threatening situation, most often through some form of divine intervention. The court stories in Daniel 1–6 are a collection of independent narratives. In terms of style, *excess* is the word that comes to mind. Repetition, length of description, and the severity of the punishment are elements in these stories. In the story of the fiery furnace, the king is given to fits of rage, and the furnace is heated to the point where the men who threw the Jews in it were killed! The overall structure is comedic. It follows a "U" shape that moves from stability to crisis (conflict or contest) to resolution of victory or salvation for the protagonist through divine intervention.

The context for the opening stories of Daniel is exile. After Babylon's defeat and destruction of Jerusalem in 586 BCE, they took their defeated enemies captive. Specifically, they took those of the aristocracy and those with assets, abilities, and skills that that were of use to the conquering nation. "People of consequence" formed the diaspora. The young men in Nebuchadnezzar's court are "royal descendants and members of the ruling class from the Israelites—good-looking young men without defects, skilled in all wisdom, possessing knowledge, conversant with learnings, and capable of serving in the king's palace" (Dan 1:3-4). These young men of privilege became commodities of the Babylonian Empire. The identity crisis they experience from exile is one of language, status, class, location, diet, culture, religious practices, and even their names.

Naming is very important in the Bible, as one's name conveys familial ties, identity, and even destiny. The stories in Daniel document the name changes of the young Jewish men in the Babylonian court, from Daniel, Hananiah, Mishael, and Azariah to Belteshazzar, Shadrach, Meshach, and Abednego. The customary practice of changing the names of captives is more than a matter of language or pronunciation. Renaming attempts to erase the "other" identity of the captive.[3] The captives do not forget their names given at birth—they simply remember to answer to different names in different contexts. Two different names are a reality of life in the diaspora and an outward sign of dual consciousness. The exiled community must navigate between two different languages, customs, and religions—all things that contribute to identity.

The stories about these young men in the Babylonian court are stories about survival. They are set up as conflicts or contests. In some stories, the Jews compete with the Gentiles in ability to serve the king and in other stories, the characters "challenge" the existing Babylonian order by being observant Jews. The stories in chapters 1, 2, 4, and 5 are contest stories; accounts where Daniel (and friends in chapter 1) is able to achieve a goal that the king's sages cannot, proving the superiority of Daniel's God and religion. Chapters 3 and 6 are stories of a conflict.[4] Jealous courtiers create scenarios where the religious observances of Daniel, Hananiah, Mishael, and Azariah come into direct opposition of the king's rulings. The consequences of this defiance are a fatal punishment, except they are miraculously preserved by God. In the court tales, the foreign king is depicted as

3. There is an iconic scene in the television miniseries *Roots* where the African slave Kunta Kinte has to literally have his old name beaten out of him before he will accept the "slave name" of Toby.

4. Lee Humphreys uses the terms "contest" and "conflict" to describe the two types of court tales in Daniel in "A Lifestyle for Diaspora: A Study of the Tales of Esther and Daniel," *JBL* 92: 211–23.

unreliable at best, and at worse he is rash, given to fits of rage to the point of madness. The Israelite men in the court demonstrate wisdom and are willing to die for their faith practices. The end of every story is the same. The God of the Jews delivers, and proves to be the true God.

The final episode of the story of Daniel in the lion's den is an iconic court tale that reflects a world view on top of another world view. Daniel's rise to prominence incites jealousy in the other officers. Unsuccessful in finding any flaws in Daniel, they convince the king to establish an edict that creates a conflict with Daniel's piety. Daniel's practice of prayer becomes criminalized and he is sentenced to a death penalty that the king is unable to rescue him from. God "shut the lions' mouths" and they brought Daniel no harm. The king responds by throwing Daniel's enemies into the lions' pit, along with their families, and by making a new decree that Daniel's God "is the living God." This is an extremely satisfying story for a community whose experience of exile may feel like living on the edge of a lions' pit. Daniel is above reproach, an ideal representative of the diaspora. He is not only rescued but his enemies are punished along with their families. To that end the stories affirm the power of God over the powers of the Babylonian, Persian, and Greek empires, while affirming and reinforcing the identity of the current audience.

Another element in the first chapters of Daniel is dreams and their interpretation. Dreams introduce another plane of existence into the narrative. They interrupt the affairs of the foreign kings with messages from God. As interpreter, Daniel symbolizes the diaspora existence of balancing two realities and allowing them to inform one another.

The interpretation of dreams in the first section forms a bridge with the second section of the book. In chapters 7–12 Daniel, the interpreter of dreams, has visions that are beyond his understanding. They interrupt the dismal reality of persecuted Jews with another, supernatural realm.

The Apocalyptic Imagination

The word *apocalypse* means to uncover or reveal, and the term apocalyptic can be used to describe a world view, a community, and a type of literature. Apocalyptic literature is "a genre of revelatory literature with a narrative framework, in which a revelation is mediated by an otherworldly being to a human recipient, disclosing a transcendent reality that is both temporal, insofar as it envisages eschatological salvation, and spatial insofar as it involves another, supernatural world."[5] It usually has the following characteristics:

1. Use of the first person in the account
2. Coded language, such as animal symbolism and numerology
3. Interpretation of visions by celestial intermediaries
4. Periodization of history, ending in a decisive triumph of good over evil
5. Emphasis on the disclosure of divine mystery[6]

Apocalyptic literature is the product of a community that needs to access an alternate reality. Scholars debate over what constitutes an apocalyptic community. It is safe to say that apocalyptic communities have experienced some form of overwhelming cognitive dissonance. The universe, as they have always understood it, no longer exists and the trauma of that experience opens the door to another reality that interacts with and informs the one they occupy, allowing them to function and establish an identity in this other, unexplained world. The context for the second half of Daniel is the worsening politics of the diaspora known as the Antiochene crisis. The political struggle of the superpower nations of Greece and Rome intersected with the machinations of the Jews who curried favor through exploiting of their own people and temple. It was a time of pernicious persecution and exploitation of the Jews, which included desecration of the temple.

The dreams in Daniel explain God's role in a world that does not make sense, while identifying the role the Jewish diaspora has in it. The apocalypses in Daniel are rhetorical—they aim to convince the audience that God's sovereignty is transcendent, working in, through, and around

5. John J. Collins, *Apocalypse: The Morphology of a Genre*, ed. J. Collins, Semeia 14 (Atlanta: Society of Biblical Literature, 1979).

6. Choon Leong Seow, *Daniel* (Louisville: Westminster John Knox, 2003), 10.

history to accomplish God's plan. The dreamer is a portal who provides access to a divine sense of reality that supersedes the known, physical world. The messenger Gabriel is dispatched to interpret the visions. The excess in the court tales is matched by the elaborate detail of the visions in the second half of the book. The images are complex and hallucinogenic, going to great lengths to describe an otherworldly realm that will have an impact on what happens in the earthly realm.

Visions and dreams are not subject to the rules of time and space of the waking world. Similarly, the court tales of Daniel and the Apocalyptic visions in the book respond to events in history but are not bound by them. The experiences of the diaspora are shaped imaginatively to create a dialogue around survival. The Jews will have to use multiple methods to maintain their identity. The dual-consciousness that exile demanded of them is the very skill that grants them access to the heavenly realm from which they can witness God's sovereignty. The presence of divine mystery in apocalyptic material means that the meaning of the text is truly dialogic with new meaning unfolding every day.

CHAPTER 24
THE BOOK OF THE TWELVE

May the bones of the twelve prophets
sprout new life from their
burial places,
because they comforted Jacob
and rescued them
with hopeful confidence.

—Sirach 49:10

The prophetic corpus has been divided into the categories of former and latter, major and minor. There are four scrolls of the former prophets: Joshua, Judges, Samuel, and Kings. On balance, there are four scrolls for the latter (writing) prophets: one each for Isaiah, Jeremiah, and Ezekiel, and one for the Book of the Twelve. Within the latter prophets, there is another designation of major and minor. Isaiah, Jeremiah and Ezekiel are the Major Prophets. In Christian circles, we call the Book of the Twelve the "Minor Prophets." Though it only means that these books are shorter, this is an unfortunate name, because there is so much powerful theology in the Book of the Twelve and these prophets should in no way be considered less significant than their three colleagues.

The term *the twelve prophets* can be traced to 200 BCE. In Sirach 49:10 we read, "May the bones of the twelve prophets sprout new life from their burial places." This reference supports the idea that the texts of the twelve prophets were considered a scribal unit at that time, further proved by the oldest manuscript of the Book of the Twelve found among the Dead Sea Scrolls, dating from the second century BCE. They were most likely copied together so that the smaller books would not be lost. Although they share a scroll, these individual books cover a period of approximately four hundred years. The books range in length from one chapter to fourteen, and they represent a wide variety of traditions and theologies. These twelve books are a literary unit because they have been copied together. Together, they fill a scroll and approximate the length of one of the Major Prophets. Thus, the Twelve Prophets is a construct, a category created out of proximity for the sake of survival.

Historically, the prophets Hosea, Amos, and Micah are located in the eighth century BCE, alongside Isaiah. Nahum, Habakkuk, and Zephaniah are contemporaries of Jeremiah in the seventh century BCE. Haggai and Zechariah 1–8 are late sixth-century BCE texts, which places them on a timeline after Jeremiah, Ezekiel, and Second Isaiah. We locate Malachi and Zechariah 9–14 in the fifth century BCE, and Joel in the postexilic Persian period, fifth or fourth century BCE. Together, these twelve prophets bear witness to a people's anticipation, experience, and response to the trauma of exile and their theologically imaginative responses.

The Day of the Lord

Several books in the Minor Prophets refer to "the Day of the Lord." The day of the Lord is an undesignated time in the future when the Lord will come to earth and establish justice, set things right, and restore God's people. A dominant theme in the collective imagination, it is a time of fulfillment of God's promises that is referred to and reinterpreted in the prophetic corpus.

Hosea: A Marriage of Metaphor

Mid-eighth century

Northern kingdom of Israel

OUTLINE	THEMES
1–3 Marriage 4–10 Broken Covenant 11–14 Call to change heart and life	God's Covenant with Israel Israel's unfaithfulness/infidelity God's response of punishment God's response in call to reconciliation

Chapters 1–3: Marriage

The book of Hosea begins with God's command, "Go, marry a prostitute and have children of prostitution, for the people of the land commit great prostitution by deserting the LORD." The command is issued as a sign-act, an action taken by a prophet as an object lesson for the word of the LORD. This marriage is the ultimate object lesson. Hosea's personal life is the arena in which the complicated relationship between God and God's people is worked out. His wife Gomer and her children are objectified in the service of YHWH's passionate discourse about Israel's unfaithfulness. This sign-act is so preposterous that scholars have debated whether the marriage is actually real.[1] Our focus will be the literary phenomenon of the marriage as metaphor. How does this unseemly marriage inform Israel's identity?

Metaphor, as previously discussed, is one of the primary modes of communication in scripture. Something known is used to describe something that is unknown. Metaphor is intentionally provocative and at times unsettling as it invites us, rather forces us, to see something in a new way. It is also the case that when a metaphor becomes familiar and overused, it loses some of its power to make meaning. Based on this understanding, it follows that metaphor is highly contextual. When the book of Hosea uses marriage as a metaphor, it makes certain cultural assumptions. Marriage relationships in Hosea's time were "asymmetrical." Women did not enjoy the same rank, rights, or privileges as men. To the husband belonged the position of power, authority, and control of the wife, particularly over her sexuality and sexual fidelity. The husband had every right to punish a wife who violated the terms of the marriage covenant. The wife's responsibility

1. Alice A Keefe, "Hosea" in *Fortress Commentary on the Bible*, ed. Gale Yee, Hugh Page Jr., and Matthew Coomber (Minneapolis: Fortress, 2014), 826.

was to bring honor to her husband—and so, immediately, the command to Hosea to marry a wife of prostitution is counter to the expectation that a wife bring honor. The marriage is doomed from the very beginning.

The metaphor of marriage also brings all the power of intimacy. Hosea's words "are more transparent to the love and anguish of God than those of any other canonical prophet."[2] It doesn't take long for things to take a wrong turn in this marriage and the book takes us through the dramatic shifts from anger to pleading and back again. Hosea, the husband, represents God, and the wife Gomer represents Israel. Gomer's sexual infidelity represents Israel's apostasy and Hosea's rage is God's rage over the betrayal. The oracles in Hosea are effective in revealing the vulnerability of the husband and the emotional hurt caused by the wife's betrayal. In this cultural context, God the powerful husband keeps pleading, hoping the wife Israel will return. The shifts between angry threats and abject pleading form a pattern recognizable in abusive relationships. When husband/God is the abuser of wife/Israel, it doesn't take much to shift over to the behavior of husband and wife in other contexts, where the husband, by virtue of his position, is "supported" in the abuse of his spouse.

In this difficult interpretive space, the interpreter is helped to remember the function of rhetoric. The powerful images of the unfaithful wife are intentionally provocative and intended to manipulate a male audience. In a communal identity focused on controlling women, God's command to Hosea makes absolutely no sense. The prophet elicits the audience's rage at God's command and Gomer's behavior only to turn it back on the audience, identifying Israel itself as the wife of whoredom. This would be an interesting twist because it would be calling men women, and whores at that! All this for the sake of demonstrating the seriousness of Israel's betrayal.[3] The dialogue in Hosea is one of actions and words. Israel is unfaithful and God responds in word and deed. Even the dialogue is unequal. Gomer does not speak for herself. The only words she has are

2. Ellen Davis, *Opening Israel's Scriptures* (Oxford: Oxford University Press, 2019), 238.

3. Renita Weems, *Battered Love, Marriage, Sex and Violence in the Hebrew Prophets* (Minneapolis: Augsburg Fortress, 1995), 68.

the ones her husband gives her. The husband in this story, whether it is YHWH or Hosea, is the one who wields the power.

Chapters 4–10: Broken Covenant

The largest section of Hosea, the oracles against adulterous Israel, begins with a covenant lawsuit. Covenant is the rubric that undergirds relationships in Hosea. Israel is in a covenant relationship with God, and has pledged fidelity to her husband. God is the offended party who "sues" his wife for a lack of "loyalty." The poetry of the oracles takes us from God's betrayal, to anger, to pleading for his wife's return and back to anger. The text leaves the reader with a sense of disorientation. God is not logical. There is a cosmic element to the oracles. As the covenant lawsuit calls the creation as witness, the oracles reveal that the land itself will feel the consequences of Israel's infidelity. The exodus will be undone. The order established in creation will be undone. Primordial chaos will return. The covenant God makes with the people is in the very fiber of creation. When God created the world, God had a plan, an order for things, and Israel's disobedience is not just about her covenant with God, but about the very structure of the world. The message for the people of Israel is that there is no Israel without YHWH. The power differential of marriage in the ancient Near East supports this perspective.

Chapters 11–14: Final Call to Change Hearts and Lives

In the final chapters of Hosea we encounter another relationship, that of parent and child. Again, YHWH is the one in charge and the people are responsible for complying. The portrayals of Israel as disobedient wife and now wayward child make a compelling case for God's anger. The people are wrong and God is justified in demanding justice. This fierce love of God for his people/wife/child leads to "divine" punishment, but then morphs into God's invitation for the people to return.

God's "taking back" of the wayward child or adulterous wife is depicted as an act of love. God has every right to abandon, punish, and destroy. Yet God longs for restoration. The use of the metaphors of marriage and parenthood leave us with an unsettling image of God. The people of God are in a covenant relationship, but they are not equal partners by any stretch of the imagination. In this construct, obedience is the duty that wife/child Israel owes her. Obedience, cloaked in the language of devotion, is the rule of the day, and a means of survival cloaked in the language of devotion. The metaphors are effective, evocative, and simultaneously dangerous.

Joel: Invasion/Day of the Lord

Fifth–fourth century BCE

Southern kingdom of Judah

OUTLINE	THEMES
1:1–2:27 Lament 2:28–3:21 Restoration	The Day of the Lord

The first part of the book of Joel is a lament in response to a locust plague. The plague may indicate that "the Day of the Lord," which is the time when God will return and set things right, is approaching. Considering that possibility, the second part of the book looks beyond the current situation and imagines the end time, when the people and land will be restored while their enemies are punished. The explanation of the plague as an intentional act of God creates space to imagine that once the people change their hearts and lives, they will be restored, and God will reserve punishment for their enemies. Although it only has seventy-three verses, Joel is memorable for its poetic call to turn back to the Lord, which is used by a number of Christian traditions in the Ash Wednesday liturgy.

> Tear your hearts
> and not your clothing.
> Return to the Lord your God,
> for he is merciful and compassionate,
> very patient, full of faithful love,
> and ready to forgive. (Joel 2:13)

The poetry of this little book is also remembered for the apocalyptic vision that brings a word of promise for Judah:

> After that I will pour out my spirit upon everyone;
> your sons and your daughters will prophesy
> your old men will dream dreams,
> and your young men will see visions. (Joel 2:28)

This future vision of the Day of the LORD is significant in its inclusivity, and with the expectation that God's return and restoration is not just a return to how things were, but a return to how things were meant to be. In the oracle of this prophet lies a hope for a future that is beyond our imagination.

Amos

Eighth century BCE

Northern kingdom of Israel

OUTLINE	THEMES
1:1 Superscription 1:2–2:16 Oracles against the nations, Judah and Israel 3–6 Oracles against Israel 7–9 Visions	Godliness = Justice and Righteousness

Amos has the distinction of being one of the first "writing prophets."[4] The book opens with the superscription (1:1), that is, the prophet's "calling card." The authority of the prophet lies in his call and in his work of speaking for YHWH. Here Amos identifies himself as a shepherd from Tekoa (the southern kingdom). He locates his prophecies within a particular time period by naming the southern and northern kings who

4. This term refers to collections emerging in the eighth century of written prophecies that are attributed to an individual. This development may be the result of increasing literacy. Michael Coogan, *The Old Testament, A Historical and Literary Introduction to the Hebrew Scriptures* (Oxford: Oxford University Press, 2013), 311.

occupied the throne during his prophetic career, Uzziah and Jeroboam, and placing his work on the timeline before a disaster (two years before the earthquake). Amos was called from his vocation as a shepherd of Tekoa in the south to bring a word of Judgment to the north when the north was experiencing a time of financial prosperity.

> These are the words of Amos, one of the shepherds of Tekoa. He perceived these things concerning Israel two years before the earthquake, in the days of Judah's King Uzziah and in the days of Israel's King Jeroboam, Joash's son. (Amos 1:1)

The prophet is tasked with transmitting the words and perspectives of the LORD, to the LORD's people, and in so doing to initiate a dialogue. That is to say, the prophetic word is intended toward something: repentance, comfort, or remembrance. This "word of the LORD" is poetic prose that employs imagery and symbolic language. The senses are in the service of conveying the word. Sometimes the prophet communicates visions that must be translated into a verbal format. And the prophetic word employs rhetoric of which the oracles of Amos are beautiful examples.

The book opens with a sweeping group of oracles against the nations, 1:3–2:16. The genre of oracles to the nations is a prophetic word issued against those nations outside of God's kingdoms of Israel and Judah, who clearly do not follow in the way of YHWH. The nations, in order of appearance, are Damascus, Gaza and Ashdod, Tyre, Edom, Ammon, and Moab. These nations surround the nations of Judah and Israel. Moreover, they are interrelated with the northern kingdom at this time. Furthermore, nations such as Moab, Edom, and Ammon are groups of people who share history and blood with the Israelites. In location and history, these "nations are close to home." One by one, nation by nation, the oracle speaks to the surrounding foreign nations by naming their offense and then their punishment before circling in, literally and literarily, to address Judah and then Israel. In Amos, the sins of the nations and those of God's people are tied to what we call social justice. Amos uses the form of "oracles to the nations" to indicate that God's people are guilty of the same sins that their enemies have permitted. Moreover, because of their special relationship with God, Israel and Judah will be held to a higher level of responsibility because of God's faithfulness to them. The geographical closeness and shared history in the oracle raises a question about this special status. Does their identity as God's people make them immune to God's wrath? That question is quickly resolved as the oracle moves from the surrounding nations to the southern kingdom of Judah and finally to the nation of Israel. This time, the oracle of woe to the nations includes God's own people. The length of the oracles is telling: the words of woe and condemnation to the nations are two to three verses long. The indictment against Judah is two verses. In contrast, the oracle against Israel is eleven verses long. If being God's people affords Israel special treatment, they are also eligible for special treatment when they violate God's commands.

The oracles follow a formula:

> The LORD proclaims:
> For three crimes . . .
> and for four I won't hold back the punishment

The format for the woe oracles is an *X* + *Y* formula, designed to emphasize the final element. In Proverbs the formula appears in the words of Agur: "Three things are too wonderful for me, four that I can't figure out." In Proverbs, all four examples are listed. Another example of this literary formula appears in Proverbs 6:16-19: "There are six things that the LORD hates, seven things detestable to him." Again, all seven examples are listed. In Amos's use of the formula only one example, the fourth one, is specifically mentioned. The effect upon a reader familiar with the motif is one of additional emphasis on the final item. There is no lead-in, or warm-up. Rather the prophet goes right to the heart of the matter, mistreatment of one another. Human rights and social justice are the reasons for indictment and in this regard, Judah and Israel are not exempt. They too have mistreated "the least of these" and for this reason, they are not acting like covenant people. To the extent that they behave like those who do not know YHWH, they are the focal point of the oracle to the nations. They are the *Y* of the *X* + *Y* formula. It's one thing for the nations of Edom and Moab to mistreat their own, but Israel and Judah are not like the other nations. The people who have been redeemed have no excuse and they cannot hide behind their religious rites.

The genre of oracle to the nations usually condemns foreign nations for their treatment of God's people, Israel and Judah. In Amos's remix of the oracle to the nations, the sin of each nation is its mistreatment of one another. When the indictment comes to Israel, the format is expanded to include more than one offense and to hold up in contrast all of God's faithfulness to them. Israel and Judah are not like the other nations. They are a people in relationship with YHWH and they deserve special treatment. In this instance, the special treatment is the extended oracle of woe and punishment. The opening oracle not only announces punishment but alerts the people to the fact that their covenantal status is about additional responsibility as much as it is about special favor. Amos conveys the message that they are not beyond punishment, in fact they are held to a higher standard.

This theme in Amos is used in support of many liberation theologies—here we have scripture that eloquently makes the case that YHWH is concerned for the poor. In modern history, Martin Luther King Jr.'s use of Amos 5:24, "But let justice roll down like waters, and righteousness like an ever-flowing stream," has forever connected the words of this prophet to the cause of civil rights in the American imagination. For all of the ways in which Amos's words inspire the imagination of liberation theologies, they also contain a warning against the limits of such use. Israel's identity is rooted in her history as a nomad and slave. Here is a nation who knows oppression, yet in a time of prosperity, the affluent members of the community appear to have forgotten where they came from, acting like the other nations. Because liberation theology is always identity centered, those who invoke it are in the business of forming identities. Those who remember and name their marginalization must, like Israel and Judah, be mindful of their ability to become oppressors.

The theme of identity as God's people continues throughout the book. In the second segment, the oracles against Israel are rooted in their special relationship with YHWH: "You only have I loved so deeply of all the families of the earth" (Amos 3:2). After this proclamation, the oracle moves to a series of rhetorical questions beginning with "Will two people walk together unless they have agreed to do so?" This is the first in a series of seven questions, which move from benign questions to questions about hunter and prey and conquest of a city. The final question, "If disaster befalls a city, is it the LORD who has done it?" is ominous, hinting at an intended punishment. Like the oracle in 1:2–2:16, the questions take the reader on a journey to the point of the whole oracle. The people have sinned and there is a price to be paid.

This second part of the book alternates between detailing Israel's sins, describing punishment, and inviting them to repentance. In light of these sins, Israel's unique relationship with YHWH is challenged when God invites the people to look at the other nations like the Philistines and then asks, "Are you better than these kingdoms?" In chapter 9, God further challenges the people by asking,

> Aren't you like the Cushite to me,
> people of Israel? . . .
> Haven't I brought Israel up from the land of Egypt,
> and the Philistines from Caphtor and the Arameans from Kir? (Amos 9:7)

Israel's covenantal relationship makes demands on the people of God. Without the covenant, they are just like any other nation. Along with the visions in the third section of Amos, the prophetic oracles challenge the assumptions of the Israelites regarding the nature of their relationship with YHWH. Covenant is about so much more than worship.

Obadiah

Sixth century BCE and later

Southern kingdom of Judah

OUTLINE	THEMES
1:1-14 Oracle against Edom 1:15-21 Israel will triumph over Edom	Oracle against Edom

The twenty-one verses of Obadiah's prophecy are directed toward Edom, the region on the southeastern border of Judah. The Edomites are the descendants of Esau, Jacob's twin brother, and the story of the brothers' lifetime of conflict in the ancestral narratives has the etiological function of explaining and justifying Judah's hatred of their cousins in Edom. Psalm 137 and the prophets Jeremiah and Amos recount the Edomites cheering on the Babylonians as they destroyed the temple with the famous words, "Tear it down, tear it down!"[5] The language of Obadiah reflects the particular hurt that Judah experienced from Edom. It recounts the things that Edom did in response to the injury. This betrayal was "salt in the wound" for Judah at its lowest moment:

> You should have taken no pleasure over your brother
> on the day of his misery;
> you shouldn't have rejoiced over the people of Judah
> on the day of their devastation;
> you shouldn't have bragged
> on their day of hardship. (Obad 1:12)

If Edom occupied some space in between estranged relative and stranger, the prophet Obadiah confirms that they are completely "other." Obadiah brings a word of retributive justice. A part of God's restoration of Judah involves the punishment of Edom. In Obadiah's theological universe, God's restoration is inseparable from the destruction of those who caused them harm.

Jonah: Oh the Irony

OUTLINE	THEMES
1 First Commission to Nineveh 2 Swallowed 3 Second Commission to Nineveh 4 Sulking	God's relationship with the "Nations"

5. Ps 137:7; Jer 49:7-22; Amos 1:11-12.

The story of Jonah, the prophet swallowed by a great fish (a whale in popular culture) is one of the biblical narratives that continues to capture the imagination of readers. In terms of genre, the book has very little in common with the other Minor Prophets. This short book, containing only one oracle, has two commissions in its four chapters. In chapter 1 there is the initial commission, as the word of the LORD instructs Jonah to prophesy to the inhabitants of Nineveh. Jonah runs in the opposite direction and finds himself in a great storm on board the boat he thought would be his escape. Thrown overboard, he is swallowed by a great fish, and in chapter 2 prays to the LORD.

Jonah's Prayer

Jonah's prayer is a psalm of thanksgiving: one offered after God's deliverance. It uses water imagery, but makes no specific reference to his circumstances inside the fish. Often Psalms uses symbolic language to describe their situation, but the genre supports the idea that the psalm was added to the tale at a later time. In its final form, the psalm of thanksgiving is a turning point in the narrative, indicating Jonah's submission (albeit temporary) to God's commission.

At the conclusion of his prayer of thanksgiving, the fish vomits him up. In chapter 3, the LORD's word comes to the prophet for the second time, instructing him to prophesy to the city of Nineveh. This time Jonah follows the LORD's command, and the people respond to the word of the LORD and change their hearts and lives. In the final chapter, Jonah sits outside the city, sulking that the LORD will not utterly destroy the city. The LORD challenges Jonah's assumptions about the extent of God's mercy and the intended recipients of that mercy. This short book is grand in scale and ironic in tone. The prophet is reluctant to fulfill God's commission because he would rather see the people of Nineveh receive God's punishment.

The literary shaping of Jonah has each of the first three chapters ending with a dramatic action and the fourth chapter ending with a question. Chapter 1 ends with Jonah being thrown overboard and swallowed by a fish. Chapter 2 ends with the fish vomiting up the prophet onto dry land. The third chapter ends with God's decision to withhold punishment because of the people's repentance. The end of chapters 1 and 2 point to God's power over creation. God creates the storm and sends the fish to follow Jonah. In chapter 3, the final action indicates God's sovereignty. At the end of the fourth chapter, God asks Jonah to remember God is creator of the entire world and that God's sovereignty will demand us to envision a God who does more than we imagine.

Micah: Who Is Like YHWH?

Eighth century BCE

Southern kingdom

OUTLINE	THEMES
1:1 Superscription 1:2–2:13 Oracles of Judgment 3:1–5:15 Jerusalem's fall and aftermath 6:1–7:20 Covenant dispute	Social Justice

The seven chapters associated with Micah of Moresheth have made a lasting impression. Micah was a contemporary of the prophet Isaiah, and he is mentioned in the book of Jeremiah, but the content of the book is not all the product of the time of the prophet's life in the eighth century. Chapters 1–3 are attributed to Micah. The second part of the book, chapters 4–7, comes from a later time period, dating to the exilic period and postexilic period. Thus within the book there is a dialogue that extends from before the punishment of exile to a future beyond it. The different time stamps in Micah affirm that there is a future after the punishment. The words in the first half of the book are not limited to a single moment in time. Even the words of punishment are followed by words of promise. Thus in Micah, judgment is inevitable, but so is a future beyond the judgment.[6] There is a literary pattern in Micah's multilayered dialogue

6. Judy Fentress-Williams, "Micah," in *The Women's Bible Commentary*, ed. Carol Newsom, Sharon Ringe, and Jacqueline Lapsley (Louisville: Westminster John Knox, 1998), 326.

that includes words of promise on the other side of judgment. Chapters 1–3 are oracles of judgment. Chapters 4–5 cast a vision for the future—one of restoration, with "a new Jerusalem, new exodus, a new David and a new Jacob."[7] The final section of the corpus, chapters 7–8, returns to the future with a covenant lawsuit in which YHWH lays out his claim against the people. The final words of Micah are words of promise. Thus the dialogic patterns in Micah that shift from judgment to promise, and condemnation to hope, instill a sense of hope or expectation that God will not forsake the people.

Similarly, the messages in this short book have continued to speak to those who listen, shaping the theological imagination of its audiences. It is in Micah we find the question, "With what should I approach the LORD?" which is answered,

> He has told you, human one, what is good and
> what the LORD requires from you:
> to do justice, embrace faithful love, and walk humbly
> with your God. (Mic 6:6-8)

Micah depicts a peaceable world where "nation will not take up sword against nation; they will no longer learn how to make war." Images and words from this prophetic collection, such as the peaceable kingdom and calls to social justice, are woven into Judeo-Christian traditions and imagination. Unlike Amos, which places social justice and religious ritual as two divergent paths and choices, Micah imagines a world where the two elements coexist.

The message of social justice that Micah articulates makes use of gender-specific imagery that supports a worldview of women in limited roles of daughters, wives, and mothers. In this way Micah reminds us that prophets, ancient and modern, are never completely free from the social contexts that produce them and to whom they prophesy. The very words we use to describe this new way of being that God calls us to is tied to our broken world. It imagines us out of one limited existence by invoking another. This is why prophecy continues to speak beyond its time, and this is

7. Rachel Baughman, notes on "Micah," in *The CEB Women's Bible* (Nashville: Abingdon Press, 2016), 1162.

why the image of a woman bringing forth new life in 4:9-10 is powerful. The woman in labor symbolizes the nation's vulnerability and suffering in exile. It also is known to have an end, which if all goes well, results in new life. The image of the woman suffering also sheds light on our understanding of limited prophetic language. We suffer under these restrictive and diminished roles, but they will have an end, and there will be new life on the other side. The peaceable kingdom will be revealed in new ways.

Nahum

The LORD is a jealous and vengeful God:
the LORD is vengeful and strong in wrath
The LORD is vengeful against his foes
he rages against his enemies. (Nah 1:2)

Seventh century BCE

Southern kingdom of Judah

OUTLINE	THEMES
1:1 Superscription 1:2-15 2:1-13 3:1-19	Oracle against Empire

After the superscription in 1:1, the prophecy of Nahum plunges us into an ongoing dialogue. What prompts the words of Nahum 1:2, where "vengeful" appears in three out of four lines? Why do we need to know that God is strong and vengeful?

The words of the prophet are cast as an oracle about Nineveh, the capital of the Assyrian Empire. Nineveh was a great city. It was so great that its very name was synonymous with wealth and power. In evoking Nineveh, the prophet not only addresses Assyria, but sets up the city as an archetype for the evil empire.

As the victim of Assyria's oppression, we observe in the words of Nahum a people who do not have the military might to defend themselves. Assyria will be punished, but it will not be at the hands of Judah, but rather another superpower, Babylon. Even as the people hope for Assyria's punishment, there is the acknowledgment that they are incapable of executing justice on their own. The vengeance they are incapable of in the physical world finds expression in the words of the prophet. God is vengeful, God is powerful, and God will utterly destroy. In the words of Nahum we also observe the extent to which oppressed people can still be complicit in the oppression of others. The gendered language of Hebrew means that cities are feminine. Thus the imagery of Nineveh's destruction is infused with the cultural values of the time. The city is subjected to the ultimate walk of shame. She is a woman carried away (2:7), a "whore" and "mistress of sorceries" (3:4) who will be exposed (3:5). No one will lament for her (3:7). The vitriol of the judgment reflects the pain of those who have "suffered from your continual cruelty" (3:19).

These prophetic words are a placeholder, a memorial to the rage and pain that result from oppression. The Bible does not shy away from the emotions of this chronically oppressed community, nor does it set up boundaries between the word of the LORD and the pain of the people. It ends in a question indicating that Nahum is a dialogic response to trauma that invites a response from the audience. It is a word, but it is not the last word.

Habakkuk

Seventh century BCE

OUTLINE	THEMES
1:1–2:20 Dialogue with the Lord 3:1-19 Prayer	Dialogue about suffering and chaos

We don't know anything about Habakkuk as a historical figure, but he is a figure of legend.

The book of Habakkuk is a unique literary composition. It is three chapters long and divides into two parts. Part 1 (chapters 1–2) is a dialogue between the prophet and YHWH. The prophet issues a complaint in 1:2-4, with questions around suffering and violence in the world. The prophet's search for justice is elusive, and "becomes warped" (v. 4). The LORD's response in 1:5-11 is to promise more of the same. God tells Habakkuk that the foreign nation, the Chaldeans, will continue to afflict

God's people, who will continue to suffer. Habakkuk tries again in 1:12–2:1, and this time does not describe the suffering but describes God. Using creation imagery, the prophet describes humans like "creeping things with no one to rule over them" (1:14). This description of humanity is a contradiction of Genesis 1:28, where humanity has rule over the creeping thing. The prophet casts the world's state as creation in upheaval and out of order, implying that injustice and suffering in the world operate against the world order God created. Moreover, in this second complaint, the prophet takes a stand (literarily), awaiting God's answer:

> I will take my post,
> I will position myself on the fortress,
> I will keep watch to see what the Lord says to me
> and how he will respond to my complaint. (2:1)

The prophet's position at the fortress is an image of one who trusts in God's sovereignty in the midst of confusing circumstances. The LORD answers him, again with another message of judgment and doom.

The dialogue between God and Habakkuk concludes with the prophet's prayer in which Habakkuk acknowledges God's sovereignty. God is creator and warrior. The overall dynamic of the book, along with a lack of specific historical references, is not specific to a particular time and place but rather one of universal human questions to the state of the world with God's responses. In the end, the only response is one that acknowledges God's greatness and hopes in God's deliverance. The genre of the final part of the dialogue, a psalm of praise, conveys the notion that our only proper response to the utter glory of God is one of praise.

Zephaniah

I will wipe out everything from the earth, says the Lord. (Zeph 1:2)

Seventh century BCE

Southern kingdom of Judah

OUTLINE	THEMES
1:1–2:3 Day of the Lord 2:4-15 Oracles against the nations 3:1-20 Wait for me	The Day of the Lord is utter destruction The LORD will restore

At first glance, the book of Zephaniah is more of a diatribe than a dialogue. There is something about Zephaniah that is over the top, beginning with the superscription. Unlike other prophetic superscriptions, Zephaniah gives a detailed genealogy going back three generations, to include his great-grandfather, King Hezekiah. Not only is he a descendant of Hezekiah, but most likely related to the current king, Josiah.[8] After the superscription, in 1:1, the opening oracles of Zephaniah are graphic and unrelenting. The overall effect of the words is that of an assault. The oracle employs hyperbole. If the LORD destroys the whole world in verses 2-3, why does he have to mention that he will destroy Judah and Jerusalem? Likely the oracle is ordered for rhetorical effect. The LORD will not destroy the world, including Judah and Jerusalem. Rather, the LORD will destroy the whole world because of Judah and Jerusalem? Verses 2-4 depict universal destruction that reminds us of the undoing of creation experienced in the flood. The chaos that existed prior to creation is identified in verses 4-6, with Judah's practices of worshipping foreign gods. This is the return to primordial chaos that threatens to undo the order of creation.

The description of the utter destruction is followed by another iteration of the Day of the LORD, in 1:7-18, where the prophet's description reminds us of Amos. This Day of the LORD is not a good one for Judah, but one of judgment. In the same way that the opening oracles shift from the world to Judah, the reverse happens here as the oracles move from the Day of the LORD for Judah to oracles to the nations again in 2:4-15. But this time the transition is interrupted by an invitation, a call to repentance in 2:1-3. For all of the heavy-handedness of these judgment oracles, the hope

8. Both Hezekiah and Josiah receive high praise. Second Kings 18:5 says of Hezekiah, "There was no one like him among all of Judah's kings—not one before him and not after him." Second Kings 23:25 says, "There's never been a king like Josiah, whether before or after him, who turned to the LORD with all his heart, all his being, and all his strength, in agreement with everything in the Instruction from Moses."

for restoration can be identified in two places: most obviously, the call to repentance indicates that there is still the potential for reconciliation. Less obvious is the invitation extended in the oracle of judgment itself. God's threat to utterly destroy is just that. The announcement of punishment is not the act itself. So why would God spend so much time talking about and describing what was going to happen? So long as there is dialogue, there is the potential for restoration. It is the absence of conversation, even a difficult, or primarily one-sided one, that works against relationship.

For those who remain after the barrage of judgment, there is this word,

> Then I will change the speech of the peoples into pure speech,
> that all of them will call on the name of the LORD
> and will serve him as one. (Zeph 3:9)

Zephaniah 3:9-13 is a promise of restoration, followed by a call to worship, to "rejoice," "shout," "rejoice and exult" (3:14). Gendered language and imagery is used to describe the renewed relationship. Daughter Zion is told that the Lord will "bring all of you back, at the time when I gather you" (3:20).

The promise at the end of the book does not mitigate the problematic gender images. As we come toward the end of the Minor Prophets, it is worth noting that the pervasive use of metaphor based in gender roles weighs down the metaphor so that it appears to prescribe and affirm of a culture's established practices and values. The goal of the metaphor is to stretch the imagination of the audience beyond what is in order to imagine a better reality. When it works well, a metaphor would not only work to restore the relationship between God and God's people, but in so doing would inspire changes in the ways humans interact with one another—even or especially in the most intimate of relationships.

Haggai

Sixth century BCE

After the exile

OUTLINE	THEMES
1:1-14 Build the temple 1:15-23 Be strong	The temple's restoration

Haggai is tied to the time after Cyrus's decree that the temple in Judah be rebuilt. The prophetic text consists of four reports of God's command to build the temple. The language in the first command evokes David's desire to build a temple:

> Look, I'm living in a cedar palace, but god's chest is housed in a tent! (2 Sam 7:2b)

> Is it time for you to dwell in your own paneled houses while this house lies in ruins? (Hag 1:4)

By casting the command to rebuild as a "remix" of David's desire to build the first temple, Haggai reestablishes the temple with the continuation of the Davidic monarchy. The temple is more than a place to worship. With it comes the presence of God in the holy of holies and God's promise to the Davidic monarchy. For this reason, the book concludes with the prophet's address to Zerubbabel, a descendant of David (2:20-23). The oracle has two parts: first, with language that evokes the exodus, God promises to tear down and overthrow "kingdoms" and "nations." Then, God will establish Zerubbabel, "because I have chosen you, says the LORD of heavenly forces" (2:23). The establishment of the temple is part of the restoration tied to the second year of the reign of Darius (520 BCE). In Jewish tradition, Haggai, Zechariah, and Malachi are the last prophets.[9]

Zechariah

Sixth century BCE

Southern kingdom

9. Ehud ben Zvi, "The Twelve Minor Prophets," in *The Jewish Study Bible*, ed. A Berlin and M. Z. Brettler (New York: Oxford University Press, 2004), 1244.

OUTLINE	THEMES
1:1-6 Invitation 1:7–6:15 Visions 7:1–14:21 Oracles	God remembers God will rebuild and re-establish

Like the prophet Micah, there is meaning in the prophet's name. Zechariah means "YHWH remembered." This prophet is called to bring a word of the LORD to a community that needs to be reminded, decades after the exile, that God will fulfill God's promises. Like many prophetic collections, the book comprises more than one collection.

The first eight chapters of Zechariah are a collection of oracles and visions that are tied to a specific time, 520–518 BCE. Each vision is tied to activities connected with the construction of the new temple.[10] The visions of the new temple offer the audience an alternative to their memories of the temple that was lost. The visions intend to redirect them so they can begin to look forward and not behind. Once they can "see" differently, they will be better able to "hear" the words of the Lord in the remainder of the book, chapters 9–14. This collection of oracles looks out from the turbulent present, not to the past but to the time when God's reign is established over all the earth. The literary structure works to reposition a community from loss to expectation:

> A day is coming that belongs to the LORD,
> when that which has been plundered from you will be
> divided among you. (14:1)

Malachi: The "Other" Last Word

Fifth century BCE

After the exile

10. Marvin Sweeney, *Tanak: A Theological and Critical Introduction to the Jewish Bible* (Minneapolis: Fortress, 2012), 364.

OUTLINE	THEMES
1:1 Superscription 1:2–3:21 The disputes/speeches 3:22-24 Conclusion	The Day of YHWH

Malachi is the last book in the collection of the twelve. The superscription at the beginning is simple: "A pronouncement. The LORD's word to Israel through Malachi." There is no historical information on Malachi, and the meaning of his name, "my messenger" or "my angel," leads some scholars to surmise the prophet did not even exist. Such a name could be either a proper name or a title. A messenger or angel is an intermediary who, like a priest, "instructs Israel in the name of God and petitions God in the name of Israel."[11] For this reason, other scholars question Malachi's vocation—is he a prophet or a priest? The genre of Malachi is not the expected prophetic oracle. Rather, the book consists of six disputation speeches, a series of questions and answers from the LORD. It is an extended dialogue about Israel's identity. The speeches engage current assumptions (fifth century BCE) with long-standing traditions and teachings. In addition, the book is in dialogue with the other prophetic voices that are on the scroll.

At the heart of this book is the battle for identity. Jews in the Persian period have many voices and perspectives vying for their attention and numerous influences have contributed to the shaping of their identity. The very genre of the book, the disputation speech, is the essence of dialogue. Each speech is formed in response to behavior and each one intends to elicit a particular response. Malachi expounds on the temple, worship, and the Day of YHWH, with the goal of grounding the people's identity in the Sinai covenant.

"He [YHWH] Hates Divorce"

The metaphor that is often used to talk about covenant is that of marriage. To the extent that family units in this historical context are rooted in marriage, it is the foundation for stability in the community. Traditionally in the prophetic corpus, YHWH describes

11. Jon D. Levenson, *Sinai and Zion: An Entry into the Jewish Bible* (Cambridge: Harper & Row, 1987), 126.

> Israel as a bride, beloved and chronically unfaithful, breaking the covenant, again and again, with God in the position of the beleaguered husband trying to make the marriage work. In Malachi, God takes on the perspective of a wife who is sent away because her husband is unfaithful. It is in the context of this extended metaphor that we find the words "he [YHWH] hates divorce" (2:16). Is the divorce referred to here symbolic, literal, or both? Divorce is permitted in Levitical law. Moreover, in the Persian period, Jewish men put away their foreign wives as an act of piety. It is safe to say that the images in Malachi are in service to what is understood as the primary relationship in the book and that is the one between YHWH and the people.

In the ordering of the Hebrew Bible, Chronicles is the last book, and it ends with a decree from Cyrus, king of Persia to the Jews in the diaspora, to build a temple in Jerusalem. In Hebrew, the very last words are "Let him go up," and these "last words" can be interpreted as words of hope.[12] The ordering of the Old Testament ends with the book of Malachi. The final three verses are believed to be two postscripts. The first refers to Moses. Malachi 4:4 simply states, "Remember the Instruction from Moses, my servant, to whom I have Instruction and rules for all Israel at Horeb." The English translation capitalizes the word *Instruction* because it refers to *Torah.* By invoking Moses and the Torah or Instruction, the book directs the audience back to the desired point of origin and orientation. The identity of the people begins and remains with the covenant at Horeb. Malachi 4:5 references the prophet Elijah, who also stood on Mount Sinai or Horeb (1 Kgs 19:1-18), and foretells the sending (resending) of the great prophet, whose return will precede "the great and terrifying day of the LORD." Verse 6 concludes the book with a command toward reconciliation:

> Turn the hearts of the parents to the children
> and the hearts of the children to the parents.
> Otherwise, I will come and strike the land with a curse.

Reconciliation is the way that Israel will prepare for the day of the LORD. This reconciliation is cast within the construct of family, parents, and children. On that day, the enemies, the "arrogant ones" and "all those doing evil" (4:1) are burned, while the "sun of righteousness will rise on

12. Davis, *Opening Israel's Scriptures* (Oxford: Oxford University Press, 2019), 413.

those revering my name; healing will be in its wings (4:2). This image, "of the sun with wings is common in Assyrian pictures" . . . as a force that "ushers in vindication for the righteous"[13] even as the wicked are destroyed. The moment of reconciliation is followed with the threat of punishment, "lest I come and strike the land with a curse" (4:6). The last word of the Minor Prophets, and of the Old Testament, is *herem*, curse or total destruction. In Judaism, the response to this harsh ending comes in the way it is read. When this passage is publicly read in the synagogue, the reader goes back and repeats the words about the coming of Elijah.[14] Similarly, in Christianity, the word *herem* is not the last word, but a word of longing at the end of one chapter or testament, which creates expectation in the second testament about the one Elijah or an Elijah figure will precede.

Make Sure Not to Miss . . .

- Jonah's Prayer, Jonah 2
- Oracle to the nations, Amos 1:2–2:16
- Swords into plowshares, Micah 4:3
- But you of Bethlehem of Ephrathah, Micah 5:2
- "Let justice roll down like waters . . . ," Amos 5:24
- "What does the Lord require of you . . . ," Micah 6:8
- "Your sons and your daughters shall prophesy . . . ," Joel 2:28

13. William P. Brown, *Obadiah through Malachi* (Louisville: Westminster John Knox, 1996), 204.

14. Robert Alter, notes for Malachi in *The Hebrew Bible: A Translation with Commentary* (New York: W. W. Norton and Company, 2019), 1394.

THE NEW TESTAMENT

Part One

THE GOSPELS

"Prepare ye the way of the Lord . . ."

—*Godspell*

Gospel: The word *gospel* comes from the Old English *godspell*, which is a contraction of the two words *gōd*, "good" and *spell*, "news" or "story." The English word is a translation of two words in Latin, *bona annuntiatio* or *bonus nuntius* from ecclesiastical Latin, and *evangelium*, from the Greek, both meaning "good news" or *evangel.*

The New Testament begins with the good news, the gospel of Jesus, who is called the Messiah or anointed one, *Christos* in Greek. The four books designated as Gospels—Matthew, Mark, Luke, and John—tell the story of the life of Jesus of Nazareth and, although they form a particular genre, share some characteristics with ancient biographies.[1] The ancient biographies of "classical heroes and philosophers" would have had three components: the origin and early days of the hero; his works and accomplishments; and his death and its significance.[2] Beyond these shared characteristics, however, each of the Gospels has its own unique voice and perspective in the manner in which it details Jesus's life, teaching, and ministry. Yet every Gospel follows a similar narrative arc and ends with accounts of Jesus's betrayal, prosecution, conviction, execution, and then his resurrection. Although the Gospels do not adhere to the same chronology, they do make narrative sense and succeed in their goal to proclaim and preserve the story of the risen Christ, the returning Messiah. In this sense, the Gospels are testimony, a true statement or story by a witness, which

1. Unlike ancient biographies, the Gospels devote an inordinate amount of attention to the death of Jesus. For this reason, some scholars designate the Gospels as a subgenre of ancient biography.

2. John Y. H. Yieh, *Conversations with Scripture: The Gospel of Matthew* (New York: Church Publishing, 2012), 11.

come decades after Jesus left his disciples with the promise of his return. For first-century Christian communities, living in the shadow of the Roman Empire, these testimonies functioned as origin stories that explained how things came to be and reoriented the hearers so they remembered and were strengthened in their identity. The life, death, and resurrection of Jesus is the departure point of the Christian imagination.

The testimonies of the Gospels were intended as performance texts.[3] The "spell" part of *godspell*, connotes a "spoken word or set of words meant to have magic power."[4] The language, repetition, imagery, and word choice of the Gospel writers contributed to telling the story of Jesus to an audience in a way that had the power to change lives. The rules of oral/aural culture are geared toward "event" and not "chronology." In the context of the early church, the story of the good news was told to encourage believers and bring nonbelievers into the fold. Thus, when Jesus speaks in the text, the audience heard his words, sayings, parables, and prayers being repeated and retold. Those words, which appear in some English print Bibles in "red letters," were kept alive for the early church audiences.[5] In other words, the proclamation of the gospel was liturgical. Moreover, when the gospel was performed, it did more than affirm an identity for its audience. It laid out a program of action. The kingdom of God that Jesus represented stood in bold opposition to the empire of Rome and to all other earthly empires. When the good news was proclaimed, it was an act of resistance against these worldly powers of oppression. In this way, the proclamation of the gospel was a subversive act. It restructured the world created by the empire through assigning new identities and acknowledging an alternative kingdom. The Gospels in the New Testament are the receptacles for these oral traditions.[6]

---

3. Joanna Dewey, *The Oral Ethos of the Early Church* (Eugene, OR: Cascade, 2013), xvi.

4. Tom Boomershine, *Story Journey: An Invitation to the Gospel as Storytelling* (Nashville: Abingdon Press, 1988), 16.

5. A "red letter" edition Bible is one with the purported words of Jesus in red print.

6. The written record of an oral tradition preserves it, and also restricts it. The written form cannot convey the nuance and subtleties of a performed narrative.

Roman Rule, Greek Culture, and the Children of Abraham

The setting for these origin stories is Judea, an area under Roman occupation, in the first century CE. Rome had asserted itself as a superpower, effectively taking control of the Mediterranean area, in the mid-second century BCE. In 64 BCE, the Roman emperor Pompey conquered Jerusalem and the surrounding areas of Samaria, Judea, and Galilee and Rome remained in control.[7] Thus Jesus was born into and lived his life in a place that was under Roman authority. He lived, ministered, and was executed in occupied territory. For the Jewish population, which made up a small percentage (5–10 percent) of the empire, Rome dominated and shaped their economic situation, culture, and religion.

The impact of Roman rule on people's economic lives in Judea was significant. Excessive taxes pushed some into poverty and plunged others deeper into poverty. There was no middle class, only the rich and the poor. One-fourth to one-third of the Roman population was enslaved.[8] People in such an economy experience food insecurity, inadequate healthcare, higher rates of disability and mortality, and the despair that accompanies these circumstances.[9] Moreover, the "pervasive presence of the Roman colonial domination" was evidenced in the abusive treatment of the people by the military who policed the population.[10] Jews under Roman domination were an endangered people.

The term *Greco-Roman* is used to describe the world and culture of the Mediterranean from the time of Alexander the Great until the fourth century of the Roman Empire. Alexander was more than a military leader and conqueror. He understood that conquest involved more than military might, and so he imposed his Greek culture, which he believed to be superior, on every territory he conquered (a process known as Hellenization). He

7. Mark Allan Powell, *Fortress Introduction to the Gospels*, 2nd ed. (Minneapolis: Fortress, 2019), 7.

8. Powell, *Fortress Introduction to the Gospels*, 7.

9. Obery Hendricks Jr., *The Politics of Jesus: Rediscovering the True Revolutionary Nature of Jesus's Teachings and How They Have Been Corrupted* (New York: Three Leaves Press, 2006), 50–53.

10. Hendricks, *Politics of Jesus*, 54.

promoted the use of Greek language, architecture, culture, and religions.[11] Thus, when Rome came to dominance, it integrated its own culture with this Hellenization and produced a world represented in the Gospels that was multicultural and polytheistic.

The children of Abraham, a minority population, were unique in this world because of their monotheism. The rest of the Greco-Roman world, for the most part, was polytheistic, and this put the monotheistic Jews at risk of being absorbed into the larger Greco-Roman culture that surrounded them. However, Judaism in the Second Temple period (515 BCE–70 CE) was not a monolith.[12] Despite the exilic and postexilic writings that tried to shape a single Jewish identity, the experience of the diaspora under a variety of dominant world powers resulted in a multifaceted Judaism representing different understandings of Torah and how to live under Roman oppression. The religious groups mentioned most frequently in the Gospels are the Pharisees and the Sadducees, but they were not the only ones.

- The Sadducees were of priestly descent and formed the aristocracy of Jerusalem. The term *Sadducee* is probably a Greek rendering of the Hebrew word *Zadokim* or *Zadokites*, descendants of Zadok the high priest (2 Sam 8:16-18).[13] Associated with the temple itself, with connections to the Roman authorities, they were conservative in their interpretation of scripture and only acknowledged the Torah or Pentateuch (not the Prophets or any Writings in use) as authoritative.[14]

- The Pharisees took their name from a term that could connote lawyer (interpreter of the Torah), teacher, or rabbi (one who expounds, or explains the Torah). This group would have been associated with the local synagogues and would have seen it as

11. Bart Ehrman, *The New Testament: A Historical Introduction to the Early Christian Writings* (Oxford: Oxford University Press, 2000), 19.

12. The Second Temple Period is the time from 515 BCE, when the temple was built by the Jews who returned from Persia, until 70 CE, when it was destroyed.

13. Hendricks, *Politics of Jesus,* 57.

14. John T. Carroll, *Jesus and the Gospels: An Introduction* (Louisville: Westminster John Knox, 2016), 13.

their job to ensure proper interpretation of the teaching of the Torah. They determined what obedience to the Torah looked like. Their "oral laws" prescribed the way to keep the "written law" given by Moses.[15] Both the Pharisees and Sadducees were keepers or guardians of the practice of early Judaism. In the Gospels they have numerous encounters with Jesus, who not only does not feel compelled to follow in their designated proper path but declares himself to be the Son of God, an alternative way, the true path to God.

- The Samaritans were the descendants of the northern tribes (Israel) and considered themselves to be the true adherents of the faith, recognizing only the books from Moses (Pentateuch/Torah) as sacred scripture. The level of hostility between Jews and Samaritans was high, as each group claimed to be the legitimate heirs of Abraham. This tension helps us understand why the Samaritan woman at the well (John 4) is surprised that Jesus even speaks to her, and also provides the proper context to the parable of the good Samaritan.

- The Essenes (Qumran community) were an esoteric faith community that separated itself to maintain holiness. Many scholars believe that the ruins at Qumran are those of the Essenes. In their essentially monastic community, they prepared and awaited the imminent "Day of the Lord," when God would overthrow the Roman Empire and deal with the corruption in Jewish leadership.

- The Zealots were an aptly named group of revolutionaries. They believed in using military force and engaged in guerilla warfare against the Roman Empire.

Composition History and the Synoptic Gospels

The Gospels, all written between 60 and 90 CE, come after Paul's letters chronologically, dated between 49 and 60 CE. Their placement at the

15. Ehrman, *The New Testament*, 39.

beginning of the canon indicates that Christ is the point of orientation in the New Testament. All four of the Gospels were produced by anonymous writers. The names associated with and serving as the titles for the Gospels represent a tradition of the early church and are not meant for historical identification. Although the biblical ordering of the Gospels is Matthew, Mark, Luke, and John, the majority of scholars agree that the chronological sequence for the Gospels is Mark, Matthew, Luke, and John. Luke's Gospel is the first part of a two-volume work that includes the book of Acts.

The first three Gospels in the New Testament (Matthew, Mark, and Luke) are known as the Synoptic Gospels and share many similarities in content and chronology. Most scholars believe that these similarities reflect a common source. The fourth, John's Gospel, tells its story in a way that is over 90 percent unique.[16]

The term *synoptic* means "see (optic) together (syn)" and this "single lens" is evident in the content of Mark, Matthew, and Luke. All three follow the same order, the same "narrative framework." Moreover, there are portions of material in all three Gospels that are "nearly identical."[17] Ninety percent of the content of Mark is in Matthew's Gospel, "often in the same words and same order."[18] Luke uses about half of Mark, changing some terminology from Greek to Aramaic.[19] The examination of what brought about this strong commonality between the three, along with the unique elements in each one, coupled with the desire to understand their individual composition histories, is known as the "synoptic problem." The quest for answers to the questions raised by scholars seeking to solve this problem, resulted in a theory of composition analogous to the source-critical theory for the Pentateuch in the Old Testament.

One of the most widely accepted theories about the composition of the Gospels is known as the four-source hypothesis. This hypothesis as-

16. Powell, *Fortress Introduction to the Gospels*, 182.

17. Luke Timothy Johnson, *The Writings of the New Testament* (Minneapolis: Fortress, 2010), 144–45.

18. Warren Carter and Amy-Jill Levine, *The New Testament: Methods and Meanings* (Nashville: Abingdon Press, 2013), 18.

19. Carter and Levine, *The New Testament*, 54–55.

sumes that Mark is the earliest Gospel and that both Matthew and Luke use Mark as a source. In addition, Matthew and Luke have similar material that does not come from Mark. This shared material is believed to come from a source known as *Q*, from the German word for "source," *Quelle*. In addition to *Q* and Mark's Gospel, Matthew has content that is unique to Matthew and, similarly, Luke has content unique to itself. These sources are called *M* and *L*, respectively. The chart below is a visual image of the hypothesis:

Gospel Chart[20]

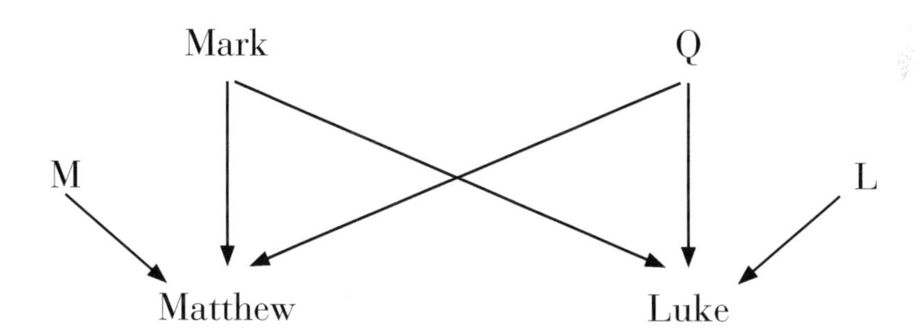

Elements in the Gospels

Birth Narratives

Two Gospels record Jesus's birth. Following a genealogy that connects Jesus to both David and Abraham, the Matthean birth narrative opens with the claim, "This is how the birth of Jesus Christ took place" (Matt 1:18). From the start, the narrative, which comprises three parts—the announcement of Jesus's birth, the visit of the magi, and the flight to and return from Egypt—is aimed at proclaiming that Jesus is the Christ, the Messiah. In the opening of the narrative, we are told that Jesus's mother,

20. Google images from Wikimedia Commons, The_Four-Source_Hypothesis.png, https://commons.wikimedia.org/wiki/File:The_Four-Source_Hypothesis.png.

Mary, was engaged to a man named Joseph and became pregnant before they were married. Joseph, who plays the major role in this version, would have been within his rights to expose Mary to public scorn, but he decided to dismiss her privately to protect her. Before he could take action, an angel from the Lord appeared, announcing, "Don't be afraid to take Mary as your wife, because the child she carries was conceived by the Holy Spirit. She will give birth to a son, and you will call him Jesus, because he will save his people from their sins" (Matt 1:20-21).

The account is presented as fulfillment of the prophet Isaiah's words: "The young woman is pregnant and is about to give birth to a son, and she will name him Immanuel" (Isa 7:14). The New Testament writer is using a second-century Greek translation that presumes the word *virgin* for the Hebrew word, *young woman,* in Isaiah. Jesus's genealogy, birth, and childhood are contained in the first two chapters of Matthew, in which Matthew proclaims the good news in the story of a child—the long-awaited one has arrived and the time for the Messiah has come.

Matthew's account frames Jesus's birth as a fulfillment of prophecy. Five times in these first two chapters, the writer uses the formula, "This fulfilled what the Lord had spoken through the prophet."[21] The multiple references to prophetic texts expose Matthew as making a proclamation rooted in the prophetic word, and interpreting the prophetic word so that the audience recognizes Jesus as the Messiah. This audience is familiar with the words of the prophets and expects the Messiah.

Luke's birth narrative is actually the story of two births. Stories about John the Baptist's and Jesus's births begin in chapter 1 and, while also including elements of prophetic foretelling, focus more on relationships. The story of John the Baptist's birth comes first and incorporates the Old Testament motif (e.g., Abraham and Sarah) of the barren wife. Zechariah (an Aaronide priest) and his wife Elizabeth are older and childless. An angel appears to Zechariah and tells him that Elizabeth will have a son, and his name is to be John. John, like Samson, is to be a special child, dedicated to the Lord and made to stay away from wine and liquor. The angel says that the child "will be filled with the Holy Spirit even before his birth" (Luke 1:15).

21. Matthew 1:22; 2:5, 15b, 18, 23b.

Luke is careful to highlight the birth of Jesus taking place in Bethlehem, which connects him to David and directs us to the prophetic text in Micah 5:2,

> As for you, Bethlehem of Ephrathah,
> though you are the least significant of Judah's forces,
> one who is to be a ruler in Israel on my behalf will come out from you.

The Luke narrative emphasizes the movement of Mary and Joseph from Nazareth to Bethlehem in response to Caesar's tax decree. There they find lodging in a guest room (possibly located by a barn stall attached to a house or a cave) where animals were housed and fed. In that space, the baby Jesus is placed in a manger or feeding trough. Jesus's birth is witnessed to by heavenly forces, in the form of angels, and human ones, in the person of ordinary, most likely poor, shepherds from the countryside. The story first moves inward, to the manger, and then spreads out to the shepherds who "reported what they had been told about this child" (Luke 2:17). In this birth account, the hearer learns about who Jesus is through connections and relationships to people and places.

Teaching, Sayings, and Parables

In all four Gospels, Jesus devotes much time to teaching, expounding on, and explaining the Torah or law, and to describing the kingdom of God or heaven. Jesus uses proverbs and prophecy, particularly in the Synoptic Gospels, and talks about God's vision of the future and his own purpose in coming to gather the disciples. These elements are particularly evident in the lengthy "discourses" in the Gospels of Matthew and John. However, one of the most memorable forms used for teaching about such things is not these lectures but the short, pithy parable. There are twenty-three parables in the Gospel of Matthew, eight in Mark, and twenty-four in Luke.[22] The Greek cognate for parable, *parabole,* means "putting things side by side." Parables are extended metaphors. Like metaphor, a parable lays two things, often two unrelated things, side by side and in that pairing asks

22. Of the twenty-three parables in Matthew, eleven are unique. Two of the eight parables in Mark are unique and eighteen of the twenty-four parables in Luke are unique.

the reader to make sense of them. With this pairing, parable uses ordinary language to express something extraordinary—the known conveys the unknown. Each parable takes us into an ordinary, yet alternate universe so we can learn some aspect of God or of God's kingdom, which is transformative. This extended metaphor is not a means to an end. The meaning is found "only within the story" but "is not exhausted by the story."[23] Thus, when Jesus uses parables, he is extending an invitation to the audience to see, hear, feel, and understand differently. With the words "the kingdom of heaven is like . . ." or "a man had two sons . . ." or "there was a rich man . . . ," Jesus seeks to awaken the hearer's theological imagination. This "primal form" of communication is designed to engage head and heart. Moreover, this intentionally symbolic language reminds us that any attempts to speak about the divine can never be completely literal. The words used to describe the love and knowledge of God should always strain against the limitations of language. When we understand how parables work, we can conclude that engaging the parables is a spiritual exercise. When he told parables, Jesus was forming followers into disciples.

Miracles

The Gospel story of Jesus's life and ministry is also characterized by narratives describing his miracles. Jesus performs these supernatural acts, primarily healings, in each of the Gospels.[24] The miracles are evidence that he is more than just another teacher, and these acts mark him as a prophet at least of the stature of Elijah. Miracles serve a variety of functions in the Gospels. In Mark, Jesus's miracles are a part of the "messianic secret," where Jesus does the miraculous and then tells the witnesses to tell no one. In Matthew, the miracles are fulfillment of prophecy and a "lesson" for Jesus's rivals, who attack him based on legal technicalities. In some instances, miracles are Jesus's way of shifting the paradigm. In Luke, for example, Jesus's miracles are connected to the sociopolitical context of em-

23. Sallie McFague, *Speaking in Parables: A Study in Metaphor and Theology* (Minneapolis: Fortress, 1975), 13.

24. Whereas the Synoptic Gospels speak of miracles, the Gospel of John will refer to Jesus's miraculous works as signs.

pire, so in Luke, miracles are often a political act. Miracles can sometimes be an interruption in a story, or they can be the purpose. Always, miracles are an opportunity for wonder. Throughout, miracles are a reminder of Jesus's divinity interfacing with the needs of humanity, be they political, physical, spiritual, or psychosocial. The miracles invite the audience into an encounter with the Son of God.

Miracles in the Gospels fit into the following categories:

- Healing: for example, Jesus's healing of the woman with the issue of blood in Mark 5
- Raising of the dead: for example, raising Lazarus in John 11, raising Jairus's daughter in Mark 5
- Exercising power over elements or the natural world: for example, feeding the five thousand in Matthew 14, stilling the storm in Matthew 8, Mark 4, and Luke 8
- Performing an exorcism: for example, healing the Gerasene demoniac in Luke 8

Through telling the stories of Jesus working these miracles, the Gospels highlight Jesus's power over humans, spirits, elements, and matter, which sets the stage for the all-important miracle of forgiving sins.

The modern reader's response to the miraculous is often colored by a post-Enlightenment perspective in which science rules and so there is a tendency to look for a logical explanation for any apparently supernatural act. In Matthew, Jesus feeds multitudes (four thousand in 15:32 and five thousand in 14:31) with only a small amount of bread and a few fish. Some modern interpreters "explain" this story as an example of sharing. The little boy who offers his food inspires others to share their food. But sharing is not what these Gospel stories proclaim. In the Gospel accounts there is not just enough to feed those in the crowd but also baskets of food left over. There is not scarcity; there is an abundance and this abundance is an important characteristic of the kingdom that Jesus has come to proclaim. The Gospel stories present Jesus performing a supernatural act and exerting power over the natural world in a way that meets a human need and points to a God who is able to come into the world but is not limited by the world. It is this "otherness" of God that is the subject of these stories and explaining the supernatural in natural, psychological, or scientific terms is inappropriate and counter to the goals of the Gospels.

Passion Narratives[25]

The story of Jesus and the good news is rooted in the suffering, death, and resurrection of Jesus, the Christ, known as the "Passion narrative." Although each of the Gospels has a unique understanding of Jesus and tells its story with a particular audience and end in mind, arguably each one is, in effect, an extended Passion narrative. From a literary perspective, the death and resurrection of Christ is the chronotope of chronotopes. It is the event around which everything in the New Testament writings revolves, and it is the event that invites the Hebrew Bible and its emphasis on what it means to be God's people into a new dialogue. Christ's incarnation, death, and resurrection will force the Gospel writers to revisit, reinterpret, and reconfigure their identity, and the identity of their audiences, as God's people, and this new identity will eventually result in a new religion. Behind the stories of Jesus's life, ministry, death, and resurrection in the Gospels, we observe a small group of Jews seeking to establish and maintain their identity, as they define and redefine what it is to be the people of God. At the center of this movement is the person, work, and witness of Jesus the Christ. What follows is a brief sketch of each Gospel with some attention to distinguishing literary characteristics.

---

25. *Passion narrative* is the term that defines the suffering (passion), death, and resurrection of Jesus.

CHAPTER 1
MATTHEW: THE IDENTITY REMIX

OUTLINE	THEMES
1:1–4:16 Genealogy, birth, and early days 4:17–16:20 Public ministry in Galilee 16:21–28:20 Journey to Jerusalem, crucifixion, death, and resurrection	Jesus is the Messiah or Christ, the Son of God Immanuel, God with us Righteousness redefined The church/ecclesia

The term *remix* originally referred to the reuse of elements of one song in another. The most common types of remix were sampling, that is, taking a segment of one song and using it as a foundation for another, and the extended cut, that is, using a longer version of an original release for another purpose or audience (such as a dance club). Remixing music also involved adapting a piece of music from one genre to another, introducing another artist into an existing work, or creating a cover, that is, one artist's version of another artist's work. Of the four Gospels, Matthew, with a likely composition date of 80–90 CE, is the ultimate remix of the Hebrew Bible. The author uses his twenty-eight chapters to sample and extend elements of the Hebrew scriptures as he tells the story of Jesus. This version of the good news is informed, shaped, and supported by the Torah and the prophetic witness to the Messiah or Christ. The writer of the Gospel makes approximately sixty-eight Old Testament references. Jesus is portrayed as the embodiment of the one who was attested to in scripture and who will cause the audience to hear familiar scriptures in a new way. For example, when Jesus began his ministry in Galilee, Matthew explains it this way:

> He left Nazareth and settled in Capernaum, which lies alongside the sea in the area of Zebulun and Napthali. This fulfilled what Isaiah the prophet said:
>
> "Land of Zebulun and land of Napthali,
> alongside the sea, across the Jordan, Galilee of the Gentiles,
> the people who lived in the dark have seen a great light." (Matt 4:13-16a)

Here we observe that Matthew takes great pains to use language that echoes the prophetic word. Another example of Matthew's remixing of prophecy can be seen in the account of Jesus's triumphal entry into Jerusalem. Reflecting on the prophet's words in Zechariah 9:9, Matthew takes the poetic word of the prophet and puts it into the narrative. Zechariah prophesies,

> Rejoice greatly, Daughter Zion
> Sing aloud, Daughter Jerusalem.
> Look, your king will come to you.
> He is righteous and victorious.
> He is humble and riding on an ass,
> on a colt, the offspring of a donkey. (Zech 9:9)

Zechariah's prophecy takes the form of parallelism, the association of one line to another. This type of poetic repetition allows for the second or subsequent line to bring something the first line does not, in this instance, pointing out that the ass upon which Jesus rides is a colt. In Matthew's remix, the symbolic language of Zechariah does not easily translate into Matthew's prose. Jesus instructs the disciples to "untie them and bring them to me," a "donkey tied up and a colt with it" (Matt 21:2b, a). Jesus sat on "them" (Matt 21:7)—picture that! In Mark, Jesus rides on a colt (Mark 11:7), and Luke has Jesus ride upon a colt "no one has ever ridden" (Luke 19:30). Matthew's strident commitment to the prophetic passage has Jesus riding on both the donkey and the colt.

Evidence of Matthew's remixing can also be observed in the structure of the book, the opening genealogy, and the Sermon on the Mount discourse. The structure of Matthew's Gospel follows the three-part outline characteristic of ancient biography:

1. Jesus's early years (1–4)
2. his work and ministry (5–25)
3. his death and resurrection (26–28)[1]

The beginning of each section is marked with the phrase, "from that time . . ."[2] In this Gospel we also observe an envelope structure. The book begins and ends by establishing Jesus's identity as Immanuel, "God with us." Another structural feature in Matthew is the organization of Jesus's teachings into five discourses, modeled after the five books of the Torah.

The Gospel opens with a bold claim supported by a genealogy. It begins, "A record of the ancestors of Jesus Christ, son of David, son of Abraham." Genealogies matter greatly in the ancient world and ours. As observed in the *toledot* formulas in the Old Testament, genealogies serve a variety of functions. Genealogy has the literary function of transitioning the story from one place to another, or setting the stage for the narrative to come. In a culture that ties identity to name, family or kinship group, and land, genealogy is historical, political, and social. It is the way a family system establishes pedigree and places individuals in the larger tapestry of the whole people. Thus, by his intentional shaping of Jesus's background, Matthew establishes Jesus's identity and his people past, present, and future.

Matthew's genealogy is divided into three sections—three sets of fourteen generations. One extends from Abraham to David, one from David to the Babylonian exile, and the final one from the Babylonian exile to the birth of Jesus. Scholars believe that the practice of *gematria*, meaning conveyed by numerical code, is at work here. The Hebrew letters of the alphabet also represent numbers, and the three letters in David's name have

1. John Y. H. Yieh, *Conversations with Scripture: The Gospel of Matthew* (New York: Church Publishing, 2012), 9.

2. Matt 4:17 and 16:21.

a numerical equivalent of fourteen.[3] The emphasis on David supports Matthew's claim that Jesus is the Christ, since the prophetic witnesses proclaimed the Messiah would be a descendant of David. The form of the genealogy in three sections also suggests that every fourteen generations, something important happens. Thus, it is indeed time for the Messiah to arrive. Matthew's genealogy omits and moves family members around, even leaving out three kings to achieve this fourteen-generation pattern. He does not include everyone[4] and does not intend to.

Matthew's obvious selectivity in this construction of Jesus's genealogy raises a question about the presence of the women, Tamar (Gen 38), Rahab (Josh 2), Ruth (Ruth 1–4), wife of Uriah (Bathsheba in 2 Sam 11 and 1 Kgs 1), and Mary, Jesus's mother. The inclusion of any women in such a list is unusual. Genealogies were usually patrilineal. In royal annals, the queen mother could be, but was not always, named. This makes the list of women who are remembered additionally puzzling. If women are to be included, certainly it should not be these women! Rahab, Ruth, and Uriah (Bathsheba's husband) are Gentiles. Tamar, Ruth, and Mary conceive under unusual circumstances. The wife of Uriah (also mother of Solomon) comes into David's royal family under the shadow of an abuse of power, sexual assault, deception, trickery, and murder.

Historically, interpreters have argued the presence of the Gentile women is an indication that Jesus came to save not only the Jews but all humanity. Others have argued that these women are listed to remind the audience that Jesus came to save sinners.[5] A literary reading sees genre as a major clue in understanding the inclusion of the names. The writer of Matthew is tracing Jesus's bloodline for an audience with specific expectations about the Messiah as descendant of David and inheritor of David's legacy. The inclusion of Tamar, Rahab, Ruth, the wife of Uriah, and Mary

3. Suzanne Watts Henderson, *New Testament Conversations: A Literary, Historical and Pluralistic Introduction* (Nashville: Abingdon Press, 2019), 123.

4. Warren Carter and A. J. Levine, *The New Testament: Methods and Meanings* (Nashville: Abingdon Press, 2013), 23.

5. Gentiles, by virtue of worshipping false gods, would fit in the category of sinner. While it is true that Rahab is a sex worker, she is also a person of faith (Josh 2:9-13). Moreover, the men listed in the genealogy would fit into the category of sinner, so Matthew wouldn't need to include women to have sinners on the list!

upsets the proverbial apple cart by using the traditional form to challenge and expand the vision of those who demand that the Messiah, the one who would free the people from Roman oppression and restore Israel as a nation, comes from the "right people." A literary reading sees the genealogy as a remix of the genre.

If one goal of genealogy is to establish pedigree, then the genealogy is necessary. Equally necessary is a broader understanding of the kingdom of God. Matthew uses the genealogy to remind the people that God is often found in the questionable situations and unusual circumstances that are characteristic of life in the margins. With this remix of genre, the writer of Matthew casts Jesus in a much larger role than simply that of the one coming to give relief from Roman rule. In fact, Jesus's ministry in Matthew is seen as an ongoing work of fulfillment of the Torah, which requires a new understanding of the law. Jesus will check off all the necessary boxes, but with the greater goal of subverting the entire system and ushering in the kingdom of God. In this way the genealogy foreshadows Jesus's entire ministry, whose expansiveness will challenge our understanding of identity.

Matthew's account of Jesus's story moves from his birth and early years to the ministry of John the Baptist. John is cast as the one who exercises the prophetic voice and plays the part of the forerunner to the Messiah in the narrative trajectory. John precedes Jesus in birth, in ministry, and in death. John calls the people to repentance. Dressed in camel's hair like the prophet Elijah, John baptizes the repentant and prophesies (Matt 3). In keeping with the prophetic tradition, John proclaims, "Here comes the kingdom of heaven!" It is John who baptizes Jesus in the Jordan River. John is arrested and eventually executed. In the overall structure of the book, the account of John the Baptist serves as a transition from Jesus's birth narrative to his ministry as an adult as it indicates the overall shape of the narrative.

The Sermon on the Mount

Jesus makes five great speeches or "discourses" in Matthew: the Sermon on the Mount (chs. 5–7), the Missionary Discourse (ch. 10), the

Parables on the Kingdom of Heaven/God (ch. 13), the Community Discourse (ch. 18), and the Speech on the End Times (chs. 24–25). These five speeches and the material preceding each one makes for a division of Matthew into five books, an analogy with the five books of the Torah/ Pentateuch.

The Sermon on the Mount is the first and best known of the discourses.[6] It begins with what we know as the Beatitudes, which are followed by a series of teachings using the metaphors of salt and light and including teaching on earthly versus heavenly treasure, trees and fruit, a house on a firm foundation versus one built on the sand, and prayer (i.e., the Lord's Prayer in Matt 6:9-13). Jesus expounds on the law, using the phrases, "you have heard that it was said . . . but I say to you. . . ." With this teaching on the law combined with his location on a mountain, Jesus is depicted as the new Moses who has an even greater authority and brings a new dispensation of the law.

The Beatitudes

Happy are people who are hopeless, because the kingdom of heaven is theirs.
Happy are people who grieve, because they will be made glad.
Happy are people who are humble, because they will inherit the earth.
Happy are people who are hungry and thirsty for righteousness, because they will be fed until they are full.
Happy are people who show mercy, because they will receive mercy.
Happy are people who have pure hearts, because they will see God.
Happy are people who make peace, because they will be called God's children.
Happy are people whose lives are harassed because they are righteous, because the kingdom of heaven is theirs.

The title given to this section of the discourse, Beatitudes, comes from the Latin translation of the Greek word for *makarios*, "blessed" or "happy." This is the Greek translation of the Hebrew word '*ashre,* that is, the same word that appears in Psalm 1, a wisdom psalm that outlines the walk of

6. Mark Allan Powell, *Fortress Introduction to the Gospels* (Minneapolis: Fortress, 2019), 100–101.

the righteous one.[7] The Beatitudes evoke the wisdom traditions of the Old Testament in form and content. The form of the Beatitudes is that of a two-part saying. First a human character or behavior is listed, and then the consequential blessings of such a character or behavior are presented.[8] The subjects of the Beatitudes are all, like those of the proverbs, elements of life. However, while the didactic nature of the material is evident, the meaning of the Beatitudes is more elusive. Taken at face value, there is a disconnect between parts one and two of each saying. In a sense, the Beatitudes are like riddles, or words of the wise, which must be unlocked. Here we observe the wisdom tradition as it invites listeners to see and hear differently. The Beatitudes offer comfort to people who are suffering by offering another perspective on their situation. As the last line of the Beatitudes proclaims, and the sermon as a whole illustrates, the kingdom of heaven is something that exists as an alternate reality to Roman domination. This is the point of the Sermon and the Gospel itself, to proclaim the onset of the kingdom of heaven. With Jesus, the kingdom of God or heaven has been realized. This is an essential message to the community of believers who first received Matthew's Gospel.

The Passion Narrative in Matthew

The last section of Matthew's biography tells the story of Jesus's betrayal, trial, crucifixion, and resurrection.

- Plot to kill Jesus by chief priests and elders
- A woman anoints Jesus with perfume
- Judas betrays Jesus
- Preparation for Passover/Last Supper
- Jesus prays in Gethsemane
- Jesus is arrested

7. The word *Makarios* is in Psalm 1:1 of the Septuagint, the Greek translation of the Hebrew Bible.

8. Yieh, *Conversations with Scripture*, 45.

- Jesus appears before Caiaphas, the High Priest
- Peter denies Jesus three times
- Jesus goes before Pilate and is sentenced to death
- Jesus is crucified
- The temple curtain is torn and holy people raised
- Jesus is buried in the tomb of Joseph of Arimathea
- Mary Magdalene and the "other" Mary testify to the resurrection
- Jesus appears to and commissions the disciples

In Matthew's Gospel, the Passion narrative is similar to the one in the Gospel of Mark, perhaps reflecting Mark as a source, but with some additional unique elements. In Jesus's encounter with Pilate, for example, the writer of Matthew includes a scene with Pilate's wife, who warns her husband to "leave that righteous man alone. I've suffered much today in a dream because of him" (27:19). When he is unable to dissuade the crowd that demands Jesus's crucifixion, Pilate washes his hands so as to claim that he is "innocent of this man's blood" (27:24).[9] The warning dream of Pilate's wife evokes the dreams at the beginning of the Gospel in which an angel reassures Joseph that it is appropriate to marry Mary (1:20), the magi are warned not to return to Herod (2:12), and Joseph is instructed to take his family to and return from Egypt (2:19-22). The dreams at the beginning of the narrative are evidence of God's hand in human events. Although there is no mention of an angel or God in the report of Pilate's wife's dream, the message that Jesus is a "righteous man" fits with the larger themes of the narrative and supports the identity construct of Jesus, who is the embodiment of righteousness.

Also unique to Matthew's narrative is the apocalyptic tone and the description of supernatural events, reflecting creation's response to Jesus's death:

9. Henderson, *New Testament Conversations*, 136.

> Look the curtain of the sanctuary was torn in two from top to bottom. The earth shook, the rocks split, and the bodies of many holy people who were dead had been raised. After Jesus's resurrection they came out of their graves and went into the holy city where they appeared to many people (Matt 27:51-53).

In Matthew, Jesus's crucifixion is literally and figuratively earth-shattering. The earthquake results in a resurrection of "many holy people" (27:52), who like Jesus, "appeared to many people" (27:53), signaling the unleashed power of resurrection as a result of Jesus's sacrificial death. The curtain in the temple being torn in two, from the top to the bottom, signals the end of the separation between God and humanity, realized through Jesus's death. These elements set the stage for the resurrection of Jesus. In the crucifixion account we observe some of the same literary devices used in the birth narrative. In addition to the dreams used as warning, there are the witnesses of nature. In the Passion narrative there is an earthquake and in the birth narrative there is the star. With these devices Matthew signals the confluence of the God of creation and the creation. The very earth bears witness to the events of Immanuel, God with us.

The concluding words of Matthew, traditionally known as the Great Commission (28:18-20) are a remix of the Great Commandment. In Deut 6:4-9, Moses commands the people about to enter the promised land to "love the Lord your God with all your heart." These words are followed with the instruction to "recite . . . talk . . . [and] write" these commands to "your children." In Matthew, Jesus, the new Moses, commissions his followers to make disciples by teaching not just their children but "all nations," a reference that recalls God's original promise to Abraham in Genesis (Gen 12:3b). The commissioning speech follows a traditional formula. First, as we would expect, the authority of the speaker is established, "I've received all authority in heaven and on earth" (28:18). Next, comes the command to act: "Therefore, go and make disciples of all nations, baptizing them in the name of the Father and of the Son and of the Holy Spirit, teaching them to obey everything that I've commanded you" (28:19-20a). Finally, Jesus offers the assurance of God's ongoing presence with those being commissioned: "Look, I myself will be with you every day until the end of this present age" (28:20b). The good news of Matthew ends, as it begins, with the proclamation of Immanuel, "God is with us." In the person of Jesus the Christ, the kingdom of God/heaven is made available to all humanity. The Great Commission returns us to the theme of the genealogy, that the work and ministry of Jesus reaches beyond a single family or tribe or nation. The work of Jesus is for the world.

Elements Unique to Matthew[10]

Genealogy

Birth narrative

- Visit of the Magi (2:1-12)
- Flight to Egypt (2:13-21)
- Fulfilling of the law (5:17-20)
- The Antitheses (5:21-24, 27-28, 33-38, 43)
- True piety (6:1-15, 16-18)
- Pearls before swine (7:6)
- Mission for Israel (10:5-6)
- Invitation to rest (11:28-30)
- Peter tries to walk on water (14:2-31)
- Peter is blessed (16:17-19)
- How much forgiveness? (18:21-22)
- Titles prohibited (23:7-12)
- Pharisees denounced (23:15-18)

10. Powell, *Introducing the New Testament,* 108.

- Death of Judas (27:3-10)
- Pilate washes his hands (27:24-25)
- Guard at the tomb (27:62-66; 28:11-15)
- The Great Commission (28:16-20)

Miracles

- Resurrection of the saints at crucifixion (27:52-53)

Parables

- Weeds and wheat, treasure, pearl, net (13:24-30, 36-52)
- Unforgiving servant (18:23-35)
- Laborers in the vineyard (20:1-16)
- Two sons (21:28-32)
- Bridesmaids (25:1-13)

CHAPTER 2

MARK: THE SECRET IDENTITY

Mark's Gospel "resists easy characterization,"[1] especially when compared to the other Synoptic Gospels. This first and shortest Gospel has no birth narrative. Also missing is the level of detail we find in Matthew and the literary sophistication we experience in Luke. At first glance, the book appears episodic in nature. There is movement, but it is not always linear. The brief, and not always connected episodes, combine with the frequent use of the Greek word *euthys*, translated as "immediately" (used forty-two times), to give the impression that the writer of Mark is in a hurry.[2]

A second glance, however, reveals an intentional shaping of the material with Old Testament images and apocalyptic motifs.[3] This intentional shaping of a familiar story makes Mark an ideal performance text. Repetition, location, and intercalation as organizing principles assist an audience in following the story. Additionally, the Gospel of Mark uses time to emphasize the sense of urgency with which the story is told. Mark's use of time evokes the "adventure time" of Greek drama. And, if that is not enough, the original ending of this Gospel is a cliffhanger. All these elements are in service to Mark's story of Jesus and the revelation of his identity as the Messiah at his crucifixion.

---

1. Luke Timothy Johnson, *The Writings of the New Testament*, 149.

2. Mark Allan Powell, *Introducing the New Testament: A Historical, Literary, and Theological Survey* (Grand Rapids: Baker Academic, 2009), 130.

3. Ched Myers, "Mark's Gospel," in *The New Testament—Introducing the Way of Discipleship*, ed. Wes Howard-Brook and Sharon Ringe (Maryknoll, NY: Orbis, 2002), 43–44.

OUTLINE	THEMES
1:1-15 Baptism and opening proclamation 1:16–8:26 Jesus's ministry 8:27–13:37 On the way to the cross 14:1–15:47 Jesus's suffering, death, and burial 16:1-8 Epilogue: Resurrection and silence	Messianic mission realized through the cross The realm of God comes to earth

The text of Mark can be divided into two sections or "acts" based on geography. Act 1, Mark 1:1–8:21, takes place in the countryside of Galilee. Act 2, Mark 8:22–16:8, is centered in and around Jerusalem. Both sections have similar elements: a call to discipleship (1:1-20 and 8:22–9:13), an extended sermon (4:1-34 and 13:1-37), and a "passion" tradition (6:14-29 and 14:1–15:39).[4] This kind of repetition is the narrative form of parallelism, a literary tool we observed in the Psalms and in some of the prophets. With parallelism in poetry, the second line includes something the first line did not (*a* and what's more, *b*). In the Gospel of Mark, the repetition of narrative elements look to the "what's more" that is the crucifixion. Thus, Mark uses geography and repetition to shape his Gospel to point to the crucifixion as the climax of the story.

A date of 70 CE is generally assigned for the Gospel's composition, and the anonymous author is believed to have been a Greek-speaking Jew. The early church attributed the Gospel to one named Mark.[5] Mark's Gospel was initially received by an audience who had experienced the trauma of Roman persecution, either by personal experience or by bearing witness to someone else's experience.[6] Some scholars argue Mark was written for survivors who saved their lives at great cost, perhaps by hiding or by

4. Myers, "Mark's Gospel," 47. Myers argues for a "rough symmetry" in Mark consisting of six elements.

5. Papias claims that the Gospel writer named Mark was the interpreter of Peter who wrote down what he said. Some scholars believe this Mark is the John Mark mentioned in Acts 12:12, 25; 15:37-39 and in some epistles (Colossians, Philemon, 2 Timothy, and 1 Peter).

6. Serene Jones, *Trauma and Grace: Theology in a Ruptured World* (Louisville: Westminster John Knox, 2009), 14.

denying Christ.[7] To connect with such an audience, Mark takes them back to the Crucifixion—the foundational trauma of the faith—and invites them to see it as the moment Christ's identity and purpose is revealed. As a performance text, this Gospel invites people into the moments of Christ's life and ministry on this earth as a template for living in their own current context. This life of Jesus is to be the lens through which they interpret their life experiences and find meaning in them. The audience is to identify with characters in the story and to journey with Jesus to the awful and awesome transformative event (chronotope) of the cross. In this context, the performance of Mark is a political act that invites the audience into a theological response to empire.

The opening words of the Gospel speak about the Messiah, and come from the book of Isaiah, a prophet especially known for theopolitics—the intersection of the workings of the political realm and God's movement in the world. In Isaiah, the prophet brought a word from the LORD as an alternate reality to the political machinations of the day. By choosing to place Isaiah's words at the beginning of this Gospel, the writer reminds the audience of a God whose plan and purpose supersede that of any earthly ruler, even of the Roman emperor.

> The beginning of the good news about Jesus Christ, God's Son, happened just as it was written about in the prophecy of Isaiah:
>
> Look, I am sending my messenger before you.
> He will prepare your way,
> a voice shouting in the wilderness:
> "Prepare the way for the Lord;
> make his paths straight." (Mark 1:1-3; cf. Isa 40:3; Mal 3:1; Exod 23:20)

Although this opening statement tells the reader that Jesus is the Christ, that is, Messiah, the one talked about by the prophets, it takes time for the characters in the Gospel to come to this realization. And Jesus doesn't help. He performs miracles and then instructs the witnesses and beneficiaries to tell no one. In Mark 1:43, for example, he instructs the man he healed not to say "anything to anyone." He instructs evil spir-

7. Powell, *Introducing the New Testament*, 144.

its "not to reveal who he was" (3:12). He brings a dead child back to life and gives the witnesses "strict orders that no one should know what had happened" (5:43a). When Peter proclaims that Jesus is "the Christ," he orders the disciples "not to tell anyone about him" (8:30). Even the parables he uses to teach are mystifying to outsiders and, at times, are not clear even to his closest followers. In Mark 4:1-9, for example, Jesus teaches with the parable of the seeds scattered on different soils. The story of the farmer gives four scenarios of planting and produce, concluding with the provocative words, "Whoever has ears to listen should pay attention!" When asked to explain this parable, Jesus responds to his followers and the disciples in the ambiguous words, "The secret of God's kingdom has been given to you but to those outside everything comes in parables" (4:11). Jesus refers to the kingdom of God as "secret," and then recites and evokes the prophet Isaiah's words, "This is so that they can look and see but have no insight, and they can hear but not understand. Otherwise they might turn their lives around and be forgiven" (Mark 4:12; cf. Isa 6:10). The secrecy around Jesus's teaching and ministry raises questions about his identity and the purpose of his ministry. The author of the Gospel depicts Jesus as someone who does not fit into any known category. Is he a teacher or a prophet or a rabble-rouser? The constant movement and short episodic nature of the book can give the impression that the audience is being asked to play a game of "Clue." How are we to assemble the evidence provided to determine the identity of this Jesus? It is not until the crucifixion that everything that has come before makes sense. In fact, it is the crucifixion that is the lens for understanding everything we need to know about Jesus in Mark's Gospel. For this reason, some describe the Gospel of Mark as a Passion narrative with a long introduction. If you want to know who this Jesus is, look to the account of his suffering and death. It is in this "moment" that his identity is clear. The messianic secret helps the Christian community for whom the Gospel was written to understand that not everyone will recognize Jesus's identity. There will be opposition and even persecution of those who know him. The crucifixion of Christ is the defining moment and event not only for Jesus, but for this community familiar with persecution. Every time they hear the story, their identity is affirmed.

Time plays an important role in the way the story in the Gospel of Mark is told. In particular, the writer employs various understandings of time. The Gospel tells its story using time as humans understand and experience it. The Gospel also uses "ritual" or "mythic" time, which interrupts the daily activity of humanity and invites the audience into a broader understanding of their existence and purpose, allowing an identity that originated in the past to inform their present and future. Experiencing events in mythic time enables humans to consider a reality that is broader than the one they encounter in the present. In this way the Gospel of Mark is a formative text that becomes liturgical as it invites the audience to remember and rehearse a formation story. Mythic time also serves as a reminder that some moments have more weight or meaning than others.[8] Mark's story of Jesus is always moving between human time and mythic time, with the understanding that the eternal holds sway over the human understanding and experience of time.[9] Once we recognize this, we can conclude there are only two "moments" in time in Mark's Gospel: the moment when Christ's ministry begins and the one when Christ is realized as the Messiah.

Jairus's Daughter and the Bleeding Woman

Another characteristic of Mark's Gospel is intercalation, which is an interruption or an insertion in the narrative. By interrupting one story with another, the writer creates a dialogue between the two stories and the audience. The combination of the stories of Jairus's daughter and the bleeding woman, which appears in all three Synoptic Gospels, is an example of interruption. Matthew tells the story in 138 words, Luke in 280 words, but the usually abrupt writer of Mark devotes 374 words to

8. Brenda Deen Schildgen, *Crisis and Continuity: Time in the Gospel of Mark* (Sheffield: Sheffield Academic Press, 1998), 12.

9. Schildgen, *Crisis and Continuity*, 13.

the story.[10] Mark's version is a brilliant example of this Gospel writer's "signature move" with intercalation. The story begins with Jesus crossing the lake to an awaiting crowd. Jairus, a synagogue leader, "came forward . . . fell at [Jesus's] feet" (5:22) and pleaded with Jesus to come to his home and heal his daughter. Jesus goes with him but, on the way, a woman, who had been bleeding for twelve years, makes her way through the crowd, and rather than seeking to get Jesus's attention, simply touches his clothes. Upon so doing she is healed. Jesus senses what has happened and he "interrupts" the movement toward his particular mission in order to locate and speak to the person who anonymously sought out healing. He asks, "Who touched my clothes?" The question, as his disciples point out, is ridiculous considering Jesus is surrounded by a large, jostling crowd. Jesus's question, however, is intended to invite the woman to identify herself so that she can be acknowledged and declared healed. While that interaction is taking place, word comes that Jairus's daughter has died. Jesus, however, is undeterred in his healing mission to the child, just as he was undeterred in seeking out the woman in the crowd. He continues in spite of the reports that the girl is dead and, when he comes to her, brings her back to life, saying, "Young woman, get up." The writer makes a point of saying that the child was twelve years old.

These two stories of healing are interwoven so that one interrupts the other literally and literarily. The woman who has been bleeding for twelve years is one who has lived on the margins of society, but, armed with determination, makes her way through the crowd to reach her goal. This woman who is isolated from the community by her illness is called "daughter" by Jesus and in so doing he welcomes her back into the community. The girl does not come to Jesus at all. Rather, her father comes on her behalf. One has someone come on her behalf and another comes on her own. One is driven by her own faith and the other benefits from the faith of her father. Jesus heals them both. They are both someone's daughter and Jesus heals both the one on the margins and the one encircled by her family.

---

10. Vernon K. Robbins, "The Woman Who Touched Jesus's Garment: Socio-Rhetorical Analysis of the Synoptic Accounts," *New Testament Studies* 33 (1987): 503.

Imagine the experience of being among those who first heard these stories. The two previously unrelated women intersect in the narrative because of Jesus and because of their need, which only he can meet. The woman has been suffering for twelve years, the span of the little girl's life, whose life appears to be threatened by a recent sickness. For an oppressed community, these two women embody both long-term and recent trauma. The audience knows what it is to live under the shadow of ongoing oppression and they also know what it feels like to have a traumatic event. Through the intercalation, Mark's Jesus offers two steps necessary to recover from trauma. The interruption allows for the healing steps to come in the right order. Jesus tells one daughter, "Your faith has healed you," and to another daughter Jesus says, "Young woman, get up." Those who have experienced trauma must first be made whole before they can move forward.

The Passion Narrative in Mark

In the last three chapters of Mark we come to the point of the Gospel. Here we find the narrative of Jesus's death (and resurrection), including the following components:

- A woman anoints Jesus with expensive perfume.
- The disciples share a Passover meal.
- Jesus predicts Peter's denial of him.
- Jesus prays in Gethsemane.
- Jesus is arrested.
- Jesus is put on trial before the Sanhedrin.
- Peter denies Jesus.
- Jesus is tried before Pilate.
- Jesus is crucified.
- Jesus is buried.
- The tomb is found empty by three women.

This account of the passion begins and ends with women. In Mark 14:3, an unnamed woman anoints Jesus with valuable oil, an act he explains to those around him in this way: "She has anointed my body ahead of time for burial" (v. 8). This early anointing turns out to be a good thing because the women who come to anoint Jesus's body after his hasty burial at the end of the story encounter only an empty tomb. Mary Magdalene, Mary the mother of James, and Salome make their way to the tomb to anoint the body of the crucified Jesus, who had been placed in the tomb without the customary preparation, only to find the stone that had been laid at the entrance rolled away. Entering the tomb, the women find a man in a white robe who announces that Jesus is risen and instructs the women to tell the disciples. The women, however, "overcome with terror and dread . . . fled from the tomb. They said nothing to anyone because they were afraid" (16:8). This is a dramatic ending for the performance of the Gospel, leaving the audience to remember the event and inviting them to take up the command themselves to "tell the disciples" (16:7), to finish the story themselves. These last words are "words of re-gathering, re-union, and hope."[11]

The persecuted community would not have heard the story of Jesus's crucifixion without some level of anguish or experienced the good news of Jesus's resurrection without remembering and experiencing his suffering. Through Mark's narrative, they are able to encounter the traumatic story of Christ's crucifixion from a place of their own trauma. Through the performance of the Jesus story, they are reminded that suffering is a part of the revolutionary work of the Gospel. The original ending leaves the audience to the moment of shock and wonder over the realization of the resurrection, still trying to understand all of its implications.

The ending of Mark received mixed reviews among its earliest audiences. Two alternative endings were suggested and have become a part of the Markan tradition. The shorter ending, of one verse (v. 9), is assigned to the fourth century. In the longer ending (vv. 9-20) the women report the resurrection, Jesus appears to Mary Magdalene and to two other disciples,

11. Emerson B. Powery, "Mark," in *True to Our Native Land: An African American New Testament Commentary*, ed. Brian Blount (Minneapolis: Fortress, 2007), 152.

and later to the eleven disciples with a commission, after which he is taken up into heaven. These twelve verses are written and function like a report, simply listing the things that Jesus did, as if checking off a list. The goal in the second ending seems to be to include the elements of the resurrection narrative that belong to the tradition and were omitted by Mark. However, as a performance vehicle, the original ending to the Gospel preserves the fear and hope of a people who suffered on account of this good news, and leaves the question ever before the reader. How will you respond to the empty tomb?

Elements Unique to Mark

- Parable of seed growing secretly (4:26-29)
- Healing of deaf and mute man (7:31-37)
- Healing of blind man of Bethsaida (8:22-26)
- Teaching on salt (9:49, 50b)
- Young man in the garden who runs away (14:51-52)[12]

12. Powell, *Introducing the New Testament*, 131.

CHAPTER 3

LUKE: AN INCLUSIVE IDENTITY

OUTLINE	THEMES
1:1-4 Prologue 1:5–2:52 Birth narratives and childhood 3:1–4:13 Preparation for ministry 4:14–9:50 Jesus's ministry in Galilee 9:51–19:28 Jesus's journey to Jerusalem 19:29–21:38 Jesus's ministry in Jerusalem 22:1–23:56 Jesus's trial and death 24:1-53 The resurrection	The good news is for everyone

The writer of Luke's Gospel makes his purpose clear from the very beginning: "I have also decided to write a carefully ordered account for you, most honorable Theophilus. I want you to have confidence in the soundness of the instruction you have received" (Luke 1:3-4). This Gospel is, indeed, a carefully ordered account of the life of Jesus addressed to Theophilus, which means "friend of God," and could refer to an actual individual or a group, or it could merely be a literary device.[1] Written sometime between 80 and 90 CE, the Gospel of Luke was the first part of a two-volume work that included the book of the Acts of the Apostles. The author is aware that there are other traditions about Jesus and seeks to

1. Christian E. Hauer and William A. Young, *An Introduction to the Bible: A Journey into Three Worlds* (Upper Saddle River, NJ: Prentice Hall, 2001), 276.

establish the teachings he holds as those that can be confidently believed. Luke is known for the author's beautiful writing style. The level of sophistication in the language and the skillful use of biblical prophetic tropes suggest that the writer was well educated in Greek and mindful of Jewish tradition. Luke is distinguished from the other Gospels by the representation of women characters and its particular attention to the poor.

Luke's Gospel, like Matthew's, begins with a familiar biblical motif, the miraculous birth narrative, with a twist. The first chapter sets the stage for the birth of not one but two characters, John the Baptist and Jesus. Beginning with the announcement of John's birth, Luke creates a dialogue between the two birth narratives. In both stories we find an obstacle to conception and a divine messenger or angel with a promise or prophecy about the child. An angel announces John's birth to his father, Zechariah, and the angel Gabriel tells Mary, his mother, about Jesus's birth. Both prospective parents are told what is expected of them and the names to be given to the children. The text shifts from one account to the other, until the two unborn children are brought together by their mothers when Mary visits her cousin Elizabeth, the mother of John. The leaping of the baby in Elizabeth's womb is followed by Mary's song of praise (the Magnificat), John the Baptist's birth, and Zechariah's prophecy about his son (1:67-79).

The narratives of the birth announcements in chapter 1 are dominated by speech. In each story, there are words of prophecy that function as prediction, followed by responses from the recipient. Mary responds to Elizabeth's prophetic word with the Magnificat, and Zechariah's disbelief results in speechlessness (1:20), followed by his prophecy after his speech is restored. The opening chapter concludes with John's birth, one prophecy fulfilled as it anticipates the birth of Jesus.

Mary's Magnificat and Zechariah's Prophecy

Luke 1 contains the birth narratives for Jesus the Messiah and John the Baptist. The narratives and characters are intertwined. Mary, mother of Jesus, and Elizabeth, mother of John the Baptist, are cousins. Mary is visited by an angel and told of her child's birth. She then visits her cousin Elizabeth, who is also pregnant with a promised child. Elizabeth, upon seeing Mary, is filled with the Holy Spirit as the child leaps in her womb. She prophesies over Mary, "Happy is she who believed that the Lord would fulfill the promises he made to her." Mary's response is the Magnificat (the Latin word for glorify/magnify), a song of praise to God modeled after Hannah's Song in 1 Samuel 2. John's father, the priest Zechariah, is unable to speak because he doubted God's promise of a child (Luke 1:20). After John's birth, Zechariah prophesies over his child. Like Mary's Magnificat, the first part of Zechariah's prophecy attests to God's faithfulness and is confident in God's salvation. Mary's and Zechariah's prophetic words are an example of Luke's literary technique of pairing, one version of the story that features a man and one that features a woman.[2] In Luke 1, we observe two examples of Luke's pairing. First, both Elizabeth and Zechariah are filled with the Spirit and prophesy. Second, although Mary's words are deemed a song, her words carry the same prophetic weight as Zechariah's. Beyond Luke's male-female pairing, we also observe in this chapter the pairing of Mary and Elizabeth as the bearers of promised children, and the connection between Mary's song and that of Hannah.

Luke's account of Jesus's birth is a beloved and familiar biblical story—it's the one Linus recites in *A Charlie Brown Christmas*. This is a beautifully written narrative that includes details highlighting both the contexts and locations of the events described and easily lends itself to orality. The locations of the manger and the shepherd's field are transformed into sacred spaces, and the birth of this child is infused with hope and expectation. The author of Luke uses location to move the reader to the place of the child's birth. In response to a Roman edict that everyone must be registered for tax purposes, Joseph and his pregnant fiancée move from Nazareth in Galilee to Bethlehem. In Bethlehem they are located inside a stable, probably adjacent to a guesthouse. There the child is born and laid in the manger or animal feeding trough. Then the story shifts outside to shepherds guarding flocks in the field. Then, with a motif borrowed from the prophets, comes an angel accompanied by the heavenly forces erupting into praise, "Glory to God in heaven, and on earth peace among those whom he favors." If we follow the rubric of movement and location, the opening narrative moves from larger place to smaller one, from region to city to a stable and, finally, to a manger. From this smallest place, both Jesus and the narrative move out to proclaim the news to shepherds who

2. Jane D. Schaberb and Sharon Ringe, *Gospel of Luke*, in the *Women's Bible Commentary*, 497.

will themselves bear witness to the child. This birth is not only a fulfillment of a prophetic word but it is an event heralded to the common folks, shepherds, people on the margins who eked out a meager existence. Thus, the tone is set in Luke that the good news extends to the poor and the dispossessed—everyone!

Luke's attention to poverty is also evident in this Gospel's version of Matthew's Sermon on the Mount, which takes place not on a mountain but on a plain. Once again, location is important. This location evokes the prophetic words of Isaiah echoed by John the Baptist: "Every valley will be raised up, and every mountain and hill will be flattened" (Isa 40:4; cf. Luke 3:5). Jesus moves from mountain to plain and stands "on a large area of level ground" (Luke 6:17). Luke's Beatitudes, still evoking the form of wisdom teachings, are grounded in the realities of current human experience. Whereas in Matthew's account Jesus says, "Happy are people who are hopeless," Luke's Gospel has Jesus say,

> Happy are you who are poor,
> because God's kingdom is yours.
> Happy are you who hunger now,
> because you will be satisfied.
> Happy are you who weep now,
> because you will laugh. (Luke 6:20-21)

In Luke, the current physical experience of poverty is not to be escaped. When Jesus later comes to the synagogue in Nazareth and reads from the scroll, it is Isaiah 61:1-2 that he chooses, verses proclaiming that the Lord has anointed him to "preach good news to the poor." It is stories like these, focusing on poverty and economic oppression, that have led to Luke's Gospel being called the social justice gospel. The people to whom Jesus came understand the realities of poverty and, in Luke's Gospel, Jesus cares about the day-to-day concerns of the poor and the systems that kept people in poverty.

Some readers interpret Luke's recognition and inclusion of women in his Gospel as further proof of the author's commitment to social justice. Luke has more material about women than any of the other Gospels. One way in which Luke incorporates women into the narrative is by employing a literary device known as "pairing." He tells a story featuring a man and then one with a woman as the subject. This functions like a form of the parallelism that we see in Hebrew poetry. For example, in Luke 7, Jesus heals the servant of a Roman centurion and then the son of a widow. In Luke 8, he exorcises a demon from a man and then heals two women. Additional examples of pairing in Luke include the following:

- Jesus's followers are listed, male (Luke 6:12-16) and female (Luke 8:1-3).
- A woman is healed on the Sabbath (Luke 13:10-17) and a man is healed on the Sabbath (Luke 14:1-4).
- The parable of a man losing and finding his sheep in Luke 15:4-7 is paired with the story of the woman who loses and finds a coin in 15:8-10.[3]

The literary technique of pairing trains the reader to anticipate more. If followers are male, we should expect female; when a story has a wealthy person, we can anticipate someone from another part of the economic strata. Pairing is another way that Luke's Gospel acknowledges the humanity of the shepherds and the Samaritans, the poor and wealthy, men, women, and children. In so doing Luke recasts the story of Jesus as Messiah for all humanity.

Women in Luke

Luke has more content about women than the other Gospels. The Gospel story begins with birth narratives featuring Mary, the mother of Jesus and Elizabeth, mother of John the Baptist. The prophetess Anna appears alongside Simeon in Luke 2. A woman washed Jesus's feet early on in the story as an introduction to a parable (7:36-50). Women were listed with the disciples, Mary Magdalene, Joanna, Susanna, and so on (8:2-3). Women are featured in parables. Memorable examples of women in this category include the woman with the lost coin and the woman who gets justice from the unjust judge (18:1-8). Women are healed (Jairus's daughter), the bleeding woman (8:40-56), the disabled woman (13:11-13), and they are beneficiaries of hearing like the widow whose son is raised (7:11-17). The widow with her small offering is a story in the narrative complex of

3. Mark Allan Powell, *Fortress Introduction to the Gospels*, 2nd ed. (Minneapolis: Fortress, 2019), 148.

> Jesus teaching at the temple (21:1-4). Mary and Martha appear in 10:38-42. Furthermore in chapter 24, it is the women who discover the empty tomb and they are the first witnesses to the resurrection.
>
> The presence of women is not to be equated with a presumed equality of women. Although the women are included and highlighted, they are also cast in roles of subservience.[4] Perhaps their presence reflects an "attempt to legitimate male dominance in the Christianity of the author's time."[5]

The Good Samaritan

One of Jesus's most well-known parables, the good Samaritan, is unique to Luke's Gospel. In it we observe both Jesus's use of parables to teach and Luke's skill in storytelling. Here is a parable that has captured the Christian imagination, particularly as it pertains to identity. The parable is Jesus's response to a question, a story within a story. As such, it reminds us that stories and their meanings take their cues from the material that surrounds them. Our context provides us with clues for how we are to hear and interpret a story. First, we recognize that the parable takes place within an exchange between Jesus and a legal expert or lawyer whose purpose is to "test Jesus." He asks, "Teacher . . . what must I do to gain eternal life?" (10:25). Jesus responds with a question: "What is written in the Law? How do you interpret it?" (10:26). The legal expert gives the right answers, the "great commandment," also known as the *shema* from Deuteronomy, and a command from Leviticus 19:18 that is known familiarly as the second great commandment.[6] Although Jesus affirms his response, the man is not satisfied. In fact, the narrator tells us that he "wanted to prove that he was right," which leads to the next question: "and who is my neighbor?" (10:29). We can only guess at how the legal expert wanted to "prove he was right," but once the legal expert reveals

4. Jane Schaberg and Sharon Ringe, "Gospel of Luke," in *The Women's Bible Commentary*, ed. Carol Newsom, Sharon Ringe and Jacqueline Lapsley, 493.

5. Schaberg and Ringe, "Gospel of Luke," in *The Women's Bible Commentary*, 493.

6. "Israel, listen! Our God is the Lord! Only the Lord! Love the Lord your God with all your heart, all your being and all your strength" (Deut 6:4-5).
"You must love your neighbor as yourself: I am the Lord" (Lev 19:18b).

the real question, Jesus responds with a parable. A man journeys from Jerusalem to Jericho. He is robbed, beaten, and left on the side of the road. A priest comes along, and upon seeing him crosses over to the other side of the road and passes by. The same thing happened when a Levite encountered the man on the way. Then, a Samaritan came along and "was moved with compassion," took care of the man, and took him to a place where he could recuperate at the Samaritan's expense. Jesus concludes the story with the question: "Which one of these three was a neighbor to the man who encountered the thieves?" (10:36). The legal expert answered, "the one who demonstrated mercy," to which Jesus instructs "Go and do likewise" (10:37).

Jesus's storytelling is didactic. He first responds to the question with a question, and then answers the question with a story. The question is rooted in the Torah or Instruction of Leviticus. The law states God's people are to love their neighbor. The legal expert's question reflects the history of interpretation around this teaching. How far does this love extend? Who is my neighbor? The parable answer draws on wisdom traditions as it invites the man to learn from observation. In so doing, Jesus invites the legal expert and audience to interpret the law through the experiential lens of the man who has been beaten by robbers. On the roadside, outside of the places where the constructs of social status hold sway, every person who passes by has an opportunity to claim their humanity and assist the man in trouble. It is ironic that the person who helps is a Samaritan, a despised other. Another irony is that the legal expert who attempts to test Jesus is tested and bested by the teacher as it is the legal expert who ends up answering questions and receiving additional instruction.

The parable's lasting significance exists because of humanity's ongoing practice of maintaining lines of distinction along constructed lines that only insiders can understand. The parable invites listeners into an alternate universe where they find themselves by the side of the road either as a passerby or as a victim of violence. In what circumstances must our constructs of identity be put aside? How often do our identity constructs contribute to the suffering and death of others?

The Passion Narrative in Luke

Luke's account of Jesus's death and resurrection begins in Luke 22 and includes the following elements:

- Plot to kill Jesus
- Preparation for Passover
- Passover Meal/Last Supper
- Peter's denial predicted
- Jesus prays
- Jesus is arrested
- Peter denies Jesus
- Jesus is taunted
- Jesus appears before the council
- Jesus appears before Pilate
- Jesus comes before Herod
- The people choose Barabbas
- Journey to the cross; Simon of Cyrene
- Jesus dies
- Jesus is buried
- Empty tomb witnessed by Mary Magdalene, Joanna, Mary the mother of James, and the other women with them

Luke's account of the resurrection in chapter 24 has the same level of detail and narrative beauty as the story of Jesus's birth in chapter 2. Like the birth narrative, the event is facilitated by women. Three named women, Mary Magdalene, Joanna, Mary the mother of James, and "the other women with them," discover the empty tomb in their attempt to do women's work, namely tend to the corpse. Two angels appear to them when they enter the tomb and tell the terrified women about the resurrection. The women "remember his words" (24:8), and act on them, which is in contrast to the response of the male disciples, who initially discount the women's story and do not believe them (24:11). Also in similarity to the birth narrative, the resurrection account moves from location to location. The women come to the tomb and everything emanates, comes and goes, from that space. The tomb is recast not as a place for the dead, but as an incubator or womb from which new life comes. This is a powerful image for a community of faith in times of difficulty. Jesus's resurrection reminds the church that their suffering may result in glory. After the appearance of the angels to the women, Jesus himself appears to two followers on the Emmaus road (one of whom has a Greek name), and then finally to the disciples. The ordering of the appearances speaks to the identity of the Christian audience who receive it. Followers of Christ are women and men, Gentile and Jew, those steeped in the tradition and new converts. Jesus appears and is present to all. This Jesus came for all humanity, and it is to all humanity that Luke offers a "carefully ordered account for you . . . to have confidence in the soundness of the instruction you have received" (Luke 1:4). The Gospel's story continues in Acts, where the events in Jerusalem spread out from that place to the world.

Elements Unique to the Gospel of Luke

- Announcement of John's birth (1:5-25)
- Announcement of Jesus's birth (1:26-28)
- Mary visits Elizabeth (1:39-56)
- John's birth (1:57-80)
- Jesus's birth in a manger (2:1-20)
- Presentation in temple (2:21-38)
- Jesus visits the temple as a child (2:41-52)
- Genealogy (3:23-38)
- Good news to the poor (4:14-23, 25-30)
- Woman anoints Jesus's feet (7:36-50)
- Women disciples (8:1-3)
- Rejection by Samaritan village (9:51-56)
- Return of the Seventy (10:17-20)
- Mary and Martha (10:38-42)
- Zacchaeus (19:1-10)
- Jesus before Herod (23:6-12)
- Sayings at the cross (23:28-31, 34, 43, 46)
- Jesus on the road to Emmaus (24:13-35)
- Jesus appears to the disciples (24:36-49)
- Jesus's ascension (24:50-53)

Miracles

- Miraculous catch of fish (5:1-11)
- Raising of widow's son (7:11-17)
- Healing crippled woman (13:10-17)
- Healing of man with dropsy (14:1-6)
- Ten lepers healed (17:11-19)

Parables

- Two debtors (7:40-43)
- Good Samaritan (10:29-37)
- Friend at midnight (11:5-8)
- Rich fool (12:13-21)
- Severe and light beatings (12:47-48)
- Barren tree (13:1-9)
- Cost of discipleship (14:28-33)
- Lost coin (15:8-10)
- Prodigal son (15:11-32)
- Shrewd manager (16:1-12)
- Rich man and Lazarus (16:19-31)
- Widow and judge (18:1-8)
- Pharisee and tax collector (18:9-14)

CHAPTER 4

JOHN: IDENTITY THROUGH *LOGOS*

In the beginning was the Word
and the Word was with God
and the Word was God. (John 1:1)

OUTLINE	THEMES
1:1-18 Prologue 1:19–12:50 The Book of Signs 13:1–20:31 The Book of Glory 21:1-25 Epilogue	The mystery of the incarnation Jesus is God's beloved Son New birth

John is the last of the Gospels in both canonical order and date of authorship, probably written between 95–105 CE. The exquisitely elusive words of this Gospel are directed to a faith community struggling with their identity. Externally, there are the ongoing pressures from the Roman Empire. (Scholars debate the extent of that pressure.) Internally there are divisions over doctrine. The community to whom the Gospel is addressed is most likely diverse in ethnicity and religious backgrounds. There are competing theologies and doctrines, primarily centered on the answer to the question of who Jesus is. In response to this confusion, the Gospel presents a metaphorical universe, one that stands in stark contrast to the audience's fractured reality, crafted to introduce them to the Jesus they all thought they already knew.

Many of the elements that are standard in the Synoptic Gospels are absent from John's. There is no birth narrative or story of Jesus's baptism by John. There is no account of Jesus's temptation or transfiguration. John's Jesus does not eat with sinners or teach in parables. No demons are exorcised nor are the disciples called to deny themselves and leave their actual homes and families.[1] The writer of John acknowledges these differences as he articulates his purpose in the penultimate chapter:

> Jesus did many other miraculous signs in his disciples' presence, signs that aren't recorded in this scroll. But these things are written so that you will believe that Jesus is the Christ, God's Son, and that believing, you will have life in his name. (John 20:30-31)

It is only after the audience experiences the Gospel narrative that the writer discloses this Gospel's intention. John's approach is decidedly focused on the alternate universe he is creating, an alternate universe that invites the audience to know Jesus intimately, so that they will "believe," or "go on believing."[2] John's Gospel seeks to encourage and unify believers even as it seeks to bring new ones into the fold.

Famously described by Clement of Alexandria as the "spiritual gospel,"[3] John presents the mystery of Jesus. The prologue of John's Gospel is similar to a prophetic call narrative, containing the themes and theology of the book. The opening words, "in the beginning," intentionally evoke the opening words of Genesis, taking the reader back to what we know as the beginning of time, placing Jesus in a cosmic genealogy. Unlike the writer of Mark's Gospel, the writer of John is in no hurry. The words matter, in fact "every word counts": as John expands on the creative act of God's speech in Genesis 1, this Gospel will create Jesus "out of words."[4] John is less interested in the audience knowing Jesus's earthly lineage than his divine origin, and he presses the limits of language so that we might

1. Allan Powell, *Introducing the New Testament: A Historical, Literary, and Theological Survey* (Grand Rapids: Baker Academic, 2009), 178.

2. The tense of this phrase in John 20:31 could be present or aorist tense. If present, it should be translated "believe," but if aorist, it is translated "go on believing."

3. Powell, *Introducing the New Testament*, 169.

4. Wes Howard-Brook, "John's Gospel's Call to Be Reborn of God," in *The New Testament—Introducing the Way of Discipleship*, ed. Wes Howard-Brook and Sharon Ringe (Maryknoll, NY: Orbis, 2002), 81.

truly understand who this Jesus is. He is the word, *logos*, the metaphor selected so John can help the reader approach the mystery of the incarnation. In Greek thought, the word is more than language but "the rational principle" that belongs to human beings.[5] The writer of John casts *logos* as "event rather than system."[6] This is a dynamic way of knowing, achieved through experience. *Logos* is the creative force behind new life that comes to us though the organizing "metaphor . . . of birth."[7]

The language in John is so highly metaphorical and intentional that it forces the reader to engage the text on its terms. The prologue of the Gospel (1:1-18) assumes the form of a chiasm, a literary feature of John. Intentionally structured to emanate from, or point to a center, the shape of the prologue directs the audience to the purpose of the passage in 1:12-13.

A 1:1-5 Relationship of *Logos* to God, creation, humanity
  B 1:6-8 Witness of John the Baptist
    C 1:9-11 Journey of Light/*Logos*
      D 1:12-13 Gift of Authority to Become Children of God
    C' 1:14 Journey of *Logos*
  B' 1:15 Witness of John the Baptist
A' 1:16-18 Relationship of *Logos* to Humanity, "Recreation, God"[8]

John 1:12-13 offers a groundbreaking identity, namely "children of God," like the beloved son Jesus, "born not from blood . . . but . . . from God" (1:13). The cohesion of the Johannine community will be rooted in relationship, as every member takes on the same identity as a member of God's beloved family.

This new identity can only be attained by engaging metaphor, something we observe in Jesus's encounter with Nicodemus the Pharisee in

5. Howard-Brook, "John's Gospel's Call to Be Reborn of God," 81.

6. Carol Newsom, "Bakhtin, the Bible and Dialogic Truth," *Journal of Religion* 76, no. 2 (April 1996): 294. Newsom describes Bakhtin's dialogic truth using the phrase "event" not "system" to connote a dynamic experiential definition of truth that I believe is at work in John's Gospel.

7. Howard-Brook, "John's Gospel's Call to Be Reborn of God," 83.

8. Howard-Brook, "John's Gospel's Call to Be Reborn of God," 82.

chapter 3. The religious leader comes to Jesus "at night," seeking to know who Jesus is but doing so privately. A person of his station, a protector of the establishment, has something to lose by visiting the controversial teacher. Their exchange begins not with a question, but with a statement of acknowledgment by Nicodemus. "Rabbi, we know that you are a teacher who has come from God, for no one could do these miraculous signs that you do unless God is with him" (John 3:1). Jesus's response presumes an unspoken question. "I assure you, unless someone is born anew, it's not possible to see God's kingdom" (3:3). This statement makes as much sense to Nicodemus then as it does to us now, so we understand Nicodemus's follow-up question. "How is it possible? . . . It's impossible to enter the mother's womb for a second time and be born, isn't it?" (3:4). Jesus goes on to talk about flesh and spirit, and Nicodemus goes on to ask again, "How are these things possible?" (3:9). Nicodemus's question originates from his understanding of how the world operates—what is "possible." The answer is metaphorical, otherworldly. Jesus's response offers heavenly answers to Nicodemus's concerns over earthly things. Like God's call to Abraham, taking on this new identity in Christ, being born again, will require a complete abandonment not just of one's current identity, but of the very paradigm that creates that identity.

From a literary perspective, Nicodemus's night visit provides a platform for Jesus to articulate a metaphor for new life. However, Nicodemus comes to, and presumably leaves, Jesus in literal and perhaps theological darkness. At least, there is no record of any immediate response to Jesus's final comments. We do encounter Nicodemus again in chapters 7 and 19, where he exists in the "shadows," a secret follower who still maintains his status as a Pharisee. In chapter 7 he "defends" Jesus by reminding the opposing Pharisees that "our law doesn't judge someone without first hearing him and learning what he is doing, does it?" (7:51). In chapter 19:38-42, he is with Joseph of Arimathea, another secret follower of Jesus "because he feared the Jewish authorities" (19:38). He assists with Jesus's burial by purchasing the myrrh and aloe for burial.

Nicodemus's storyline likens the challenge of following Jesus to the disconnect between metaphorical and literal language. Understanding

Jesus's references to being "born again" requires the reader to leave behind the "world as we know it," and the particular challenge for Nicodemus the Pharisee is to leave behind the world where he enjoys privilege. The hardship of leaving his position as a Pharisee is as difficult as understanding what Jesus is talking about when he says, "You must be born anew" (3:7). Being identified with Christ requires abandoning one way of being for another, unknown way. Being born as children of God is not without the pain of labor, and this new identity with God is only possible through metaphor.

The metaphorical language of John constantly demands that the audience be willing to leave the known world for the imaginative universe that is evoked in Jesus's teaching. Whereas the symbolic and metaphorical language in the Synoptic Gospels is used to teach about the kingdom of heaven/God, the metaphorical language of John's Gospel is centered around Jesus. In John we observe again the way that scripture demands that the audience engage the text on its own terms. Jesus's language embodies the Bible's "tyrannical . . . claim to truth," which seeks not to "flatter us," but rather to "subject us."[9] This is particularly evident in what scholars refer to as the "I am" statements.

"I Am" Statements

The importance of metaphor is evidenced in the way in which Jesus discloses his identity to his audience in John's Gospel, employing a series of metaphorical rather than literal statements that demand that we exercise our imagination. Jesus says,

> I am the bread of life (John 6:35); I am the living bread (John 6:51).
>
> I am the light of the world (John 8:12; 9:5).
>
> I am the gate (John 10:7, 9).
>
> I am the good shepherd (John 10:11, 14).
>
> I am the resurrection and the life (John 11:25).

9. Erich Auerbach, *Mimesis: The Representation of Reality in Western Literature* (Princeton, NJ: Princeton University Press, 2003), 14–15.

I am the way, and the truth, and the life (John 14:6).

I am the vine (John 15:1, 5).

These statements are often placed in a context in which the audience is required to move from the literal or physical world to embrace another way of shared life together in community. For example, Jesus describes himself as the bread of life in the same chapter where he feeds the five thousand (John 6:1-14, 26-40).

In John 6, Jesus introduces his metaphorical bread of life in a lengthy discourse. A crowd of people who have followed him to the shore of the Sea of Galilee needs food. Jesus supplies it miraculously and then leaves. The next day the people pursued Jesus to the other side of the sea, and he begins to instruct them by saying, "I assure you that you are looking for me . . . because you ate all the food you wanted" (6:26). Once again the literal and the metaphorical collide when he turns the attention of his audience away from the literal food he had provided the previous day and talks about manna eaten by the Israelites in the wilderness as the bread of God, and then tells them that he is that bread. The listeners ask, "How can this man give us his flesh to eat?" Jesus insists that he is the bread from heaven and that "whoever eats this bread will live forever" (6:58). The disciples responded, "This message is harsh. Who can hear it?" (6:60).

Using the platform of providing actual bread for the body, Jesus makes a transition to describing himself as the bread they need most of all. Without warning, Jesus employs metaphor to move from the physical world where his listeners experience physical hunger to the real world where, unbeknownst to them, they are experiencing great spiritual hunger. This Jesus can take care of both, and he uses an experience they are familiar with to expose them to another reality. The "sign" does the work of metaphor in that it uses the familiar to introduce the audience to the unfamiliar.

Much the same thing can be said of the other metaphors that Jesus makes use of in identifying himself. The audience who hears all the "I am" statements knows what a gate, a shepherd, a vine, and a light are, but their knowledge is limited to the physical things they can see or feel. When Jesus inserts himself into the equation, the world they know becomes what

C. S. Lewis described as "shadowlands."[10] This may be why the miraculous acts in John are called signs. The work of the signs is to show the people who Jesus is, and in seeing Jesus through the shadowy mystery they can come to understand and know God.

One of the most compelling "I am" statements is found in John 15, where Jesus claims, "I am the vine." This image evokes the prophet Isaiah (Isa 5), who uses the vineyard image to describe Israel's relationship with God. In John 15, Jesus expounds on the nature of the relationship between Jesus, God the father, and the disciples using this image. These words, delivered before his crucifixion, provide the disciples with a paradigm for their relationships with God and each other going forward. They will thrive only as they are connected to the source and as they are tied to each other.

In addition to the seven metaphorical "I am" statements, the writer of John's Gospel has Jesus utter seven absolute "I am" sayings. Jesus says,

- "I Am" in response to the woman at the well when she says, "I know that the Messiah is coming" (John 4:25-26).
- The disciples were understandably afraid when they saw Jesus walking on the water, and he said to them, "I Am. Don't be afraid" (6:20).
- "If you don't believe that I Am, you will die in your sins" (8:24).
- "When the Human One is lifted up, then you will know that I Am" (8:28).
- "Before Abraham was, I Am" (8:58).
- "I am telling you this now, before it happens, so that when it does happen you will believe that I Am" (13:19).

10. In *The Last Battle*, the final volume of the Chronicles of Narnia, the characters discover upon entering Aslan's realm that the world they lived and died in was merely a "shadowland" of Aslan's realm. These two realms evoked in the popular fiction draw on the imagery we see in John's Gospel. Jesus introduces the ultimate reality to a people who have lived in the shadows.

- To those seeking to arrest him, Jesus asked, "Who are you looking for?" They replied, "Jesus the Nazarene," to which he responded, "I Am" (18:4-5). When he answered in this way, they fell. Jesus repeated the question: "Who are you looking for?" Again they replied, "Jesus the Nazarene," and he said, "I told you, 'I Am'" (18:7-8).

The absolute "I am" statements begin and end with Jesus. These words evoke God's revelation to Moses on Mount Horeb/Sinai. When Moses asked the god of the mountain his name, the response was "I am/will be what I am/will be."

The Passion Narrative in John

In John's Gospel, Jesus's death and resurrection takes place in the wake of the resurrection of Lazarus. This sign, with its prophetic overtones reminiscent of Elijah (1 Kgs 17), is perceived by the religious leaders as a threat to institutional religion, and we see their response played out as the narrative action shifts to Jesus's crucifixion (John 11:48-50).

- The chief priests and Pharisees plot to kill Jesus.
- The disciples prepare for the Passover.
- Mary anoints Jesus's feet.
- Jesus enters Jerusalem.
- Jesus talks about his death.
- Jesus washes the disciples' feet.
- Last Supper
- Jesus announces his betrayal.
- Commandment to love
- Jesus announces Peter's denial.
- Teaching
- Jesus prays in the garden.

- Jesus is arrested, tried, beaten, and crucified.
- Jesus is buried in the tomb of Joseph of Arimathea.
- The risen Jesus appears to Mary Magdalene.

The account of Jesus's appearance to Mary Magdalene in the garden, unique to John, is one of the more iconic Gospel narratives. Mary makes her way to the tomb "while it was still dark" only to find the stone removed. She runs to tell Peter, who comes and, indeed, finds the tomb empty, at which he "saw and believed." Peter leaves, but Mary remains, weeping. There she has an encounter with Jesus, whom she doesn't recognize until he calls her by name, saying "Mary." In calling her name, Jesus invites Mary out of her confusion and grief to recognize him. He is inviting her to remember that she does in fact know him, and she can recognize him as the risen Lord if she will focus on his voice. The story of Jesus's recognition is not just about the event but about the disciples' ability to see and interpret the signs to discover the truth that is always a mystery: Jesus is fully divine and fully human. He died and is now alive, and his followers have the gift of the companion to lead them through the challenges of a shared Christian life together.

As the last of the Gospels in both order and date, John's focus on knowing Jesus more than proclaiming the kingdom of God may also reflect an acknowledgment that the expected return of Jesus, the *parousia,* has not occurred. This delay resulted in a shift in understanding about the identity of the church as something beyond waiting for the return. Now they must become a community of those who identify with Christ and are the children of God. Until Christ's return, the language and the alternate universe that it calls into being casts them as waiting for new life supported by birth imagery. In this sense the birth narrative in John is not for Jesus but for the people who will become the Children of God in the world.

Elements Unique to the Gospel of John

- Calling of Andrew, Philip, and Nathaniel (1:35-51)
- Changing water into wine (2:1-12)
- Night meeting with Nicodemus (3:1-21)
- Meeting with the Samaritan woman at the well (4:1-42)
- Healing of the man at Bethsaida's pool (5:1-18)
- Saving a woman from stoning (7:53–8:11)
- Healing of a man born blind (9:1-41)
- Raising of Lazarus (11:1-44)
- Washing of disciples' feet (13:1-20)
- Prayer for believers (17:1-26)
- Resurrection appearance to Thomas (20:24-29)

Part Two

THE ACTS OF THE APOSTLES

CHAPTER 5
THE ACTS OF THE APOSTLES

OUTLINE	THEMES
1–7 Jerusalem 8–12 Judea and Samaria 13–28 Out in the world	The Holy Spirit The church in Jerusalem and beyond

Although written by the same author who penned the Gospel of Luke, the book of Acts is more than "Luke, the sequel." It differs from the Gospel in genre and emphasis. The main character in Luke is Jesus, and the Gospel makes a claim about Jesus in and beyond history. The book of Acts, which takes place in a post-Jesus world, is presented in the form of ancient historiography with a focus on events in the life of Jesus's followers that contributed to the origin of what would become the church in and beyond Jerusalem. The book's placement, between the Gospels and the Letters, supports the overall structure of the New Testament by providing a transition from the life of Jesus to the establishment and growth of the church in Jerusalem, Judea, and the world beyond.[1] The main character in Acts, however, is not the highlighted individuals, especially Peter and Saul/Paul, but rather the Holy Spirit. The people who act here do so in supporting roles. To the extent that the book is in no way limited to the twelve apostles and the action comes from the Holy Spirit, the assigned title, the Acts of the Apostles, should signal the reader to read between the lines—this is a history of identity and identity politics. And the identity is that of the people of God as those who believe in Jesus.

1. Asia Minor, Greece, and Rome.

As a history of the early church, Acts is a "selection and interpretation of events from a certain perspective and within certain agendas."[2] One agenda of the early church is to construct an identity made up of followers of Jesus after the ascension. Up until this moment, the followers of Jesus were those who literally followed Jesus; this relatively small group will develop into a movement known as the Way. As the Way expands geographically and grows in membership, it must renegotiate its identity again and again. Jesus's original followers were Jews, believers in the God of Israel. How does that identity change when Gentiles come into the fold? To what extent does Greco-Roman culture interact with and influence the identity? In its effort to construct an origin story for an increasingly large and diverse community, Acts makes use of literary devices and subgenres, like speeches, travel narratives, dialogues, miracles, and sermons.[3] Additionally, Acts shapes its story by making use of characterization and location, with a particular focus on two important men: Peter and Saul, who would become Paul. In the first part of Acts, Peter shapes this identity as a disciple, preacher, miracle worker, and leader who comes to the fore at the celebration of Pentecost. The expansion of the church in the latter chapters is associated with the Apostle Paul.

Pentecost

Acts begins in anticipation of Pentecost. Chapter 1 contains a summary of the events that took place between Luke's story of Jesus's resurrection and his ascension. The risen Jesus is described as being with his disciples for forty days, preparing them for his departure. He instructs them to wait in Jerusalem for the promised Holy Spirit. When the disciples ask if it is Jesus's intent to restore the nation of Israel, Jesus replies,

2. Justo González, "Acts of the Apostles," in *The New Testament—Introducing the Way of Discipleship,* ed. Wes Howard-Brook and Sharon Ringe (Maryknoll, NY: Orbis, 2002), 105.

3. Bart Ehrman, *The New Testament: A Historical Introduction to the Early Christian Writings* (Oxford: Oxford University Press, 2000), 123.

> It isn't for you to know the times or seasons that the father has set by his own authority. Rather, you will receive power when the Holy Spirit has come upon you, and you will be my witnesses in Jerusalem, in all Judea and Samaria, and to the end of the earth. (Acts 1:7-8)

Immediately after giving these instructions, Jesus ascends into heaven and two heavenly messengers appear and send the disciples on their way to Jerusalem. Acts recounts that the "family of believers was a company of about one hundred twenty persons" (1:15). It is upon this group of followers, "all together in one place" (2:1), that the promised Holy Spirit descends in chapter 2. The arrival of the Holy Spirit is the point of orientation for the book as a whole and is also the moment the church is born. The time and location of the Holy Spirit's arrival is no coincidence.

The historian of Acts describes the event of the Holy Spirit's arrival so that it is in dialogue with Pentecost, the Jewish holy day referred to in the Hebrew scriptures as the Festival of Weeks. Locating the event in Jerusalem signals its significance. Pentecost takes place fifty days after Passover and commemorates God's providence and the giving of the Torah on Mount Sinai.[4] Thus the dispensation of the Spirit at this time sets up a dialogue between the Law (Instruction) and the Spirit. The Holy Spirit's arrival on Pentecost both honors and redefines the holy day. In the accounts of the earliest days of the church we observe a tension between the Instruction, which comes to represent the establishment, and the Spirit, which is a constantly moving target.

The Pentecost event happens in Jerusalem, which is the location of the temple where the God of Israel is worshipped, and the city that would also become the epicenter of the early church. Jerusalem is the place from which it all emanates. As the "headquarters" of the early church, the choice of location brings with it certain assumptions. In particular, Jerusalem is a reminder of Christianity's rootedness in Judaism, its practices and people. As the church grows, it must reckon with the expansion beyond that ethnicity and practices—for example, circumcision and the dietary laws. One identity trope in Acts is that of being rooted and formed in Judaism, but not limited to Judaism. The event that takes place in Jerusalem is intended

---

4. The name "Pentecost" signals the fifty-day period between the two holy days.

to demonstrate that God's power extends beyond Jerusalem to "all Judea and Samaria, and to the end of the earth" (Acts 1:8). This is evidenced in the Spirit giving the disciples the ability to speak in other languages. Also, although the Holy Spirit comes to the disciples in Jerusalem, it comes not in the temple, but rather in a house, which foreshadows the form of many first-century churches that will meet in houses. Instead of being worshipped in one centralized location, the gift of the Holy Spirit will enable Christians to experience God as mobile. The presence of God will be with them as it was in the tabernacle in the wilderness.

The gift of the Holy Spirit is God's ongoing presence and power, and the book of Acts offers an account of how the Spirit empowers and supports this newly birthed, revolutionary movement. The book's structure reflects the movement of the disciples as they bear witness to Christ in Jerusalem, Judea, and Samaria, out to the world. The geographic pattern reflects the expansion of the movement to include Gentiles.

Pentecost and Babel

The story of Pentecost is often compared or paired with the story of the Tower of Babel. The latter comes at the end of the primeval history and signals the beginning of divisions among humanity on the basis of language and by extension, geography, ethnicity, and race. The dispensation of the Holy Spirit does not eliminate the other languages, nor does everyone find commonality in one. Rather, the disciples are gifted with the ability to speak in other languages. The ability to communicate in other languages, polyglotism, is a gift not only for the one who receives the message, but for the one who gives it. Multiple languages improve and enhance the cognitive abilities of the learners. Theologically, the event of Pentecost births the church in diversity. From a dialogic perspective, there could be no better beginning to the Christian movement. The foundation of the faith is tied to a variety of sounds, figures of speech, sound pairs, and worldviews. In other words, Christianity in its nascent form embraces polyphony,[5] which means that Peter will not be the only leader of the church.

5. Polyphony is a musical term that refers to two or more melodic parts that are sounded together. It is also used in dialogic criticism to refer to the "'many-voicedness' of texts in which characters and narrator speak on equal terms." Sue Vice, *Introducing Bakhtin* (Manchester: Manchester University Press, 1998), 6.

St. Peter, the Apostle

In the Gospels, the composite image of Peter, also known as Simon and Simon Peter, is complex. Capable of both great insights and major mishaps, he is depicted as impetuous and daring, often speaking without thinking. He is the disciple who risked walking on the water to meet Jesus (Matt 14:29). He is the one who cut off the ear of the high priest's servant (Luke 22:49-51; John 18:10-11) when the soldiers came to arrest Jesus. He initially refused to have Jesus wash his feet (John 13:8), and he is the one who is remembered for denying Jesus three times. He is also the disciple who answered correctly, when Jesus asked his followers (Luke 9:18-20; Matt 16:13-16; Mark 8:27-29), "Who do the crowds say that I am?" and also when he asked, "And what about you? Who do you say that I am?" In Matthew's account of this exchange, Jesus's response to Peter's statement includes the words, "I tell you that you are Peter. And I'll build my church on this rock. The gates of the underworld won't be able to stand against it" (Matt 16:18). This statement is particularly important to Peter's role in Acts and in the church that is ultimately built. Jesus changed his name from Simon or Simeon to Cephas, an Aramaic name with the Greek equivalent of *Petras,* which means "rock."

The initial days after Pentecost are marked by amazement. It is after the indwelling of the Holy Spirit in Acts that Peter is transformed from the unpredictable follower of Jesus in the Gospels to the apostle who takes a leadership role in the early church in the book of Acts. In chapter 2, Peter is the preacher who delivers a famous Pentecost sermon that uses the prophetic text of Job and the Psalms in an interpretation of Israel's history that argues that Jesus is the Christ. On that day three thousand people "accepted Peter's message" (2:41). Peter then heals a lame man and upon seeing a crowd of people, delivers another sermon (3:12-26). Angry and, perhaps frightened, the religious leaders put Peter and John, who was with him, in prison and then had them questioned by the Sanhedrin. When confronted by the religious leaders, "Peter, inspired by the Holy Spirit" (4:8), addressed them with such force that they were "caught by surprise by the confidence" with which these men, whom they understood "were uneducated and inexperienced" spoke (4:13). Everything that has happened in these days, from teaching and preaching to imprisonment and persecution by religious gatekeepers to miracles and phenomenal growth, is recorded with a sense of wonder. The arrival of the Holy Spirit allows the followers of Jesus to move forward with power and authority through any kind of trial, challenge, or conflict.

In these first chapters of Acts, readers can see the words of Jesus's commission (Luke 24:47-48) come to fruition as the Holy Spirit empowers the disciples to be witnesses to Christ in Jerusalem. The Holy Spirit enables the disciples to preach with power and also to live in a new kind of community. All those who identified themselves as followers of Christ sold their possessions, pooled the funds, and allowed the apostles to decide how the funds would be used (Acts 2:42-47 and 4:32-35). All that is described in the early chapters of Acts confirms that the Holy Spirit truly is the "heavenly power" (Luke 24:49) needed to bear witness to Jesus. The Holy Spirit is the transforming force in the lives of the main human actors, Peter and Paul in particular.

Stephen and Philip

Although Peter and Paul are the most familiar characters in the book of Acts, others play important roles as well. The stories of both Stephen and Philip serve the literary function of transitioning the focus of the narrative from Peter to Paul. Stephen's story begins with Peter and ends with Paul. A crisis of church administration and mission introduces Stephen in the narrative. The Greek-speaking Christians claimed discrimination at the hands of the Aramaic-speaking Christians when it came to the daily distribution of food to their widows. The solution arrived at by the "the twelve" was to appoint deacons, seven men, to serve tables. One of these deacons was Stephen, a man "full of faith and the Holy Spirit" (6:5 NRSV) who "stood out among the believers for the way God's grace was at work in his life" (6:8). The presence of the Holy Spirit in Stephen led to opposition. Stephen gives a sermon (nearly one thousand words) that so enrages the religious leaders and the crowd of those who witness it that they drag Stephen out of the city and stone him. Present at the stoning of

Stephen, holding the coats of those who participated, was a young man named Saul, who "was in full agreement with Stephen's murder" (8:1).

Philip's story focuses on the promised spread of the gospel to Samaria, where Philip is sent, and ultimately to "the end of the earth" (1:8). After a successful mission to Samaria, the writer of Acts describes Philip's encounter with an Ethiopian eunuch, an encounter that is facilitated by the supernatural agency. An angel instructs Philip to take a desert road where he encounters an official of the Ethiopian Queen Candace. The man is reading the prophet Isaiah, which, he admits to Philip, he is unable to understand. Philip explains the passage and proclaims the good news of Jesus so powerfully that the official requests baptism. After Philip baptizes the eunuch, the "Lord's Spirit suddenly took Philip away" (8:39). This supernatural transport is reminiscent of Elijah, who was transported in 1 Kings 18:12 and 2 Kings 2:1. Thus, Philip's mission is told in a way that looks back and evokes the words of the prophet Isaiah and the stories of the prophet Elijah and also looks forward, to the scope of Paul's missionary work to Gentiles beyond Jerusalem and Samaria.

Women in Acts

In the book of Acts, the representation of women can be used to measure the extent to which the early church was countercultural or fell prey to the patterns of the patriarchy of the external society and culture of the time. The early Christian community was, in many ways, a countercultural witness to the alternative kingdom of heaven that opposed the patterns of the Roman Empire. Material goods were shared, and women had more equality (1:14; 2:42-44; 5:32-35). The text confirms the presence of women in the house on Pentecost (1:13-14), so we know they were recipients of the Holy Spirit. Women were teachers (18:26) and patrons (16:11-15). They offered hospitality (12:12) and exercised prophetic gifts (21:9).[6] And yet, women in the book of Acts remain, for the most part, in obscurity, leading scholars to conclude that by the time Acts was written,

6. Ginger Gaines-Cirelli, "Acts," in *The CEB Women's Bible* (Nashville: Abingdon Press, 2016), 1372.

the egalitarian vision that characterized the early church was already being subsumed by the culture of the Greco-Roman world. The Edenic moment of full humanity for all disciples of Christ gave way to a post-Edenic world weighed down by hierarchy and difference.

Sometimes history is less about the facts and more about the way a story is told. In the case of the portrayal of women, the story is told in a way that tells about the moment the church was infiltrated by the brokenness of patriarchy. The portrayal of women in Acts, then, is not a historically accurate account of women's roles in the church but it is a painfully honest portrayal of the distance between the Pentecost community and the institutional church.

St. Paul, the Apostle

Paul's identity is intentionally constructed in Acts. In chapter 13, the narrative of Saul in Cyprus reveals that Saul also has a Roman name, Paul. The two names signal his dual identities as a Jew who is also a Roman citizen. Born in Tarsus, he was educated by Gamaliel, a prominent Jewish teacher. He spoke Aramaic and Greek, and he would go on to carry the message of the gospel as a Jew to the Gentiles.[7] Originally introduced by his Hebrew name Saul, he first appears in the text as one who supported the stoning of Stephen and who, zealous in the practice of his religious beliefs, goes on to become an active persecutor of Christians. On the road to Damascus to arrest followers of Jesus, he has an encounter with Jesus, an iconic conversion experience. This encounter with the risen Lord and the commission by Jesus earns Saul the title "apostle." In his letter to the Corinthian church, Paul describes his status as apostle: "[Jesus] appeared to Cephas, then to the Twelve . . . and last of all he appeared to me, as if I were born at the wrong time" (1 Cor 15:5, 8). The encounter on the road to Damascus is like the call narratives of the prophets, and lends him an authority that he will need to carry out his mission to take the gospel to the Gentiles.

---

7. F. Scott Spencer, "Saul/Paul," in *The CEB Study Bible*, ed. Joel B. Green (Nashville: Abingdon Press, 2013), 243 NT.

Paul's church-planting journeys take him from Jerusalem to modern-day Greece, Turkey, Spain, and Italy's capital city of Rome. He corresponds with his church plants and with congregations with whom he hoped to become acquainted. In his letters we find a master of rhetoric, an apologist for the gospel, and an eloquent theologian. The effectiveness of Paul's letters is evidenced in their continued use and presence in Christian faith communities today. Not everyone agrees with or likes Paul, but his contribution to Christian theology is undeniable. Paul is the director of formation for those first fledgling Christian communities who responded to the gospel message but had to figure out what it meant to be a Christian in day-to-day life. There were practical issues to navigate, including around dietary laws and ritual observances, which were grounded in doctrinal concepts like righteousness, grace, faith, and works.

Paul and Barnabas, who is called by the Holy Spirit to accompany Paul on his first missionary journeys, were sent by the Greek church in Antioch to the Jerusalem council in chapter 15. There they met with James and other leaders of the Jerusalem church to negotiate requirements of circumcision for male Gentile Christians. One cannot help but wonder if the obsession with male genitalia would be lessened had women had a more prominent role! Nevertheless, the men came to the agreement that Gentiles would not have to be circumcised but must refrain from "the pollution associated with idols, sexual immorality, eating meat from strangled animals, and consuming blood" (15:20b). This record demonstrates that some regulations in the life of the church are arrived at through compromise and shaped by context.

Paul's roots in Judaism, which will play a role in his letters, allowed him to explain the Jewish foundation of certain aspects of the faith even as he redefines them. His letters to the churches he plants are a record of his formative teaching to them as he responds to their specific contexts and needs. Because Christianity is birthed out of Judaism, and the early church included Jewish and Gentile members, the construct of identity for this new people of God often struggled around both religious practices, such as circumcision, and theological concepts, like the grace of God. These matters are both recurring themes in Paul's letters to the churches.

The book of Acts ends with Paul in Rome preaching and teaching, before his trial and martyrdom. For the reader, a conclusion with Paul still active in ministry serves as a nice transition to the Pauline and deutero-Pauline letters that follow Acts in the canon. The open-ended ending of the book is, however, unsettling. Readers seek a conclusion that answers their questions. What happens to Paul and the expanding church? What happens to the church in Jerusalem? Is the conflict between Jewish and Christian believers finally resolved? Although some answers are provided in the epistles themselves, the nonconclusive ending serves as a reminder that the work of the Holy Spirit with which the story began is unending. This is indeed a book about the Acts of the Holy Spirit and not the Apostles.

Diaspora and Empire

The locations that shape the book of Acts begin with Jerusalem and emanate "to the end of the earth" (1:8). Perhaps the most important location, identified by theologian Willie Jennings, is not a particular geographic place but rather the space between diaspora and empire. The early church is birthed out of a diaspora community that is under the regime of the Roman Empire. As the fledgling community of faith evolves it does so "caught up in the grip of diaspora and empire."[8] This tension and this dynamic are defining characteristics of the church. It is present in the representation of women and the ongoing struggle to include Gentiles. This defining characteristic of the church continues to be repeated by followers of Christ who must discern the voice of the Holy Spirit out of all other voices that seek to influence and shape the church.

8. Willie James Jennings, *Acts: A Theological Commentary on the Bible* (Louisville: Westminster John Knox, 2017), 6.

Make Sure Not to Miss . . .

- Pentecost, 2:1-41
- Office of deacons created, 6:1-7
- Stephen's stoning, 6:8–7:60
- Philip and the Ethiopian, 8:26-40
- Saul's conversion, 9:1-32
- The Jerusalem Council, 15:1-35
- Paul travels to Rome, 27–28

Part Three

THE LETTERS

Twenty-one of the twenty-seven New Testament books are letters, which means the majority of sacred writings in the canon of the early church take the form of dialogue, that is, conversation between parties separated by distance. In this way ancient letters are like old voicemail messages, which capture a moment in time, a part of a larger conversation, and thus reading the letter requires a different type of imagination. The vast majority of the letters are "occasional letters," written under specific circumstances to address a particular situation. The original audience believed the writer to be present in the letter itself, so it was read (or heard, since the letters were originally read aloud) as a reflection of the author's unique personality and beliefs.[1]

The Gospels and Old Testament stories take the reader on a journey into an alternate narrative universe. The rules of engagement resemble those for reading fiction. With the letters, the reader approaches and engages the material with an approach similar to reading nonfiction. The letter reader is like a detective, listening for clues in the references, figures of speech, historical references, and tone, since these elements may provide a window into the day-to-day matters of concern to the writers and the communities to whom they were addressed. Through the letters we learn about the variety of challenges encountered by the early believers and the churches they were a part of and how those challenges were unique to each context. We are also able to consider how circumstances change over time and how interpretation of scripture and practices adjusted. For example, we have more than one letter to the church at Corinth, and from that extended dialogue, we are able to imagine

1. *Harper's Bible Commentary*, ed. James L. Mays (San Francisco: Harper and Row,1988), 1120.

how the church changed over time. Together, the letters give us a mosaic image of the early church that is simultaneously fascinating, reassuring, incomplete, and troubling.

Written by Paul, James, Peter, John, Jude, and other church leaders, the canonical ordering of the letters begins with Paul's letters to churches and to individuals (ordered by length), followed by Hebrews (which reads like a sermon), followed by the letters written by James, Peter, John, and Jude. Of the twenty-one letters, thirteen are associated with the Apostle Paul, although not all are actually authored by him, and are categorized as either Pauline or deutero-Pauline. Other categories for the non-Pauline Letters are the Pastoral and the General (Catholic) letters.[2] The New Testament letters follow the literary conventions of letter writing in the Greco-Roman world. Their structure usually includes a greeting, thanksgiving, and a stated theme, followed by the body of the letter, and the closing formula.

Because these letters address first-century Christian communities, they form a dialogue with the book of Acts, at times corroborating or contradicting an event in Acts history, which makes no reference to the letters. The letters are also evidence of events in the Roman Empire and Greco-Roman world and where this growing movement fits in. Letters are also in dialogue with the Gospels—how does the church interpret, understand, and utilize the good news of the gospel, and how did faith communities interpret and reinterpret Jesus's words in light of their circumstances? Letters are in dialogue with each other, inviting us to discern how context and community play a role in the formation of the communities. In the end, the letters then and now form an ongoing dialogue with readers. The rhetoric and imagery of the letters transcend their earlier contexts. They are a part of the Christian canon that is interpreted and reinterpreted. For that reason, they continue to form identity.

2. Mark Allan Powell, *Introducing the New Testament: A Historical, Literary, and Theological Survey* (Grand Rapids: Baker Academic, 2009), 216.

Pauline and Deutero-Pauline

We begin with letters from Paul, a dominant figure in the early church. His missionary work and letters have irrevocably shaped the Christian tradition. The letters are ordered from longest to shortest, Romans to Philemon. Of the thirteen letters associated with the apostle, scholars agree that seven of this group were written by Paul: Romans, 1 Thessalonians, 1 and 2 Corinthians, Philemon, Galatians, and Philippians. This assessment is made on the basis of literary style (vocabulary, writing style, and composition), theology (consistency in what Paul says about God and Jesus), ethics (whether the letters reflect the radical freedom and equality that defines the Way), and fit with the overall narrative (whether the letter fits within the witness in Acts and the other letters).[3] These criteria are complicated and imperfect and a detailed discussion is beyond the scope of this work. However, if this assessment is correct, almost half of the letters attributed to Paul are pseudonymous, meaning they were written by followers of or in the tradition of Paul. These non-Pauline Letters are included in the canon, and thereby considered and reckoned with as inspired writings.

As a part of the Christian canon, the ongoing formation of the first-century church, as seen in the letters, is a snapshot of an identity in process. How, then, does one interpret and apply these texts in faith communities today? Some Christian congregations cite passages from these texts to justify a refusal to ordain women as clergy. Others cite Paul's proclamation that there is neither "Jew nor Greek . . . slave nor free . . . male and female" (Gal 3:28), to take the opposite position. The church in its current manifestation continues to struggle with an identity birthed out of Pentecost and shaped by its current context and culture. In this regard, how one reads matters greatly. The tools of the detective to uncover context, authorship, editing, and style will take the reader to a certain point. The interpretation of these clues requires a holy imagination.

3. Luke Timothy Johnson, *The Writings of the New Testament* (Minneapolis: Fortress, 2010), 256.

The Pastoral Letters

First and Second Timothy and Titus are called the Pastoral Epistles or Letters because they address general, pastoral concerns, particularly around leadership structure. These concerns are addressed to a time in the development and growth of the Christian tradition (third generation of Christian experience, 90–110 CE), when Domitian was the Roman emperor. The Christianity of the Pastoral Letters is not the same Jesus movement that characterized the early church, where the Holy Spirit was depicted like a character that moved the people of the Way to a radically expansive vision of the kingdom of God. Rather these letters depict the transmission and transformation of a faith tradition from one generation to the next.[4] The Pastoral Letters fit under the category of "pseudonymous" Pauline authorship.[5] Paul's authorship of these letters is disputed because they seem to reflect a later time in the life of the church. Had Paul written them, they (2 Timothy and Titus) would have been his last letters before his martyrdom.

The conceptual grouping of these letters together reveals a converging image of the Christian communities—one that is rooted in Judaism but not bound by its practices. In these letters we observe the Christian assemblies attempting to maintain a unique identity through teaching, even as it is shaped by Greco-Roman culture and values.

General Letters

The General or Catholic letters are James, 1 and 2 Peter, 1, 2, and 3 John, and Jude. This term indicated letters addressed to the church at large, more so than a specific congregation. Even these general audiences had a specific worldview in mind, which is why it is important to remem-

4. Clarice J. Martin, "1–2 Timothy and Titus (the Pastoral Epistles)," in *True to Our Native Land: An African American New Testament Commentary,* ed. Brian Blount (Minneapolis: Fortress, 2007), 409.

5. Pseudonymous authorship refers to a practice where a disciple of the "author" writes in the name and presumed tradition of the author. The disciple writes to "honor—but adapt—the idea of an earlier author." Martin, "1–2 Timothy and Titus," 410.

ber that all the letters are dialogues. All of them, even those composed for more general use, were written to be read aloud. The general letters signal an acknowledgment on the part of the early church that the growth of the church would demand more than occasional letters. Yet even the general letters are a reflection of a particular moment in time and a specific worldview. Because of their intended broader audience, the general letters demand a dialogic reading.

CHAPTER 6

ROMANS

OUTLINE	THEMES
1:1-7 Greeting 1:8-14 Thanksgiving 1:15-17 Theme: The Gospel is the power of salvation 1:18–15:43 Body of the letter 1:18–4:25 God's response to sin 5:1–8:39 The impact of Christ's death and resurrection 9:1–11:36 God's faithfulness and Israel's future 12:1–15:13 Faithful living 15:14-33 Paul's mission and God's plan 16:1-27 Closing	The gospel: Christ's death and resurrection have the power to save Righteousness redefined Grace

Paul's letter to the church of Rome was written between 57 and 58 CE and is one of the apostle's later letters. However, because the letters are presented in the canon by length from longest to shortest, Romans serves as the gateway to the other New Testament letters. This is a fortuitous placement, for it is arguably the most influential of all Paul's writings. In Romans, Paul offers what is frequently described as a definition of what it means to be a follower of Jesus. He expounds on God's righteousness, the nature of grace, justification, salvation, and the relationship between the spirit and the law. And he does so with great effectiveness—so much so that a virtual "who's who" of Christian thought leaders including Augustine, Martin Luther, and John Wesley cite Romans as a transformative text in their personal formation.[1] Romans is foundational for many teachings and traditions in Christianity. In fact, many describe Romans as the biblical book containing the foundations of systematic theology, that is, an ordered and coherent summary of all things that are foundational to the faith tradition. One scholar lists ten ways that Paul describes the work of Christ—eight of which can be found in Romans:[2]

Justification—Humanity is acquitted, righteous before God	Rom 3:21-26
Salvation—Humanity is rescued from evil and wrath	Rom 5:9; Phil 3:2
Reconciliation—Humanity is restored to right relationship with God and one another	Rom 5:10-11; 2 Cor 5:18-19
Expiation—Humanity's sins are blotted out, wiped away	Rom 3:25
Redemption—Humanity is bought back from slavery to sin and death	Rom 8:18-23; 1 Cor 7:23
Freedom—Humanity set free from sin and the law	Rom 8:2; Gal 5:1
Sanctification—Humanity is made holy	1 Cor 1:2, 30; 6:11
Transformation—Humanity is changed into the image of God	Rom 12:2; 2 Cor 3:18
New Creation—Humanity is given new life	2 Cor 5:17; Gal 2:20–6:15
Glorification—Humanity shares in the glory of God	Rom 8:18, 21, 30; 1 Thess 2

Paul writes to the church at Rome, a community he did not know, at a critical time in his own ministry. He writes not only to expound on fundamental teachings for the growing religious community, which must form an identity that is inclusive of both Jewish and Gentile believers, but he

1. Mark Allan Powell, *Introducing the New Testament: A Historical, Literary, and Theological Survey* (Grand Rapids: Baker Academic, 2009), 255.

2. Joseph Fitzmyer, *Paul and His Theology: A Brief Sketch*, 2nd ed. (Englewood Cliffs, NJ: Pearson, 1989), 59–71.

writes primarily to introduce himself. In telling his story he makes a case for the Christian faith. In Romans we observe that Paul is both a master of rhetoric, and also a gifted storyteller.

Whatever else it does, Paul's letter to the Romans offers a summary of the gospel Paul proclaimed.[3] However, when one considers the genre, whether letter or theological discourse, and the context in which it was written, it is more useful to describe Romans as practical theology, or Paul's embodied theology rather than systematic theology.

Introduction: 1:1-7

Paul's opening greeting begins with one long sentence, which, like much of the letter, sounds more doctrinal than dialogical. This is clearly not the standard opening for a conventional piece of Greco-Roman correspondence. The letter's addressees are not mentioned until verse 7. Instead, Paul's focus is on himself in relationship to Jesus. Paul describes himself as *doulos,* a servant or a slave. With this term he invites the audience into a very particular theological landscape. In the Greek culture and philosophy, freedom was prized as the pinnacle of human achievement within society. Slavery would be the antithesis of this desired status. In the Roman world, enslavement was a symbol of the empire's power over its subjects or the evidence of wealth and economic influence. So Paul's use of *doulos* is designed to grab the attention of the readers to whom the letter is directed. No one wants to be a *doulos,* but by using this word to describe himself and his relationship to Christ, he introduces or evokes a sense of indebtedness, calling to memory those who found themselves in slavery for a debt they could not pay. Moreover, with this word, often translated as "servant" rather than "slave," Paul also aligns himself with other servants and their roles. In the Septuagint, the Greek translation of the Hebrew Bible, the term refers to "people used by God to carry forward God's purpose," a concept further developed in Isaiah to depict God's

3. Thomas L. Hoyt Jr., "Romans," in *True to Our Native Land: An African American New Testament Commentary,* ed. Brian Blount (Minneapolis: Fortress, 2007), 250.

slave or servant as someone who must be prepared to suffer and die.[4] Christ is the ultimate example of this *doulos,* and he is the one to whom Paul is now *doulos.*

The introduction goes on to specifically root Jesus's identity in the line of David, and proceeds to claim him as "God's Son," the one resurrected from the dead, and the conduit of God's grace to all who are "called" by Jesus, including "Gentiles" (Rom 1:4-6). With that compelling description, Paul sets the tone for this letter. By introducing himself as a willing servant of the ultimate servant who effectively makes God's grace available to everyone, Paul tells his audience what is to be expected of them.

After the introduction comes a thanksgiving for the people of the Roman church in 1:8-15, which is followed by a statement of the letter's theme in 1:16-17:

> I'm not ashamed of the gospel: it is God's own power for salvation to all who have faith in God, to the Jew first and also to the Greek. God's righteousness is being revealed in the gospel, from faithfulness for faith, as it is written, *The righteous person will live by faith.*[5]

This statement is a personal one. It is Paul's testimony. In a corporate setting we would see this as Paul's "branding" or mission statement. The gospel, the good news, as proclaimed by Paul, not only saved him but has the power to save all who believe, Jews and Greeks. Salvation is the formative event, and the central action that changes everything. Salvation is the transformative event that makes both Jews and Gentiles God's people. In some of the early churches, the Jewish community struggled to accept Gentiles. It is possible that in the Roman church, the opposite was the case and that part of Paul's work was to explain Israel's role in God's story of salvation.[6] Here the apostle exercises his gifts as a storyteller in reviewing the gospel story that includes him. In proclaiming this gospel through story, Paul essentially invites his readers to give up and abandon

4. Hoyt, "Romans," 250.

5. The italicized words represent a citation of Habakkuk 2:4.

6. Leander Keck, notes on "Romans," in *The Harper Collins Study Bible* (New York: HarperOne, 2017), 1910.

the other stories that have shaped their lives[7] and claim the story of God's righteousness. Because God's righteousness by its nature extends to all of God's creation, it is as they receive it, their origin story. In this way, the common narrative allows all followers of Jesus to be grafted into one tree (Rom 11:16-24).

In the body of the letter (1:8–11), Paul expounds on the righteousness of God. For Paul, God's righteousness has two sides and works in two different directions. God's righteousness refers both "to God's holy character and covenant faithfulness."[8] God's righteousness is beyond humanity. We cannot approach it or maintain it. God is righteous and we are not: "there is no righteous person, not even one" (3:10). In Judaism the law was the bridge to righteousness, yet generation after generation of Jews were unable to uphold the law. Gentiles, who were not under the law's jurisdiction, still by their conscience had a sense of the law when they "instinctively do what the Law requires . . . show the proof of the Law written on their hearts" (2:14a, 15a). Both Jew and Gentile, one through teaching and the other through instinct, were given the opportunity to follow God's righteousness and both failed. Paul then argues that God's righteousness continues to be made known to us through God's faithfulness. In contrast to humanity's inability to be righteous on its own, God extended righteousness to God's people in covenant faithfulness. Paul's use of the term *covenant* introduces a history of God's relationship to humans to those who may not know it (Gentiles), and reinterprets that history for those who do (Jews). Covenant is the basis upon which God and God's people entered into and maintained relationship, the solemn promises they made to each other. Israel's history is one of the people's repeated failure to keep their promises. The covenant is broken again and again, but God's righteousness compels God to repeatedly attempt to make and remake covenant. Jesus is the working solution, the one who bridges the divide between God and humanity through "justification." Thus, in Romans, Paul presents God's righteousness as both the thing that creates a

7. A. Katherine Grieb, *The Story of Romans* (Louisville: Westminster John Knox, 2002), xx–xxi.

8. Michael Gorman, notes on "Romans," in *The CEB Study Bible*, ed. Joel B. Green (Nashville: Abingdon Press, 2013), 278 NT.

chasm between God and humanity and the thing that motivates God to bridge that divide. God's righteousness is what ultimately saves us. This is the story that Romans tells again and again.

Paul's knowledge and brilliant interpretation of the law in the body of Romans, perhaps reflecting his education as a Pharisee, result in a powerful and memorable statement on the nature of God's righteousness. What was written as a letter of introduction to the Roman church now functions as a letter of formation for later generations of God's people. Paul offers up his own story and identity as a model for all believers, and this letter is the communal narrative or, more accurately, the meta-narrative of the work of Christ. This story of one man's identity as Jesus's willing servant supersedes, shapes, changes, and replaces all other stories and identities, with the goal of forming every listener into a *doulos* for Christ.

CHAPTER 7
1 CORINTHIANS

OUTLINE	THEMES
1:1-3 Greeting 1:4 -9 Thanksgiving 1:10-17 Church divisions and Paul's teaching 1:18–15:58 Body of the letter • 1:18–4:21 Paul's message • 5:1–6:20 Immorality and lawsuits • 7:1-40 Marriage and divorce • 8:1–11:1 Food • 11:2-34 Worship • 12:1–14:40 Gifts of the Spirit and love • 15:1-58 The Resurrection • 16:1-24 Conclusion	Unity in Christ Held together by love

Corinth, located on an isthmus between two port cities, was a large and prosperous urban center. This large and prosperous city was first destroyed and later rebuilt by Rome. When Rome destroyed the city, many of the inhabitants were enslaved, and many of the people in the newly formed Roman colony were former slaves. [1] Less than one hundred years after Rome made Corinth its colony, the Apostle Paul brought the gospel message to the city and founded a Christian community. The Christian community that was formed in Corinth was also a traumatized one. Its Christian identity is shaped by its political history, its Greek heritage, its

1. Richard Hays, *1 Corinthians,* Interpretation: A Bible Commentary for Teaching and Preaching (Louisville: Westminster John Knox, 2011), 3.

geographic location, its diverse population, and the message of the gospel, which means that Paul's message of Jesus was interpreted through the multiple and diverse lenses. It should come as no surprise that the church at Corinth was marked by division.

Based on references to other letters that were sent, scholars agree that 1 Corinthians is not Paul's first letter to the church, but most likely the second. Similarly, 2 Corinthians is probably Paul's fourth letter. Here is an ongoing dialogue between the apostle and the community around the practical issues in the day-to-day life of the church and why they matter. It is a work of practical theology.[2]

Paul's letter to the Roman church was a personal and theological introduction resulting in overarching doctrinal statements easily lending themselves to broad application. In contrast to Paul's testimony in Romans, his letters to Corinth are very much occasional letters, addressed to a specific church and particular sets of circumstances. For all the specificity of each letter to the Corinthian church, the general dynamics of forming a unified body out of a diverse population is an ongoing theme in Christian communities, and for this reason, the letters to the church at Corinth continue to inform the church today. In some ways, the dynamics of 1 Corinthians work like case law. Paul speaks first to a situation and then uses it as a platform to connect it to a larger, theological or legal principal. He begins by addressing a specific issue, and then offers his prescription, which he then supports with a theological basis. This dynamic combined with Paul's rhetorical skills result in some of the most beautiful literature in the Bible (1 Cor 13). This book, then, in its form is a perfectly imperfect composite, much like the community to which it is addressed.

In the first chapter, immediately after the greeting and thanksgiving, Paul speaks to the issue of internal divisions and rivalries that are threatening the unity of the church (1:10). The rival groups are claiming allegiance to different leaders: Paul, Apollos, Cephas, and Christ. There is no division in Christ, Paul declares, and all are to proclaim "Christ crucified." Paul wants to clarify that Christ is not simply another teacher. Rather, Christ is the epicenter of the entire movement; the story of Christ's crucifixion is the origin story for

2. Charles L. Campbell, *1 Corinthians* (Louisville: Westminster John Knox, 2011), 4.

the church. Just as Abram was called to leave everything that represented his identity in Genesis 12, so too are the members of this church in Corinth called to abandon their own individual stories and adopt the story of Jesus as their point of origin. Any and all identity of the church of Corinth is rooted in Christ as "God's power and God's wisdom" (1 Cor 1:24). Christ is the foundation of the church (1 Cor 3:10-11). Paul's job as an apostle is that of a "manager" who must "prove to be faithful" (1 Cor 4:2).

From this position as father, manager, and apostle over "beloved children," Paul moves to address the next issues of concern: sexual immorality and lawsuits in the church. Paul's point is not just to offer condemnations of these behaviors but also to emphasize that these offenses have an impact both on those involved and the rest of the community. In fact, they threaten the unity of the community. Paul then moves on to other specific issues, including marriage in light of the anticipated *parousia* or second coming, whether it was permissible to eat meat sacrificed to idols, the protocol for worship, and the Lord's meal. In each situation, Paul has to navigate the existing differences of class, race, ethnicity, and so on, and help the audience to be governed by a commitment to the unity of the congregation and an awareness that Christ's return is imminent.

To drive this point home, Paul offers an object lesson in 10:1-13 that is a remix of Israel's history in the wilderness. His retelling is typological. Using a Christian lens, Paul highlights patterns to incorporate the predominantly Gentile Corinthian church into Israel's sacred history.[3] The experiences are cast as more spiritual than physical. Paul describes the crossing of the Sea of Reeds as a baptism "into Moses." Mannah becomes "spiritual food" that they all ate, and "all drank the same spiritual drink." In Paul's telling of the past, the rock from which water came "was Christ." In his rendition, the Corinthians review Israelite history with the benefit of looking at "their" past, and this time, making the right choices. Paul says, "These things happened to them as an example and were written as a warning for us to whom the end of time has come" (10:11). Paul's appropriation of the wilderness tradition establishes an interpretive relationship

3. Campbell, *1 Corinthians*, 163.

that is "metaphorical, holding together two dissimilar situations" (Israel and Corinth) for new insight.[4]

Perhaps the most familiar portions of this letter come in chapters 12 and 13. In chapter 12, Paul teaches on spiritual gifts, which are varied in nature, but all bestowed by the Holy Spirit. These gifts are given to individuals in the church to strengthen and support the body of believers, for "the common good" (1 Cor 12:7). It does not take much imagination to surmise that the diversity of gifts is a potential problem in a diverse community and a stratified society. People on the lower end of the socioeconomic strata with highly valued gifts suddenly have an opportunity to be elevated. Those with more status and wealth might feel entitled to one of the important, or visible, gifts. In emphasizing the common source and purpose of the gifts, Paul wants to stop the believers from comparing gifts or competing with each other. He wants to move them from an understanding of gifts as commodities to one of gifts as equipment for service. To this end, he makes masterful use of metaphor. In imagining the church as Christ's body, Paul offers as a point of orientation something they are all familiar with—their bodies. From this point of familiarity, Paul invites the audience to an understanding of the mystical by imagining Christ's one body with many parts, all of which are necessary. Every part of the body (gift) has a purpose and cannot exist on its own. Paul's ability to make use of literary technique in developing an argument is on display here as he switches the Corinthians from their immediate and specific context to a symbolic one, which enables them to see themselves and their gifts differently. They are fully embodied and part of a larger, greater body, and the key to understanding a spiritual truth can be found in their physicality. But the brilliance of Paul's move to re-situate the Corinthians from competition to cooperation is not where the letter ends.

In the next chapter he goes beyond simply seeking cooperation to speaking of love. Chapter 13 is relatively short, comprising only thirteen verses, and more poetic than prose in form. Paul waxes eloquent on the nature of love (*agape*), what it is and isn't, and with his power of persuasion, makes the most compelling case for why it is to be pursued and

4. Richard Hays, *Echoes of Scripture in the Letters of Paul* (New Haven, CT: Yale University Press, 1993), 161.

valued above all other gifts. He uses hyperbole in the introduction to establish the fact that nothing compares to love, not the gifts of prophecy, faith, generosity, or the tongues "of human beings and of angels" (13:1-3). It is the greatest of gifts. Next, Paul outlines what love is, in action and attitude (13:4-7), which concludes with the all-encompassing line "endures all things" (13:7b). In the final section, Paul expounds on the enduring nature of love and concludes as he began, with hyperbole that extols the power of love: "Now faith, hope, and love remain—these three things—and the greatest of these is love" (13:13). Unlike the other gifts, which are bestowed by the Holy Spirit on individuals, *agape* love is one that everyone can have, and it is the one that is not simply bestowed—it must be pursued. In the Corinthian context, Paul's exquisite words about love are not romantic. They are practical and necessary for this and any community that is prone to division.

In chapter 14, Paul returning to the subject of spiritual gifts addresses how gifts are to be exercised in the church. Here, Paul seemingly takes a position against women prophesying in public (14:3b-35). Interpreters of this passage struggle with a teaching that seemingly contradicts other things Paul has said. In chapter 11, he talks about how women who speak in church should be attired (which is conservative but not prohibitive); in 12, the gifts of the Spirit are open to everyone; and when he speaks about prophecy in 14, it appears to be inclusive. All told, the injunction against women prophesying doesn't fit well with the rest of the book.[5] Because these verses appear in different places in various manuscripts, some scholars conclude they are a "marginal gloss," added later by someone other than Paul.[6] Another possibility is that Paul issued this command based on a need to control the worship in this particular context. Tied to this is the possibility that the ban against women speaking is specific to the context of church versus the home, such that women could prophesy in home settings but not in church. Some wonder whether the prohibition is only against wives and not single women.

5. Campbell, *1 Corinthians*, 241.

6. Jouette Bassler in "1 Corinthians," in *The Women's Bible Commentary*, ed. Carol Newsom, Sharon Ringe, and Jacqueline Lapsley (Louisville: Westminster John Knox, 2012), 564–65.

The debate on women's roles in the church continues as those in the Christian tradition attempt to make sense of a ban such as this against the larger witness of Paul and scripture in this book and beyond. Teachings that support a hierarchy based on gender, class, and race stand in opposition to the liberating power of the resurrection. Part of what Paul teaches in 1 Corinthians is that liberation is not freedom to do just anything.

This struggle to interpret all of scripture in its historical and current context itself is an ongoing identifying marker of the church. Although Paul espoused unity, the church continues to struggle with cultural values in and out of the text. Does unity come at women's expense? This is no simple matter of choosing a Christian culture over a worldly one, but rather, which biblical or Christian culture will we espouse? In these epistles we are reminded that "from the very beginning the church has never represented a community of people who lived in harmony and unity." Rather it is comprised of people who "negotiate their differences . . . to create a community reflective of God's love, grace and acceptance."[7] Theologian Kelly Brown Douglas puts it this way; "The fact of the matter is, calling ourselves church is aspirational."[8]

Paul's position on women in the church and all other matters are shaped under the rubric of his teaching on the resurrection in chapter 15. Here Paul first establishes the centrality of the resurrection—it is why Christians can have hope beyond their current existence and it is what makes Christ more than another rabbi. The resurrection "sets people free from the tyranny and fear of death."[9] The resurrection of Christ is transferred onto the body of Christ, which will experience the transformation and resurrection of their bodies. Paul's detailed teaching on the resurrection informed and continues to inform Christian doctrine and theology. In the shape of this book, it forms a lovely inclusion with the opening of the letter. First Corinthians begins with the death of Christ and ends with Christ's resurrection, and the church will find its purpose and identity in the liminal space between those two events.

---

7. Guy Nave, "2 Corinthians," in *True to Our Native Land: An African American New Testament Commentary*, ed. Brian Blount (Minneapolis: Fortress, 2007), 308.

8. Kelly Brown Douglas, "In This Kairos Time Will We Embody the Church?" *Sojourners*, March 26, 2020.

9. Campbell, *1 Corinthians*, 244.

CHAPTER 8
2 CORINTHIANS

OUTLINE	THEMES
1:1-2 Greeting 1:3-7 God's comfort and deliverance 1:8-11 Deliverance from suffering 1:12–13:10 Body • 1:12–2:13 Paul's recent actions • 2:14–7:4 The apostolic ministry • 7:5-16 Paul responds to the church's response • 8:1–9:15 The collection for Jerusalem • 10:1–13:10 Future plans to come to Corinth 13:11-13 Closing and blessing	Paul's authority as apostle Strength and weakness in Christ

To describe the Bible as a dialogic text is to acknowledge that the text as we have it is a compilation of sources that have come together over time from different sources. It is an acknowledgment that some sources were oral before they were written, and that these various sources represent multiple perspectives. These sources, strands, and voices that are joined together in scripture constitute a conversation and the truth of scripture is dialogic—it comes out of the conversation. It should also be reiterated that the dialogues of scripture are not always smooth or harmonious. In fact, it may that the harmonious dialogue is the exception. Second Corinthians is a letter that demands a dialogic approach, because it comprises many exchanges that need adjudicating. Understanding this letter will require an approach that identifies some of the dialogues in the texts and "seeks intersection rather than integration of divergent viewpoints and it provides a platform for them to encounter each other without necessarily coming into agreement."[1] For our examination of the text, we identify four dialogues.

The first dialogue begins with the name, signaling it is not the first or only voice in the dialogue. In fact, the name of the book is misleading. The canonical letter we call 2 Corinthians is most likely the fourth in a series of letters, of which we only have two. The letters we have are part of a larger drama between Paul and the church he established in Corinth. As these are occasional letters, a first observation is that the circumstances behind the first letter are not those that give rise to the second. Moreover, we do not have all the other correspondence, and so a part of interpreting this text will require piecing together the sequence of events, and filling in the gaps created by the other letters. Fortunately, some of these events and other letters are referred to in the book of Acts and 1 and 2 Corinthians, and with these materials we arrive at a reconstruction of events.

Paul, the Church at Corinth, and the Letters

- Paul established the church at Corinth.
- They wrote him (1 Cor 7:1).
- He wrote them (1 Cor 5:9); we do not have this letter.
- He wrote them again (this is 1 Corinthians in the NT canon).
- Paul sent Timothy to Corinth (1 Cor 4:17; 16:10-11).
- The "super-apostles" come to Corinth and criticize Paul.
- Timothy reports to Paul.

1. Raj Nadella, *Dialogue Not Dogma: Many Voices in the Gospel of Luke* (Edinburgh: T&T Clark, 2011), 112.

- Paul has a "painful" visit to Corinth where he was wronged (2 Cor 2:1-11).
- Paul wrote another letter "of tears" (2 Cor 1:23–2:4; 7:5-11).
- 2 Corinthians is believed to be fragments of earlier letters—scholarship is divided on which fragments are in this letter.

With these events in mind, we come to a second dialogue created by the units of material in the letter. While there is general agreement that Paul wrote 2 Corinthians, there is no agreement around the unity of the letter.[2] Sudden shifts in subject and style suggest that the canonical edition of 2 Corinthians is made up of multiple Pauline Letter fragments, forming a dialogue that ranges in tone from joy, pride, and consolation (7:4) to contention and sarcasm (12:11-13). Diverse in tone and content, a number of literary devices are at work in this letter. The patchwork of the letter reflects both the multiple contexts from which Paul writes and the myriad issues that are ongoing for the Corinthian community. For all of its complicated composition history, 2 Corinthians contains compelling elements, both theologically and literarily.

A third dialogue that informs this letter is the subtext of conflict. The religious leaders referred to as the super-apostles brought a different teaching to the church and led them in a different direction. They criticized Paul, which led to Paul's "painful" visit to Corinth, where he was hurt by a member of the faith community. Second Corinthians comes after that situation is resolved, but a significant part of 2 Corinthians is dedicated to affirming Paul's authority as an apostle and the integrity of his ministry (2:14–7:4). This section is a response to those who called Paul's authority into question.

Some of what makes 2 Corinthians a memorable letter is a fourth dialogue, which comes from Paul's use of Old Testament images, motifs,

2. There are some scholars who argue that some portions of 2 Corinthians are additions from a non-Pauline source.

and characters to illustrate his arguments and form his audience. Through these Old Testament lenses the audience can discern broad themes of "affliction" and comfort, "weakness and power . . . authority and integrity."[3] Moreover, using these Old Testament references, Paul is forming a Christian identity for a primarily Gentile audience, out of his interpretation comes a remix of the past Israelite story.

Second Corinthians begins as expected with the salutation. Paul identifies himself as "an apostle of Christ Jesus by God's will." This is how Paul self-identifies in most of his letters. This time, it is from the tentativeness of the past difficulties with this community that Paul begins by claiming his status as apostle, "one called." His call is the source of his authority to proclaim and preach.

The opening salutation is followed by the expected "thanksgiving" with a twist. For this letter, the thanksgiving is replete with references to suffering, trouble, and comfort (1:3-7). Paul is not subtle here. He does not want the audience to be "unaware . . . of the troubles we went through in Asia" (1:8). Here Paul reminds the readers that trouble, both his and others, is what it means to share in Christ's suffering. He is equally confident in God's ability to rescue "us" from any trouble. In recounting his suffering, he established a trajectory of our suffering being met by God's comfort, facilitated through the Holy Spirit. The pattern of suffering and comfort is the pattern of death and resurrection, a foundational tenet of the Christian faith. It is a recurring motif in 2 Corinthians that allows the disparate units "to encounter one another without coming to agreement."[4]

This letter from the apostle is personal to the extent that Paul defends himself and his ministry to a church that is not only divided but has challenged his authority as apostle and minister of the gospel. In Romans, Paul introduces himself to a church he did not establish. In 2 Corinthians, Paul presents himself to a community who has forgotten what is most important about him. The rival missionaries' challenge to Paul's authority evokes

3. Guy Nave, "2 Corinthians," in *True to Our Native Land: An African American New Testament Commentary*, ed. Brian Blount (Minneapolis: Fortress, 2007), 308.

4. Nadella, *Dialogue Not Dogma*, 112.

a similar situation in Jeremiah, where rival prophets discount the word of the prophet. The self that Paul presents is a literary construct, layered and dialogic. The identity he constructs is the foundation upon which he calls the Corinthian church to a new identity.

These broad themes of affliction and comfort, weakness and power, authority and integrity evoke the ministry of the prophets Moses and Jeremiah. In 2 Corinthians, Paul remixes prophetic elements to form an identity for this predominantly Gentile audience. By incorporating the prophets of old, specifically Jeremiah, Paul places himself in a powerful line of succession. He constructs an unofficial genealogy that cannot be challenged by the super apostles. Moreover, with this family history, Paul invites the mainly Gentile church to claim this story as their heritage as well.

In 2 Corinthians 1:12–2:2 Paul moves from explaining his change in plans to defending his status as apostle. In this segment the motif of letter is used to describe Paul's former letter (2:3), to reference "letters of introduction" (3:1-2), which are not needed because the church itself is the letter of commendation, "written on our hearts" (3:2). Paul then moves to describing the church as "Christ's letter," not "written on tablets of stone but on tablets of human hearts" (3:3). From this description Paul shifts to Moses's tablets of stone that are to be replaced with a new covenant, language that evokes the prophet Jeremiah. Paul uses the elements of writing, letter, and writing surface to take his audience on a historical journey that includes the giving of the law at Sinai, Moses's role as prophet, and Jeremiah a prophet in the tradition of Moses who suffers and prophesies about a vessel on the potter's wheel that is broken and reformed, and then speaks of a new covenant. Paul weaves together these words and images from the past to show the church in Corinth that God's revelation always opens up before us, but it is always facilitated by those God calls. Moreover, the images from the past are utilized to form and reform a dynamic understanding of God's work, facilitated by the Holy Spirit.

It is out of his identity as apostle that he continues to call the church at Corinth to this new, Christ-centered identity: "So then, if anyone is in Christ, that person is a new creation" carries echoes from the Major Prophets, reaching back to the "new thing" in Isaiah 43:18-19, and the new covenant in Jeremiah. Just as Jeremiah imagines a law written on hearts and not on stone, so too does 2 Corinthians invite the church to see themselves as born anew, created afresh in Christ, allowing for a new identity, a new understanding of God's work in the world, a new everything! The teaching of the super-apostles does not reflect this newness of life, but is tied down to old understandings of God's work in the world.

The Israelites remembered their origins in story and in the names of the ancestors, "Abraham, Isaac, and Jacob." The family of the Corinthian church does not have such a shared story. In the letters, Paul constructs and relays a story of the people so that they can live with intentionality and purpose. This knowledge is much needed both to combat false teaching and in the face of suffering.

In 2 Corinthians, Paul uses his own suffering as a teaching opportunity. With the technique that is present in some of Paul's other writings, his own experience becomes the model from which he proclaims that in suffering, the body carries Jesus's death so that "Jesus's life can be seen." In suffering, Christians reenact the work of Christ's redemption, which makes room for the power of the resurrection.

In this letter, Paul struggles between the two realities of external and internal pressure. To the challenge of external suffering he offers consolation and to the reality of his own weakness he looks to God's strength. In 2 Corinthians 12, the apostle speaks about his own weakness, an undisclosed "thorn in my body," in addition to the afflictions in the beginning of the letter. Although not specified, the imagery of the thorn allows for pain, perhaps ongoing discomfort, impairment, even disfigurement. It may have been the source of humiliation during his painful visit. His request for relief is answered by God, but not in the way that he or any of us would hope. Instead of removal, God promises, "My grace is enough for you, because power is made perfect in weakness" (2 Cor 12:9). Paul's body is the object lesson in this passage. His physical being is surrounded by God's supernatural presence. Although the body is the point of departure, it is not the point of orientation. The chapter begins with a vision and ends with a word from the Lord. This is the answer for a church that will continue to struggle with its diversity, difference of opinion, and fractures in the culture itself. The church at Corinth will have to imagine a reality that is greater than the options before it and larger than the sum total of its parts. In the spirit, they will be transformed "from one degree of glory to the next degree of glory" (2 Cor 3:18).

CHAPTER 9

GALATIANS

OUTLINE	THEMES
1:1-5 Greeting 1:6-9 Astonishment 1:10–6:10 Body of the letter 1:10–2:21 Paul's testimony 3:1–5:12 Abraham 5:13–6:10 Fulfillment of the law 6:11-18 Closing	Freedom in Christ

Reading Galatians feels like walking into an ongoing argument. You may feel awkward, embarrassed, and confused as to what exactly is going on. Clearly Paul has issues with the churches of Galatia. Instead of the thanksgiving that we traditionally expect to see after the greeting, Paul moves to immediately chastise them: "I am amazed that you are so quickly deserting the one [me, Paul] who called you by the grace of Christ to follow another gospel" (1:6). We aren't told who the Galatians have begun to follow or what other gospel they have turned to, but Paul's displeasure with their behavior is clear from the beginning of the epistle.

Paul founded the church in the area called Galatia, which included the cities of Iconium, Lystra, and Derbe.[1] The name Galatia could also refer to the Celtic tribes in the northern area.[2] The exact identity of these people is debated. The people in these Roman provinces were most likely

1. Luke Timothy Johnson, *The Writings of the New Testament* (Minneapolis: Fortress, 2010), 302 NT.

2. Frank J. Matera, "Galatians Introduction," in *The CEB Study Bible*, ed. Joel B. Green (Nashville: Abingdon Press, 2013), 353 NT.

pagans, who according to Paul quickly received the gospel and the Holy Spirit and then, perhaps almost as quickly, were converted to a competing gospel, described by Paul as "another gospel" (1:6), an attempt to "change the gospel of Christ" (1:7). Perhaps the Galatians were not open to the true gospel so much as they were just open. Now Paul is seeking to reinforce the teaching behind the Galatians' experience of the gospel of Jesus Christ as proclaimed by him, and to firm up their identity.

At issue here is the ongoing debate that has plagued other churches around Jewish practice in Christianity. The earliest groups of people who believed in Jesus were Jews. As recorded in the book of Acts, the "establishment," Jewish Christians, seek to maintain order in the growing church by attempting to form the new Gentile Christians according to the Torah and the keeping of the commandments. This seems to be the basis of the argument that the false teachers who have "bewitched" the Galatians are making. Paul writes to clarify that righteousness comes not from the law but from the Spirit of God. The central event in the Christian life is the crucifixion and resurrection of Jesus. This is the defining moment in the history of God's relationship with humanity. The crucifixion creates a new future and recasts the past. The cross reframes every moment before it, and Paul does not want the church in Galatia to be saddled down with obsolete terminology and inadequate paradigms.

After chastising the church for being so easily swayed, Paul seeks to redirect them with a carefully constructed argument in which Paul's rhetorical genius is evident. He begins by establishing himself as an authentic apostle, one called by God, and therefore, one who did not need to rely on the Jewish establishment in Jerusalem for validation. Paul wants the Galatians to learn from his own story. When one receives a direct call from God (as did Paul and the church at Galatia), the opinions of the religious establishment must be subject to godly authority. The encounter with God is the foundation of faith, not the traditions of the religious community. What has worked for Paul must then work for the church at Galatia.

In 2:1-10 Paul offers a summary of the Jerusalem conference, where Paul's God-given commission to preach to the Gentiles was confirmed and there was agreement that circumcision would not be required of the

Gentiles. The same Spirit that led him to Jerusalem to settle this matter is the same Spirit that called the Galatians when Paul visited them. It follows then that the Galatians' salvation was not bestowed by the church. Rather, salvation is a gift from God, made possible by the righteousness of God.

In Galatians we observe the same ongoing struggle that characterizes other Christian communities—the struggle between the Spirit and those entities that limit the Spirit, be it the flesh, the empire, or religious tradition itself. This is not the first time Paul has been confronted with this scenario. This struggle for an identity between the dynamic Spirit and all other institutions and empires is a recurring theme. Yet, we observe in the occasional letters how Paul forms an argument that is suited to each community and their specific context.

In order to illustrate his point for the Galatians, Paul takes an iconic identity story, the story of Abraham the patriarch, and interprets it in a way that changes everything. In chapter 3, Paul begins with Abraham as an example of righteousness: "Abraham believed God and it was credited to him as righteousness" (Gal 3:6; Gen 15:6). In Paul's reading of this passage and its tradition, he affirms Abraham's faith in God's word, all the while arguing that God's word "preached the gospel in advance to Abraham" (Gal 3:8). In other words, in God's word to Abraham was a gospel yet to be revealed. In dialogic theory, God's word is characterized by its unfinalizability. There is a dynamic element to God's word (the Spirit) that allows new understandings to be birthed, and it is in this space that the community of faith in Galatia finds its way into the story. The Spirit makes room for everyone to be "God's children through faith in Christ Jesus" (Gal 3:26), joining a family where baptism is the mark of adoption. It is this reality that allows Paul to proclaim "there is neither Jew nor Greek . . . slave nor free . . . male and female" (3:28). Some scholars argue these words are tied to the baptismal rite, uttered as one goes into the water to proclaim a new reality.[3] Thus every time we hear them, they serve the liturgical function of renewing baptismal identity.

3. Carolyn Osiek, "Galatians," in *The Women's Bible Commentary*, ed. Carol Newsom, Sharon Ringe, and Jacqueline Lapsley (Louisville: Westminster John Knox, 2012), 572.

Paul goes on to make sure the church knows that freedom in Christ is not intended to look like what has gone before, with another example from the Abraham story. God calls Abraham to be the father of a great nation. The child of promise in Abraham's story is Isaac, born of his wife, Sarah. Even though Ishmael is the firstborn, born of the Egyptian slave Hagar, it is Isaac who is the heir of the promise. Paul takes the origin story and embarks on an allegory presenting Abraham's two sons, Ishmael and Isaac, as the sons of slavery and freedom, based on the status of their mothers. Ishmael is the son of slavery, and as Paul sees it, Ishmael is present-day Jerusalem, for they are enslaved to the authority of the Instruction of Sinai (4:25). Isaac, born to a free woman represents all those "conceived by the Spirit" (4:29). In its traditional rendering, Ishmael is the son of slavery and Isaac the son of freedom. Paul uses the story of these two sons, one born to the promise and the other under normal circumstances, to explain the difference between the new and old covenants. In casting the story this way, Paul not only shows the Gentiles that they are the legitimate children of God but instructs Jewish Christians that the commandments they uphold are a part of the old ways, the old covenant. In a brilliant literary move, Paul's analogy places Jewish Christians with Ishmael, who in his remix of the story, represents the natural way or the old covenant. Notice also the powerful images of birthing that call attention to the matriarchs in the ancestral stories.

All Christians, Jewish and Gentile, are called to follow the Spirit in the new covenant. The outward sign of the new covenant is not the adherence to practices, such as circumcision, but is the fruit of the Spirit: "love, joy, peace, patience, kindness, goodness, faithfulness, gentleness, and self-control. There is no law against things like this" (Gal 5:22-23). The fruit of the Spirit invites the hearers and readers to imagine a new understanding of what it means to be grafted onto the tree, or into the family of Abraham. The signs of belonging are not the outward markings of the body, but rather the manifestation of the spirit in the exercise of these "fruits."

CHAPTER 10
EPHESIANS

OUTLINE	THEMES
1:1-2 Greeting 1:3-14 Blessings 1:15-19 Prayer 1:20–3:13 God's power is our victory 3:14-21 Prayer 4:1–6:20 Life as victorious people 6:21-24 Closing words	Household of God Armor of God

Although Paul spent more time in Ephesus than anywhere else, the letter to the Ephesians is likely a pseudonymous work, written by a disciple of Paul.[1] The clues to authorship include the fact that Ephesians, much like Colossians, has a long sentence structure that is uncharacteristic of the undisputed Pauline Letters. Moreover, there are a few substantial differences in the perspective and teaching in the body of the letter. In Ephesians, the return of Christ is not imminent, and there is an absence of specific and personal details that also raise questions about Pauline authorship.[2] The letter is believed to have been written in the latter third of the

1. The act of writing under a pseudonym was a common practice and a way of honoring the one under whose name the author writes. It is also a way of continuing a particular tradition of school of thought. See Timothy G. Gombis, "Ephesians Introduction" and notes on "Ephesians," in *The CEB Study Bible*, ed. Joel B. Green (Nashville: Abingdon Press, 2013), 363 and 370 NT.

2. E. Elizabeth Johnson, "Ephesians," in *The Women's Bible Commentary*, ed. Carol Newsom, Sharon Ringe, and Jacqueline Lapsley (Louisville: Westminster John Knox, 2012), 576.

first century CE, later than the other letters attributed to Paul.[3] This later dating is seen in its assumption of a more established church structure. Scholars also believe the similarities between Ephesians and Colossians support the possibility that the writer of Ephesians draws on the Colossian letter. Ephesians, unlike the majority of the Pauline Letters, does not address a specific crisis. Rather, it is general in scope, outlining a Christian identity for application in the wider church.

After the greeting, the opening blessing and prayer in Ephesians are triumphant in tone, pointing to and placing everything under Christ. The author proclaims the security of the believer in earth and in heaven. The people of God are redeemed and have an inheritance. Moreover, "God put everything under Christ's feet and made him head of everything in the church, which is his body. His body, the church, is the fullness of Christ, who fills everything in every way" (1:22-23). Here the writer puts first things first in acknowledging the centrality and supremacy of Christ.

In the first two chapters, the family language emphasizes familial relationship, focusing on the rightful place and inheritance in the family. The writer assures his Gentile audience of their status in God's family. They are saved (2:1-10), and they are made right with God—reconciled (2:11-22). Chapter 3 explains that the spreading of the gospel to the Gentiles was always a part of God's plan, and it is the writer's hope that the Ephesians and those who come after them will be able to receive and comprehend that which is beyond knowing, namely the love of Christ (3:16-19). The language in these verses is arresting: "I ask that you'll have the power to grasp love's width and length, height and depth, together with all believers" (3:18). Part of the import of this letter is to make sure these new converts understand their place as cherished members in the family of God. The letter here assures the Gentiles they are not an afterthought but were always in God's "secret" plan. Moreover, with their salvation they have an inheritance. In the ancient world, inheritance and love were not necessarily connected. A loved child might not inherit due to birth order or the status of their mother or the child's gender. However, the recipients of this letter are part of a family in which they are loved and will inherit as a result

3. Johnson, "Ephesians," 576.

of their faith in Jesus Christ and the God who has "put everything under Christ's feet" (1:22). The abundance of the creation is theirs. Thus, in this first part of the letter, the writer outlines orthodoxy, the belief system that underlies the faith with family language. The images of inheritance connote belonging and a stable future.

Based on these outlined beliefs, in chapter 4 the church at Ephesus is invited to move from an understanding of their Christian identity to an understanding of Christian ethics, and how to live "as people worthy of the call you received from God." An ethnically diverse faith community, the people of the Ephesian church have come to the faith from different paths. It is important to the author of this letter that unity be an identifying characteristic. Everyone is a part of one body, of which Christ is the head (4:16). That there should be a noticeable difference between their previous (Gentile) life and their life as people who follow the example of Christ is the focus of chapter 5. This distinction between Gentile and Christian life is based not in ethnicity but in spirituality. To this end, the letter exhorts the community to live in the "light of the Lord" (1:8) and to be "filled with the Spirit" (5:18). The language is consistently aspirational, making an appeal to the audience in ways that are reminiscent of Leviticus's appeal that holiness is for everyone. This unified and holy living is presented as a metaphorical body in the household where Christ is the head.

Chapter 6 introduces the symbolic household over which Christ is the head. The instructions for community life fall under the category of "household codes." In these codes, the household is structured in such a way as to support and honor the patriarch, the head. Wife, children, slaves, and animals all have a role in maintaining the necessary order. As expected, children are commanded to obey their parents (6:1) and slaves their masters "with fear and trembling and with sincere devotion to Christ" (6:5), and wives are instructed to "submit to their husbands" (5:24). In Ephesians we observe that with the household code structure is an expectation of mutuality. Parents are instructed not to "provoke your children to anger." Husbands are told to "love your wives just like Christ loved the church and gave himself for her" (5:25). Masters are told to "treat your slaves in the same way [that they treat their masters]" and to "stop threatening them . . . because you . . . have a master in heaven. He does not distinguish between people on the basis of status" (6:9). The writer of Ephesians most certainly espouses a household code as part of the life of faith, but hopefully not as an end in itself. The model of the household is used to describe how the ideal church community should operate.[4] Christ, not the legal codes of Judaism nor the philosophies of the Gentiles, will determine the beliefs and behaviors of the church.[5] A hopeful reading of this passage sees a seed planted that Christians living in the world could subvert oppressive earthly systems in their service to Christ.

Ephesians describes a layered Christian identity, one that moves from internal to external. It begins with inheritance or birthright. Then it takes on a role within the organization of the household, and it is followed by the way one is to present oneself in the outside world. The movement from internal identity to external presentation is developed through the metaphor of clothing, using the image of putting on armor. This imagery of armor is one that presumes that Christians must be prepared to face a hostile environment and need the protection of God. The writer closes out the letter with an extended description of "the armor of God" (6:10-17).

> Finally, be strengthened by the Lord, and his powerful strength. Put on God's armor so that you can make a stand against the tricks of the devil. We aren't fighting against human enemies but against rulers, authorities, forces of cosmic darkness, and spiritual powers of evil in the heavens.

The Roman soldier would have been a familiar figure to the people of Ephesus. And the writer uses the image of a soldier equipped for battle and wearing "the whole armor of God" (NRSV) instead of the armor of Rome, to demonstrate to this community that they are in fact engaged in warfare, against "rulers, authorities, forces of cosmic darkness, and spiritual powers of evil in the heavens" (6:12). In this battle imagery we observe the apocalyptic overtones that are characteristic of Ephesians and

4. Timothy G. Gombis, "The Household Code," in *The CEB Study Bible*, 370 NT.

5. For more information on household codes, see page 331.

Colossians that "place human freedom within the context of a struggle for the cosmos."[6] Donning the armor of God is the behavior of a Christian with a particular understanding of their identity and the environment they inhabit. They must be intentional and on guard like a soldier and equipped to live out their faith in a spiritually hostile environment. In this passage the listeners are told repeatedly to "stand," "stay alert," and "pray." Moreover, the image implies that the church must be equipped to be on the defense and offense as followers of Christ, against its "enemies." The images of a household and an army work together to show that the church is being called to a life of unity and discipline where there is a hierarchy of one head, one commander, and that one is Christ.

Household Codes in the New Testament

Household code is the term designated to describe passages of scripture found in Colossians 3:18–4:1; Ephesians 5:21–6:9; 1 Peter 2:18–3:7; 1 Timothy 2:8-15; 5:1-2; 6:1-2, and Titus 2:1-10 and 3:1. The household code is the model for the Greco-Roman household. Aristotle supported the notion that the ideal household order had a man in authority over everyone else, including the wife, slave, and children. Roman culture, for its part, was hierarchical and androcentric. Thus household codes were the standard model. In an increasingly diverse world, the codes explained the role of the subordinates in submitting to the husband/master/father. The maintenance of this order at the family level ensured the stability of society at large. Thus, much was at stake in the family unit as it was considered the building block of the larger community.

This hierarchical structure was pervasive in the Greco-Roman world, with the exception of the early church. Acts describes the church as a community where goods were shared in common, and women and slaves were included. Churches started by the Apostle Paul had women in leadership, and Paul famously proclaimed in Galatians 3:28 that in Christ, "there is neither Jew nor Greek; there is neither slave nor free; nor is there male and female, for you are all one in Christ Jesus," and in Colossians 3:11 and Ephesians 2:11-12. So where would statements that support a household of subservient woman, children, and slaves fit into the church's identity? Was there a shift in Paul's teaching, from one code to another? Did he simply contradict himself, or was his position on women opposed by other church leaders?

6. Luke Timothy Johnson, *The Writings of the New Testament* (Minneapolis: Fortress, 2010), 373.

The place of household codes in the church then and now is a source of ongoing study and debate. At stake is the role of women in leadership in the church, subjugation of entire groups of people (slaves), and the centrality of male leadership. The challenges of household codes are the challenges of biblical interpretation at the intersection of religion and culture. Does the freedom proclaimed in the gospel transform culture or is it subject to culture?

A few points for consideration are as follows:

1. Authorship: Are the letters that espouse household codes Pauline or are their Pauline authorship disputed? If all the passages that support household codes are found in the disputed letters of Paul, then interpreters can acknowledge the difference of opinions in the early church among leadership on this topic. Even if Paul did not support these codes, the books are a part of the New Testament canon, and are regarded as having authority for the church.
2. Context for letters: We know that many of the New Testament letters were written to communities to address a specific situation or circumstance. Is it possible that the household codes in these letters were primarily circumstantial and not universal?
3. Relationship between the Christian community and the world: Some of the letters that espouse the household codes are written during the time described as the delayed parousia. The church had expected it to occur by now, and in the ongoing negotiation with and persecution under the Roman Empire, Christians were trying to survive. Were the household codes seen as a way in which these marginal communities could assimilate and make themselves less threatening?

These points for consideration all fit under a larger issue around biblical interpretation. Clarice Martin's work on household codes offers a unique perspective. Her womanist approach is integrated and intersectional. In her history of interpretation, she includes the experience of African slaves in America who read these passages through the lens of liberation theology—a theology that itself expanded to include women.

The trajectory of the household codes in the letters may in fact present us with a religious movement that over time became less countercultural for its own survival. Subsequent generations in this same faith tradition read the text in an expansive and inclusive direction for their own survival as well.

Did the church take existing household codes and "Christianize" them, making Christ the reason for supporting the hierarchical order?

Did Christianity threaten the patriarchy, and were the household codes an attempt to keep persecution at bay and assure the ruling powers that Christians didn't need to be feared? If so, this act of assimilation came at a great price, for which communities of faith continue to pay.

From a dialogic perspective, the household codes are an example of an ongoing conversation around identity in the Christian community. Where and when will the church's identity be countercultural for the sake of the gospel? Will assimilation or respectability be the goals of Christ's followers?

CHAPTER 11

PHILIPPIANS

OUTLINE	THEMES
1:1-2 Greeting 1:3-11 Thanksgiving and prayer 1:12-26 Paul's imprisonment 1:27–2:18 Follow Christ's example 2:19–3:16 Examples of imitating Christ, good and bad 3:17–4:9 Appeal to live the Christian life 4:10-20 Thanking the Philippians for their gift 4:21-23 Closing words	Joy God's faithfulness

Philippians is a small letter, only four chapters long, that has had a tremendous impact. Its message of joy rooted in God's faithfulness has made it a "fan favorite" in Christian tradition. Written by Paul from prison, such a message is particularly effective. Although the specific cause of the imprisonment is never identified, Paul makes it clear that his future is uncertain, and his life is at risk. Nevertheless, he is convinced that his situation is a part of God's plan to advance the gospel and that "Christ's greatness will be seen in my body . . . whether I live or die" (1:20). Paul's confidence and joy are rooted in God and not his circumstances, and this is the message he conveys to the Philippian church.

Included in this missive is a hymn that outlines the presence and mission of Christ as God who took on flesh and offered himself as sacrifice and is now exalted. These words, presumably from a preexisting text that would have been familiar to the church at Philippi, functioned as a creed or confession, and they continue to have that function in Christian communities to this day. The contrast in genre from prose to hymn grabs the attention of the reader and invites the reader into an alternate space. The hymn has a liturgical function, as it presents the familiar into the text, and as an element of worship creates the opportunity for a shared encounter with God. Perhaps this is the source of Paul's confidence and joy in the midst of imprisonment.

Paul then moves from his own situation to that of the church in Philippi. A flourishing commercial center in Macedonia, Philippi was along one of the major trade routes in the area.[1] Like other early churches, the Philippians were experiencing harassment, but Paul reminds them that this treatment is to be expected from those who reject the good news.[2] And he goes on to challenge the authority of those, known as "Judaizers," who promoted circumcision as a requirement for salvation. Paul reminds the church of his own credentials as a Pharisee, a "Hebrew of the Hebrews," and emphasizes that the only thing of value is "knowing Christ Jesus." The church, Paul tells them, should focus on "the righteousness of God that is based on faith" (3:9) not particular religious practices like circumcision or other earthly things.

Philippians does differ from the other letters in the canon in that it addresses a specific issue involving particular individuals rather than the church as a whole is addressed, namely a rift between two women, Euodia and Syntyche, who are leaders in the Philippian churches. More important than the nature of the dispute is the fact that the reference documents women in leadership in the New Testament church and clearly recognizes them as "women who have struggled together with me in the ministry of the gospel," women who were valued by Paul.

As in other letters, Paul does the work of formation for the early church by describing what the Christian community should look like, what it means to "carry out your own salvation with fear and trembling"

1. Bart Ehrman, *The New Testament: A Historical Introduction to the Early Christian Writings* (Oxford: Oxford University Press, 2000), 312.

2. Jerry L. Sumney, "Philippians Introduction," in *The CEB Study Bible*, ed. Joel B. Green (Nashville: Abingdon Press, 2013), 374 NT.

(2:12). In Philippians, Paul not only gives directions for how to behave, "Become imitators of me and watch those who live this way" (3:17), but in chapter 4 he instructs the Philippians on how to think. He urges them to "focus your thoughts on these things: all that is true . . . holy . . . just . . . pure . . . lovely . . . and all that is worthy of praise" (4:8-9). He directs them away from worry and toward prayer as a pathway to peace and joy, a pathway that offers this community a means of achieving stability in turbulent times.

CHAPTER 12

COLOSSIANS

OUTLINE	THEMES
1:1-2 Greeting 1:3-8 Thanksgiving 1:9–4:6 Body 4:7-18 Greetings and blessings	The Ethics of the Church

Colossians is a circular letter, that is, one intended for more than one audience (4:16), addressed to the people of Colossae, a town located in what is now modern-day Turkey. Like the letter to the Ephesians, its Pauline authorship is disputed by scholars because, although the teaching is Pauline, the style and vocabulary differ from those of the undisputed letters. At the time of the letter's writing, the population of the city and of the church was primarily Gentile, specifically Greek and Phrygian. In the second century there was an influx of Jewish settlers into the city, and this added diversity, particularly with respect to religious practices, may have resulted in the difficulties that contributed to the reason for the letter.[1] At issue for the church in Colossae, a church that Paul himself did not found, is the need for the Gentile Christians to adhere to Jewish practices, such as circumcision, dietary laws, and keeping the Sabbath. Once again, non-Jewish converts need to be formed in what, according to Paul's teaching, it means to be a Christian. The religious and cultural soil out of which Christianity comes is Jewish. The writer of Colossians wants the church to be mindful of its Judaic roots, but not bound by Judaic practices. Pauline

1. Ralph P. Martin, *Ephesians, Colossians, and Philemon,* Interpretation: A Bible Commentary for Teaching and Preaching (Louisville: Westminster John Knox, 1992), 81–82.

rhetoric consistently and continuously purports Christ and Christ alone to be the center of the faith.

The traditional thanksgiving in the letter is followed by a hymn that begins with creation and interprets the very beginning of the world in such a way that identifies Christ's existence and centrality to both faith and practice.[2] The placement of a hymn or poetry in the midst of prose is a powerful literary device, serving to make its content stand out, requiring that it be noticed. It also serves an almost liturgical or creedal function by inviting the readers to participate, to join in a call-and-response to the tenets of the faith. In this sense, the hymn brings everyone into a shared space and a communal experience of witness to the work of Christ, who was there from the very beginning. The hymn reminds Jewish Christians that it was always a part of God's plan to bring Gentiles into the fold and incorporates the Gentile Christians into the family of faith, the body of Christ. The hymn itself is a means of formation.

From the hymn the writer recounts Paul's work and suffering for the sake of the gospel. Here his teaching is introduced by reminding the audience of his authority and brings the audience into a desired space so that he can identify the issue at hand: "Don't let anyone judge you about eating or drinking . . . these religious practices are only a shadow of what was coming—the body that cast the shadow is Christ" (2:16-17).

Removed from the events of the death and resurrection of Jesus by several decades, chapters 2 and 3 use those events as a motif to help the hearers of the letter understand what it means to serve Christ. Christians symbolically die to one way of life and rise to another, where the old rules and regulations no longer apply. Now our lives are "hidden with Christ in God" (3:3). In this new way of being there is "neither Greek nor Jew, circumcised nor uncircumcised, barbarian, Scythian, slave nor free, but Christ is all things and in all people" (3:11).

This new way of being, where there is neither "Greek nor Jew . . . slave nor free" is followed by another iteration of the household codes, one in which there are indeed slaves and masters and rules for their relationship. Slaves are told to obey their "masters on earth in everything . . . with

2. J. R. Daniel Kirk, notes on "Colossians," in *The CEB Study Bible*, ed. Joel B. Green (Nashville: Abingdon Press, 2013), 383 NT.

the single motivation of fearing the Lord" (3:22). These instructions, like those in Ephesians, have a very long and tormented history of interpretation. In the United States, these scripture passages were used, not only to justify the institution of slavery but also to elicit unquestioning obedience and loyalty from their African captives as decreed by God with their masters as God's representative. The legislation in Colossians continues to include the masters: "Masters, be just and fair to your slaves, knowing that you yourselves have a master in heaven" (4:1). The command to masters in 4:1, not always as carefully observed as the command to the slaves, is designed to impose a sense of balance in the household of faith. It superimposes God's role as the master in the ultimate household code over an existing earthly one. However, the reminder that there is a master in heaven did not eliminate the existence of the institution of slavery nor the devaluing of humanity upon which slavery depends. To the contrary, the master in this paradigm, like the husband in Ephesians, is a demigod, giving almost divine status to the human "in charge."

The prominence of household codes in the Greco-Roman world and their presence in several of the epistles raises the issue of the interaction between and influence of the larger culture and society on the Christian movement. Strict adherence to these codes cannot be the way forward, since, in his closing, the writer of the letter names among his coworkers a slave and a woman who hosted a house church.[3] One explanation for the seeming contradiction between teachings that both proclaim the freedom in Christ and still seem to impose the hierarchy in the surrounding culture is the suggestion that the Christians, by practicing their freedom in Christ, would ultimately transform the existing social structure of the Greco-Roman world. In the same way that the presence of Gentiles changes the definition of being Christian, so, too, this explanation proposes, would the presence of Christians in the world change the world.

If this was, indeed, the expectation of the letter's writer, it was not and has not yet been achieved. What we observe in the letters and in the subsequent history of the church is the opposite—a shift from a community that was originally otherworldly and countercultural to one that

3. Lloyd A. Lewis, "Colossians," in *True to Our Native Land: An African American New Testament Commentary*, ed. Brian Blount (Minneapolis: Fortress, 2007), 386–87.

adopts the values and becomes a part of the dominant culture. Christianity has become respectable in the eyes of the world, but in doing so it moves away from its origins. Early followers of Christ lived an alternative lifestyle, sharing everything they earned, and caring for each other's needs (Acts 4:32-35). Women who co-labored with the Apostle Paul (Phoebe, Prisca, etc.) seemed to move with freedom and be treated with equality. The household codes, like Paul's arguments against marriage (1 Cor 7:1-7), may have been the result of his belief, shared by much of the early church, that the focus of the Christian life should be on the coming *parousia*, Christ's return. In fact, Paul's ministry was shaped by the conviction that this event was imminent. In practical terms this meant that there were matters that Paul addressed or chose not to address that mattered less in light of the push to win souls for Christ in the short time that remained.

Responding to the matters related to the household codes and references to slavery and the treatment of women is impacted by issue of Pauline authorship of Colossians. It appears as if the arguments that proclaim an alternative to the household codes, that in Christ there is neither "Jew nor Greek . . . slave nor free . . . male and female" (Gal 3:28), show up in the earlier letters and undisputed letter. It is in the later letters, those that may be the product of subsequent generations, that the church takes up the cultural norms that the early church attempted to move away from. As more time passes, however, and the expectation of an imminent return of Christ is further removed from the life of the church, the heirs of the tradition will begin to understand these texts and to envision their place in society differently.

This shift, if it is an accurate depiction of the development of Christianity, raises questions about Christianity and religion in general and its role in the world. To what extent does a religion challenge the status quo, and when does it succumb to it? In Ephesians, the household code, which aims to incorporate everyone into one body in Christ, does so at the expense of the full personhood of every member. Such a movement appears to be an imaginative religious identity succumbing to the status quo in the culture.

CHAPTER 13

1 THESSALONIANS

OUTLINE	THEME
1:1 Greeting 1:2-10 Thanksgiving 2:1–3:13 History with the Thessalonians 4:1–5:24 Instruction 5:25-28 Greetings, closing remarks, benediction	Remain faithful in Christ

Scholars agree that 1 Thessalonians is most likely the earliest of Paul's letters and thus the first New Testament text. The church in Thessalonica was founded by Paul along with Silvanus (Silas) and Timothy, and the approximate date of the letter is 51 CE. Paul sent Timothy to check on the community and, based on Timothy's report, Paul sent this letter to reassure and instruct the congregation. The letter contains the traditional elements of a greeting and an extended thanksgiving, followed by exhortation and closing greetings. First Thessalonians is a parenetic letter (*parenesis* means moral exhortation), consisting of three elements: memory, model, and maxims.[1] This Hellenistic style of writing is seen in a number of Paul's letters.

After the greeting, Paul offers thanks for what God has done in their midst, particularly the evidence of faith, hope, and love (1:2-10). He reassures the Thessalonians that they are "loved by God," and lets them know

1. Luke Timothy Johnson, *The Writings of the New Testament* (Minneapolis: Fortress, 2010), 261.

they are "constantly in our prayers" (1:4, 2). In this way, the thanksgiving section is a preview of the "memory" that comes in the next section of the letter.

In the body of the letter, chapters 2 and 3, we observe the first two elements of a paranetic letter, that is, memory and model. The people are called to remember their reception of the gospel and to see how Paul models faithfulness, even when he is separated from them. First, Paul recounts the story of the church. He reminds the Thessalonians of his ministry there and how they received the message of the gospel. He then assures them of his desire to see them "face-to-face" (2:17). But he reminds them that when he could not come, he sent Timothy, and now sends a letter to encourage them to remain faithful to "the Way."

In chapter 4, we find the third element of *paranesis*, maxims. Paul outlines what godly living looks like; "to stay away from sexual immorality" (4:3), "live quietly, mind your own business, and earn your own living" (4:11). The challenge of living a godly life is then joined by advice on how to respond to the challenge of grief concerning what happens to those who die. Remember the early church believed Christ's return was imminent. With the *parousia*, or return, delayed, Paul offers much-needed, practical answers about what is expected of the faithful believer and what will happen to those who are alive and those who are dead at the Lord's coming, whenever it may occur. In 4:13-18, Paul declares that when the Lord returns, those who have died will be raised and taken along with those living. In these few short verses are words that continue to support a belief about life and death in Christ, and a reunion with Christ known as the "rapture," the event of Christ's return to gather his followers and take them away. According to the book of Acts, after Jesus literally ascended into heaven, the disciples were then addressed by "two men in white robes" who said, "this Jesus, who was taken up from you into heaven, will come in the same way that you saw him go into heaven" (Acts 1:10-11). These words and Paul's interpretation of them are foundational for teaching about Christ's return, and these words continue to be used in funeral liturgies throughout Christianity. The church in Thessalonica found (and the church today still finds) encouragement "with these words." More detail about the rapture comes in 5:1-11. Paul wants the church to know what he understands is coming so that they are rooted in an identity as followers of Christ who have a certain future in uncertain times.

Paul's letter closes with the additional instructions to love and respect each other and to "rejoice always. Pray continually. Give thanks in every situation because this is God's will for you" (5:16-18). The benediction in verses 23-24 is followed by a final greeting in verses 25-28, which includes the instructions that the letter be "read aloud to all the brothers and sisters." The influence of Paul's first letter is proof that the parenetic letter is still effective today. Christian communities continue to be shaped by the exhortation to moral living and explanation of what happens to those who have died.

CHAPTER 14
2 THESSALONIANS

OUTLINE	THEMES
1:1-2 Greeting 1:3-11 Thanksgiving 2:1-17 The Day of the Lord 3:1-15 Community instruction 3:16-18 Final greetings and benediction	Continue to remain faithful

A significant amount of time passes between the writing of 1 and 2 Thessalonians, but some of the same concerns are important to the congregation. Like 1 Thessalonians, the second letter, which was probably not written by Paul, also addresses the Lord's return, "the Day of the Lord," but from a different perspective. This second letter addresses a community who is afraid the Day of the Lord has already happened. The terminology comes from the Old Testament prophetic tradition.[1] The Day of the Lord is the occasion of God coming to earth and setting things right, doing justice, and restoring a world that has lost its way. The Israelites often looked forward to this day as the moment when God would vindicate them against their enemies. However, not all the prophets supported this view. In some prophetic traditions the people were told they too would have to answer to God for their sins on that day.[2] The reference is absorbed into the early church's understanding of the *parousia*, Christ's

1. References to the Day of the Lord appear most frequently in Joel, Isaiah, and Zephaniah. See *The Anchor Bible Dictionary,* vol. 2, ed. D. N. Freedman (New York: Doubleday, 1992), 82.

2. Amos 5:18-20.

return, and just as the Day of the Lord is interpreted and reinterpreted in the Old Testament, the return of Christ is formed and reformed in the doctrine of the early church. Second Thessalonians provides a corrective to 1 Thessalonians, which describes Christ's return as sudden, "like a thief in the night" (1 Thess 5:2). The author of the second letter lists specific signs that will precede the Lord's return, giving the community something to look for as they wait.[3] Scholars believe that the author of this letter was aware of the first letter and writes "to correct or supplement the earlier letter as a way of continuing Paul's legacy."[4]

Like the first letter, the letter encourages the community. The words of encouragement are in response to the struggles of the community. They are reminded that God will judge those who are harassing them. The faithfulness that is encouraged in 1 and 2 Thessalonians does not only address their behavior to one another. This faithfulness will require the community to reinterpret the words of the tradition in light of their current circumstances.

---

3. Love L. Sechrest, "2 Thessalonians Introduction," in *The CEB Study Bible*, ed. Joel B. Green (Nashville: Abingdon Press, 2013), 397 NT.

4. Sechrest, "2 Thessalonians Introduction," in *The CEB Study Bible*, 397 NT.

THE PASTORAL LETTERS

First and Second Timothy and Titus are called the Pastoral Letters because they address general, pastoral concerns, particularly around leadership structure. These concerns are addressed to a time in the development and growth of the Christian tradition (third-generation correspondence, during the years 90–110 CE) when Domitian was the emperor. The Christianity of the Pastoral Letters is not the same Jesus movement that characterized the early church, where the Holy Spirit was depicted as a character that moved the people of "The Way" to a radically expansive vision of the kingdom of God. Rather these letters depict the transmission and transformation of a faith tradition from one generation to the next.[1] The epistles fit under the category of "pseudonymous" Pauline authorship.[2] Paul's authorship of these letters is disputed because they seem to reflect a later time in the life of the church. Had Paul written them, they (2 Timothy and Titus) would have been his last letters before his martyrdom.

In genre, the Pastoral Letters are separated from the occasional letters in that they are not written to a specific congregation under a singular set of circumstances. However, the context of the letters is the occasion. These letters were produced at the intersection of a historical-political moment and a developmental stage in the life of the church. Thus we could aptly name them the "Particular Pastoral Letters." In other words, these instructions for pastors are for a particular group of leaders at a specific time.

1. Clarice J. Martin, "1–2 Timothy and Titus (The Pastoral Epistles)," in *True to Our Native Land: An African American New Testament Commentary,* ed. Brian Blount (Minneapolis: Fortress, 2007), 409.

2. Pseudonymous authorship refers to a practice where a disciple of the "author" writes in the name and presumed tradition of the author. The disciple writes to "honor—but adapt—the idea of an earlier author." Martin, "1–2 Timothy and Titus," 410.

The conceptual grouping of these letters together reveals a converging image of the Christian communities—one that is rooted in Judaism but not bound by its practices. In these epistles we observe the Christian assemblies attempting to maintain a unique identity through teaching, even as it is being shaped by Greco-Roman culture and values.

CHAPTER 15

1 TIMOTHY

OUTLINE	THEMES
1:1-20 Introduction 2:1-15 Steps for correction 3:1-13 Instructions for God's household 3:14–6:19 Instructions for Timothy as a leader 6:20-21 Closing	Lessons for leaders

Timothy is a "child" of Paul, a member of the inner circle who was sent to Ephesus. Two letters bear his name and, based on their content, the first could have been generated at a time early in Paul's ministry and the second one in the time immediately after Paul's death.[1] Both letters might be called "third-generation correspondence." The first generation is represented by Lois, Timothy's grandmother, and the second generation by Eunice, his mother. The listing of Lois and Eunice is a genealogy of faith, one that not only speaks to Timothy's pedigree as a Christian but expresses a hope for the ongoing transmission of the faith.[2] The opening instruction in 1 Timothy speaks to this hope and emphasized the importance of a safeguard against "wrong teaching" (1:3). This letter aims to set the record straight and to provide "sound teaching" (1:11) in the

1. Clarice J. Martin, "1–2 Timothy and Titus (the Pastoral Epistles)," in *True to Our Native Land: An African American New Testament Commentary,* ed. Brian Blount (Minneapolis: Fortress, 2007), 409.

2. Cynthia Long Westfall, "1 Timothy Introduction," in *The CEB Study Bible*, ed. Joel B. Green (Nashville: Abingdon Press, 2013), 404 NT.

face of those who have "missed this goal" (1:6). The emphasis on the true faith acknowledges the presence of other, alternative practices and beliefs. Christianity is old enough and widespread enough that attention is directed toward the establishment and maintenance of orthodox doctrine and governance. What was once a movement, known as "the Way," is now an institution.

The institutional nature of the church is evident in some of the regulations in 1 Timothy that bear the mark of "household codes." The influence of these codes, which defined the particular hierarchical order common in the Greco-Roman world of the time, is apparent in the Pastoral Letters.[3] For example, when it comes to women, control is the rule. Women, according to 1 Timothy, should focus more on doing good and less on tending to their appearance. Moreover, a wife should "learn quietly with complete submission" and seek neither to teach nor "control" her husband. Instead, "she should be a quiet listener" (2:11-12).

Were this an occasional letter, one written to a specific congregation for a particular purpose, our interpretation would include an examination of the context that might help us deal with this teaching. In 1 Timothy, the occasion is not an event but a mindset, an assumed understanding of the nature of women and men. The espoused hierarchy is justified through an interpretation of Genesis 3, which argues that Adam was created first and that Eve was deceived by the serpent, not Adam. This interpretation of Genesis 3 does not take into account the first creation story, in which both male and female were made in God's image, and, arguably, at the same time. Moreover, the interpretation in 1 Timothy is selective in what it remembers of the story. The story of Adam and Eve's disobedience in the garden of Eden is recast in order to support the secondary status and role of women. This teaching exists as one (albeit limited) reading of a previous text and stands as an example of scripture being used to justify a particular social order. The writer of 1 Timothy favors a Christian identity that is hierarchical and privileges men, a position that is in sync with the culture of the time. This is an example of a reading of the text in the service of the status quo.

3. See "Household Codes" on page 331.

In chapter 3 we find additional regulations reflecting church structure. There are guidelines for offices of supervisor/bishop, servant/deacon, and elders in "God's household" (3:15). The guidelines build on the hierarchical nature of the household code and promote the idea that all the leaders, who are specifically a part of God's household and under God's authority in the church, are male. The letter also includes a list of "duties" for the community, including how to treat older men and women and care for the widows. These instructions are phrased in words reminiscent of the commandment to "honor" one's father and mother and reflect practices rooted in the early Israelite community.

CHAPTER 16
2 TIMOTHY

OUTLINE	THEMES
1:1-7 Introduction 1:8-18 No shame for the testimony of the Lord or Paul 2:1-21 Pass on the message, share the suffering 2:22-26 Avoid behavior that causes conflict 3:1-9 Avoid ungodly people 3:10-17 Take Paul as your model 4:1-8 Timothy's commission and Paul's departure 4:9-22 Closing	Pass on the faith Suffer for the faith

Second Timothy reads more like a collection of final instructions than a traditional occasional letter. Written by an author who claims to be Paul in prison awaiting a second trial and most likely death, the text speaks sharply about how to behave in "the last days." It is from this context that Timothy is reminded to remain true to the "testimony about the Lord of me, his prisoner" (2 Tim 1:8). Timothy is reminded that suffering comes with Christianity at this point and is encouraged to follow Paul's example and to "continue with the things you have learned" (3:14).

Second Timothy follows the form of a parenetic letter, with the three-part model of memory, model, and maxims. The audience is reminded of their identity in Christ and of the example of the presumed author, Paul. Upon that foundation, the letter issues instruction on how to behave in the world. The instructions in this brief letter are not without literary finesse. In chapter 2, the writer uses the images of a soldier, an athlete, and a farmer to encourage the community to endure. This notion of work to be done on the other side of salvation is expressed in the metaphor of the different types of bowls in a mansion. Some are for garbage and others are "set apart as a 'special bowl'" (2:20-21).

In this small letter we find the declaration that "every scripture[1] is inspired by God and is useful for teaching, for showing mistakes, for correcting, and for training character" (3:16). Also in 2 Timothy we find the instruction to "make an effort to present yourself to God as a tried-and-true worker, who doesn't need to be ashamed but is one who interprets the message of truth correctly" (2 Tim 2:15). With the ever-present pressures of the past (Jewish practices and law) and the present (Greco-Roman household codes), what might it mean to interpret the message of truth correctly?

1. Scripture here refers to the Hebrew Bible/Old Testament.

CHAPTER 17
TITUS

OUTLINE	THEMES
1:1-4 Greeting 1:5-9 Appointing elders 1:10-16 Correcting rebellious people 2:1–3:8 Teaching people how to be godly 3:9-15 Closing	Good and godly behavior

Titus was a Gentile convert, and like Timothy was a part of Paul's ministry team on his third missionary journey.[1] Also like Timothy, Titus was assigned to represent Paul. Titus served in Corinth and Crete. Like the letters to Timothy, the letter to Titus provides instructions for church officers (elders) and what godly behavior should look like. Consistent with the messages in 1 and 2 Timothy, the establishment of the early church places godly men, who have a consistent understanding of the teachings, in positions of authority. The hierarchy of the household codes is again evident, with instructions for older men, older women, younger men, and slaves.

The ministry and letter of Titus is evidence that the church was expanding to include Gentiles. This diversity will force the church's identity to expand. In fact, it is hard to read the Pastoral Letters without feeling the tremendous desire behind them to establish a Christian identity that was consistent and compatible with the larger society. It is also hard to

1. Cynthia Long Westfall, "Titus Introduction," in *The CEB Study Bible*, ed. Joel B. Green (Nashville: Abingdon Press, 2013), 424 NT.

read this letter and not reflect on their legacy. The overlay of household codes on Christian identity has had devastating results in the past and that extend to our current context. In this small collection of letters, we also document the larger and ongoing dialogues within the faith tradition itself. Will Christianity remain as a countercultural witness to the liberating power of God through Jesus, or will it become yet another institution that supports the status quo and reaps its benefits? How do we decide what matters most? This is the ongoing struggle for the church as an institution. Here are some observations.

- Clarice Martin points to a rejection of the slave codes in the New Testament by African American churches, and a simultaneous endorsement of the call for the subjugation of women.[2]
- White women in Christianity have struggled and continue to struggle with recognizing the full humanity of people of color, especially women of color.
- Center-left denominations throughout Christianity continue to struggle over the full inclusion of LGBTQIA Christians.

The growth of the church and the inclusion of Gentiles demanded an ongoing renegotiation of identity. There are moments in this history when that identity includes radical hospitality and other moments when it embraces the status quo.

2. Clarice Martin, "The *Haustafeln (Household Codes),*" *in Stony the Road We Trod* (Minneapolis: Fortress, 1991), 206–31.

CHAPTER 18

PHILEMON

OUTLINE	THEMES
1-3 Greeting 4-7 Thanksgiving 8-16 The appeal for Onesimus 17-21 Encouragement to do what is right 22 Potential visit 23-25 Closing	Onesimus the slave

Philemon is a Pauline letter, most likely his last one, written while he was imprisoned in Rome. It is short, only 335 words in Greek, written without a scribe and to an individual rather than a church. The brief letter is being carried to Philemon by the hand of Onesimus, whom Paul calls "my child," but who is in fact a slave of Philemon. Although the letter does not tell us how Onesimus came to be with Paul, we can presume he either ran away, or was "lent out" by his master to Paul.[1] After the opening greeting, Paul makes an appeal to Philemon on behalf of Onesimus, that he may be received as "more than a slave—that is, a dearly loved brother." This is an appeal "through love," not a "command . . . to do the right thing" (vv. 16, 8). What exactly is it that Paul is requesting of Philemon? The options in the text include

1. Lloyd A. Lewis, "Philemon," in *True to Our Native Land: An African American New Testament Commentary,* ed. Brian Blount (Minneapolis: Fortress, 2007), 437.

1. allowing Onesimus to continue to serve Paul, verse 13
2. receiving Onesimus back without penalty, verses 15 and 17
3. setting Onesimus free, verse 16[2]

It is not possible to discern from Paul's words whether Paul is addressing the institution and practice of slavery generally or is simply concerned with the treatment of one slave, Onesimus. What we know for sure is that Paul's relationship with this slave has led him to make an impassioned request that this slave be considered a "dearly beloved brother." Ultimately, in this letter Paul invites Philemon to "experience the disquieting nature of the gospel."[3] In usage over time Paul's words have stirred up hope for those who are subject to institutions and practices that make sisters and brothers "other." African American slaves and their descendants have read this little letter for its potential in speaking to the power of the gospel not only to transform lives but ultimately to transform powers, principalities, and institutions.

---

2. Emerson Powery, notes on "Philemon," in *The CEB Study Bible*, ed. Joel B. Green (Nashville: Abingdon Press, 2013), 431 NT.

3. Lewis, "Philemon," 443.

CHAPTER 19

HEBREWS

OUTLINE	THEMES
1:1–2:18 Introduction 3:1–12:29 Body 13:1-25 Conclusion	The saving power of Christ The finality of Christ

Hebrews is unlike any other epistle. In fact, it bears a closer resemblance to a sermon than a traditional letter. The writer, who is unknown to us, describes the writing as a "message of encouragement" (13:22). This unusual book does not begin with the expected greeting but rather with what might be described as an instruction. The opening words, beginning with "in the past" (1:1), outline the way God worked with "our ancestors" as a foundation for explaining what God is doing now, "in these final days." The original language of Hebrews is not the more common *koine* Greek we are accustomed to in the New Testament; rather, its eloquence comes from the literary style of the elevated Greek in which it is written, signaling a literary and rhetorical intentionality one anticipates in a good sermon. Hebrews seeks to encourage its recipients by strengthening their identity as a part of the salvation story and using that identity as the justification for being faithful to the way, even in the face of difficult circumstances.

Hebrews uses Old Testament scripture, motifs, theology, and metaphors as a platform to explain what it means to be a Christian in the present. Moving back and forth from exposition to exhortation,[1] the writer

1. Luke Timothy Johnson, *The Writings of the New Testament* (Minneapolis: Fortress, 2010), 413.

rehearses the role of temple and tabernacle, sacrifice, and priest to lay a foundation for the exaltation of Jesus as the messenger, sacrifice, and advocate like no other. In days past, the high priest was the highest level of access one had to God. Hebrews declares Jesus to be the ultimate high priest in the order of Melchizedek (Gen 14:17-24). Jesus is better than the angels, greater than Moses and Joshua, and the ultimate sacrifice. More than an extension of Judaism, or even fulfillment of prophetic promises, Jesus is everything.

This carefully constructed sermon demonstrates a detailed knowledge of Hebrew scripture and Jewish practices that leads some to conclude it was intended for a Jewish audience. The book's assigned title, "To Hebrews," reflects this assumption. Other scholars point to the stylized Greek and assume the audience was mixed, or even wholly Gentile. What we can affirm is that the writer seeks to encourage a congregation of believers by reminding them of who they are. The exposition of the letter is impassioned and intentional—forming or reminding the congregation of their story, rooted in Israel, although not limited to Judaism, and finding its ultimate expression in Jesus. The exhortation comes naturally from the exposition. Once the audience realizes their true identity, their purpose becomes clear. The "mission statement" of the church is rooted in the church's identity in Christ. The exhortation is dialogic in nature, inviting the audience to join the author on a journey to the desired destination. The pronouns *us* and *we* are used generously, along with questions that are designed to elicit a response.[2] Whether the earlier audiences were Jewish, Gentile, or a combination, Hebrews aims to create a definitive, Christian audience. The writer of Hebrews carefully examines concepts that are foundational to Israel's identity and remixes them so that they are infused with Christian theology. Two examples are covenant and faith.

At the heart of God's relationship with God's people in the Hebrew Bible is covenant, a term that is deeply rooted in Jewish identity. The Torah or law formed a type of covenant, a contract that defined the existence and nature of the divine-human relationship. God formed individual covenants

2. Thomas G. Long, *Hebrews,* Interpretation: A Bible Commentary for Teaching and Preaching (Louisville: Westminster John Knox, 1997), 6.

with Noah, Abraham, and David. God made a covenant with the people of Israel at Sinai that outlined the terms by which they would be "related" to one another. The history of Israel can be summarized as a story of the people breaking the covenant and God renewing the covenant. The word for covenant in Greek, *diathēke*, has multiple meanings. It can mean both "contract or covenant," which is consistent with its usage in the Old Testament, or it can mean "will or testament." In Hebrews 9:15-22, the author explores this second meaning of covenant, arguing that Christ's sacrifice sets us free from our obligation to the old covenant and makes us heirs of an "eternal inheritance" (9:15), a new covenant. This new covenant includes Christ's return to earth to "save" those who are "eagerly waiting for him" (9:28), the event that comes to be known as the *parousia* or second coming.

Chapter 11 begins with the words "Faith is the reality of what we hope for, the proof of what we don't see" (1:1). The remaining thirty-nine verses offer a historical and theological treatise on faith in action, beginning with creation, and moving from the primeval history to the founding ancestors, the exodus and entrance to the promised land, then the judges and monarchy, naming specific examples of ancestors in the faith who experienced victory or suffered as a result of their faith. The writer concludes the chapter, "All these people didn't receive what was promised, though they were given approval for their faith. God provided something better for us so they wouldn't be made perfect without us" (11:39-40). In other words, it is time for the community to whom Hebrews is directed to take their place in the tradition as keepers and purveyors of the faith. They are to join the "great cloud of witnesses" and to take hold of "the baton" that has been passed to them. This phrase introduces the metaphor of the life of faith as a relay race that we are offered in 12:1: "So then, with endurance, let's also run the race that is laid out in front of us." The image speaks to the form and focus of the runner (12:1-3) and to the type of race. This is a long-distance race, one that requires discipline on the part of the runner.

This sermon to the Hebrews includes a benediction in the final chapter:

May the God of peace,
who brought back the great shepherd of the sheep,
our Lord Jesus,
from the dead by the blood of the eternal covenant,
equip you with every good thing to do his will,
by developing in us what pleases him through Jesus Christ.
To him be the glory forever and always. Amen. (13:20-21)

As expressed in the benediction, Hebrews encourages and equips a bedraggled community to persevere by rehearsing their identifying markers, like covenant and faith, past, present, and future so that they can see a purpose in their current circumstances and a hope for their future.

CHAPTER 20
JAMES

OUTLINE	THEMES
1:1 Greeting 1:2-27 Major themes 2:1–5:6 Body 5:7-20 Conclusion	Faith and action (works)

The short and provocative letter of James is addressed to "the twelve tribes who are scattered outside the land of Israel," from "James, a slave of God and of the Lord Jesus Christ" (Jas 1:1). A number of traditions identify this James as James the brother of Jesus, although the author never makes that claim, and there were other well-known disciples also named James.[1] If the letter is written by the brother of Jesus, it is ironic that Jesus is barely mentioned. Whatever his identity, this James writes to followers of Christ in the diaspora.

The letter is perhaps best described as "Christian wisdom literature."[2] In James, the author draws on the Old Testament wisdom tradition and mixes it with teachings that resemble the Sermon on the Mount,[3] encouraging the audience to endure hardships and to "stand firm during testing" (1:12). This "standing firm," however, is by no means intended as a sta-

1. We know of James the son of Zebedee (Matt 4:21), James the son of Alpheus (Matt 10:3), James the brother of Jesus (Mark 6:3), James the younger (Mark 15:40), and James the father of Judas (Luke 6:16).

2. A. Katherine Grieb, "Catholic Epistles," in *The New Testament—Introducing the Way of Discipleship*, ed. Wes Howard-Brook and Sharon Ringe (Maryknoll, NY: Orbis, 2002), 177.

3. Bart Ehrman, *The New Testament: A Historical Introduction to the Early Christian Writings* (Oxford: Oxford University Press, 2000), 332.

tionary position. James calls the community to demonstrate their faith in the living out of their daily lives. He contends, "Faith without actions is dead" (2:26). Thus, the call to Christian identity here is one of steadfastness in beliefs that are to be demonstrated by the works that one does and not just the words one proclaims. One gets the sense in reading James that this letter is directed to mature Christians, those who are looking to know more about the life of faith that they have begun. The tone of the letter is direct, and the expectations for its audience are high.

James's teaching on faith and works is in the form of a diatribe, a dialogue between the writer and an imagined interlocutor.[4] In this diatribe the writer invites the audience to listen in on a performed conversation, to step back and consider the argument from a distance. Although James reflects a different understanding of faith and works, it does not stand in opposition to Paul's view (Rom 2:6; Eph 4:12).[5] Paul argues against the concept that works lead to justification and faith, rather that Christ is the way to salvation. James's teaching, from a different context and using a different lens, can be best understood in dialogue with Paul. Whereas Paul works to distinguish a community of faith as separate from the "works-oriented" community, James comes later to restore balance to the relationship. Works do not replace faith, but they are the product, the evidence of faith.[6] This pairing of works as the result of faith is tied to examples of economic justice. James wants the community to know that Christianity is a religion that acts in the world as a result of its faith rather than using faith as an excuse to hide from the world.[7]

In the final chapter, James instructs the community on behavior in anticipation of the *parousia*, the return of Christ. They are to be "patient as you wait for the coming of the Lord" (5:7), with the added admonition to

4. Christian E. Hauer and William A. Young, *An Introduction to the Bible: A Journey into Three Worlds* (Upper Saddle River, NJ: Prentice Hall, 2001), 349.

5. Patrick J. Hartin, "Faith and Works," in *The CEB Study Bible*, ed. Joel B. Green (Nashville: Abingdon Press, 2013), 457 NT.

6. Thomas G. Long, *Hebrews*, Interpretation: A Bible Commentary for Teaching and Preaching (Louisville: Westminster John Knox, 1997).

7. Gay Byron, "James," *in True to Our Native Land: An African American New Testament Commentary,* ed. Brian Blount (Minneapolis: Fortress, 2007), 467.

"Look! The judge is standing at the door" (5:9). In this section, the writer specifically warns the rich against exploiting the poor (5:1-6) and against participating in systems that benefit one community at the expense of another.[8] The letter does not end with a standard conclusion, but rather continues with instructions, echoing the sentiments expressed at the beginning of the letter: wait with patient faithfulness, pray and help those who "wander from the truth" (5:19). For James, this act of keeping people on the right path is the holding position until the *parousia.*

8. Byron, "James," 469.

CHAPTER 21
1 PETER

What happens to a dream deferred?

—Langston Hughes, "Harlem"

OUTLINE	THEMES
1:1-2 Greeting 1:3-12 Thanksgiving 1:13–2:10 Right behavior and identity 2:11–4:11 Right behavior in society and household 4:12–5:11 Words of encouragement 5:12-14 Conclusion	Faithful and righteous living Endurance

The salutation of 1 Peter 1:1-2 identifies St. Peter as the author and the audience as "God's chosen strangers in the world of the diaspora." Here a Jewish author writes to Gentile Christians in language that intentionally casts them as the "new Israel," and nonbelievers as the "Gentiles."[1] The language and content of the letter reflect a date for composition somewhere between 60 CE, if the Apostle Peter did write it, and 65 CE, if it is written by one of his disciples. First Peter speaks to a time in which (1) the return of Jesus, the *parousia*, had not yet occurred; (2) persecution of Christians by the Roman Empire was increasing; and (3) questions were being raised about the essential tenets of the faith.

1. Christian E. Hauer and William A. Young, *An Introduction to the Bible: A Journey into Three Worlds* (Upper Saddle River, NJ: Prentice Hall, 2001), 350.

The letter instructs the Christians to endure suffering, but it also pushes them to maintain a righteous lifestyle while they wait, or better said, endure suffering by maintaining a righteous lifestyle. The writer does this by reminding the audience of their legacy as God's chosen people, the image of a new Israel (1:2–2:10).[2] Their example as Christians under persecution is to serve as a living witness, a means by which others may see and be converted.

Whereas the early church was initially called to be outwardly counter-cultural, this later letter exhorts the community to adopt a more practical strategy and live as "immigrants and strangers in the world" (2:11), and to "submit to every human institution" (2:13). It is "God's will that by doing good you will silence the ignorant talk of foolish people" (2:15).

The language of this letter intentionally sets up a contrast between the reality of the current situation of the audience and its meaning for their identity as Christians. They are suffering, but this is their calling (2:21). They are following in Christ's footsteps and, for that reason, they are not defeated. Christ's suffering ends in victory, and this narrative of Christ is the template for their lives. They wait, but they are full of hope. The language in 1 Peter is triumphant, establishing an alternate reality that is realized in their behavior. The writer of 1 Peter urges the community to be firmly rooted in their identity in Christ so they will be ready for his return. This is the endgame strategy.

---

2. A Katherine Grieb, "1 Peter," in *The New Testament—Introducing the Way of Discipleship*, ed. Wes Howard-Brook and Sharon Ringe (Maryknoll, NY: Orbis, 2002), 180.

CHAPTER 22
2 PETER

OUTLINE	THEMES
1:1-2 Greeting 1:3-11 Grace for a godly life 1:12–2:21 Apostolic reminder 3:1-14 Answers to issues 3:15-18 Conclusion	God's judgment Knowledge of God The end times

The second letter of Peter speaks to the delayed return of Christ, the rumors that Christ is not returning, and the possibility that, if Jesus is not returning, a righteous life is not required. The belief in the imminent return of Jesus was a hallmark of the early church and the basis for its understanding of the requirements of the life of faith. Now, as the church continues to live into a hope deferred, it is necessary to make sense of what the ongoing delay means and how they are to now understand all the teachings in a way that might bring meaning to the delay.

Second Peter is addressed to "those who received a faith equal to ours through the justice of our God and savior Jesus Christ," from Peter, "a slave and apostle of Jesus Christ" (1:1). Identified as "my second letter to you," there are connections with the earlier epistle and also references the Pauline letters (3:1, 15). The letter comes at a time when people still know the "teachings and memories associated with the original apostles" along with other teachings that have developed as the church has matured.[1]

1. Matthew Skinner, *A Companion to the New Testament: The General Letters and Revelation* (Waco, TX: Baylor University Press, 2018), 68.

Most scholars believe 2 Peter is not an independent letter but rather an adaptation of the letter attributed to Jude, as 2 Peter draws heavily on the images, language, and teaching in Jude to remind the audience of God's power and divine judgment, which is for Christians and non-Christians alike. Those who are followers of Christ must live in the knowledge of God, or, in the vernacular, "act like you know," so that the church will be found "pure and faultless" (3:14). Like Jude, 2 Peter concludes with a benediction that instructs its audience to "be on guard so that you aren't led off course into the error of sinful people, and lose your own safe position. Instead, grow in the grace and knowledge of our Lord and savior Jesus Christ. To him belongs glory now and forever. Amen."

CHAPTER 23
1, 2, AND 3 JOHN

The Johannine Epistles

The Johannine epistles—1, 2, and 3 John—are associated with the Gospel of John, along with the Revelation of John, to form a unit called the Johannine tradition. This tradition is a literary construct centered around John's Gospel. 1, 2, and 3 John are associated with John's Gospel because they too are highly symbolic and emphasize the tensions within the community and faith and those between the faith community and the world.[1] In its attempt to provide direction, the Johannine Epistles employ imagery made familiar by the Gospel of John, such as darkness and light, good and evil, death and life. In the world created by the author(s), it is easy to designate true believers from the rest of the world. Love is the standard, more accurately, love in action. One's faith confession was only as good as one's life in community.[2] Nowhere else in the New Testament is the "ideal of peace and unity and love so clearly expressed—and so clearly at odds with the community's own experience."[3] Here is an internal identity that is formed in opposition to the outside world. In this regard, the way of love is an act of resistance and these three

1. Luke Timothy Johnson, *The Writings of the New Testament* (Minneapolis: Fortress, 2010), 466.

2. Wes Howard-Brook, "John's Gospel's Call to Be Reborn of God," in *The New Testament—Introducing the Way of Discipleship*, ed. Wes Howard-Brook and Sharon Ringe (Maryknoll, NY: Orbis, 2002), 101.

3. Johnson, *The Writings of the New Testament*, 467.

short letters are propaganda. 3 John is a letter or recommendation for the messenger, and 2 John is an introduction to 1 John.

1 John

OUTLINE	THEMES
1:1-4 Prologue 1:5–3:10 God is light 3:11–5:12 God is love 5:13-21 Epilogue	True versus false teaching Love

First John, the first of three letters attributed to John, refers to no author, has no greeting or announcement, and does not follow the traditional form of an ancient letter. However, its message is clearly written in the metaphorical language we recognize from John's Gospel, perhaps indicating why the unnamed author is identified with the author of the Fourth Gospel. Such words as *life* and *death*, the *truth*, *brothers* and *sisters*, *little children*, *antichrist*, the *world*, and *light* and *darkness* are used as a platform from which the author calls the community to uphold the true teachings, which are evidenced in the following:[4]

- **Righteous living:** God's light reveals our sin. We are called to live in the light, so we must live righteously (keep God's word). With our behavior, we choose to live in light or in darkness.
- **Love:** Love is the measure by which God's children are identified. Those who belong to God will love God and their neighbors.

These two core beliefs are the identifying markers for the community of faith.

The intent of this message is clearly stated as making sure that the faith community remains resolute and is not dissuaded by the faction referred to as "antichrists." This term refers to a group that broke away from the Johannine community, teaching that Jesus was fully divine, but actually

4. Joel S. Kaminsky, Joel N. Lohr, and Mark Reasoner, *The Abingdon Introduction to the Bible: Understanding Jewish and Christian Scriptures* (Nashville: Abingdon Press, 2014), 356.

a spirit appearing to be human.[5] This message denies the apostolic witness and contradicts the Gospel accounts that Jesus is God incarnate. The writer of 1 John wants to maintain orthodoxy, holding to the authorized tenets and teachings of the faith, the "true" gospel. But 1 John's call to orthodoxy is not framed as a detailed list of rules and regulations. Rather it is presented through the symbolic language of light versus darkness and love of God versus love of things of the world. These words call up images that provide the rubric of the truth and community that are the identifying markers of people of faith.

The call to protecting the faith in 1 John comes with a sense of urgency and universality in 1 John. In 2:12-14, the writer uses repetition to emphasize that his message is for everyone:

- Little children, I am writing to you . . .
- Parents, I am writing to you . . .
- Young people, I'm writing to you . . .
- Little children, I write to you . . .
- Parents, I write to you . . .
- Young people I write to you . . .

Each of these lines ends with a summary of the message:

- . . . because your sins have been forgiven through Jesus's name
- . . . because you have known the one who has existed from the beginning
- . . . because you have conquered the evil one
- . . . because you know the Father
- . . . because you have known the one who has existed from the beginning
- . . . because you are strong, the word of God remains in you, and you have conquered the evil one

5. Christian E. Hauer and William A. Young, *An Introduction to the Bible: A Journey into Three Worlds* (Upper Saddle River, NJ: Prentice Hall, 2001), 352. This teaching is known as Docetism, which is taken from the Greek word for "appear."

First John is both a message of exhortation and one of hope. The warning against false teaching is balanced with the assurance that the true disciples of Christ will walk in truth because God is light (1:5–3:10). They will be identified by their love for each other because God is love (3:11–5:12).

2 John

OUTLINE	THEMES
1-3 Greeting 4 Thanksgiving 5-6 Live in love 7-11 Don't love deceivers 12-13 Benediction	Love one another Reject false teachers

Second John, unlike 1 John, is in the traditional form of a letter. The greeting identifies the author as "the elder" who writes to the "chosen gentlewoman and her children." This unusual description of the audience is generally taken as a reference to the church, which would be consistent with the practice of assigning the female gender to countries, lands, cities, and the church. The noun "lady," *kyria,* is the feminine form of *kyrios*, the masculine form meaning "lord." The usage of the term strengthens the image of family for this community. In the beloved community, do the roles of lady and lord function with mutuality or do they reflect the patriarchal structure of the outside world? How far does the unique identity as God's family extend? The theme of love, which was given significant attention in 1 John, is picked up in this letter as is the warning about false teachers. In 2 John, the church is specifically admonished against receiving those who do not uphold the right teaching.

3 John

OUTLINE	THEMES
1-2 Greeting 3-4 Thanksgiving 5-12 Exhortation 13-15 Benediction	Continue to love Hospitality as an expression of love

The last of the Johannine Letters is a letter of introduction from "the elder" to a congregational leader identified as "Gaius." This very brief letter, only fifteen verses in length, focuses on the theme of adherence to the truth that appears in the other two Johannine Letters. The writer praises Gaius for his hospitality to those who carry the letter(s) to the community of faith and also identifies one who "doesn't welcome us." In these few verses, the adherence to the truth is placed in dialogue with the themes of hospitality. The writer asks the community to be hospitable and then condemns one who has not been. Some writers believe the letter settles a dispute between rival leaders, not based on doctrine, but on the exercise of love in hospitality.[6]

6. Robert W. Wall, "3 John Introduction," in *The CEB Study Bible*, ed. Joel B. Green (Nashville: Abingdon Press, 2013), 489 NT.

CHAPTER 24
JUDE

OUTLINE	THEMES
1-2 Greeting 3-4a Purpose 4b-16 Problems and warnings 17-23 Encouragement for the faithful 24-25 Conclusion	God's judgment

Jude is addressed to "those who are called, loved by God the father and kept safe by Jesus Christ," from "Jude," whose identifying markers are "slave of Jesus Christ and brother of James." Assuming that the James referred to is James the brother of Jesus, then the Jude would also be Jesus's brother and his familiarity with Jewish texts and traditions is understandable.

The letter is short, and wastes no time in getting to the point, namely an expression of outrage about unorthodox teaching from "godless people" who have used the doctrine of grace as an excuse for immorality. Drawing examples from the Hebrew scriptures, including the stories Sodom and Gomorrah, Cain, the sons of Korah, disobedient angels in 1 Enoch, and Balaam, Jude illustrates the consequences of disobedience to God, bearing witness to the connection between faith and obedience. The imagery is evocative and to the point. The false teachers are "waterless clouds . . . fruitless autumn trees, twice dead, uprooted." Jude's message here is that God's grace is balanced by God's righteousness and righteous judgment. Jude evokes the tone of prophetic oracle and for that reason it is important to remember that oracles of woe and warning function to bring the listeners back into right relationship and this hope is expressed and reinforced in the benediction:

> To the one who is able to protect you from falling,
> And to present you blameless and rejoicing before his glorious presence,
> To the only God our savior, through Jesus Christ our Lord,
> Belong glory, majesty, power and authority,
> Before all time, now and forever. Amen.

Part Four

REVELATION

CHAPTER 25
REVELATION

OUTLINE	THEMES
1:1-8 Introduction 1:9–11:19 First cycle of visions 12:1–16:21 Second cycle of visions 17:1–18:24 The fall of Babylon 19:1–20:15 Visions of the last things 21:1–22:5 Vision of the New Jerusalem 22:6-21 Conclusion	Jesus Christ is Lord of all

Revelation is the last book of the New Testament, the "last word" of the Christian canon, the last act in the large arc of biblical narrative known as the salvation history. Genesis is the story of the world's beginnings, and the Apocalypse/Revelation of John reveals the end and the recreation of a new heaven and earth.[1] However, this conclusion to the biblical story is unsettling. John is hard to navigate. The images are overpowering and the material "does not move in a straight line."[2] The Apocalypse of John abounds with imagination. The only way to engage the book is to leave the known world behind. It also helps to focus on the plot.[3]

1. Tina Pippin, "Revelation/Apocalypse of John," in *The Women's Bible Commentary*, ed. Carol Newsom, Sharon Ringe, and Jacqueline Lapsley (Louisville: Westminster John Knox, 2012), 627.

2. Brian Blount, "Revelation," in *True to Our Native Land: An African American New Testament Commentary*, ed. Brian Blount (Minneapolis: Fortress, 2007), 523.

3. Blount, "Revelation," 523.

Scholars attribute the authorship of the book to "a follower of Christ" named John about whom nothing more than his name is known. Early on, Christian tradition associated the John who authored this book with John the apostle and Gospel writer. The writer locates himself on the island of Patmos, but his reason for being there is not specified. The book was most likely written in stages, as indicated by what are possibly allusions or references to the Roman Emperor Nero (54–68 CE) and also to events that occurred in the emperor Domitian's reign (81–96 CE). Both rulers are associated with periods of persecution of the church. The book in its final form most likely appeared at the end of the first century.[4] This "revelation of Jesus Christ . . . to his servant John" is born out of crisis. The crisis of persecution contributes to the genre of the book. Revelation is apocalyptic literature,[5] part of a genre that reflects a worldview that seeks to expose or reveal a truth.[6] Apocalyptic literature is defined as

> a genre of revelatory literature with a narrative framework in which a revelation is mediated by an otherworldly being to a human recipient, disclosing a transcendent reality, which is both temporal insofar as it envisages eschatological salvation, and spatial insofar as it involves another, supernatural world.[7]

Many scholars believe this genre is the product of a community whose present circumstances are sufficiently oppressive and threatening as to press them to explore an alternate reality, another realm. Apocalyptic literature speaks to the current world order by revealing such an alternate reality. John's heavenly perspective, which is gained through the trance state in which he experienced the vision that he records, provides the vantage point from which to describe events in the spiritual realm, which in turn offer insight into what is going on in the earthly one. In this way, the

4. David E Aune, notes on "Revelation," in *The Harper Collins Study Bible* (New York: HarperOne, 2017), 2308.

5. The revelation of John is apocalyptic, but it also has the elements of a letter and prophecy.

6. Stephen Cook, *The Apocalyptic Literature* (Nashville: Abingdon Press, 2003), 22.

7. John J. Collins, "Introduction: Towards the Morphology of a Genre," in *Apocalypse: The Morphology of a Genre*, ed. J. Collins, *Semeia* 14 (Atlanta: Society of Biblical Literature, 1979), 9.

writer provides the audience with a way forward, a sense of purpose in the current circumstances and hope in the world to come.

The visions in apocalyptic literature are highly symbolic, sometimes cryptic and requiring interpretation. Revelation is no exception to this. The cast of symbolic characters in Revelation includes a celestial woman, a serpent or dragon, four horsemen, the lamb, a child, a land beast, a sea beast, the whore of Babylon, a bride, and Jezebel. Thus, for all of the uncovering that is implied by the word and the genre of apocalypse, interpretation is required. However, in spite of this need for interpretation, there is also an element in apocalyptic literature that resists any simple, symbolic, allegorical, or historical reading. Revelation will demand that the reader come to the book on its own terms and enter a "new symbolic universe."[8] One does not simply interpret Revelation, one experiences it.

Revelation can be divided into two parts. The book begins with messages to the seven churches in Asia Minor (2:1–3:22) and then, in a second section, offers a series of visions (4:1–22:5). The book is better navigated if one begins with the first of the visions in the second section, those in chapters 12–14.[9] These visions present a woman laboring to deliver a child while a serpent or dragon waits to kill it. The child is "snatched up to God and his throne" (12:5). In the next scene the dragon participates in a battle against the angels in heaven and is defeated, "thrown down to the earth" (12:9). He then pursues the woman on earth, unsuccessfully, and determines to "make war on the rest of her children, on those who keep God's commandments and hold firmly to the witness of Christ" (12:17). One cannot ignore the trauma that informs these images. These "children" could represent the church, and this vision sets the backstage for their current persecution. The dragon enlists the help of a beast from the sea, which in turn summons another beast. These beasts could represent Rome and the empire of Asia Minor, which contains the entities that institute and enforce the worship of Rome. The mythic proportion of the imagery provides a scaffolding that may sustain a community, but the language

8. Cook, *The Apocalyptic Literature*, 194.

9. Blount, "Revelation," 523.

is not bound to one set of circumstances. The imagery opens a window through which we glimpse a world much larger than the one we occupy.

Knowing the supernatural backstory to Revelation's current sociopolitical circumstances provides the early church with knowledge that will inform how they live in turbulent times. Assimilation and accommodation for the sake of ease and comfort are not an option.[10] This community must understand all that is at stake. The heavy symbolism of the book reminds the audience that they are participants in a much larger drama, namely a supernatural battle of cosmic proportion. There will be suffering, and there will be casualties, but with victory even death will be destroyed, opening the way to a new heaven and a new earth. This new reality, reassuring as it may be, cannot be contained.

This acknowledgment and movement into an alternate reality is a tried-and-true survival tactic. In Revelation, the act of interpretation is less about deciphering the text so that it makes sense in our realm and more about entering into the space that a symbolic world offers when the current environment is dangerously hostile.

The glory of the victory at the end is portrayed with the same depth of symbolism as the description of the cosmic battles that precede it. The details in the final vision, which describes the "last things," are the words and images upon which the persecuted church hangs its faith. There is a promise of a celebration that takes the form of a wedding feast between the bride/church and the Lamb/Christ. This metaphor is based on one we see in prophetic literature where Israel is God's bride. The enemies are defeated. The dragon/snake/Satan is thrown into the abyss for one thousand years; the martyrs for the faith are enthroned and favored. Satan is released one last time to deceive, and then he is "thrown into the lake of fire and sulfur," where he will remain with the beast and the false prophet "forever and always" (20:10). This is followed by the Final Judgment (20:11-14), and then a description of the new heaven and new earth. In this place, there is no more mourning, crying, pain, or death. Out of the chaos of the present circumstances, the church is promised an eternal life where they are in the presence of "the Lord God Almighty and the Lamb." In

10. Blount, "Revelation," 524.

this place there is the tree of life and there is no more curse. The end of all things returns us to an Edenic place, which is described using symbols from the larger narrative of identity. This is the hope of the persecuted.

The persecution of the late first-century church is a specific crisis that gives rise to the apocalypse. The perspective of John's letter is universal, applying not just to the embattled Christians but to the whole world. It is two-dimensional, with heaven and earth within its scope, and it uses "elaborate and often bizarre imagery and cryptic symbol" to convey its message.[11] This imagery allows for an excess of meanings so the Apocalypse of John, or Revelation, continues to arrest the attention of Christian communities.

Perhaps like no other book, Revelation invites us to consider both the limits and the endless possibilities of language. Humans use language to talk about a God who is beyond their comprehension. The symbolic world that is represented in imaginative writing allows us to glimpse into an alternate universe inhabited by light and darkness, beasts and angelic beings that help us to better understand our purpose and role in this created order. Not unlike the primordial chaos God subdued at the very beginning, the narrative arc in this final example of biblical literary imagination offers an ending where an awesome/awful God is victorious over the forces that would consume us.

11. Sophie Laws, *In the Light of the Lamb: Imagery, Parody, and Theology in the Apocalypse of John* (Wilmington, DE: Michael Glazier, 1988), 13–14.

BIBLIOGRAPHY

Achebe, Chinua. 1959. *Things Fall Apart*. New York: Penguin Books.

Alter, Robert. 2019. *The Hebrew Bible: A Translation with Commentary*. New York: W. W. Norton and Company.

Armstrong, Karen. 1996. *In the Beginning: A New Interpretation of Genesis*. New York: Alfred A Knopf.

Ballentine, Samuel E. 1989. *Leviticus*. Interpretation: A Bible Commentary for Teaching and Preaching. Louisville: Westminster John Knox.

Berlin, Adele. 1985. *The Dynamics of Biblical Parallelism*. Bloomington: Indiana University Press.

Blount, Brian K., ed. 2007. *True to Our Native Land: An African American New Testament Commentary*. Minneapolis: Fortress.

Boomershine, Tom. 1998. *Story Journey: An Invitation to the Gospel of Storytelling*. Nashville: Abingdon Press.

Brown, William P. 1996. *Obadiah through Malachi*. Westminster Bible Companion. Louisville: Westminster John Knox.

———. 2002. *Seeing the Psalms*. Louisville: Westminster John Knox.

Brueggemann, Walter. 1982. *Genesis*. Interpretation: A Bible Commentary for Teaching and Preaching. Louisville: Westminster John Knox.

———. 1995. *The Psalms and the Life of Faith*. Minneapolis: Fortress.

———. 2003. *David's Truth in Israel's Imagination and Memory*. Minneapolis: Fortress.

Buchmann, Christina. 1994. *Out of the Garden: Women Writers on the Bible*. New York: Fawcett Columbine.

Byron, Gay. 2016. *Womanist Interpretations of the Bible: Expanding the Discourse*. Atlanta: SBL Press.

Campbell, Charles. 2018. *First Corinthians*. Interpretation: A Bible Commentary for Teaching and Preaching. Louisville: Westminster John Knox.

Campbell, Douglas. 2018. *Paul, An Apostle's Journey*. Grand Rapids: Eerdmans.

Carr, David M. 2014. *Holy Resilience: The Bible's Traumatic Origins*. New Haven, CT: Yale University Press.

Carroll, John T. 2016. *Jesus and the Gospels, An Introduction*. Louisville: Westminster John Knox.

Carter, Warren, and Amy-Jill Levine. 2013. *The New Testament: Methods and Meanings*. Nashville: Abingdon Press.

Childs, Brevard S. 1962. *Myth and Reality in the Old Testament*. Eugene, OR: Wipf and Stock.

———. 1970. *Biblical Theology in Crisis*. Philadelphia: Westminster.

———. 1974. *The Book of Exodus: A Critical, Theological Commentary.* Old Testament Library. Louisville: Westminster.

———. 1979. *Introduction to the Old Testament as Scripture*. Philadelphia: Fortress.

———. 2000. *Isaiah: A Commentary.* The Old Testament Library. Louisville: Westminster John Knox.

Collins, John J., ed. 1979. *Apocalypse: The Morphology of a Genre, Semeia* 14. Atlanta: Society of Biblical Literature.

Cook, Stephen L. 2003. *The Apocalyptic Literature.* Nashville: Abingdon Press.

Craig, Kenneth. 1995. *Reading Esther: A Case for the Literary Carnivalesque*. Louisville: Westminster John Knox.

Davis, Ellen. 2000. "Critical Revisioning: Seeking an Inner Biblical Hermeneutic," *Anglican Theological Review* 82, no. 4, 733–51.

———. 2019. *Opening Israel's Scriptures*. Oxford: Oxford University Press.

Dewey, Joanna. 2013. *The Oral Ethos of the Early Church*. Eugene, OR: Cascade.

Douglas, Mary. 1999. *Leviticus as Literature*. Oxford: Oxford University Press.

DuBois, W. E. B. 1982. *The Souls of Black Folk*. New York: Penguin.

Ehrman, Bart. 2000. *The New Testament: A Historical Introduction to the Early Christian Writings*. Oxford: Oxford University Press.

———. 2001. *A Brief Introduction to the New Testament.* Oxford: Oxford University Press.

Exum, J. Cheryl. 2005. *Song of Songs: A Commentary.* Old Testament Library. Louisville: Westminster John Knox.

Fentress-Williams, Judy. 2012. *Ruth*. Abingdon Old Testament Commentaries. Nashville: Abingdon Press.

Fishbane, Michael. 1998. *Biblical Text and Texture: A Literary Reading of Selected Texts*. Oxford: Oneworld.

Fretheim, Terrence E. 1991. *Exodus*. Interpretation: A Bible Commentary for Teaching and Preaching. Louisville: Westminster John Knox.

Gafney, Wilda C. 2017. *Womanist Midrash*. Louisville: Westminster John Knox.

Gray, John. 1964. *I & II Kings*. Old Testament Library. London: SCM.

Grieb, A. Katherine. 2002. *The Story of Romans*. Louisville: Westminster John Knox.

Hallo, William. 1979. "Leviticus and Ancient Near Eastern Literature." In *Leviticus: A Modern Commentary*. New York: Jewish Publication Society.

Halpern, Baruch. 1988. *The First Historians: The Hebrew Bible and History*. San Francisco: Harper & Row.

Hauer, Christian E., and Williams A. Young. 2001. *An Introduction to the Bible: A Journey into Three Worlds*. Upper Saddle River, NJ: Prentice Hall.

Hauerwas, Stanley. 2006. *Matthew.* Brazos Theological Commentary on the Bible. Ada, MI: Brazos.

Hays, Richard. 1997. *First Corinthians*. Interpretation: A Bible Commentary for Teaching and Preaching. Louisville: Westminster John Knox.

Henderson, Suzanne Watts. 2019. *New Testament Conversations: A Literary, Historical and Pluralistic Introduction*. Nashville: Abingdon Press.
Hendricks, Obery M. 2006. *The Politics of Jesus*. New York: Three Leaves/Doubleday.
Hirsch, Edward. 1999. *How to Read a Poem: And Fall in Love with Poetry*. New York: Harcourt.
Howard-Brook, Wes, and Sharon Ringe, eds. 2002. *The New Testament—Introducing the Way of Discipleship*. Maryknoll, NY: Orbis.
Jennings, Willie James. 2010. *The Christian Imagination: Theology and the Origins of Race*. New Haven, CT: Yale University Press.
Johnson, Luke Timothy. 1986. *The Writings of the New Testament: An Interpretation*. Minneapolis: Fortress.
Kaminsky, Joel S., Joel N. Lohr, and Mark Reasoner. 2014. *The Abingdon Introduction to the Bible: Understanding Jewish and Christian Scriptures*. Nashville: Abingdon Press.
Kirk-Dugan, Cheryl A. 1997. "Exorcising Evil." In *A Womanist Perspective on the Spirituals*. New York: Orbis.
Kugel, James. 1981. *The Idea of Biblical Poetry*. New Haven, CT: Yale University Press.
Lathrop, Gordon. 1998. *Holy Thinks: A Liturgical Theology*. Minneapolis: Fortress.
Laws, Sophie. 1988. *In the Light of the Lamb: Imagery, Parody and Theology in the Apocalypse of John*. Wilmington, DE: Michael Glazier.
Levenson, Jon D. 1987. *Sinai and Zion: An Entry into the Jewish Bible*. Cambridge: Harper & Row.
Levine, Amy-Jill. 2014. *Short Stories by Jesus*. New York: HarperCollins.
Liss, Hamma, and Manfred Oeming. *Literary Construction of Identity in the Ancient World*. Winona Lake, IN: Eisenbrauns.
Long, Thomas G. 1997. *Hebrews*. Interpretation: A Bible Commentary for Teaching and Preaching. Louisville: Westminster John Knox.
Martin, Ralph. 2991. *Ephesians, Colossians and Philemon*. Interpretation: A Bible Commentary for Teaching and Preaching. Louisville: Westminster John Knox.
Matthews, Victor H. 2002. *A Brief History of Ancient Israel*. Louisville: Westminster John Knox.
McFague, Sallie. 1975. *Speaking in Parables: A Study in Metaphor and Theology*. Minneapolis: Fortress.
Metzger, Bruce M., and Michael D. Coogan, eds. 1993. *The Oxford Companion to the Bible*. Oxford: Oxford University Press.
Milgrom, Jacob. 2004. *Leviticus: A Continental Commentary*. Minneapolis: Fortress.
Miller, Patrick. 1986. *Interpreting the Psalms*. Philadelphia: Fortress.
———. 2009. *The Ten Commandments*. Interpretation: Resources for the Use of Scripture in the Church. Louisville: Westminster John Knox.
Moore, Stephen. 1989. *Literary Criticism and the Gospels: The Theoretical Challenge*. New Haven, CT: Yale University Press.
Murphy, Roland. 1990. *The Tree of Life: An Exploration of Biblical Wisdom Literature*. Grand Rapids: Eerdmans.

Nelson, Richard D. 1987. *First and Second Kings*. Interpretation: A Bible Commentary for Teaching and Preaching. Louisville: Westminster John Knox.

Newsom, Carol, Sharon Ringe, and Jacqueline Lapsley. 2012. *Women's Bible Commentary*, 20th anniversary ed. Louisville: Westminster John Knox.

O'Brien, Julia M. 2008. *Challenging Prophetic Metaphor: Theology and Ideology in the Prophets*. Louisville: Westminster John Knox.

O'Connor, Kathleen. 2011. *Jeremiah: Pain and Promise*. Minneapolis: Fortress.

Olson, Dennis. 1996. *Numbers*. Interpretation: A Bible Commentary for Teaching and Preaching. Louisville: Westminster John Knox.

Page, Hugh. 2010. *The Africana Bible: Reading Israel's Scriptures from Africa and the African Diaspora*. Minneapolis: Fortress.

———, et al. 2013. *Israel's Poetry of Resistance*. Minneapolis: Fortress.

Pardes, Ilana. 1992. *Countertradition in the Bible: A Feminist Approach*. Cambridge, MA: Harvard University Press.

Plaut, W. Gunther et al. 1981. *The Torah: A Modern Commentary*. New York: The Union of American Hebrew Congregations.

Polzin, Robert. 1989. *Samuel and the Deuteronomist: A Literary Study of the Deuteronomistic History, Part Two: 1 Samuel*. Bloomington: Indiana University Press.

Powell, Mark Allan. 2009. *Introducing the New Testament*. Grand Rapids: Baker Academic.

———. 2019. *Fortress Introduction to the Gospels*. Minneapolis: Fortress.

Russaw, Kimberly D. 2018. *Daughters in the Hebrew Bible*. Lanham, MD: Lexington Books/Fortress Academic.

Sakenfeld, Katherine Doob. 2003. *Just Wives? Stories of Power & Survival in the Old Testament & Today*. Louisville: Westminster John Knox.

Schildgen, Brenda Deen. 1998. *Crisis and Continuity: Time in the Gospel of Mark*. Sheffield: Sheffield Academic.

Schneider, Tammi J. 2008. *Mothers of Promise*. Grand Rapids: Baker Academic.

Seow, Choon Leong. 2003. *Daniel*. Louisville: Westminster John Knox.

Skinner, Matthew. 2018. *A Companion to the New Testament: The General Letters and Revelation*. Waco, TX: Baylor University Press.

Smith, Mitzi J. 2011. *The Literary Construction of Other in the Acts of the Apostles: Charismatics, the Jews and Women*. Eugene, OR: Pickwick.

Speiser, E. A. 1981. *Genesis*. The Anchor Bible Commentary. New York: Doubleday.

Stulman, Louis. 2005. *Jeremiah*. Abingdon Old Testament Commentaries. Nashville: Abingdon Press.

Sweeney, Marvin A. 2012. *Tanak: A Theological and Critical Introduction to the Jewish Bible*. Minneapolis: Fortress.

Van Wijk-Bos, Johanna. 2019. *The End of the Beginning: Joshua and Judges*. Grand Rapids: Eerdmans.

Vice, Sue. 1997. *Introducing Bakhtin*. Manchester: Manchester University Press.

Walker, Alice. 1983. *In Search of Our Mother's Garden*. New York: Harcourt Brace Jovanovich.

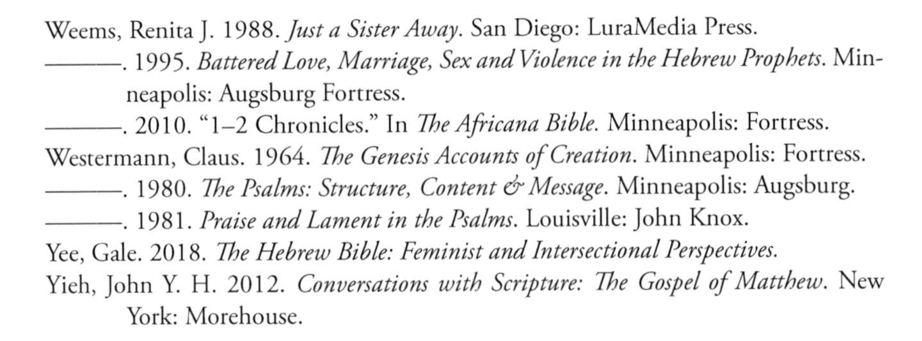

Weems, Renita J. 1988. *Just a Sister Away*. San Diego: LuraMedia Press.

———. 1995. *Battered Love, Marriage, Sex and Violence in the Hebrew Prophets*. Minneapolis: Augsburg Fortress.

———. 2010. "1–2 Chronicles." In *The Africana Bible*. Minneapolis: Fortress.

Westermann, Claus. 1964. *The Genesis Accounts of Creation*. Minneapolis: Fortress.

———. 1980. *The Psalms: Structure, Content & Message*. Minneapolis: Augsburg.

———. 1981. *Praise and Lament in the Psalms*. Louisville: John Knox.

Yee, Gale. 2018. *The Hebrew Bible: Feminist and Intersectional Perspectives.*

Yieh, John Y. H. 2012. *Conversations with Scripture: The Gospel of Matthew*. New York: Morehouse.

Made in United States
Orlando, FL
12 January 2022